The River We Have Wrought

The River
We Have Wrought

A History of the Upper Mississippi

John O. Anfinson

University of Minnesota Press
Minneapolis • London

The University of Minnesota Press gratefully acknowledges the generous assistance provided for the publication of this book by the Hamilton P. Traub University Press Fund.

The maps in the book (Figures 2 and 26) were created by Parrot Graphics.

Published by the University of Minnesota Press
111 Third Avenue South, Suite 290
Minneapolis, MN 55401-2520
http://www.upress.umn.edu

Printed in the United States of America on acid-free paper

Library of Congress Cataloging-in-Publication Data

Anfinson, John O.
    The river we have wrought : a history of the upper Mississippi / John O. Anfinson
        p. cm.
Includes bibliographical references and index.
    ISBN 0-8166-4024-6 (PB : alk. paper)
    1. Mississippi River—History. 2. Mississippi River—Environmental conditions.
3. Human ecology—Mississippi River. 4. Mississippi River—Navigation—History.
I. Title.

F351 .A58 2003
386' .3'09775—dc21

                                                            2002011941

12 11 10 09 08 07 06 05   10 9 8 7 6 5 4 3 2 1

For Caitlin and Eric

Contents

Acknowledgments ix

Introduction xi

1. **Innumerable** 1

2. **This Splendid Juggernaut** 29

3. **The Bounty of Providence** 53

4. **Making the Mississippi Over Again** 81

5. **Highway of Empire** 101

6. **So Nearly Perfected by Nature** 125

7. **Cradle, Home, and Place of Sojourn** 145

8. **A Marooned Interior** 175

9. **Straining at the Chains** 197

10. **An Inland Empire's Need** 213

11. **This Noble River** 239

Epilogue: Fourth River 275

Notes 293

Index 349

Acknowledgments

As with most books, the foundation of this one is built on research. Without trained and experienced archivists, this book would have been impossible. Throughout my uncounted visits to the Minnesota Historical Society, and while at the National Archives in Chicago, Illinois; College Park, Maryland; and Washington, D.C., and other archives, the archivists have guided me through endless shelves of historic documents to the manuscript collections I needed.

To Paul Walker, Bill Baldwin, and Marty Reuss of the U.S. Army Corps of Engineers, Office History, I owe a special debt. They provided considerable advice and help with many aspects of this project, from research suggestions to manuscript review. Historians Charles Parrish, of the Corps' Louisville District, and William Willingham, formerly with the Corps' North Pacific Division, and Tom Pullen, a biologist with the New Orleans District, also provided comments on early drafts of the manuscript. A number of former and current employees of the St. Paul District deserve special thanks, including David E. Berwick, Jane Carroll, Jean Schmidt, and Al Santo.

Mark Neuzil from the University of St. Thomas in St. Paul, Philip Scarpino from Indiana University at Purdue and Purdue University at Indiana, Todd Shallat from Boise State University, and Robert Kelley Schneiders from Texas Tech University at Lubbock thoroughly reviewed the manuscript and wrote substantial and detailed comments that have helped improve this study greatly.

I must thank Todd Orjala, acquisitions editor for the University of Minnesota Press, for two things. He relentlessly pursued this manuscript, despite a variety of obstacles, and he has expanded the University of Minnesota Press's interest in the Mississippi River.

I owe my greatest debt and gratitude to my family. I have watched my daughter, Caitlin, and my son, Eric, grow faster than I could write this book. Deb showed remarkable patience, encouragement, and support.

Introduction

On February 20, 1931, the Izaak Walton League's Minnesota division issued a notice about "Two Big Meetings."[1] The first was scheduled for Wabasha, Minnesota, in six days, and the second for Winona, Minnesota, on March 7. Both meetings focused on the 9-foot channel project for the upper Mississippi River. Under this project, Congress directed the U.S. Army Corps of Engineers to construct twenty-three locks and dams from just above Red Wing, Minnesota, to Alton, Illinois. Although the Corps had improved the river for navigation under a series of major projects since the Civil War, the river had remained too shallow and unpredictable. Railroads dominated shipping in the Midwest. By 1918 no packets or raftboats made the trip from St. Louis to St. Paul. The 9-foot channel project, navigation boosters insisted, would finally create a river that could compete with railroads and entice commerce back to the river. The project threatened, however, to transform the upper Mississippi River's character. This is why the Izaak Walton League issued its notice. The League predicted that the new dams would kill a river already reeling from excessive pollution, siltation, and wetland drainage. At the meetings, the League's chapters from Minnesota, Wisconsin, Iowa, and Illinois declared their opposition. For the first time, conservationists opposed a major navigation project for the river; for the first time, they challenged the once dominant vision for the great river. That vision, which dated to the Midwest's earliest settlement, held that shipping was the river's highest purpose.[2]

Despite the conservationists' challenge, the Corps completed the project in 1940. The predictions of navigation boosters and conservationists have come true, although not exactly as they imagined. Where every previous project had failed, the 9-foot channel project brought commerce back to the river. That success has been at a tremendous cost, according to modern conservationists. As their predecessors warned— for different reasons—today's conservationists believe the river is facing an ecological crisis. The 9-foot channel's success and consequences have led to a new debate over the upper Mississippi River's future, a debate that most Midwesterners and most Americans are unaware of. Yet the debate's outcome will define the future of the river's ecosystem and the Midwest's economy, and with both, the nation.

Many environmentalists fear the upper Mississippi River is headed toward an ecosystem collapse. Sooner than we can imagine, backwaters, side channels, and main channel habitat will disappear as will much of

Figure 1. A fifteen-barge tow passing through Lock and Dam No. 6 at Trempealeau, Wisconsin. Photograph by Mark Krumholz; courtesy of the St. Paul District, U.S. Army Corps of Engineers.

the wildlife that depends on them. Fewer songbirds will pipe their voices through the river bottoms. Fewer shotguns will bang out at the millions of ducks and geese that use the upper Mississippi as a flyway, and fewer fish will swim in its waters.

To farmers, agricultural corporations, barge line companies, and others dependent on the river to ship their products, the Mississippi is faltering in a different way. It is a vital transportation artery that has become clogged. As the race with other nations for agricultural markets quickens, the river is not up to the contest. Those troubled about the river's ecosystem and those worried about shipping warn of dire outcomes if their concerns are ignored.

What the region and nation have done to make the upper Mississippi River navigable is the problem, some environmentalists argue. The reservoirs created by the upper river's twenty-nine locks and dams (some were built before the 9-foot channel project, and some after), they contend, have imposed an order on the river that is not ecologically sustainable. During normal and low flows, the reservoirs hold back the river's waters and slow its pace. Sediment is filling the backwaters. Before the Corps built the dams, the river had a more pronounced annual pulse. Spring high water gave way to low water during late summer and fall. At low water, sediment along the channel and in the backwaters compacted and dried out, a process critical for some aquatic plants. Because the dams hold the river artificially high, large areas no longer dry out, and the sediment stays soft and loose. Seeds of some important emergent aquatic plants cannot germinate. The wind and boats stir the sediment, creating conditions in which submersed aquatic plants cannot root themselves firmly and do not receive enough light to thrive. Without these plants, waterfowl have to alter their migration route or face starvation. Wind-driven waves, blowing across the large reservoirs, are eroding islands, eliminating unique habitats and adding to the sediment that is filling the river. The river's bottom is leveling out. The deep holes outside the main channel that bass and other fish need to winter over are disappearing. These are just some of the more critical of the effects identified by environmental interests.[3]

Radical critics of the locks and dams want them removed, which would end commercial navigation and limit recreational boating. Most ecologists and river managers hope the locks and dams can be operated to re-create the river's natural cycle. However, except for a few dams at the lower end of the system, regulating the dams to mimic the natural cycle is problematic. For the best ecological results, the Corps would have to lower the river during the late summer and fall, when most commercial navigation takes place. Navigation supporters argue that closing the river to shipping would devastate farmers, grain companies, and consumers. Without the Mississippi, the cost of shipping grain, fertilizer, coal, and other commodities would rise dramatically, and the region could no longer compete in world agricultural markets.

So much traffic now moves on the lower part of the upper Mississippi that the locks cannot handle it quickly enough, leading to costly delays. Responding to the navigation industry, Congress authorized more than $50 million for the Corps to study how to improve the lock and dam system to allow for more traffic. The navigation study has become the focus of a debate over how to manage the river now and in the future.

Can the river's ecosystem stand more traffic? Is the existing navigation system already unacceptably changing the river's ecosystem, even without additional traffic? How will the region's economy suffer without further navigation improvements? Should the nation maximize the river's economic or environmental qualities? These are questions facing the Midwest and the country.

The debate over how to manage the river would be occurring even without the navigation study. Questions about what to do with the upper Mississippi River will not go away, regardless of what Congress decides this time. The river will be a critical transportation route as long as agriculture remains central to the Midwest's economy. The river's ecosystem will remain essential to many fish, plants, and animals and to the humans that value them. The debate has no easy answers. It may be, as Richard White suggests about the clash over managing the Columbia River for salmon or dams, that "our society faces exactly the kind of dilemma it is least prepared to deal with; the quarrels ... cannot be settled by dividing the pie."[4] If this is true for the upper Mississippi River, whose interests should take priority? This book provides the context for trying to answer these questions.

There is no comprehensive history of the upper Mississippi River that examines the origins of navigation improvements and how the conservation movement rose to challenge navigation's supremacy. Yet, besides nature, navigation improvements have been among the most powerful forces reshaping the river. Who fought for the projects and why? What exactly were they fighting for? What arguments and issues did they use? What was the national sentiment when Congress authorized each project? How have the visions Americans have held for the upper Mississippi River and its purposes evolved? What important compromises did conservationists initially win and how? Answering these questions will give the reader a greater appreciation for how we got to where we are today and some idea of the potential to influence what the past has bestowed upon us.

Steamboat traffic began on the upper Mississippi River in 1823, and by the eve of the Civil War had entered its packet boat heyday. But Congress provided little funding for navigation improvements before the war. Constitutional objections concerning the role of the federal government in internal improvements and the lack of political and economic strength in the early Midwest stymied most efforts to improve the river for navigation. (I distinguish between improving the river for navigation and improving the river. Throughout the history of navigation improvements, navigation boosters and others believed they were improving the river, perfecting what nature had begun.) Congress did fund minor work at the Des Moines and Rock Island Rapids but did not back comprehensive navigation improvements for the upper river. Chapter 1 examines the character of the natural river, the origins and growth of river commerce, the evolution of the federal government's attitude toward navigation improvements, and the little work that was done.

Following the Civil War, Midwesterners demanded more extensive and systematic improvements. To them the river was a poorly constructed highway that promised to become the region's greatest commercial artery, if properly improved. With increasing intensity from 1866 on, they sought access to the Atlantic Ocean and the world through the Mississippi to realize their manifest destiny. That destiny, they believed, was to become a commercial and industrial power as strong as the East, as well as to be the nation's breadbasket. To fulfill this destiny, they continually lobbied Congress to reshape the upper Mississippi. In response Congress authorized four broad navigation projects: the 4-, 4½-, 6-, and 9-foot channel projects. Each depth was set against the low-water year of 1864. Under the different projects, the river ideally would carry 4, 4½, 6, or 9 feet of water if it fell as low as it did in 1864. The locks and dams today create a 9-foot channel, although the river is often much deeper.

Chapter 2 shows how the Midwest's growing population, its increasing economic and political strength, and changes in the nation's philosophy toward internal improvements led Congress to approve navigation projects for the Mississippi. In 1866 Congress authorized the Corps to create a 4-foot channel. To do so, the Corps founded three districts on the upper Mississippi (St. Paul and Rock Island in 1866, and St. Louis in 1873), establishing a permanent stake in how the river would be transformed and managed. Between 1866 and 1877, the Corps tried to develop the 4-foot channel by removing snags, cutting back overhanging trees, and dredging. Although this work made the river safer for steamboats, it did not improve navigation much and changed the river's physical and ecological character little.

As the 4-foot channel failed to improve the upper river's navigability and as railroads increasingly captured the region's passenger and grain shipping, farmers and other navigation boosters began calling for more intensive efforts. Chapter 3 looks at who lobbied for a new project and how they successfully pressured Congress into authorizing the 4½-foot channel in 1878. Chapter 4 discusses how the Corps began sculpting a 4½-foot channel in the upper river between St. Paul and St. Louis, with wing dams, closing dams, and dredging. Under this project, the Corps began transforming the river's landscape and ecology in dramatic ways.

Although the Corps built hundreds of closing dams and wing dams, river traffic continued to falter. By the first decade of the twentieth century, the river's only significant commerce—lumber—began falling with the forests of Minnesota and Wisconsin, and the 4½-foot channel could not coax traffic away from the railroads. Commerce fell so far that railroad baron James J. Hill criticized the government for wasting money trying to make the upper river navigable. Railroads could handle all the traffic above the gateway city, he contended. His speech backfired. Already worried about railroad monopolies, navigation boosters sought a more aggressive project. With a 6-foot channel, they argued, traffic would return to the river. From 1902 to 1907 they lobbied Congress to establish the 6-foot channel. Their crusade received less popular support than the previous movement, but like that earlier movement, national events gave it a power and a visibility beyond the movement's own means. Responding as much to the national context as to the regional one, Congress authorized the 6-foot channel in 1907. Under this project, the Corps constricted the river even more. The Engineers raised and extended old wing dams and closing dams and added more of both. By 1930 wing dams studded the river between St. Louis and St. Paul, and nearly every side channel had a closing dam. Chapters 5 and 6 explore the continuing fall of commerce and the movement for the 6-foot channel.

As the Corps carved the 6-foot channel into the upper Mississippi, a new vision emerged for the river. It began as a local movement to establish a national park on the Mississippi in northeastern Iowa. When this failed, Will Dilg, one of the Izaak Walton League's founders, and others mounted a campaign to set aside 260 miles between Wabasha, Minnesota, and Rock Island, Illinois, for a fish and wildlife refuge. The river's deteriorating health spurred them. Pollution, sedimentation, levees, overuse, and channel constriction were overwhelming the river's fish and wildlife. Acknowledging national support for the river's environmental and aesthetic qualities, Congress authorized the Upper Mississippi

River National Wildlife and Fish Refuge in 1924. Dilg's success reflected and redefined how many Midwesterners and many Americans thought about the Mississippi and other rivers. Chapter 7 examines how conservation interests successfully established their stake in the river.

Conservationists won a piece of the upper Mississippi at a time when navigation seemed to be fading away. Some conservationists might have thought they would soon have the river to themselves. By 1918 no through commerce moved on the upper river. Nearly every city had abandoned its riverfront, and few had facilities for loading and unloading barges. But in 1924, the same year Congress authorized the refuge, a new navigation movement began to stir. The movement would exceed any previous navigation movement in economic and political strength. It would result in a new approach to restoring commerce to the river, an approach that, when laid over the refuge, the agricultural levees, and the river's natural features, defines the upper river's landscape and ecosystem today. Chapters 8, 9, and 10 examine the final fall of river commerce and the powerful movement that rose to restore it, the movement that ended with the 9-foot channel locks and dams.

Conservationists divided in their response to the project. As the two big meetings showed, many Izaak Walton League members rejected the locks and dams. Professional biologists within the Bureaus of Biological Survey and Fisheries, precursors to the Fish and Wildlife Service, provided essential support but undermined the League's arguments. Yet, together they won important compromises. Their success, while limited, heralded a new era on the upper Mississippi River. From this time on, navigation interests have had to consider the impacts of their projects on the river's environmental qualities.

Although I briefly bring environmental and commercial navigation issues up to date in the epilogue, this history ends with the completion of the 9-foot channel project in 1940. One goal of this book is to inform people about why Congress authorized the major navigation projects for the upper Mississippi River. The 9-foot channel project was the last major project authorized for the whole upper river. Those pushing for navigation improvements today are looking for modifications to the existing system, not an entirely new project. Another goal is to explain the origins of today's controversy over the river's future. This controversy centers on the locks and dams built under this project. The debate is largely being carried on by biologists, engineers, shippers, politicians, and environmental organizations. While they have little understanding of the history, they often premise their positions on it. Finally, so much history has occurred since 1940 that the history from 1940 to the millennium's end would require another book or two.

Today the federal government is the dominant player in managing the upper Mississippi River. This rankles some states and many individuals. In November 1994, the Upper Mississippi River Basin Association (UMRBA) hosted a meeting titled "Management of the Upper Mississippi River Basin: Current Issues and Options." The association was formed in 1981 after President Ronald Reagan terminated the federally established Upper Mississippi River Basin Commission. The governors of the five upper river states (Minnesota, Wisconsin, Iowa, Illinois, and Missouri) created the association to continue a forum for discussing management and policy issues concerning the river. The association held the meeting to explore different management strategies for the upper Mississippi River. Rather than continue with the current situation, in which a plethora of federal, state, and local agencies, with the federal government clearly dominant, managed the river, the UMRBA wanted to explore models with a more coordinated approach and with more state and local control. The meeting reflected a growing interest by the states, who wanted a greater say in the upper river's management. The explanation for the current management system lies in the river's history and emerges throughout this book.[5]

Navigation opponents have often charged that the navigation projects were pork barrel. This sidetracks the current debate from important issues. To move on, we have to acknowledge that none of the major navigation projects was simply engineers' dreams, as one opponent of the 9-foot channel charged. They were not spurious projects pursued by a small, elite minority at the expense of the nation's taxpayers. To contend that they were ignores the Midwest's long and determined efforts for the projects and underestimates the breadth and depth of support behind them. The Corps did not lead the battle for any of the major projects. They did play a small, proactive role in the 6-foot channel effort but, initially, mounted the strongest opposition to the 9-foot channel. Some local projects were clearly pork barrel, intended to benefit one community and a specific politician, and even the Corps complained about these. And no coherent, private water elite rose to impose its order on the river. Since the region's origins, Midwesterners have regarded the Mississippi River as an essential component of their transportation network. Midwesterners, from small river towns to the river's large urban centers, from farmers to real-estate brokers, have pushed for the projects because they believed the region's economy depended on cheap transportation.

No two movements were alike. They evolved with the region, reflecting its changing needs and its growing economic and political power. The 4½-foot channel project's main impetus came, not surprisingly, from farmers, since they dominated the region's population and economy, but small town merchants and city boosters also backed the project. Commercial interests in the cities along the upper river had to struggle on their own to win the 6-foot channel. Dealing with economies reeling from the loss of timber shipping and manufacturing, they looked to the river as their salvation. Farmers were noticeably absent, as they enjoyed unusually good times. Nine-foot channel proponents put together the most formidable, broad-based, and concerted effort. Their movement reflected the plight of farmers in the 1920s and the fears of large, well-established commercial interests, both of which saw the river as an essential element to the region's economy.

The Izaak Walton League under Will Dilg mounted the broadest and most impressive grassroots campaign focused on the river. The 260-mile-long Upper Mississippi River National Wildlife and Fish Refuge gave the League and others concerned about the river's aesthetic and biological qualities a stake in managing the river. Ecosystem issues today are different above and below Rock Island (the refuge's southern boundary) because of the refuge.

Knowing the history of how the river came to be in its current state will, I hope, place the debate over the river's future in a fuller context. And I hope this book will interest more people in the river and its history so that the decisions made for the river are as informed and widely understood as possible. Even if some people do not agree with my narrative, I hope this book spurs them to expand the debate and delve deeper into the river's history. The river wrought for the Midwest by the Corps and others is a legacy of the dreams and desires of past generations. The river the Corps and others forge today will reflect the dreams and desires Midwesterners hold for it now.

CHAPTER 1

Innumerable

Paddling upstream from St. Louis, Missouri, to Fort Snelling, Minnesota, in 1823, the *Virginia* became the first steamboat to navigate the upper Mississippi River. It did so twice that year. Other boats plied the river—birchbark and dugout canoes, pirogues, flatboats, and keelboats—but the *Virginia* announced a new era. Italian adventurer and romantic Giacomo Beltrami, a passenger on that first voyage, captured the moment best. Upon arriving at Fort Snelling, at the confluence of the Minnesota and Mississippi Rivers, he declared: "Our passage to this place forms an epoch in the history of navigation. It was an enterprise of the boldest, most extraordinary nature."[1] One hundred and eighteen feet long, 22 feet wide, and sitting 5 feet into the water, the *Virginia* showed that under steam power, people and goods could move far more quickly and in greater numbers and quantities than on boats with poles, paddles, or sails. From this time on, most who relied on a navigable river would find its natural character troublesome and call for the river's transformation into a commercial highway.[2]

What steamboat pilots and pioneers found troublesome—sandbars, snags, fluctuating water levels, leaning trees, braided channels, and rapids—provided habitat for uncounted plants and animals, some of which have disappeared from the river, and some from the planet. Many species recoiled at American expansion, well before the federal government initiated navigation improvements. No catalogs exist of the exact variety and numbers of species, but the observations of early explorers and travelers are sufficient to show how much the river and its valley have changed. Buffalo, wolves, passenger pigeons, rattlesnakes, and the ancient paddlefish once abounded in or along the river. A massive forest blanketed the valley and its countless islands.

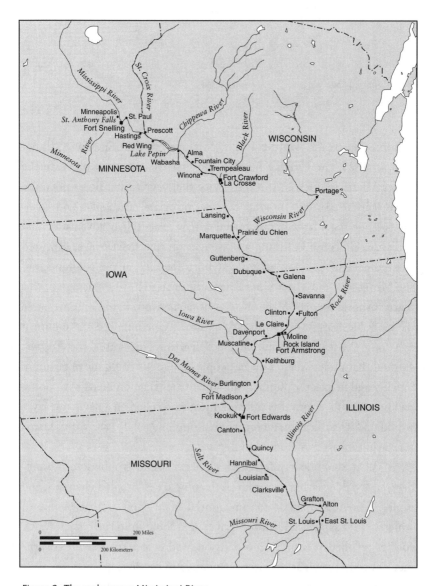

Figure 2. The early upper Mississippi River

The Heyday of the Steamboat

In twenty days the *Virginia* traveled the 700 miles between St. Louis and Fort Snelling, just above present-day St. Paul, Minnesota, despite running only during the day and stopping frequently to gather wood. But a keelboat, which had been the principal craft for hauling large loads upstream before steamboats, made only 8 to 15 miles a day upstream, unless it had a favorable wind and could unfurl its sail. Built on a keel, with ribs and planking, keelboats measured 40 to 80 feet long and 7 to 10 feet wide and had drafts—the depth of the boat below the surface—of only 20 to 30 inches when loaded. An average cargo might weigh 15 tons. One keelboat the *Virginia* overtook needed a month to travel the 425 miles from St. Louis to Galena, Illinois. Major John Biddle, a passenger on the *Virginia* during its second voyage of 1823, reported that a keelboat often required thirty-six days to reach Fort Snelling; the *Virginia* had taken only fifteen. By one estimate, steamboats reduced the shipping costs on the Mississippi River by about one-third.[3]

Steamboat traffic grew quickly after 1823, spurred mostly by the lead trade. During the late eighteenth century, fur traders and explorers learned that the Sauk and Fox Indians mined lead around Galena and in the adjoining lands in Wisconsin and Iowa. In 1807 the U.S. government asserted control of this area and began issuing permits to miners. By 1823 pioneers were streaming into St. Louis and other ports along the upper Mississippi and taking steamboats north to lead country. In 1829 the mines near Galena employed some ten thousand people. For the next twenty years, lead dominated the upper Mississippi's commercial shipping. Located on the Fever River, just upstream from the Mississippi, Galena became the busiest port above St. Louis. Between 1823 and 1847, miners excavated and shipped 472 million pounds of lead downstream. After 1847, the lead supply waned and the trade declined.[4]

Nevertheless, steamboat traffic on the upper Mississippi increased. One measure of this was the number of times steamboats docked at the upper river's port cities. Some steamboats landed only once, while others returned many times. St. Paul recorded 44 steamboat arrivals in 1841, and 95 in 1849. During the 1850s, traffic boomed. By

1857, St. Paul had become a bustling port, with over 1,000 steamboat arrivals each year by some sixty-two to ninety-nine boats. One hundred and thirteen river miles downstream, Winona, Minnesota, counted 1,700 steamboat dockings in 1857. At Davenport, Iowa, steamboats landed 1,587 times that year. The number of steamboat dockings at St. Louis grew from 1,721 in 1840 to 3,443 in 1857. In 1841, 143 of these steamboats hailed from the upper river, and by 1852, 705 originated above the Gateway City. Steamboats grew not only in number but in size and in the tonnage they carried.[5]

As rapidly as the number of steamboats increased, demand outpaced them. In 1854 the *Minnesota Pioneer*, a St. Paul newspaper, reported that passengers and freight overflowed from every steamboat that

Date	Number
1844	41
1845	48
1846	24
1847	47
1848	63
1849	95
1850	104
1851	119
1852	171
1853	200
1854	256
1855	560
1856	837
1857	1,026
1858	1,090
1859	802
1860	776
1861	772
1862	846

Figure 3. Number of steamboat arrivals at St. Paul, 1844–62. *Sources*: Frank Haigh Dixon, *A Traffic History of the Mississippi River System* (Washington, D.C.: U.S. Government Printing Office, 1909), 20; Mildred Hartsough, *From Canoe to Steel Barge* (Minneapolis: University of Minnesota Press, 1934), 100.

arrived, and that "the present tonnage on the river is by no means sufficient to handle one-half the business of the trade."[6] While two steamboats often left St. Paul each day, merchants and farmers deposited
goods and produce faster than they could carry it away. Many upper river
cities mirrored St. Paul. Each steamboat that docked created more business and a greater backlog, as more immigrants disembarked to establish
new farms and enterprises.[7]

Passenger traffic on the upper Mississippi River accelerated after
the *Virginia*'s arrival in 1823. Spurred by Indian land cessions that
opened much of the Midwest between 1820 and 1860, by Iowa's state-
hood in 1846 and Wisconsin's in 1848, and by the creation of the Minnesota territory in 1849, immigrants flowed into the upper Midwest.
Many of these immigrants came from the East; others came from
Europe, fleeing famine in Ireland and political upheaval on the conti-
nent. While some immigrants arrived by way of the Great Lakes, many
settlers entering Iowa, Minnesota, and western Wisconsin made part
of their journey on the upper river. Historian Roald Tweet contends
that "the number of immigrants boarding boats at St. Louis and traveling upriver to St. Paul dwarfed the 1849 gold rush to California and
Oregon."[8] Over one million passengers arrived at or left from St. Louis
in 1855 alone. Immigration swelled the population of the four upper
river states above Missouri between 1850 and 1860. Minnesota's population jumped from 6,077 to 172,023, Iowa's from 192,000 to 674,913,
Wisconsin's from 305,391 to 775,881, and Illinois's from 851,470 to
1,711,951. Passenger traffic became so important to the steamboat trade
that by 1850 passenger receipts exceeded freight receipts.[9]

Railroads reaching the river's east bank in the 1850s both hurt
and promoted river traffic. Railroads fed passengers and goods to
steamboats. After arriving at a railhead, many immigrants and goods
transferred to steamboats for destinations up or downstream. Railroads,
however, began segmenting the river trade. Boats that once traveled the
whole upper river made shorter trips between railheads. In 1854 the first
two railroads reached the Mississippi River: the Chicago and Rock
Island Railroad at Rock Island, Illinois, and the Chicago and Alton at

Alton, Illinois. In 1855 a railroad entered Galena. Quincy and Cairo, Illinois, became railheads in 1856; and East St. Louis, Illinois, and Prairie du Chien, Wisconsin, in 1857. La Crosse, Wisconsin, joined these cities, becoming the terminus of the Milwaukee and La Crosse in 1858. In 1856 the Chicago and Rock Island became the first railroad to cross the river. But the economic panic of 1857 and the Civil War ended further railroad expansion across the Mississippi. Despite the growing railroads, river traffic remained strong. Midwestern agricultural production explains why.[10]

Agricultural output surged with the Midwest's population. In 1850 the four upper river states above Missouri produced 12.0 million bushels of wheat and 63.6 million bushels of corn. Ten years later the wheat harvest reached 43.1 million bushels, and that of corn 124.5 million bushels.[11] While the river did not move all this grain, the agricultural boom hinted at the potential for river shipping. By 1860 agricultural production overwhelmed steamboat capacity. That spring, the *Stillwater Messenger* estimated that farmers between St. Paul and La Crosse had stockpiled 200,000 bushels of grain, hoping some steamboat might carry them away. By the beginning of the navigation season, farmers had added another 150,000 bushels. Demand spurred steamboats to start pushing barges. One barge could carry as much as 10,000 bushels of grain loaded into sacks, and some steamboats pushed five barges (a difficult proposition on the natural river). The St. Paul trade employed more than 186 barges by 1866. While some barges moved grain to railheads for transshipment, others carried their cargoes to St. Louis or on to New Orleans.[12]

Timber products became the upper river's most important commerce. The forests of Wisconsin and Minnesota possessed immense stands of white pine, and the upper Midwest's geography provided the ideal distribution system. Stout and buoyant but easily cut and milled, white pine became the primary building material for most Midwestern cities. Lumbering began in western Wisconsin and Minnesota in the late 1830s and grew swiftly during the 1840s and 1850s. The Mississippi River and its tributaries drained much of the richly timbered lands of western and central Wisconsin and northeastern and north-central Minnesota and became the avenue by which most timber moved. The Wisconsin River, which emptied most of the state's central region, ran from north-central to south-central Wisconsin and then turned south-westward to the Mississippi at Prairie du Chien. Above Prairie du Chien, and draining much of western Wisconsin, flowed the Chippewa, Black, and other rivers. On the border between Minnesota and Wisconsin, the St. Croix River supplied the Mississippi with timber from both states. Finally, the Mississippi itself drained the north-central heart of Minnesota, carrying logs and lumber to Minneapolis, which would become the largest timber milling center west of Chicago. Following the Civil War, when railroads crossed the river and crisscrossed the plains, the importance of the region's geography would become even more apparent. Complementing the timbered river basins of Minnesota, Michigan, and Wisconsin lay the sparsely timbered or timberless plains of Iowa, southwestern Minnesota, Nebraska, Kansas, and the Dakotas. Before the Civil War, however, most of the timber went to build cities along the rivers or just inland. St. Louis, with its large population and financial resources, initially dominated the lumber milling and retailing on the upper river. As early as 1844, St. Louis consumed about one-half of the sawed lumber from the upper Mississippi River.[13]

The seasons dictated the lumber industry's annual cycle. During the winter, lumber companies felled trees in the upper Mississippi's tributary valleys and stockpiled them on a streambank or rolled them onto the ice to await the spring thaw. In the spring, logs flooded the small streams and larger tributaries, sometimes causing massive logjams. On the larger tributaries, millers near the timber's source caught their logs in booms and sawed them into finished lumber. They then assembled the cut lumber and piled it onto rafts to float to lumberyards down-stream or on the main stem. Other logs, belonging to millers farther downstream or on the Mississippi, were bound into small rafts and floated to their destinations. As long as millers could float their logs downstream without losing too many, they did so. On lakes and on large rivers like the Mississippi, where logs might scatter and catch on bars or stray into back channels, lumber companies formed them into large rafts. Starting in the 1840s and lasting up to the Civil War, most rafts on the Mississippi River's tributaries drifted with the current, steered by large oars, to downstream mills and lumberyards. On Lake Pepin, a 25-mile-long widening of the river about 50 miles below St. Paul, and on other slow reaches, millers tried pushing the rafts downstream with steam-boats. These raftboats, as they became known, would not become common on the big river until after the Civil War.[14]

As steam power revolutionized shipping on the Mississippi, it also transformed lumber milling. Early sawmills relied on water power, which required a steeper drop than generally found along the main stem. Steam power allowed entrepreneurs in villages and cities all along the river and its tributaries to establish mills. When Stephan Hanks, who would become one of the upper Mississippi's renowned pilots, traveled up the river in 1842, he encountered only two sawmills on the St. Croix River, and few on the Mississippi below Hastings, Minnesota. The first steam-powered sawmill opened at Stillwater, on the St. Croix River, in 1851, and others followed quickly. Towns such as Red Wing, Wabasha, and Winona, Minnesota; La Crosse and Prairie du Chien, Wisconsin; Clinton, Davenport, and Fort Madison, Iowa; and Rock Island, Moline, Quincy, and Alton, Illinois, became important milling centers based on steam power. In 1852 Hanks reported that 135 mills operated between St. Paul and St. Louis.[15] Lumber products comprised the greatest quantity and value of merchandise shipped on the river. More than passenger traffic or grain hauling, timber shipping would benefit from the effort to transform the river from a natural stream to a commercial highway.

Since timber, grain, and passenger traffic were growing rapidly on the upper Mississippi River before the Civil War, most navigation boosters believed the river would steadily rise as the region's paramount commercial link with the eastern United States and the world. Few boosters realized what railroads would do to river commerce following the war. They had no idea that the 1850s would be thought of as the steamboat's heyday. Although railroads had begun contending for the river's traffic before the war, most navigation boosters believed that channel improvements would keep the Mississippi dominant or at least competitive.[16]

Navigating the Natural River

Before 1866 the upper Mississippi River still possessed most of its natural character, a character early explorers and travelers found beautiful (if at times annoying), steamboat pilots found perilous, and Midwesterners feared might stifle the region's progress. Leaning trees, snags, islands, sandbars, and rapids delayed or blocked navigation. While explorers and travelers commented on the variety and abundance of wildlife, they did not recognize or value the habitat the river's natural character provided.

Trees filled and enshrouded the natural river. Where boats followed the deepest channel as it hugged one shore or the other, leaning trees might sweep off poorly placed cargo or an unwary passenger. Many trees fell into the water to become snags. Snags skewered the careless and even the cautious boat. Steamboat pilots classified these frequent and treacherous hazards: sawyers swayed back and forth with the current, preachers bowed in and out of the water, planters lodged themselves in the river's bottom, and sleepers hid beneath the water's surface.[17]

American explorer Lieutenant Zebulon Montgomery Pike quickly discovered snags and other obstacles to navigating the upper Mississippi. Pike left St. Louis on August 9, 1805, in a 70-foot-long keelboat. He carried twenty men and supplies for four months. General James Wilkinson, the commander-in-chief of the western army and governor of the Louisiana Territory, had ordered Pike to discover the Mississippi's source, choose and acquire the best sites for military posts, make alliances with the Chippewa and Dakota, stop intertribal fighting, assess the fur trade, take meteorological observations, and generally evaluate the resources the United States had acquired west of the Mississippi with the Louisiana Purchase of 1803. America already owned the land east of the river (ignoring Native American claims), having acquired it through the Treaty of Paris in 1783, which concluded the Revolution. British traders still dominated the fur trade of the upper Mississippi River valley, however. The twenty-six-year-old Pike set out to proclaim the American presence.[18]

Figure 4. Zebulon Pike became the first American explorer on the upper Mississippi River. Portrait by Charles Wilson Peale. Courtesy of the Independence National Historical Park.

Pike's experiences and those of explorers and travelers who came before and after him gave the American government a good idea of what it would take to make the upper Mississippi navigable. On August 16, about 130 miles above St. Louis, a snag caught the keelboat, forcing Pike's men into the water, where they cut it from under the boat. Three days later, a snag pierced their hull, and they started sinking. Scrambling to plug the leak and bailing frantically, they rode onto a sandbar. They unloaded their slightly less than four months of provisions and replaced a broken plank. Given the size of the forests on the upper river's shores and islands, the source of snags must have seemed inexhaustible.[19]

Pike and other explorers provide sporadic but informative details about the upper river's forests. For the first part of his trip, Pike recorded some tree species he passed. From St. Louis to the Salt River, a reach of about 100 miles, he found buttonwood, ash, cottonwood, hackberry, and ash. Not far below the Salt, he saw cliffs populated by cedars to the east and sugar maple, ash, pecan, locust, and black walnut along the shores. Above the Salt River, he first mentions oak and hickory trees, noting that more oaks grew on the west side. One hundred and fifty-seven miles above St. Louis, at the Wyaconda River, oak and pecan began to dominate. Just above the Des Moines Rapids, he records only oak and ash but suggests that other species existed. He then skips up to around Rock Island, Illinois. Here prairies spread out to the west, and black walnut and hickory trees were present. Pike also observed the river's forests interrupted by prairies just above St. Louis, from the Illinois River to the Buffalo River, from the Iowa River to the Rock River, and at Prairie du Chien and La Crosse.[20]

Subsequent travelers and explorers offer more evidence of the river's immense, primeval forests, especially above Rock Island. In early August 1820, an expedition under Michigan Territorial Governor Lewis Cass came down the Mississippi River from the north and stopped at Fort Crawford at Prairie du Chien. Henry Rowe Schoolcraft, the expedition's mineralogist and geologist (and subsequently credited with identifying the Mississippi's source), could not pass up the opportunity to examine the lead mines near Dubuque, Iowa, some 50 miles downstream. Although interested in mining, Schoolcraft described the valley's flora along his route. He estimated that the river valley grew to 2 miles wide. Prairie grass covered part of the adjoining land, and a dense forest of cottonwood, elm, sugar maple, black walnut, and ash blanketed the rest. Unlike most travelers or explorers, Schoolcraft noted the "humbler growth" at the forest's edge, which included flowering poplar, dogwood, sumac, aspen, and sarsaparilla. Mature trees covered some islands, and young willows and cottonwoods populated low-lying sand-bars. Shrub oaks dotted the tall-grass prairies, suggesting an oak savannah, which "a peculiar tribe of heath-flowers" adorned.[21]

English explorer Jonathan Carver may have been the first to comment on the savannahs bordering the upper Mississippi. After descending the Wisconsin River, Carver paddled north on the Mississippi in early November 1766. Between the Wisconsin River and Lake Pepin, a reach of about 130 miles, he encountered broad, grass-covered plains on both sides. Grass also carpeted the slopes leading to the bluff tops. Small groves of oak and walnut trees spotted the prairie.[22]

Figure 5. *View on the Mississippi 70 Miles below the Falls of St. Anthony*, by Seth Eastman. Wildlife, islands, backwaters, and snags abounded on the natural upper Mississippi River. Courtesy of the Minnesota Historical Society.

The savannahs mystified Beltrami. Writing about the upper river, he saw one continuous forest, covering much of the northern United States and Canada, broken by unforested or sparsely forested prairies that sometimes ran to the river's edge. The groves of trees dotting the prairies were placed, he thought, "with so much art and symmetry, that, ... it would be impossible not to think that they had been placed there by the hand of man."[23] Although he only partially made the correlation between this landscape and humans, he later provided an explanation.

At dark, some 15 to 20 miles below Lake Pepin, the glow of a huge fire caught Beltrami's attention. "The venerable trees of these eternal forests," he exclaimed, were burning out of control. A fierce northwest wind drove the fire through the prairie and up the bluff slopes, adding to the inferno's height, so that to Beltrami the bluffs appeared like volcanoes. While his boat, the *Virginia*, had traveled only during the day, the fire, which Beltrami estimated extended for 15 miles, burned so brightly, they pushed on through the night. Native Americans, he suggested, set such fires annually to make travel on the prairies easier. Native Americans also set fires, often in the spring, to keep the forest back and encourage buffalo and other grassland species to migrate closer to the river.[24]

Three Frenchmen may have been the first to witness the Dakota deliberately setting fire to the prairie, suggesting the practice was old by Beltrami's time. In 1677 Robert Cavelier, sieur de la Salle, gained royal permission for an expedition to discover the river's mouth and source. Delays, however, left him only as far as a fort on the Illinois River, just below Peoria, Illinois, in January 1680. When directed to return to Montreal, La Salle chose Michael Accault, a voyageur, to lead an expedition to the Mississippi, accompanied by Antoine Auguelle and Father Louis Hennepin.

The small party headed down the Illinois on February 29, 1680, reaching the Mississippi in early March. As they canoed up the Mississippi, they met a Dakota party of 120 men in thirty-three canoes. After convincing the Dakota that their enemies, the Miami of Illinois, had already gone west, the two parties returned upriver. Landing near present-day downtown St. Paul, the Dakota abandoned their canoes, and as they marched overland to their villages around Mille Lacs Lake, in north-central Minnesota, they set the prairie behind them on fire. Hennepin thought they did it to hurry the Frenchmen along.[25]

The river's forest provided an endless supply of snags, leaning trees, and habitat. Each spring flood undercut the river's banks, toppling more trees into the river. While leaning trees threatened cargoes and people running too close to shore, they provided a stand for hunting birds. Schoolcraft observed many trees leaning into the river, and "perched upon these," he wrote, "we invariably find the heron, and king-fisher, who, with motionless anxiety, watch for their finny prey."[26]

Hundreds of islands divided the natural river, dispersing its waters into countless side channels and backwaters. To Pike and other novices, every island meant more channels, detours, and dead ends. The number of islands overwhelmed Pike. Only 15 miles above St. Louis, the many islands began annoying and often delaying him. They especially thwarted his progress from above the Des Moines Rapids to the Iowa River, a reach of about 70 miles. Above Prairie du Chien he complained that they were "never clear of islands...."[27] And from the Minnesota River to St. Anthony Falls, he reported, "there is almost one continued rapid, aggravated by the interruption of 12 small islands."[28] On August 4, 1820, James Duane Doty, the official journalist for the Cass expedition, grumbled that they had encountered many islands and, therefore, many channels, after heading downstream from the St. Croix River. Some channels, he explained, "are very circuitous & almost impassible. It is therefore very difficult to ascertain which are the correct ones."[29] Fifteen years later, George Featherstonaugh, a geologist and adventurer, believed that only mosquitoes outnumbered the islands. "Once or twice," he admitted, "we got into a *cul de sac* during the afternoon, and only found out our error by discovering, as we advanced, that there was no current."[30] Islands also created dangerous currents. When the river forced his lumber raft into Argo Island, near Winona, Minnesota, a raft-boat pilot cursed the island as having "a good appetite for a raft!"[31]

Climbing a bluff below La Crosse, on September 4, 1835, Feath-erstonaugh described a scene that explains how he and others could become lost among the river's islands. The scene also reveals the importance of islands as habitat. Featherstonaugh estimated that the valley spread 3 miles wide. Below him stood "an immense forest, growing upon innumerable islands, among which various streams were gliding." Some large islands held small lakes, with extensive stands of "zizania," or wild rice, and great flocks of waterfowl, beginning their fall migration, feasted on it.[32]

Pike and other travelers invaded pigeon rookeries, presumably of the now extinct passenger pigeon, on some islands. On April 12, 1806, during his return trip to St. Louis, Pike stopped at an island about 10 miles above the Salt River. Astounded, he exclaimed that "the most fervid imagination cannot conceive their numbers." In fifteen minutes his men clubbed and took on board 298 birds. "Their noise in the woods," he marveled, "was like the continued roaring of the wind. . . ." Wild peas and acorns filled the fatty, almost full-sized chicks.[33] Eighteen years later, at the head of Lake Pepin, William Keating, the geologist and mineralogist on Stephen Long's 1823 expedition, encountered a similar island rookery, and his party too killed a great number in only a few minutes.[34]

Islands also provided nesting habitat for turtles. Based on the quantity of eggs his men gathered from the sand, Keating concluded that the river's islands possessed huge turtle populations. He surmised that the turtles laid their eggs on the islands, uphill from the river, covered them with sand, and left them to incubate in the sun. He found the spiny soft shell and the common map turtle.[35]

Until the *Virginia*'s successful voyages, skeptics doubted that steamboats could navigate the Des Moines and Rock Island Rapids. The Des Moines Rapids extended 11¼ miles upstream from present-day Keokuk, Iowa, which is about 200 miles above St. Louis. Here the river had worn its bottom down to bedrock over the previous 120,000 years. No definable navigation channel flowed through the rapids, making the whole cataract treacherous during low water. At these times, boats with a draft of more than 24 inches dared not venture through the Des Moines Rapids.

Pike may have recorded the first lightering of cargo around the Des Moines Rapids, but fur traders undoubtedly knew the drill well. Pike arrived at the head of the rapids on August 20 and began ascending them, with some difficulty. Luckily, William Ewing (an agent to the Sac

Indians), a French interpreter, four chiefs, and fifteen men of the Sac came down the rapids to meet them in canoes. Lightening Pike's keelboat, they took fourteen of Pike's heaviest barrels and provided two men to guide him through the rapids. (Within a few decades, this service would become a business.) Stephen Long was not as fortunate descending the rapids. On August 4, 1817, he tried to run the rapids at low water. His boat struck the rocky bottom a number of times, hard enough to cause a leak. To keep from sinking, his men bailed constantly, until they reached Fort Edwards at the foot of the rapids.[36]

Travelers who scaled the Des Moines Rapids then faced the rapids at Rock Island, roughly 110 miles upriver. The Rock Island Rapids ran for 13¾ miles. Only 18,000 to 20,000 years old, the Rock Island Rapids still had sharp outcroppings, lying below the river's shallow surface. The rapids had navigable channels or reaches, but during low water, less than 30 inches of water covered the rapids.

On August 28, Pike found James Aird, a Scottish-born fur trader, camped at the foot of the Rock Island Rapids, undertaking a familiar exercise. Aird had breached the hull of his boat coming down the rapids, forcing him to unload and repair it. After breakfast with Aird, Pike headed up the rapids and immediately lost his rudder. While fixing it, a strong wind arose. Pike raised his sail and moved briskly but recklessly up the rapids. Had the keelboat hit a rock, he admitted, it would have sunk. He continued sailing despite meeting two of Aird's boats stranded on rocks.[37]

Skeptics doubted whether steamboats could pass the two rapids, and the *Virginia* almost confirmed their fears. On the evening of May 6, the *Virginia* paddled away from Fort Edwards, at the foot of the Des Moines Rapids. Too heavily loaded for its 5-foot draft, the boat grounded on a rock in the middle reach. Escaping with minor damage, the captain returned to the fort, presumably to lighten his load. The *Virginia* ran aground again in the Rock Island Rapids. This time the boat remained stranded for two days, until, luckily, the river rose and freed it.[38]

The river's natural pulse made the river undependable and unpredictable for navigation. Floods and low water restricted navigation or made travel dangerous. During high water, the river spread into its vast floodplains, filling lakes and sloughs and covering low-lying prairies. Spring floods could reroute the navigation channel. The rushing water undermined the river's banks, swallowing the rocks, soil, and trees that fell into it, giving birth to new hazards and habitat. Low water forced shippers to partially load their vessels and prevented them from operating on some reaches. An inadequate spring runoff, or lack of rain in the fall, or month-long droughts could restrict navigation for several weeks to an entire season. For four to five months each year, ice closed the river's upper reaches.[39]

Low water emphasized the upper Mississippi's plethora of sandbars. For navigation, sandbars posed the most persistent and frequent problem. They divided the upper Mississippi into a series of pools separated by wide shallows that snared birchbark canoes and stranded steamboats. Sandbars determined the river's overall navigability. A bad bar could separate one end of the river from the other. Normally, during the late summer or early fall, the river began falling and entered the stage steamboat pilots and Corps engineers called low water. During low water, no continuous channel existed. Deep pools might run near one bank for a short reach and then jump to the other. Or a series of deeper pools separated by shallow sandbars could be scattered across the main stem. Pilots considered deep anything over 3½ feet.

Sandbars determined the river's controlling depth—the maximum depth for navigation at low water. From St. Paul to the St. Croix River, the controlling depth at low water was 16 inches. From the St. Croix to the Chippewa River (about 150 miles downriver), it reached 18 inches. Over the next 132 miles, from the Chippewa to the Wisconsin River, the Mississippi gained only 2 inches, making the low water depth 20 inches. And from the Wisconsin to the Illinois River (a distance of about 412 miles), it attained 2 feet. By 1905, the Corps would identify 227 recurring bars between the Missouri River and St. Paul. It is not just folklore that people once waded across the Mississippi.[40]

As Pike quickly learned, sandbars interrupted navigation beginning at the Missouri River. On August 11, two days after departing St. Louis,

Pike camped just above the mouth of the Illinois River. Sandbars accounted for his slow progress. He had spent part of the day dragging his 70-foot-long keelboat over bars. Two days later bars again delayed him and again, at times, forced his men into the water to haul the keelboat over. On August 19, just below the Des Moines Rapids, sandbars ended an already bad day. Earlier, he had unloaded his boat and replaced a plank. Undaunted, Pike drove on after dark but became "entangled in sandbars," persuading him to camp for the night. Above the Des Moines Rapids, sandbars either troubled Pike less, or he quit complaining about them.[41]

Other explorers and travelers found sandbars as great a problem above the rapids as Pike did below. During the night of July 18, 1817, Long returned down the Mississippi, drifting with the current from the Minnesota River to the St. Croix, in his six-oared skiff, occasionally bumping into a sandbar. On July 27, Long met a boat carrying nine months of supplies for Forts Edwards, Armstrong (on Rock Island), and Crawford. The boat had struggled at both rapids, and sandbars had often delayed its progress. The boat had left St. Louis on June 8, seven days after Long.[42]

Three years later, the Cass expedition headed down the Mississippi from Fort Snelling (then Fort St. Anthony) to Prairie du Chien. On August 4, Schoolcraft observed that "navigation is rendered more difficult, on account of the innumerable sand bars" below the Chippewa River's mouth. He accurately noted that sandbars increased because the Chippewa carried so much sand into the Mississippi. While Schoolcraft limited his complaints about sandbars to the river below the Chippewa, Charles C. Trowbridge, another expedition member, wrote that from St. Anthony Falls to Prairie du Chien, they found "sand bars without number, which extending in every direction from the shores very much impeded our progress; and indeed we were fortunate if we did not strike 15 to 20 of them in a day...." They were traveling in birchbark canoes.[43]

George Byron Merrick captures well the perils of piloting the natural Mississippi River for the increasing number of steamboats. Born in Niles, Michigan, on the St. Joseph River, Merrick watched steamboats plow back and forth between South Bend, Indiana, and the town of St. Joseph on Lake Michigan. When Merrick was twelve years old, his family left Michigan and traveled to Rock Island. There they took a steamboat upriver to Prescott, Wisconsin, some 30 miles below St. Paul, arriving in June 1854. Merrick's father bought a warehouse on the levee from which he ran a storage and transshipping business. He also sold "boat-stores" and groceries to the steamboats that stopped at the levee. The family lived in the upper two stories, George sharing the attic with his brother.[44] From there the boys could see and hear every steamboat that stopped at or passed the levee. "And thus," Merrick recalled, "we grew into the very life of the river as we grew in years."[45] When old enough, he began working on a steamboat as a cabin boy and after one season became a cub engineer. Over the next nine years he worked his way up to become a cub pilot. But in 1862 he left the river to fight in the Civil War. After the war, he settled in New York. In 1876 he returned to Wisconsin to become—fittingly—a railway agent and later a newspaper editor and publisher.[46]

From his experiences, Merrick learned much about the natural river. The dangers of navigating the river loomed so great, he said, that pilots had to memorize "every bluff, hill, rock, tree, stump, house, wood-pile, and whatever else is to be noted along the banks of the river." A pilot, he continued,

> further added to this fund of information a photographic negative in his mind, showing the shape of all the curves, bends, capes, and points of the river's bank, so that he may shut his eyes, yet see it all, and with such certainty that he can, on a night so perfectly black that the shore line is blotted out, run his boat within fifty feet of the shore and dodge snags, wrecks, overhanging trees, and all other obstacles by running the shape of the river as he knows it to be—not as he can see it.[47]

And pilots learned "the artistic quality" of their craft, Merrick declared, "in handling of a boat under the usual conditions—in making the multitudinous crossings, . . . dodging reefs and hunting the best water."[48] As

Pike, Long, Aird, and others had learned, poor hunters often fell prey to the river they hunted.

At first Merrick called sandbars the "terror" of steamboat pilots. Reconsidering, he said "resignation" more aptly captured their attitude. Pilots, he boasted, knew where to find the deepest water, "but they also knew that when they found the best water it would be too thin to float any boat drawing over three and a half feet. With a four-foot load line it simply meant that the steamboat must be hauled through six inches of sand by main strength and awkwardness, and that meant delay, big wood bills, bigger wage-lists, wear and tear of material, and decreased earnings." And yet, he complained, "A big packet not loaded below the four-foot line was not laden to the money-making point."[49] Henry Lewis, who traveled on the upper river in 1846, 1847, and 1848 to paint a panorama of the river, claimed boats lasted only four to five years, due to the "wear and tear in getting over sandbars, etc., and the frail construction of the boat[s]...."[50] And in 1862, Nathan Daly, the son of a Minnesota pioneer family fleeing from the Dakota Conflict in Minnesota, described the effect bars could have on a steamboat's hull. Traveling down the Mississippi to Illinois, Daly's family camped for a night a few miles below St. Paul. Here, the *Northern Light*, one of the largest steamers on the upper river, passed them just after sundown. The young Daly recalled that he could "distinctly hear the grinding of her bottom on the gravel bar over which she was passing."[51] Some boats ground to a halt on sandbars. To get off, pilots sometimes used spars, long wood poles on which the front and back of the boats would be alternately jacked up and pushed forward. In this way, pilots hoped to walk their boat over the bar. If lucky, they avoided "hogging" the boat, that is, warping or breaking its hull, which they could do if they set their boat on the crest of a steep bank.[52]

While Merrick, Hennepin, Carver, Pike, Schoolcraft, and others considered sandbars, islands, leaning trees, braided channels, and snags obstacles, they marveled at the abundance and variety of fish and wildlife that depended on this critical habitat. Hennepin offered two strikingly different accounts of wildlife on the upper Mississippi. On his trip up the river, during the early spring of 1680, wildlife—food—abounded.

After entering the Mississippi from the Illinois River, he boasted that "our canoe was loaded with seven or eight big wild turkeys, which are plentiful in this country. We did not lack for buffaloes, deer, beavers, fish, or bears, which we killed when these animals were swimming across the river." But on his voyage downriver in July, game eluded Hennepin and his companion, Auguelle. Any meat they did get spoiled quickly in the midsummer heat. At times they scrambled for fish dropped by the many eagles. Another time they found an otter eating a paddlefish. They tried catching turtles but usually scared them away. When Auguelle left to hunt on the prairies along the river, Hennepin caught a large turtle with a thin shell, a snapping turtle, maybe, as it almost bit off his finger. While he was distracted by the turtle, his canoe floated away. Throwing his habit over the turtle, he waded and swam after the canoe. Upon returning to finish off the turtle, he noticed a herd of some sixty buffalo crossing the river. He called Auguelle back, and they managed to kill one. Meeting the Dakota again, Hennepin learned that large herds of buffalo grazed in the prairies back from the river. Although Keating reported that buffalo still visited the Mississippi River in 1817, by 1823 the buffalo had retreated west. Keating attributed this to the completion of Fort Snelling in 1823, but the fur trade, the horse, and other factors contributed more.[53]

Fish became a staple for most who traveled on the river. While camping on an island a short distance above Clarksville, Missouri, Pike captured 1,375 little fish. These most likely came from a backwater pool that had been cut off from the river as it fell. Twenty years later, George Catlin, a painter and adventurer, canoed down the Mississippi with a corporal from Fort Snelling. About 20 miles below Prairie du Chien, they reported taking bass from "every nook and eddy ... where our hooks could be dipped." James C. Colhoun, a member of the 1823 Long expedition, also feasted on bass near St. Anthony Falls. Keating reported that catfish weighing 142 pounds had been caught at the falls.[54] Rare today, the paddlefish, or pallid sturgeon, created the greatest interest. Its unusually long, flat snout intrigued most explorers and travelers.[55]

Rattlesnakes also fascinated Long, Schoolcraft, Beltrami, Keating, and others. Most explorers and travelers encountered rattlesnakes between Red Wing, Minnesota—then a Dakota village site—and the Chippewa River. Beltrami had heard that Lake Pepin was the "headquarters" for rattlesnakes, although he shot one near Rock Island. On July 20, 1817, just below Lake Pepin, Long's party came across three Native Americans killing a rattlesnake that had just struck one of them. They had cut out the flesh around the bite, hoping to stop the venom from spreading. Two days later, upon reaching Prairie du Chien, Long learned that a rattlesnake had bitten Captain William Le Dufphey from the American garrison there. While Dufphey's leg had swollen and turned black, he had recovered with the help of some unspecified remedies. And on May 17, 1827, Captain Robert McCabe reported, "This day killed a vast number of Rattlesnakes swimming the River from the right bank."[56] McCabe had just passed Wabasha, another Dakota village site, on a trip to pick up supplies for Fort Snelling in St. Louis.[57]

Soon, rattlesnakes, buffalo, paddlefish, passenger pigeons, and Native Americans in and along the upper Mississippi River would have to make way for the juggernaut bearing down on them. To Midwesterners and the ever increasing stream of immigrants who relied on the river as their only transportation route, it was a poorly constructed highway that promised to become the region's primary commercial artery. So with increasing intensity they demanded navigation improvements. They demanded access to the Gulf of Mexico and the world for the products of the land they would transform from prairies and forests into farm fields.

The Origins of Navigation Improvement
on the Upper Mississippi

Before the Civil War the American government generally rejected internal improvement projects for roads, harbors, canals, and rivers. Those opposed to a federal role, represented by men such as Presidents Thomas Jefferson (1801–9), James Madison (1809–17), and James Monroe (1817–25), believed that the states should undertake their own internal improvements. Having thrown off the British monarchy, they distrusted a strong central authority. They worried that if the federal government began sponsoring internal improvements, some states would use the projects to gain an advantage over others. And they feared that creating and funding a federal agency to plan and build such projects would threaten states' rights and private initiative. They asserted that the Constitution did not provide for a federal role in internal improvements. They did not inherently oppose internal improvements and recognized the need to bind the country together to improve security and spur commerce, but they feared an overbearing central government more.

Henry Clay and Presidents John Quincy Adams (1825–29) and Andrew Jackson (1829–37) supported a stronger federal role. Clay and Adams especially advocated a nationalist program of civil works. They insisted that the government had the "implied power" under the Constitution to undertake internal improvements to promote commerce and public safety and to use its peacetime army to "map strategic waterways, dredge harbors for the navy, move troops through canals, train officers in a national academy, and use these army experts to direct public works."[58] Jackson, although he vetoed four river and harbor bills, oversaw the greatest spending on internal improvements of any antebellum president.

During two periods before the Civil War, navigation boosters won some victories in Congress. The first began in 1824 and lasted until 1838. During this era, the government sponsored surveys of many of the country's rivers, harbors, and coasts. The second period lasted only for Millard Fillmore's presidency, from 1850 to 1853. For the rest of the antebellum era, those who opposed federal involvement held sway. Nevertheless, Congress spent some $43 million on waterway projects before the Civil War.[59]

Under President Monroe (1817–25), Congress began pushing for some internal improvements. In 1820 it appropriated $5,000 for a survey of the Ohio and Mississippi Rivers from Louisville to New Orleans. The most important piece of legislation, however, came near the end of Monroe's second term, in 1824, when Congress passed the General

Survey Act. Through this act, the president and Congress compromised to allow surveys for nationally significant canal and road projects. The president received the authority to choose which projects were nationally important. Congress then passed the first River and Harbor Act, which included $75,000 to clear sandbars and remove debris from the Ohio and Mississippi Rivers. Overall, eastern states, having long shouldered the costs of their own civil works projects, opposed the General Survey Act, while newly developing states west of the Appalachians supported it. The General Survey Act marked the beginning of the first era of federally backed public works. Over the next fourteen years, Congress passed an annual appropriation for waterway projects. On the Mississippi, however, most of this work took place below St. Louis.[60]

Clearing and snagging on the Mississippi River and its tributaries became especially important. In 1829 Henry M. Shreve completed the first steam snagboat, the *Heliopolis*, and began removing snags from the river. The previous year Shreve had been appointed Superintendent of Western Rivers by Secretary of War James Barbour. By 1830 Shreve had excised the most threatening snags between St. Louis and New Orleans, and within two years he could announce that other hazards endangered steamboats more than snags. Despite Jackson's reticence, the government had established a significant dredging program by 1838.[61]

The Corps did initiate some work on the upper Mississippi. At St. Louis, the main channel had begun migrating to the Illinois side, threatening the city's future as a port. After surveying the problem, Lieutenant Robert E. Lee built a wing dam in 1838 to direct the current back to the Missouri shore. Lee had come to St. Louis in 1837 to survey this problem and problems at the Rock Island and Des Moines Rapids. Recognizing that more work was necessary to keep the main channel flowing past St. Louis, Lee asked for additional funding. The citizens of St. Louis advanced him $15,000, hoping that Congress would authorize more funds soon. With the economic panic of 1837 still crippling the economy, Congress refused. Lee tried to complete the project in 1839, but an Illinois landowner won an injunction against the project and stopped it. Private interests would have to complete the project at St. Louis.[62]

Above St. Louis, the Corps began surveying and working on the Des Moines and Rock Island Rapids. Lieutenant Napoleon B. Buford conducted the first survey of the rapids in 1829. In 1836 the Corps hired Shreve, already famous for snag removal, to examine the Mississippi at St. Louis and to conduct another survey of the two rapids. Shreve might have undertaken the improvements he suggested had the Corps not assigned Lee to the projects. In 1838 the Corps began blasting rock from the Des Moines Rapids. During this season and the next, they cleared a channel 50 feet wide, 4 feet deep, and about 4 miles long through one of the most difficult reaches. Still, the Des Moines Rapids was far from navigable, and the Rock Island Rapids lay untouched.[63]

Progress on the upper Mississippi River and on most internal improvement projects ended with the economic panic of 1837 and Martin Van Buren's inauguration as president in 1838. These events concluded the era of "free spending" and the first era of federal support for waterway projects.[64] Between 1840 and 1852, Congress funded few projects for the upper Mississippi River. Navigation boosters had hoped for more when William Henry Harrison, a Whig, won the presidency in 1841. The Whig Party strongly favored federal direction of internal improvements. But Harrison died within a month of taking office, and his vice president, John Tyler, opposed federal waterway projects. While Tyler had run as a Whig with Harrison, he had been a Democrat. Once president, he leaned to his Democratic Party principles on internal improvements. The Democrats had succeeded Jefferson's Republicans as the proponents of states' rights and the opponents of federal support for internal improvements. Congress did authorize $7,500 to improve the harbor at Dubuque, Iowa, but as at St. Louis, the Corps did not finish the work. The Mexican War in 1846 and 1847 and adamant opposition by James K. Polk, a Democrat and president from 1845 to 1849, were largely responsible.[65]

These setbacks aside, Westerners were gaining strength. As early as 1815, Henry Clay, a representative from Kentucky and Speaker of the House, began promoting waterway improvements as a means of weaving the country together.[66] And in 1824, as Congress debated the General

Survey Act, Clay "insisted that Congress not only had the right but, indeed, 'a great national duty' to open the veins of commerce that bound the East to the West."[67] He captured the sentiment of many settlers in the rapidly growing West, a sentiment that would characterize water-way improvement advocates well into the next century. When President Polk criticized the Great Lakes ports as of little importance, he was denounced at the Chicago River and Harbor Convention of July 1847, which drew more than ten thousand angry waterway boosters. During the 1848 presidential campaign, waterway supporters criticized the Democrats for Polk's failure to back internal improvements.[68]

In 1848 waterway advocates celebrated the election of Zachary Taylor, a Whig, to the White House. Although Taylor died after a year and a half, his successor, Millard Fillmore, was a staunch Whig. Under Fillmore's administration, waterway projects again received support. At Fillmore's recommendation, the House passed the Western Rivers Improvement Act, which contained over $2 million for navigation im-provements. The upper Mississippi River received $90,000 for work between St. Louis and the Des Moines Rapids, $100,000 for the Des Moines and Rock Island Rapids, and $15,000 for the Dubuque harbor. For the next three years, the Corps worked on these projects. By 1856 the Corps had excavated more rock from the Des Moines Rapids and had begun blasting and chiseling a channel through the Rock Island Rapids.

Overall, however, the Corps made little progress before the Civil War. The large boats of the St. Louis–New Orleans trade still could not operate above the Des Moines Rapids, and the Dubuque harbor remained a problem. In 1857 the river claimed seven boats between Keokuk, at the lower end of the Des Moines Rapids, and St. Paul. The Rock Island Rapids had wrecked two, and the Des Moines Rapids one. The Corps simply did not have the funding or equipment to make mean-ingful navigation improvements. While the Midwest gained political strength, slavery divided northern and southern Whigs, and some states' rights advocates had become concerned about the Corps' growing role. As a result, the Whigs lost control, and with the ascendancy of Demo-cratic Party Presidents Franklin Pierce (1853–57) and James Buchanan

(1857–61), the economic panic of 1857, and the Civil War, further work on the river became impossible. Pierce and Buchanan opposed federal waterway projects, rejecting "the notion that Congress could bind the Republic through a 'general system' of public works."[69] Although Congress overrode five vetoes by the two presidents, snagging and other river work virtually died. Further attention to the river would have to wait until after the war.[70]

By the eve of the Civil War, the upper Mississippi River, already the Midwest's dominant transportation route, seemed poised to become the freeway of midwestern commerce. The region's population and agricultural production had begun blossoming, feeding a boom in steamboat traffic. Railroads fueled the boom even more. Although navigation boosters saw how quickly railroads had reached the Mississippi and how thoroughly they were intertwining the lands to the east, few imagined how completely railroads would dominate river traffic in the coming decades.

The Corps had come and gone. Administratively, it left no permanent presence and had acquired no permanent stake. Despite the Corps' work, the river remained largely natural and often unnavigable for steamboats. The Corps had begun transforming the river's natural character but had not significantly changed the river's ecosystem. Navigation boosters did not rest during the war, however. They continued fighting to make the river a reliable commercial highway, and they continued lobbying to make the Corps the agent of their vision. Few contested the vision of the river as a preordained thoroughfare of trade.

CHAPTER 2

This Splendid Juggernaut

After two years rambling through the upper Great Plains, George Catlin, adventurer, romantic, artist, returned down the Mississippi River from Fort Snelling in the fall of 1835. He mourned, wistfully, for the Native Americans and their world. He foresaw the bones of their ancestors ploughed up by impatient settlers, taking away the Native Americans' homeland and sacred ground. He knew what was coming. "I have seen thus, in all its forms and features," he proclaimed, "the grand and irresistible march of civilization. I have seen this splendid Juggernaut. . . ."[1] Returning down the Mississippi, he blanched at the growing signs of his America. Yet he marveled at its overwhelming success. The farther south he traveled, the more of it he encountered—the unstoppable rush of settlers to the Mississippi River and beyond. Catlin anticipated the cutting of the forests, the erosion of exposed riverbanks, and the flow of steamboats on the Mississippi, but he did not anticipate the direct manipulation of the river to render it navigable. Like Pike, Merrick, and others, the growing number of settlers quickly learned the great river would need some work to make it serve the coming inland empire. So they pushed for federal dollars and federal expertise with renewed vigor following the Civil War.[2]

An Early Demise

Navigation boosters found in the Civil War new arguments to improve navigation on the country's rivers. Traffic demands had overwhelmed railroads during the war, demonstrating, some boosters insisted, the country's need for a multifaceted transportation system. Never again did they want the nation's well-being to hinge on one mode. Employing an old argument with a new urgency, other boosters suggested that a diverse transportation network would reunite the country more quickly and more thoroughly by integrating the regional economies. What better example than the Mississippi River, with its north to south flow, they asked.[3]

The Civil War emphasized the problems caused by low water. Citing the drought of 1864, navigation boosters contended that "unimproved" rivers had failed to serve the nation adequately. The 1864 drought left the Mississippi and other rivers so low that little traffic moved on them. This forced the already overburdened railroads to carry even more and delayed the delivery of critical goods. For the upper Mississippi, the low water of 1864 became the mark against which Congress established project depths. That year, sandbars stopped boats with the lightest drafts from reaching St. Paul and other ports.[4]

As railroads superseded the Mississippi River, the call for navigation improvements transcended the basic need for getting goods and produce into and out of the region. Boosters now worried about who would dictate shipping costs. From 1866 on, they called for navigation improvement, as much to oppose the threat and the reality of railroad monopolies as to make the river navigable. From farmers to real-estate brokers, Midwesterners would look to the Army Corps of Engineers, knowing that just the effort to improve navigation created the threat needed to keep rail prices down. To meet the economies of scale offered by railroads, the federal government would have to spend vastly more on the river than it had. And with or without railroads, the region's increasing production made the economic constraints of the natural river—the uncertain passage and often restricted capacity—unacceptable.[5]

Steamboats began losing passengers and grain to railroads before and during the Civil War. Although early railroads reaching the upper river's east bank fostered steamboat traffic, they initiated its end as well. With each new rail connection, steamboats made shorter trips between ports. Instead of going to St. Louis or New Orleans, boats unloaded at La Crosse, Prairie du Chien, Rock Island, or other railheads. Although the natural river had been hauling grain since the birth of midwestern agriculture, railroads held too many advantages. Railroads moved their freight quicker, giving their users greater flexibility in responding to market changes. Rail lines ran more directly and could reach deep into lands served by no navigable rivers. Compatibility between rail lines made transshipment unnecessary. Trains ran when the river was high or low; they ran when the cold of winter froze it; for the most part, they ran throughout the year. Those railroads that ran east to west—especially to Chicago—took advantage of complementary markets. Midwestern farmers sent grain to Chicago. Chicago merchants and eastern manufacturers sent their goods back. Steamboats and barges delivering commodities to St. Louis or New Orleans or points in between too often returned empty.[6]

The Civil War, by closing the Mississippi, helped shift trade to the northern rail lines. But the railroads and Chicago had begun winning the Midwest's trade before the war. In part, the river's natural character pushed shippers away, and in part, the railroads and Chicago offered advantages neither the river nor its cities could match. St. Louis, the key transfer point for cargoes moving north or south, lacked sufficient warehouse and handling facilities. Since the water fluctuated as much as 41 feet at St. Louis, goods and produce had to be stored well away from the river, which increased handling costs. Like St. Louis, New Orleans needed adequate storage facilities. Produce arriving in the late summer and fall overwhelmed the city. In New Orleans's hot and humid climate, unprotected produce quickly spoiled. The far longer and more hazardous route down the Mississippi to New Orleans and on to the East Coast or Europe also discouraged shipping on the Mississippi. The eastern route, through Chicago and the Great Lakes, presented fewer problems, and many eastern cities had better harbors and storage facilities than New Orleans or St. Louis. When the Chicago and Illinois Canal, connecting Lake Michigan to the Illinois River, opened in 1848, it offered a way for shippers on the Mississippi to reach Chicago and the northern route by water.[7]

In 1850 St. Louis still moved twice as much wheat and flour as Chicago. But by 1855 Chicago and the Great Lakes had eclipsed St. Louis and the Mississippi River. Initially, the Great Lakes fostered Chicago's boom. Goods could be moved both east and west in huge vessels, lowering the cost of eastern manufactures and the price of shipping midwestern produce east. As railroads expanded from east to west, most lines fed into Chicago and then fanned out from the burgeoning metropolis. Chicago thus replaced St. Louis as the great transfer point before the Civil War.[8]

Unlike St. Louis, Chicago captured the economies of scale offered by new technologies, such as steam-powered grain elevators. These elevators allowed merchants in Chicago to take grain out of the sacks and send it on trains by the carload. Because the elevators moved vast quantities of grain from trains, sorted it by quality, and loaded it onto lake freighters, their economic benefits greatly exceeded those of shipping on the river. "By 1857," says historian William Cronon, Chicago "had a dozen elevators whose combined capacity of over four million bushels meant that the city could *store* more wheat than St. Louis would *ship* during that entire year."[9]

On the river, grain still moved in sacks. Cities along the river, subject to flooding, had not yet adopted elevators for river commerce. Loading and unloading the sacks required large crews and took much longer than moving grain by elevator. As the Midwest's grain output grew, river towns could not capture the economies offered by elevators. Shippers simply had to hire more dockworkers. St. Louis would not have an elevator until after the Civil War.[10]

By the war's end, Chicago had won the battle for the region's grain and passenger trades. Steamboats had not lost everything, but the eastern route claimed the largest percentage. Shippers on the upper river may not have noticed, because steamboat traffic boomed during the 1850s. Following the war, they could no longer ignore the railroads, Chicago, or the largely unnavigable river.

Resurrecting the River

Mustering all their arguments, cities, states, shippers, and other navigation boosters in the upper Mississippi River valley began lobbying Congress for new projects immediately after the war. They held two conventions within months of each other, where they focused on the Des Moines and Rock Island Rapids. Local business organizations hosted both meetings. At the conventions, boosters set out their agenda for the river, voiced their concerns about Chicago and the railroads, felt the growing strength of their region, and announced their vision of the Mississippi River's great purpose.

On December 15, 1865, the St. Louis Merchant's Association held the first post-war convention. Delegates complained about the problems caused by the Des Moines and Rock Island Rapids and about the number of proposed bridge crossings. During the 1865 season, they claimed, shippers had lost $500,000, due to delays at the Des Moines Rapids, and some boats still required three to five days to get through. The lumber industry, just beginning to boom, also suffered. Passage over the Des Moines Rapids could add 2 percent to the cost of the lumber. Bridges, as physical and economic threats, worried convention delegates, with good reason. In the spring of 1856, shortly after the Chicago and Rock Island Railroad bridge became the first to span the upper river, the steamboat *Effie Afton* struck a pier and caught fire, destroying the bridge and the boat. In 1857, fifty-five more steamboats struck its piers. Every bridge crossing the river represented a new hazard and an economic hinterland lost to the river's cities.[11]

On February 14 and 15, 1866, navigation boosters held a second convention, this time in Dubuque, Iowa. The Dubuque Producers Exchange hosted the meeting. As at the other meeting, the delegates wanted Congress to appropriate funding immediately for the two rapids. This time they laid out the basic tenets that would define most future navigation movements. A severe snowstorm prevented some delegates from reaching Dubuque. Most who made it came from Iowa, Illinois, and Missouri. Wisconsin sent few delegates, and Minnesota may not have sent any, due to the storm. The delegates generally represented commercial interests worried about high shipping costs.

Playing on their belief that the Midwest was the nation's breadbasket, one delegate pronounced that "the world must in a great measure be fed from the granaries and the meat of the states bordering on and tributary to the Mississippi, provided a channel of commerce can be opened by which these products can be carried to the markets of the world and bring remunerative compensation to the producer."[12] The climatic differences between regions, he noted, dictated that each would produce different commodities. Shippers needed a cheap and efficient system to distribute products between the regions. Under the existing system, convention delegates complained, eastern farmers and merchants held an advantage over those in the Midwest. On February 2, 1866, farmers could garner $1.00 for a bushel of wheat in Dubuque, $1.21 in Chicago, and $1.77 in New York. If midwestern farmers and merchants could get their products to the East more cheaply, they believed, they could reap the higher returns offered there.[13]

Aggravating the situation, midwestern farmers suffered from an agricultural depression and monopolistic railroad rates. During the Civil War, P. Robb of the Dubuque Producers Exchange explained, wheat, corn, and pork prices had been high, but with the war's end, the prices dove. At Chicago, the price of pork dropped 20 percent; wheat, 30 percent; and oats and corn, 60 percent. Yet transportation costs had remained the same. Iowa's governor William M. Stone blamed railroads, announcing that "it is obvious that the period has arrived when the commercial interests of the States bordering on the Upper Mississippi demand relief from the onerous exactions of railway monopolies,..." E. B. Washburne, an Illinois congressman from Galena, echoed Governor Stone, charging that "the oppressions and extortions of the gigantic railroad monopolies of the Northwest are operating to destroy the great interests of our people." (Throughout the nineteenth century, people referred to the Midwest as the Northwest.) Navigation improvements, the delegates insisted, would restore competition and lower regional transportation costs. Delegates feared a conspiracy against the Midwest.

Robb warned them to work hard, as "Chicago, Buffalo, the Erie Canal and all the railroads to the seaboard will combine against us."[14]

Citing the Midwest's growing output, convention delegates demanded the federal government's help. According to Robb, the five upper river states held one-seventh of the population and one-sixth of all improved land in the United States as of 1864. And still, he emphasized, the Midwest produced more than one-quarter of the value of all crops, including nearly one-half of all wheat and corn that year. It also furnished more than one-quarter of the value of all the livestock, including nearly one-third of the cattle and hogs. Overall, the Midwest produced one-third to one-half of the country's leading food staples. Robb and other delegates asserted that this output, combined with the high rates charged by railroads, required that Congress make the Des Moines and Rock Island Rapids navigable. "Now how are these improvements to be made?" Robb asked the convention. Providing the answer, he declared,

> Certainly not by individuals. It is an undertaking beyond the reach of their means or power. Nor should this be done by the several States bordering on the river. It would redound to the immediate benefit of every State in the great valley of the Mississippi, while the entire nation has a common interest in the commerce that floats upon its bosom. Where so many States are directly interested, and the whole country would be immeasurably benefitted, it becomes the especial province of the General Government to undertake and complete the work.[15]

Convention delegates agreed. To them, work of such regional and national importance transcended pork-barrel politics far more than projects for East Coast harbors, such as at Boston or Charleston.[16]

Although neither Wisconsin nor Minnesota sent many delegates, both states backed the call for navigation improvements. Notifying the East and Congress of the Midwest's growing population and economic strength, Minnesota Governor William R. Marshall exclaimed: "Truly the Great West has now a voice potent enough to DEMAND that justice be done us in this matter, at the hands of the National Government."[17]

The state legislature of Wisconsin sent a memorial to Congress the day after the convention, requesting navigation improvements at the rapids.[18]

Delegates to the convention adopted three principal resolutions. First, they demanded that the federal government immediately appropriate funding for work on the Des Moines and Rock Island Rapids. Second, they insisted that the Corps should undertake the work. The delegates agreed to let the Corps select the method, so long as the agency provided a minimum channel width of 300 feet and a minimum depth of 4 feet. Finally, the delegates asserted that the government should allow boats to pass free through any canals built to bypass the rapids. Here stood the basic tenets of future navigation improvements. The federal government would fund the Corps—at no cost to shippers— to make rivers navigable to the level demanded by navigation boosters. In the June 23, 1866, Rivers and Harbors Act, the Republican-led Congress, accepting the national importance of making the rapids navigable, answered the boosters' pleas and aimed the American juggernaut at the Mississippi and other rivers.[19]

The act signaled a new era for the country and for the upper Mississippi River. It included forty-nine projects and twenty-six surveys, and appropriated $3.7 million. The Corps used some funds to continue site-specific work started before the Civil War and other funds to initiate new, more sweeping efforts. The 1866 act authorized $550,000 for building snagboats and dredges for western rivers, and $550,000 for the general improvement of the Mississippi, Arkansas, Ohio, and Missouri Rivers. It specifically provided $200,000 for work on the Des Moines Rapids, and $100,000 for the Rock Island Rapids. Congress also instructed the Corps to survey the upper Mississippi's tributaries to assess their navigability. Anticipating the coming railroad boom, Congress funded the Corps to examine and report on railroad crossing sites that would not impede navigation.[20]

Most importantly, the 1866 Rivers and Harbors Act directed the Corps to survey the Mississippi River between St. Anthony Falls and the Rock Island Rapids, "with a view to ascertain the feasible means, by economizing the water of the stream, of insuring the passage, at all navigable seasons, of boats drawing four feet of water...."[21] Put simply, Congress ordered the Corps to establish a continuous, 4-foot channel for the upper river (based on the low water of 1864). The 4-foot channel project initiated a program that would culminate with the 9-foot channel locks and dams. To accomplish its tasks, the Corps established offices at St. Paul and Keokuk, Iowa (the latter would be moved to Rock Island in 1869). With these offices and its new missions, the Corps gained a permanent stake in managing the upper Mississippi River and emerged as the key player reshaping it.[22]

The Corps on the Upper Mississippi River

To comply with the 1866 Rivers and Harbors Act, Andrew A. Humphreys, the Chief of Engineers, ordered Brevet Major General and Major of Engineers Gouverneur K. Warren to St. Paul. Warren's arrival in St. Paul that August established the Corps as a permanent actor in managing and transforming the river. From this time forward, the Corps' role would become as deep and broad as the river itself. That role came at the insistence of the states, farmers, business interests, and the general public. All demanded the federal presence, the federal expertise, and the federal dollars.

Warren came to St. Paul a brilliant but tainted Civil War hero. He possessed a keen ability to read landscapes. At the Battle of Gettysburg, he recognized the Union Army's tenuous defense on a strategic hill called Little Round Top and diverted troops to the hill. He prevented the Confederate Army from outflanking Union troops, preserving the North's victory. Through this success and his leadership during the next twenty-six months, Warren rose from a second lieutenant to brevet major general. (Brevet is a wartime rank.) At the Battle of Five Forks, however, he crossed General Philip Sheridan and lost his command. For the rest of his career, Warren fought to restore his honor, only winning redemption after his early death.

Warren's experiences prepared him well for his duties on the upper river. He graduated second in his class from West Point on July 1, 1850, as a topographical engineer. The Corps immediately sent him to join then Captain Andrew A. Humphreys on the famous Mississippi Delta Survey. Warren spent nearly two years studying the lower river's characteristics and providing data for a comprehensive hydrographical report published by Humphreys and Lieutenant Henry L. Abbot in 1861. In 1853 Major Stephen H. Long directed Warren to undertake the third survey of the Des Moines and Rock Island Rapids. Published in 1854, Warren's thorough report surpassed the previous studies. Warren also conducted three expeditions to Nebraska and the Dakotas to map them and locate the best sites for forts and the best routes for roads. From his records and those of other expeditions, Warren assembled the most complete and detailed map of the northern plains.[23]

Figure 6. In 1866, Gouverneur Kemble Warren, the hero of the Battle of Gettysburg during the Civil War, became the first district engineer for the St. Paul District, U.S. Army Corps of Engineers. Courtesy of the St. Paul District, U.S. Army Corps of Engineers.

Further establishing the Corps' stake and role on the upper Mississippi River, Humphreys appointed Lieutenant Colonel James H. Wilson to a new office at Keokuk, Iowa, on August 3, 1868. Humphreys charged Wilson with making the Des Moines and Rock Island Rapids navigable and surveying the Rock River. Soon after, Humphreys added a survey of the Illinois River from its mouth to LaSalle in northeastern Illinois to Wilson's duties. Wilson had graduated from West Point in 1860 and, like Warren, served so well during the Civil War that he rose to the rank of brevet major general. Wilson transferred his office from Keokuk to Davenport before the year's end and then established a sub-office in Rock Island in 1869.[24]

Warren applied his quick and perceptive eyes to the upper Mississippi and its tributaries, grasping in less than a year many of the river's subtle characteristics. Before he could develop a plan for the 4-foot channel, he had to survey the upper Mississippi River. He charged men under him to complete the tributary surveys and then began the upper river survey himself. In its natural state, Warren learned, the river's navigation channel frequently changed. The Corps would have to study the river each year until they understood it better. In some reaches, sandbars moved along the channel bottom, forming drifts. A drift would start at the head of a reach and begin creeping downstream, followed by another soon after. As the river fell, the crest of each drift formed a bar that acted like a small dam. Above the bar lay a pool of water. The bar lay close to the surface, but just downstream the channel quickly deepened. Normally, the river began cutting through the steep slope on the bar's back side, and another bar formed downstream. The breach in the bar opened a path through which steamboats could more easily pass. Without enough current, the cutting down happened too slowly for navigation. When a tight series of bars formed, they could obstruct navigation altogether. In these reaches Warren found that "the river seems, as it were, lost, and indecisive which way to go and the pilot is scarcely able to find the line of deepest water even in daylight, and is unable to proceed at night with any confidence."[25] The small pools behind the bars and the natural cutting-down process would play an important part in Warren's strategy for navigation improvement on the upper river.[26]

Between 1866 and 1869, Warren sketched thirty maps of the upper Mississippi River at a scale of 2 inches to the mile. Ten sheets formed a continuous map of the river from St. Anthony Falls to the mouth of the St. Croix River. The remaining maps focused on problem reaches or detailed the river near a specific town. From these maps and from what he learned about early navigation improvements, Warren began planning the 4-foot channel project and the first attempt to conquer the upper Mississippi River.[27]

Warren contacted private companies and local interests to find out what they had done to improve the river's navigability. He learned that Minneapolis had removed boulders to encourage steamboats to travel above St. Paul.[28] At Guttenberg, Iowa, an island split the river into two channels, one passing in front of the city, and the other running along the Wisconsin side. To keep traffic flowing past their city, the citizens had attempted, unsuccessfully, to close the Wisconsin channel. Warren discovered that timber rafting companies and steamboat interests had employed wing dams to scour the channel at troublesome bars. Long piers of rock and brush, wing dams projected into the channel. Like the nozzle of a garden hose, the dams tightened and focused the river's flow to scour away sandbars. Closing dams ran from the shore to an island or from one island to another to block the flow to side channels and redirect water to the main channel. These "slight dams," Warren commented, had been somewhat successful, "indicating a way of deepening the low-water channel worthy of special attention." Overall, Warren found those who had been using the river "evince a shrewd knowledge of the action of running water and the means of temporarily controlling it, gained by their constant experience and observation."[29] He listened to these knowledgeable sources but drew his own conclusions.

Warren provided estimates for a variety of projects in his first annual report in 1867. Responding in part to Minneapolis business and political interests, he requested $235,665 to construct a lock and dam between Minneapolis and St. Paul. To create a safe and continuous

4-foot channel for the river between St. Paul and the Rock Island Rapids, Warren asked for $106,000. He also sought $96,000 to acquire and operate two dredge and snag boats and $10,000 to construct two experimental closing dams.[30]

Focusing on the river's main stem below St. Paul, Warren considered two popular schemes: channel constriction and dredging or scraping. He questioned constricting the channel with wing dams and closing dams, because it required changing the river's natural character radically. He favored a project built on the river's natural tendencies. This meant using the small pools created by sandbars to their fullest. Channel constriction would eliminate the bars and the pools, he feared, and simply funnel the sand downstream. Wherever channel constriction ended, he thought, the river would dump immense quantities of sand. Once the Corps started, it would have to constrict the entire upper river, which, he estimated, would cost some $2 million. The Corps had tried wing dams on the Ohio River before the Civil War. The mixed success and expense led Warren to question their value. The "extravagant and useless" expenditure on wing dams on the Ohio between 1830 and 1844, he wrote in 1867, "did more than anything else to bring the whole subject into disrepute."[31] While rock and brush dams excited some shippers, their effect, Warren contended, yielded temporary results, no better than dredging and scraping.[32]

Although critical of channel constriction, Warren did not rule it out. He recognized that closing dams might help. He worried, however, that anyone using a side channel, such as timber rafters, would object. The river would soon eliminate the closure anyway, he believed.[33] He admitted that wing dams might work in wide reaches. In the end, he concluded, "The natural action of the stream will suggest what is proper to be done."[34] Willing to try channel constriction, he had asked for funding to build two experimental closing dams.

Dredging and scraping had a long history. Dredging entailed scooping sand from a bar and physically placing it somewhere else, while scraping meant pulling a bar's top off and letting current carry the sand downriver. Steamboat pilots had learned that by running the paddle wheels over the crest of a bar, they helped the river cut through it, allowing the flow from the pool to deepen the cut just enough for their boat to pass. General Simon Bernard and Major Joseph G. Totten, Warren noted, had discussed the merits of dredging in their 1822 report on the Ohio River. Even then they had referred to similar work used by shippers on the Loire River in France. Dredging had also been employed at the Mississippi River's mouth.[35] "In view of the hold which this method [dredging] has taken upon the minds of river men, and the difficulties, uncertainty, and expense which attend the use of dams," Warren concluded, "I have determined to recommend the employment of these dredging machines."[36] Under his direction, the Corps initiated a program of dredging and scraping sandbars, snagging, clearing overhanging trees, and removing sunken vessels to create the 4-foot channel. This work reveals much about the natural river and how the Corps began changing it.

Warren realized that to create the 4-foot channel, he needed at least two boats, both capable of dredging and snagging. Congress agreed and approved his $96,000 request for the boats in the March 2, 1867, Rivers and Harbors Act. By the beginning of the 1868 season, he had acquired the *Montana* and the *Caffrey* and had outfitted them for scraping, dredging, and snagging. These boats were the beginning of a fleet the Corps would assemble to reshape the upper Mississippi River.[37]

Because snags and leaning trees threatened lives and property, the Corps quickly began removing them. Warren reported that during the 1869 season the *Caffrey* pulled out 235 snags and cut down 195 overhanging trees between St. Paul and Lake Pepin, some 53 river miles. The *Montana*, working between Lake Pepin and the Rock Island Rapids, a distance of about 270 river miles, wrestled out about 240 snags and cut back more than 400 overhanging trees. Leaning trees posed a particular threat where the channel hugged one bank or the other. At the head of the Nininger Bluff Bar below St. Paul, for example, a small island had formed. The main channel ran along one side, and on the other the river entered Nininger Slough. At times the main channel became impassable, forcing steamboats through the narrower side channel. This channel closed so tightly that steamboats, rubbing against one bank or the other, had worn them down. Pilots venturing so close to shore watched carefully for leaning trees. Together, the *Montana* and the *Caffrey* cut down almost 2,600 leaning trees in 1872, over 3,100 in 1876, and more than 6,300 in 1877, eliminating many of the perches from which Schoolcraft's herons and kingfishers eyed their "finny prey." In the latter year, they focused on bends where the deep channel ran near a shore, removing, in one reach, all large and small trees within 5 feet of the river. By the late 1870s, their snagging and clearing work pleased the Corps. Since the initial backlog had been taken out, they reported, few snags threatened steamboat traffic. In 1876 the *Montana* removed every snag between St. Paul and the Des Moines Rapids, for a total of only 37.[38] The Corps also extracted wrecks blocking the navigation channel or access to a port. In 1874 the *Montana* removed the wreck of a "stone-boat" in the channel above Winona and dislodged the wrecks of the *Alice* and the *War Eagle* at La Crosse.[39]

Eliminating sunken vessels, leaning trees, and snags made the upper Mississippi safer. Sandbars, however, still determined when and where steamboats plied the river. To make the river a reliable commercial artery, the Corps had to eliminate the sandbars. So Warren began scraping the river. He believed scraping would cut the worst bars down by 8 to 12 inches. This may not seem like much, but for steamboats, it meant the difference between gliding over a bar or grounding upon it. After the 1868 season, Warren optimistically reported that the dredges had secured a low water channel of 3 feet, satisfying steamboat interests. But early in 1869, Warren's scraping strategy faced a difficult test. At the start of July, more than a month early, the river had fallen to its low water stage. Despite this threat, Warren announced that the *Caffrey* had provided a channel deep enough for the biggest boats. The dredges had proved so beneficial, Warren insisted, that Congress should regularly fund them—a plea his successors would make in vain for nearly twenty years.[40]

Still, at times, the river dropped so low that it thwarted the Corps' boats. Several times during the 1871 season, low water barred the *Caffrey* from the river above Prescott, Wisconsin, at the mouth of the St. Croix River. Captain J. Throckmorton, the local assistant superintendent in charge of U.S. improvements on the upper Mississippi River, complained that the *Caffrey*, at less than 36 inches, drew too much water. Throckmorton knew the river well. In making him the assistant superintendent, Colonel J. N. Macomb, the Rock Island District commander, remarked that Throckmorton's career on the river spanned nearly forty years. Sandbars and the problems they created for boats drawing too much water irritated Throckmorton. In his 1872 report he complained that small steamers, pushing barges, frequently grounded, and his crews had to spend time pulling them off to clear the channel. He rescued thirteen steamboats and twenty barges during the 1871 season. Because new bars could develop without warning, the *Montana* operated on call, responding to urgent requests to open the channel. So many sandbars obstructed the reach between the head of the Rock Island Rapids and Lake Pepin, Throckmorton grumbled, that it was almost impossible to keep the river open. Frustrated with the temporary solution scraping offered, Throckmorton and other engineers began discussing more permanent measures.[41]

As the Corps learned more about the upper Mississippi River and as the limits of dredging and scraping became manifest, the Corps turned to channel constriction. In 1873, when high water prevented the *Montana* from dredging, the Corps decided to build two experimental closing dams. First, they went to the channel at Pig's Eye Island, 5 miles below downtown St. Paul. The island divided the river, and the navigation channel sometimes ran on the east side and sometimes on the west. Below the island no deep channel existed at low water. To eliminate the problem, the Corps closed the east channel by driving two tiers of piles, 9 feet apart, and filling between them with willow brush. They then placed sandbags on top to weigh the brush down. They knew the brush would trap the river's sediment and form a solid barrier. The dam measured 600 feet long and 6 to 10 feet deep. The *Montana*'s crew then steamed down to Rollingstone Bar, just above Fountain City, Wisconsin (107 river miles below St. Paul), and built a second closing dam. This time, as would happen in the future, they did not plug the side channel completely but left an opening for lumber rafters to drive their logs through. From these first two experimental dams, channel constriction would grow into a project that would dramatically reconfigure the upper river's landscape and ecology.[42]

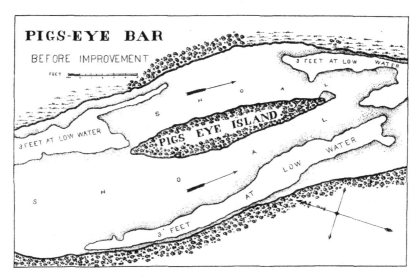

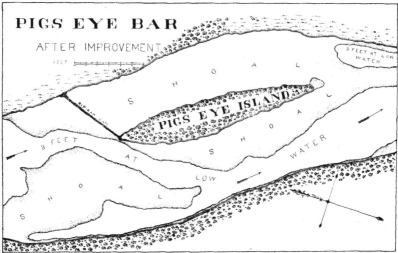

Figure 7. Pig's Eye Island before and after closing dam construction. The dam forced water away from the side channel and connected the deeper pools in the main channel. Courtesy of the St. Paul District, U.S. Army Corps of Engineers.

Anticipating that Congress would support channel constriction, Macomb tried to justify permanent funds for dredging, snagging, and clearing. In his 1873–74 annual report, he insisted that the Corps needed the appropriation "to enable us to render such temporary aid in advance of the more permanent relief which it is hoped may be afforded by a system of improvement expected to be developed from the surveys authorized at the close of the fiscal year and now in progress."[43] The surveys he referred to were for a special study titled "Report on Transportation Routes to the Seaboard," which Congress had approved by a resolution in 1872. On June 29, 1874, the Chief of Engineers had directed Macomb to survey the upper Mississippi River from St. Anthony Falls to Grafton, Illinois, to assess the feasibility of creating a channel of 4½ to 6 feet at low water.[44]

This survey reveals how much the Corps had learned about the upper river since opening its offices in 1866. Macomb hired Montgomery Meigs in 1874 to undertake the survey. Meigs had earned degrees in engineering from Harvard University and the Royal Polytechnic School in Stuttgart, Germany. He would work for the Rock Island District until 1926. Together with Charles W. Durham, Meigs began defining the channel constriction program for the upper river. Like Meigs, Durham had received his degree from Harvard and had studied in Germany, undertaking graduate courses in Heidelberg. Durham had joined the district in 1871 and oversaw the building of the first experimental closing dams. Their German training would influence how Meigs and Durham approached permanent navigation improvements for the upper river.[45]

Meigs had time only to examine the Mississippi between St. Paul and La Crosse for the congressional report. Relating common knowledge of those who knew the river, Meigs described this reach as "winding, flowing almost invariably over a sandy bottom, which changes its shape after every rise, and at low water presents serious, and sometimes impassable, obstacles to navigation."[46] The average low-water depth on the bars measured about 3 feet. And, he observed, "as most of the large steamers, and even the small ones, draw 3 feet 6 inches to 4 feet 6 inches, or 5 feet loaded, they are stopped at the bars and obliged either to spar over, or, when that is impossible, to give up the navigation altogether." Yet, he claimed, the large steamers could almost always make it up to Prescott. Meigs then provided a unique discussion of the problem and rare insights into the natural river's character:

> The trouble generally occurs just after a rise in the river. The moment the water begins rising the sand-bars begin to shift; old channels are filled; the bottom of the stream flattens out, as it were, and when the water falls again, as it generally does after a few days, the stream is spread over so great a width of river, and so flat at bottom, that it is very shallow. In the course of time the water cuts for itself a new channel through the sand; and the concentration that thus takes place restores the navigation to its usual condition until the new channel is again disturbed by a rise.

This could happen many times in a season and had surprising implications for navigation. Meigs observed that boats might struggle to reach St. Paul on a falling stage of water, lie in port a few days, and return downstream on a lower stage more easily. Steamboats made the return trip more easily because the lower river had scoured a defined and deeper—if not continuous—channel. "Any acceleration in the current of the river," he added, "immediately causes a commotion among the sand-bars, which begin to travel down stream." Based on these observations, Meigs concluded, "I am of the opinion that the safest plan of improvement will be, in general, to find the natural channel, and lead the water in that direction." Channel constriction, he believed, would achieve this.[47]

Wing dams and closing dams had been tried elsewhere in the United States to improve navigation, as Warren had pointed out. But, Meigs remarked, these efforts had taken place in rivers with rock beds or hard gravel. As Americans had little experience with channel constriction, "It is to Europe," Meigs urged, "that we must look for a perfected system of river improvements." The Germans, French, and Dutch, he reported, had been regulating streams for hundreds of years. Drawing on his education and experience in Germany, Meigs asserted that the current German method of navigation improvement "has proved itself the cheapest and most certain of lasting success."[48] This method was channel constriction by means of rock and brush dams.

Meigs stressed that a single wing dam would not work. The Corps had to place the dams in a series. As sand accumulated between the dams, plants would grow and capture more sediment. Eventually, a prairie or floodplain forest would emerge, and the river's banks would creep inward. Contrary to the common understanding, Meigs emphasized that "the production and regulation of shores, then, is the proper designation of this kind of engineering, though its object is the regulation of the channel...." By this process, he hoped, the entire upper Mississippi River would scour itself a 4½- to 6-foot channel. Further encouraging channel constriction, Meigs reported that such dams worked well in shallow and deep water. They had succeeded on the Rhine, where the river could rise 25 to 30 feet in twenty-four hours. Meigs estimated that constricting the river between St. Paul and La Crosse would cost $348,699.78.[49]

In a preliminary report dated January 6, 1875, Meigs cautioned that nowhere in the United States had anyone attempted channel constriction on such a large scale. The "importance and magnitude" of this work, he insisted, required the Corps to conduct more channel constriction experiments. The Corps did not yet understand the long-term effects of the channel constriction structures built in 1873 and 1874. And the Corps, Meigs pointed out, still needed a thorough survey of the Mississippi between La Crosse and the Illinois River.[50]

The Corps could not use channel constriction or dredging to improve navigation at the Des Moines and Rock Island Rapids. Following the Civil War, the Corps again considered how to approach the two rapids and devised two quite different plans. For the Rock Island Rapids, the Corps continued chiseling and blasting a channel through the rock to a minimum width of 200 feet and a minimum depth of 4 feet. They began removing rock in the fall of 1867 and proceeded chain by chain until, in 1886, they had excavated a nearly continuous channel. While this channel made the Rock Island Rapids more navigable, they remained dangerous.[51] At the Des Moines Rapids, the Corps determined that the most feasible and cost-effective solution would be a canal paralleling the river. Excavating the Rock Island Rapids had made sense because the Corps only needed to define a channel through a series of rock ledges. Once through a ledge, the channel became navigable until the next ledge. At the Des Moines Rapids, the shallow rock bed continued for more than 11 miles. Begun on October 18, 1867, the canal required ten years to complete.[52]

Only thirty-two years after Catlin anticipated the coming juggernaut of American expansion, its impacts on the upper Mississippi River became manifest. Agricultural settlement and logging had begun changing the river's ecosystems and landscape. Warren, in his first report on the river in 1867, noted these effects. First he mentioned the characteristics of the river's natural environment. "In the bed of the stream sometimes long water plants are stretched over the bottom by the action of the stream. In quiet places, like Lake Pepin, fields of erect aquatic plants flourish, and in places protected from moving sands, the unios grow so abundantly as to accumulate beds of their shells at least two or three feet thick."[53] Then, he began detailing the changes caused by the surging juggernaut of American settlement:

> The ploughing of the prairie, felling of forests, erection of mills, and other causes have already begun to disturb the former state of things. The water is no longer as clear and dark as it used to be, and more sand accumulates in the stream, and a noticeable quantity of saw-dust and chips from the lumber mills of the Mississippi, St. Croix, Chippeway, and Wisconsin is also deposited along the banks.

The river's bed, he observed, had already begun rising due to the inflow of new silt from freshly ploughed lands. Wave action and increased turbulence caused by steamboats and other factors had destroyed some of the riverbank's vegetation, causing erosion. He did not mention the thousands of trees harvested to fuel steamboat boilers.[54]

In the Corps' efforts to define a single navigation channel, they began transforming the river's landscape, hydraulic regime, and ecosystem, as well. They eliminated sandbars, trying to connect the deeper pools between them. They removed thousands of trees bordering the river and pulled thousands of snags from it. With far fewer snags, leaning trees, and wrecks, steamboats navigated the river more safely. Yet, these changes were temporary. If left to nature, the river would quickly replace the snags, leaning trees, and sandbars. Overall, the river remained mostly natural and largely unnavigable. The Corps simply did not have the funding, equipment, personnel, or authority to make significant and lasting changes.

For the Corps to pursue full-scale channel constriction, Congress would have to authorize a very different program, funded at a much higher level. Hope for such a program was building. Channel constriction experiments had demonstrated the potential to recast the river permanently, and the upper Mississippi River valley's economic and political clout was growing rapidly. The national mentality increasingly supported whatever efforts the Corps needed to make rivers navigable. Few if any people doubted, as a Minnesota legislature memorial implored, that "the all-beneficent Creator has graciously anticipated the wants and necessities of unborn millions in having given us exactly such a continuous means of supply and exchange from the Falls of St. Anthony to the Gulf of Mexico."[55] Navigation boosters, whether for private, local, or state purposes, all turned to the federal government and the Corps.[56]

Despite the Corps' work, railroads continued to undermine the steamboat trade. On April 15, 1874, the *Winona Weekly Republican* succinctly captured the rapid demise of the packetboat industry. "The arrival of the first boat has ceased to be the important event it used to be in days gone by," it announced, "but for the sake of history we give the arrivals of the first boats as they have occurred in Winona since 1856."

A river town, once so dependent on steamboats, had already committed them to history. Looking only to the railroad, some settlers began seeing the river as an obstacle and menace rather than a boon. Most Midwesterners, however, were not ready to give up on navigation. They could not afford to. As railroads increasingly monopolized transportation in the Midwest and as midwestern farmers sank into an economic depression, they turned to the river for relief.

CHAPTER 3

The Bounty of Providence

Immediately following the Civil War, most farmers still produced for local or regional markets. Twenty years later, they cried for cheap access to international markets for a surplus vastly beyond regional and national needs. Farmers could not turn to the upper Mississippi River, however. The largely natural river was incapable of handling the grain offered to it. Railroads bridging the upper river and spreading throughout the plains beyond offered the best outlet but often charged unacceptable rates. Out of this milieu farmers and midwestern merchants began calling for a project that would radically change the upper Mississippi River's physical and ecological character.

To make the upper Mississippi River competitive, to provide a deep and permanent channel, would take millions and require resculpting the river like no force since the glaciers. A project so massive demanded a strong and sustained political movement. Such a movement began after the Civil War and blossomed during the 1870s. While not specifically a crusade for navigation improvement, it provided the momentum. The Midwest's soaring population and agricultural output gave birth to it, but the movement expanded well beyond the Midwest. Regionally and nationally, it responded as much to railroad monopolies as to the need for a navigable waterway.

Population and Agricultural Expansion

After the Civil War, an unprecedented number of Americans hurried westward. While states east of the Mississippi River had been largely settled, the Midwest and West held millions of unplowed acres. Much of Iowa, Minnesota, the Dakotas, Nebraska, and Kansas still lay open. "The Great West was there for the taking," Gilbert Fite says in the *Farmer's Frontier*, "and men and women from the East, the Midwest, the South, Europe, and even the Orient conquered it, or were conquered by it, during the next generation."[1] They took it, of course, from Native Americans, who considered the land occupied, if not with farms, fields, fences, and domestic animals.

The pace of the Midwest's settlement and the growing size of its agricultural output between 1860 and 1880 created the need for a better transportation system and gave the Midwest the political clout to demand one. Minnesota's population grew from 172,000 to 439,700 between 1860 and 1870, and to nearly 780,800 by 1880. The number of farms in Minnesota rose from 18,181 to 92,386 during the 1860s alone. In 1860, Nebraska claimed only 2,789 farms but could boast over 63,387 in 1880, reflecting a population that expanded from 28,800 to 452,400. Settlers established farms in northwestern Iowa at a similar pace, with Iowa's population jumping from 674,900 in 1860 to 1.6 million in 1880. And the population of the Dakotas climbed from 4,837 in 1860 to almost 135,200 in 1880. Wisconsin's population jumped from 775,881 in 1860 to 1,315,497 in 1880, a 60 percent increase, while the number of farms rose by about 52 percent, from 69,270 to 134,322. Overall, the upper Midwest's population ballooned from 9.1 million in 1860, to 13.0 million in 1870, and to 17.4 million in 1880.[2]

The great number of people and farms led to an equally dramatic rise in the region's agricultural output. Oat yields in Wisconsin leapt from 11.1 million bushels to 32.9 million between 1860 and 1880. Wheat production in Minnesota climbed from 2.2 million bushels to 34.6 million during the same period. Corn production in Iowa rose from 42.4 million bushels in 1860 to 275.0 million in 1880. Illinois's corn output soared from 129.9 million bushels to 325.8 million. From 1860 to 1880 the Midwest's oat production grew from 63.0 million bushels to 270.2 million, its wheat harvest climbed from 95.0 to 329.6 million bushels, and its corn production expanded from 406.2 million to almost 1.3 billion bushels. By the 1870s the surging output demanded an outlet and contributed to a transportation crisis, but the crisis did not arise from the exceptional production alone.[3]

Railroads accelerated the pace of the Midwest's growth, and they provoked and inflamed the shipping crisis. In doing so, they added to the drive for navigation improvements as they throttled shipping on the river. In 1868 the Sioux City and Pacific Railroad reached Sioux City, Iowa, bringing settlers to the edge of the Dakotas. On May 10, 1869, Sidney Dillon, president of the Union Pacific Railroad, drove the golden spike near Promontory Point, Utah, joining the Union Pacific and Central Pacific Railroads. The nation's first transcontinental railroad, it connected Sacramento, California, with Omaha, Nebraska, and the East Coast with the West. The Northern Pacific completed a line to Moorhead, Minnesota, on the state's border with North Dakota, in 1871. The next year the Burlington reached Kearney, in south-central Nebraska, where it joined the Union Pacific. The Santa Fe reached Emporia, in east-central Kansas, in 1870 and pushed westward to the Colorado border two years later. Railroad trackage in the United States multiplied from 30,635 miles in 1860, to 52,914 in 1870, and to 92,296 in 1880. Before the Civil War only the Rock Island Railroad bridge had crossed the upper Mississippi River. Between 1866 and 1869 three more railroads bridged the river to Iowa, and by 1877 fourteen railroad bridges spanned the upper Mississippi.[4]

Each bridge captured a hinterland that had supplied the river trade. By 1878 half the southbound river tonnage that sailed past Dubuque stopped at Fulton or Rock Island, some 60 and 98 river miles downstream, respectively, and went by rail to Chicago. A year later, railroads carried "seven-eighths of the surplus products of the trans-Mississippi States north of Arkansas...." Farmers turned to railroads, in part, because the natural river, poor harbor facilities, and lack of credit at most river ports gave them little choice.[5]

The Farm Crisis

Many farmers settling on the prairies during the 1860s and 1870s lived not only on a physical frontier but on an economic one. Most spent all they had to acquire their farms and needed a couple good years to establish themselves. Their only capital came from the season's crops. Unfortunately for many settlers, the late 1860s through the mid-1870s tried them harshly. With less annual rainfall and more frequent droughts than in the East, their crops failed more often. Adding to the climatic problems, grasshoppers and prairie fires devoured their crops by the field.[6]

Midwestern farmers also faced economic forces beyond their control. During the brief recession after the war, grain prices fell. Although prices rebounded in 1866 and 1867, during the winter of 1868 to 1869, they dropped again, announcing a crisis that would deepen and become disastrous with the Panic of 1873. Prices plunged so low during the depression that farmers whose crops had evaded droughts, hail, and grasshoppers made little or no profit. Many who had moved west just after the Civil War and had invested in land and machinery when prices were good could not repay their debts. Farmers failed to control the one aspect of the price collapse within their control: overproduction. Yet most farmers did not comprehend their individual role in the crisis or were unwilling to be the ones to change it.[7]

Railroads and grain elevator operators acted in ways that made them targets of the farmers' anger, but they appeared easier to control. Shipping costs often determined whether farmers made a profit. As the farm crisis deepened, railroads tightened their command over grain shipping. While states initially sought and fostered railroad expansion, they gave little thought to railroad regulation. They soon recognized their mistake. Even before the end of the Civil War, farmers began complaining about high railroad costs. Along the Mississippi River, railroads quickly drove many packetboats out of business. Away from the river, railroads dictated the costs of transportation. Sometimes railroads charged higher prices per mile to send a bushel of grain from a point west of the river to a river port than from that same western point to Chicago. Doing so, they undercut the packetboat trade. Farmers observed that wherever waterways offered competition or the potential for it, railroads lowered their prices. This created the appearance that railroads could charge lower rates everywhere, if they wanted to. By making it cheaper to bypass the river and thereby undermining river traffic, railroads limited the region's transportation options. Farmers could have refused to use the railroads, but the river offered them little choice.[8]

Chicago's grain elevator operators also angered midwestern farmers. By 1870 Chicago's seventeen elevators sorted, stored, and transferred the flow of grain pouring into Chicago. Together, their total capacity equaled 11.6 million bushels. By contract, one railroad serviced each elevator, guaranteeing it all the grain shipped by the railroad. Working closely with each other, the elevator operators formed a single bloc. Consequently, farmers could not look for the best shipping and elevator prices.[9]

Grain grading and mixing at the elevators raised the ire and suspicion of farmers and grain traders. When grain reached Chicago, the elevators graded it by weight per bushel. An ounce one way or the other could separate one grade from another and cost ten cents or more per bushel. This might represent the difference between a profitable crop or a disaster for some farmers. Many farmers suspected the elevators of rigging their scales to lower the grade. After purchasing grain at a lower grade, some elevators mixed it with grain of a higher grade. The new mix all passed at the higher level. Given the volume of the mixed grade, the elevators could reap extraordinary profits. This practice, although not illegal, led farmers to charge the elevators with stealing the profit of their labor.[10]

A third practice by Chicago elevator operators reinforced the growing animosity of farmers. Elevator operators, because only they knew the exact amount of grain in storage, could and did manipulate the futures market to their benefit. The price of grain rose and fell on the basis of how much grain the elevators stored. If they held little grain, the price climbed. Packed elevators sent the price down. By having accurate information or by leaking false information, elevator operators could and did acquire great profits. They also earned the wrath of the grain traders and farmers.[11]

The Granger Movement

By the late 1860s these circumstances gave rise to the most powerful agrarian movement in U.S. history up to this time and to the strongest push for navigation improvement. The supporters of the movement demanded railroad reform and waterway development. The organization that galvanized and focused the farmers' unrest became known as the Patrons of Husbandry, or the Grange. Oliver Hudson Kelley, a Minnesota farmer who had moved to Washington, D.C., to work as a clerk in the Department of Agriculture, initiated the movement. On January 13, 1866, Kelley left Washington for a three-month trip through the South. The plight of southern farmers and of farmers in his home state persuaded Kelley that farmers needed a fraternal organization like the Masons, to which he belonged. Kelley returned to Washington on April 21 but left shortly afterward for Minnesota to plant his crops. In June 1867 he went back to Washington to work for the Post Office and began developing plans for the Grange with a small group of associates.[12]

Between 1867 and 1871 Kelley and the other founders established the Patrons of Husbandry. They started with a few broad objectives. They planned to educate farmers about modern, scientific agricultural methods. They hoped to bring farmers together to end their isolation and to create social and economic unity. Most founders, however, shied away from aggressive economic and political agendas.

The Granger movement's growth reflected the depth and breadth of the agricultural crisis. During the late 1860s it unfolded slowly, but in the early 1870s it spread like a prairie fire. Kelley founded the first grange, or chapter, in Minnesota in 1868. By January 1, 1871, the Grange had organized chapters in nine states, mostly in the upper Midwest. Farmers in Minnesota and Iowa avidly joined, but Minnesota had the only active state grange. Illinois and Missouri supported temporary organizations. During the year, however, Wisconsin, Pennsylvania,

South Carolina, Mississippi, Vermont, Kentucky, and New Jersey established state granges.[13]

As the farm crisis deepened and the Grange's economic program began resonating with farmers, the Grange swept over the country. By the end of 1872, the Patrons of Husbandry counted chapters in twenty-five

Figure 8. Oliver Hudson Kelley. Through the Patrons of Husbandry, or the Grange, Kelley helped persuade Congress to authorize the 4$^{1}/_{2}$-foot channel project. Courtesy of the Minnesota Historical Society.

states. Then the Panic of 1873 began. By November 1873 all but five states had granges. The number of granges multiplied from 1,362 at the beginning of 1873 to 10,029 by the end of the year. The spectacular growth continued into 1874, with 2,239 granges formed in February alone—the greatest number in a single month. In early 1875 the movement claimed 21,697 granges and 858,050 members.[14] Solon J. Buck, who wrote the classic study of the Grange, observed that although avowedly nonpolitical, "the phenomenal increase in the membership of the order during 1873 and 1874 awakened the liveliest interest, and sometimes apprehension, among politicians throughout the Union." As a result, he said, "the *New York Tribune*, referring to the Grange, declared that 'within a few weeks it has menaced the political equilibrium of the most steadfast states.'"[15]

The Grange's astonishing success came because Kelley and other radical founders advanced a strong economic program challenging the railroad monopolies and middlemen like the Chicago elevators. While most of the Washington founders opposed making the Grange an economic or political movement, Kelley pushed it into these arenas. To resolve the farm crisis, the Grangers pursued two primary economic strategies. First, they tried to reduce transportation costs, and second, they sought to eliminate middleman charges.[16]

Kelley believed that farmers had to form cooperative unions to overcome their crisis. The cooperatives would buy goods, such as farm implements, and services, such as insurance, and they would market the farmers' crops. Forming cooperatives anchored Kelly's plans. The farmers he talked to needed protection more than education. Education meant little to those suffering from droughts, grasshoppers, and falling agricultural prices. They wanted an alliance of farmers against monopolies. Cooperative marketing offered a way to attract farmers and a legitimate solution. But initially the national office opposed cooperative efforts as too aggressive. So with his direct and indirect support, the Minnesota Grange redefined the Grange's constitutional purposes, making it more radical and more active. Other states quickly followed. Kelley, however, could not move the Grange into politics.[17]

This did not stop farmers from forming or joining third parties, known as Reform or Anti-Monopoly parties. Between 1873 and 1876 the Anti-Monopolists organized parties in eleven states, including all five on the upper Mississippi River, where they enjoyed their greatest influence. Their central plank became railroad rate control. On May 5, 1873, the *St. Louis Democrat* published a letter highlighting "The Railroad Question." Signed by X. X., it began: "To the editors of the *Democrat*: It moves. The irrepressible conflict between railroad monopolists and agriculturalists has commenced." The author then invited any doubters to "pick up a paper from the most obscure county of Iowa, Wisconsin, or Michigan, Missouri, Ohio, or New York, and you will find an account of the organization of a farmers' club with vigorous resolutions on this vital topic."[18] Stories about an Illinois law dealing with railroads flanked the letter. The paper may have published its article anticipating a transportation convention being held in St. Louis in less than ten days.[19]

Illinois became the first state where an independent farmer party gained power. Once in power, the party moved to control the elevators and railroad rates. Chicago businessmen especially pressed for elevator reform. Founded in 1848 and led by some of Chicago's eminent businessmen, the Chicago Board of Trade oversaw Chicago's grain market. Fraudulent elevator practices imperiled the board's ability to manage that market and threatened to undermine trust in the grain system. Consequently, the board led the fight against elevator abuses. By 1870 Illinois's anti-railroad and anti-elevator interests forced rate control and elevator control provisions into the state's new constitution. In 1871 the Illinois general assembly then passed a series of laws forbidding all discrimination in railway charges, which became known as the Granger Laws. But in January 1873 the state supreme court ruled the laws unconstitutional. That same month farmers organized the State Farmer's Association, demanding relief from railroad abuses. In response, the legislature passed more effective and more radical laws on May 2, 1873.[20]

To insure that the laws would stay in force, Illinois farmers focused their efforts on the judicial elections of June 1873, backing candidates that favored railroad rate control. "The election which followed," said

Buck, "first displayed to the astonished politicians of the country the political possibilities of the movement; for in nearly every instance the candidate nominated or favored by the farmers was elected...."[21] Farmers then moved to influence county office elections. Their success again demonstrated the power of the farmers' resolve. Farmers or Anti-Monopoly tickets won in fifty-five of Illinois's sixty-six counties. Despite these efforts, many of the railroad abuses continued.[22]

Opposition to railroad monopolies gained strength in Minnesota in 1870, especially in the wheat-growing counties of southeastern Minnesota. The Chicago and North Western Railroad held control of shipping in this area through an agreement with the Diamond Jo Line and John Robson's Red Line packets, forming what became known as the "wheat ring." Joined by a major Milwaukee elevator operator, the ring gave preference to some large growers and monopolized the area's grain trade. Rural protests to the ring drew attention from both the Democratic and Republican conventions of 1870, and Republican Governor Horace Austin promised to challenge the railroad monopolies. During the summer and fall of 1870, the push for railroad regulation became even more intense, and in 1871 the state legislature passed two railroad laws. Under these laws, the state established a maximum charge for passengers and freight and appointed a railroad commission to gather statistics and execute the laws. As in Illinois, the railroads refused to obey the laws, and the Grangers continued their drive for regulation.[23]

During the summer of 1873, large crowds attended Granger rallies in Minnesota and called for a third party, threatening Republican party control in Minnesota. Radical Grangers formed an Anti-Monopoly party and joined the Democrats. In the fall elections, many Anti-Monopoly candidates won. The Anti-Monopolists used their new strength to pass even more stringent railroad regulations. But the laws did not account for the varied state of Minnesota railroad development. While well advanced in some areas, railroads were just entering others. Establishing rates in the different areas to meet the needs of farmers and give railroads a reasonable return on their investment became untenable, angering both interests. While railroads had refused to obey the 1871 law, they used the 1874 version to sour Minnesotans on the idea of regulation. Where the law required or allowed railroads to raise their rates to established standards, they did. Using this tactic and others, the railroads succeeded in reversing the regulations. In the fall 1874 elections, the Grangers lost their support for railroad regulation, and the legislature nullified the 1874 law, making the railway commission only advisory. This fiasco helped turn many Minnesotans to navigation improvements as a way to stimulate competition and lower rates.[24]

In Iowa and Wisconsin similar scenarios occurred. In both states Grangers supported reform parties in 1873 and won significant victories. In Wisconsin the legislature passed the Potter Law. But as in Minnesota, railroads refused to comply and had the law repealed after the next year's elections. In Iowa the Grangers and Anti-Monopolists swept to power in the November 1873 elections. They helped reelect Governor Cyrus C. Carpenter, a Republican and a strong Granger, and 50 percent of the lower house identified themselves as Anti-Monopolists, and 70 percent as Grangers. Iowa's legislature successfully passed a law establishing maximum railroad rates, and as in the other states, railroads ignored it.[25]

Early on, Grangers and state governments recognized the practical and constitutional problems of enforcing railroad rate restrictions at the state level, especially trying to regulate railroads outside their boundaries. So they pressed for national legislation. Even before the states passed their laws, the U.S. Congress had debated how to regulate railroads. During the Fortieth Congress's second session in 1867 and 1868, members began considering railroad rate legislation. During its next two sessions, Congress explored its authority to regulate interstate commerce and drafted a bill to oversee railroad rates but took no action. After 1868 an increasing tide of bills and resolutions aimed at regulating railroads fell upon Congress. The Fortieth Congress considered three resolutions. Sixteen railroad resolutions came before the Forty-second Congress, nine railroad propositions came before the House and Senate during the Forty-fourth Congress, and twenty-seven before the Forty-seventh Congress. None of these measures became law. Then in 1874, the House considered and passed the McCrary bill. This bill called for a federal commission with the power to establish rates, investigate complaints, and prepare charges against shippers that violated the act. The Senate, however, let it die. In 1878 the House considered another bill to deal with railroad abuses. It too passed the House, but the Senate again took no action. As attempts at state and federal railroad regulation failed, Grangers and other shippers pushed harder for navigation improvements.[26]

Grangers and Waterway Improvement

Kelley and Grangers in the upper Mississippi River valley saw the river as an essential route to domestic and foreign markets. They believed that if farmers could not compete successfully in foreign markets, the whole U.S. economy would suffer. America needed strong overseas outlets and a sound domestic market to remain a world economic leader, and both depended on cheap transportation.[27] In January 1869 the *Minnesota Monthly*, which became Kelley's principal voice for the Granger movement that year, carried several articles on navigation improvement. In one, Henry Eames, one of the largest grain operators in the upper Midwest, claimed that on a proper transportation system, which incorporated the Minnesota, St. Croix, and Mississippi Rivers, farmers would reap $1.25 per bushel for their wheat. "By a proper system of transportation for Minnesota," he explained, "I mean a sufficient line of barges with powerful towboats, each of which could take 100,000 bushels to New Orleans at a cost much less than to Milwaukee or Chicago,..." Eames naively predicted that when the Corps completed work on the Des Moines and Rock Island Rapids later that year, boats could navigate the upper Mississippi without breaking bulk.[28]

Subsequent writers took Eames seriously. In an April 1869 issue an article titled "How Every Man Who Owns a Farm in Minnesota Will Soon Be Made Rich by a Reduction of the Cost of Transportation of His Surplus to Market," the *Minnesota Monthly* rejoiced in the anticipation of substantial barge traffic on the Mississippi River. The news of the barge line, the journal reported, had alarmed grain operators in

New York and Buffalo, and railroads along the northern route. The grain elevator operators had sent a committee to visit the boards of trade of the Great Lakes cities "to warn them of the impending dangers of a Mississippi River competition, and the necessity of taking immediate measures to save some portion of the trade and transportation so long monopolized." Some shippers, the article claimed, already planned to reduce their rates by half. The author celebrated the opening of the Mississippi and cheered the return of competition. Expressing the Grangers' concern for a multifaceted transportation network, the article declared that "sharp competition among rival freighters is our only safety."[29] This optimism, however, was poorly founded.

Demonstrating the Grangers' early concern for improving navigation, the Minnesota State Grange convention of 1869 featured the river. Printed in the *Minnesota Monthly*'s July issue, the convention's preamble to its resolutions declared:

> The Mississippi River traverses for thousands of miles the noblest agricultural regions of the earth, running from North to South,... it is destined to become the most popular region of the world, and its waters should forever be kept free and untrammeled and open to the use of every citizen within the entire navigable length, and all obstructions, whether natural or of human device, are like impediments to the prosperity of the people who till the soil of the great valley.[30]

In the subsequent resolutions, the Minnesota Grange warned other granges to keep a vigil against steamboat monopolies and against monopolies of the river's levees and waterfronts. They especially targeted transportation monopolies such as those created by the "wheat ring." They recognized that waterway competition represented the only competition to railroads and the only way, outside of state or federal regulations, to lower rates and overcome railroad monopolies.[31]

In August 1870 Kelley left Minnesota by steamboat for St. Louis to secure direct trade arrangements between Minnesota and Missouri. During his trip, he fed the *St. Paul Pioneer Press* articles condemning railroads and the Chicago Board of Trade and promoting waterway projects. He hoped to restore the dying river connection between St. Paul and St. Louis. While railroads had received huge land grants, steamboats had not. "Railroads have got enough for the present," he concluded, calling on Congress to appropriate funding "for every navigable stream in the West" and to "open the natural outlets free to all." To restore river traffic, Kelley insisted that the Mississippi needed grants like those given to railroads, and the Grange had to establish an agent in St. Louis to buy and sell Minnesota's products.[32]

At its seventh national convention in February 1874 in St. Louis, the National Grange announced that it would work for more and cheaper transportation facilities. Colonel W. B. Smedley, Worthy Master of Iowa's Grange, largely authored a report that emphasized cheap transportation and navigation improvements. Smedley had become vice president of the American Board of Trade and Transportation, formerly known as the American Cheap Transportation Association, the previous year. Smedley charged that the United States suffered from an inadequate transportation system and unreasonable charges. As a remedy he offered a three-step program. First, the country had to make the Mississippi River navigable. Competition depended on navigation improvements. Second, Congress had to regulate railroad rates. Last, Congress had to restore the nation's foreign commerce to its previous state, which would lower freight charges and increase prices. Smedley insisted that American farmers needed foreign markets for their increasing surplus.[33]

As had the drive for railroad legislation, the push for navigation improvements drew more than farmers. St. Louis merchants were among the Mississippi River's greatest advocates. Reeling from Chicago's increasing dominance over the region's trade, they saw the river as their best counteroffensive.[34] In May 1873 cheap transportation boosters held the Western Congressional Convention in St. Louis. It attracted senators and representatives from twenty-two states, and the governors of Minnesota, Ohio, Kansas, Missouri, and Virginia. The conference organizers hoped to reveal the depth of the shipping crisis to these key political officials. The solution, they urged, lay in improving the nation's waterways for navigation, especially the Mississippi River and its tributaries. Such improvements exceeded the ability of the individual states. The federal government, they asserted, had to assume responsibility.[35]

As the economic crisis of 1873 deepened, transportation reform advocates held meetings outside the river valley as well. The National Cheap Transportation Association, organized in New York on May 6 and 7, 1873, drew representatives from most of the upper Mississippi River states. The association resolved to lobby Congress to regulate railroads and to increase other means of transportation. On May 20, 1873, the governor of Georgia called a meeting to discuss "projects of cheap transportation" between the South and the grain-growing states of the Midwest and West. Attended by the governors of some of these states and by representatives of the Grange, key cities, and organizations, the meeting focused on getting new roads and canals to facilitate commerce. Eight days later, the National Agricultural Congress met in Indianapolis to address the "transportation problem." Those who attended also called for more roads and canals and for railroad regulation. And in late October 1873, the Northwestern Farmers' Convention occurred in Chicago. While most of the two hundred delegates came from Illinois, many represented other midwestern states. Like those attending the other meetings, they sought railroad rate regulation, the construction of alternate transportation systems, including canals, and navigation improvement. By 1874, Congress could not ignore the transportation crisis.[36]

The Windom Committee

The threat of the wheat ring in the early 1870s, the commercial decline of the Mississippi River, and rising dissatisfaction with the Republican party concerned Minnesota Senator William Windom. Windom's hometown, Winona, lay on the Mississippi River in southeastern Minnesota and had been in the area controlled by the wheat ring. Windom first became a senator when Republican Daniel S. Norton died in office in 1870, and Minnesota's governor appointed Windom to fill the seat. Windom had already served in the House for a decade. Although the

Figure 9. Minnesota Senator William Windom pushed for navigation improvements for the upper Mississippi River to combat high rail rates. Photograph by Brady; courtesy of the Minnesota Historical Society.

Minnesota legislature selected someone else to finish Norton's term, Windom captured the seat in 1871. He would become one of the Senate's strongest advocates for railroad regulation.[37]

The Granger movement's rapidly growing strength in Minnesota spurred Windom to confront the transportation issue. Grange supporters, led by former Republican Ignatius Donnelly, had organized the People's Anti-Monopoly party, "with a platform striking at monopolies, advocating state railroad controls, and denouncing postwar corruption...."[38] While still in his twenties, Donnelly had become Minnesota's lieutenant governor. He moved on to represent Minnesota in the U.S. House for six years as a Republican. But in 1868 he quarreled with Minnesota's senior Republican leader, Alexander Ramsey, and failed to get reelected. Recognizing the Granger movement's growing strength and its discontent with the Republican party's failure to deal with monopolies and the farm crisis, Donnelly joined the movement in 1872. In January 1873 he organized a grange in Hastings, Minnesota, and shortly after Kelley gave him permission to organize granges nationally. As Anti-Monopoly parties threatened to undermine the Republican party's dominance in the state and nationally, Windom and other Republicans began working for railroad reform and sought ways to solve the farm crisis.[39]

Windom chaired the Senate Select Committee on Transportation to the Seaboard, putting him in good position to help both farmers and his party. In a speech before the Senate, he asserted that "it was 'an admitted fact' that present transportation facilities between the interior and the seaboard were 'totally inadequate.' These transportation networks," he charged, "were controlled by 'powerful monopolies who dictate their own terms to the people. The burdens they impose upon both consumer and producer are too grievous to be long endured.'"[40] In response, on March 26, 1873, the Senate directed Windom's committee to study the problem. The Senate was not reacting only to Windom's urging. Republican President Ulysses Grant, also well aware of agrarian unrest, had warned the Senate that "this issue would inevitably be forced on the Exec. branch,... [and] suggested that the Congress study the problem and find a solution."[41]

On April 24, 1874, Windom submitted his report to the Senate. His committee detailed the tremendous growth and the potential for even greater growth in the country's agricultural output. They also emphasized how the inadequate transportation system threatened the well-being of farmers throughout the country and the nation's place in international grain markets. They examined grain shipments from the interior to the coasts and overseas. They studied railroad practices, policies, and abuses. Exploring possible remedies to the crisis, they analyzed the benefits of building waterway projects and the authority of the federal government to regulate internal commerce and to construct internal improvements.

As Windom advocated navigation improvement and railroad regulation to solve the transportation crisis, he had to assert the right of the federal government in these arenas. So the committee began by declaring that the Constitution granted Congress certain powers over interstate commerce. Assuming Congress had the authority to regulate interstate commerce, the committee insisted its task was to determine what *"the nature, extent, and application of the powers actually delegated"* was.[42] The committee's findings attacked the states' rights and anti-federalist argument against federal support for internal improvements. After a lengthy and detailed review, the committee asserted that Congress had the right to improve the Mississippi River and other rivers for navigation. More boldly, it determined that Congress had the authority to regulate and even construct railroads to foster commerce.[43]

The Windom committee evaluated feasible and practicable ways to increase competition and reduce shipping costs. First, it examined what many hoped would work: simply promoting competition between railroads. More radically, it evaluated the possibility of building government railroad lines and letting private railroads operate them. But the committee rejected this option. After examining railroads in Europe and the United States, it found that railroads everywhere tended toward combination, which limited competition. Voicing disappointment with an unfettered laissez-faire approach, the committee reported that it had "reluctantly reached the conclusion that the reduced cost of transportation demanded by the public is not to be anticipated from unregulated competition between existing railway companies, nor in competition to be induced by the construction of additional lines under private management and control...." The committee turned to other alternatives.[44]

The committee next studied direct regulation of railroads by Congress. Here the committee determined that "the assertion of such power by the national government is of the utmost importance...." It also contended that Congress could redress some of the "evils and defects of our railway system" by government regulation. But the committee balked at full regulation. Given the complex nature of the railroad system in America, the committee declared that trying to regulate cheap rates would only "delude and disappoint the public."[45]

As a third approach, the committee considered how federally operated freight railroads could drive private rail rates down. Proponents of this solution believed that private railroads would have to match rates charged by the government railroads, and thus railroad schemes that artificially increased rates would end. Combination with the government lines would be impossible. Opponents insisted that this plan would unfairly burden the country, because such railroads could not operate at a profit. They warned that government management would cost more than private and would lead to greater abuses. And they objected that it was unfair for the government to compete against private individuals and companies. Government lines, they protested, would drive the private lines out of business. The committee rejected these claims, citing the positive experiences of government-run railroads in other countries.[46]

Finally, the committee assessed the creation of alternative transportation to railroads through federally backed navigation improvements. The Senate resolution creating the committee had especially directed them to explore this option. The committee examined existing and proposed waterways to determine the need for navigation improvements, their costs, and their existing and potential commercial benefits. They studied four major routes.[47]

For the Mississippi River, the committee began by reviewing the demise of shipping and then investigated how the United States could expand its grain exports. It undertook a detailed analysis of trade between the United States and Great Britain, examining why grain did not move in greater quantities from New Orleans to British ports. This trade was critical, because Great Britain purchased the most American grain and because world grain prices were set there. By opening the Mississippi and other rivers, the committee asserted, the United States could challenge Russia and European countries for the British grain trade, and the United States could develop its trade with Central and South America.[48]

After reviewing the advantages and disadvantages of all four proposals, the committee recommended that Congress regulate some railroads and authorize an intense program of navigation improvements. Congress, the committee suggested, should require railroads to publish their rates and fares and give reasonable notice of any changes. Windom's committee condemned railroads' purchases of parallel or competing lines as "evils of such magnitude as to demand prompt and vigorous measures for their prevention." The committee asked Congress to stop railroads from charging more for a short haul to a waterway than for a long haul to some more distant point beyond the waterway. Congress, the committee urged, should create a federal agency to collect commercial statistics. Railways and other shipping companies would have to present an annual report to the agency. States also had to assume some responsibility for railroad practices, the committee insisted. As railroad corporations received their charters in specific states, the states should deal with the problem of artificially inflated railway stocks. But, the committee noted, regulating the rates and fares of the country's 1,300 railroads surpassed the ability of Congress. The committee deferred acting on this alternative in favor of those that might solve the transportation problem more quickly.[49]

Trying to salvage some laissez-faire provision, the committee unanimously pronounced that "the problem of *cheap* transportation is to be solved through *competition*, ... rather than by direct Congressional regulation of existing lines." Congress had to prevent railroads from combining with their competitors, and the competitors needed more less-expensive routes on which to operate. For these reasons, the committee contended, the federal government or a state had to own the competing mode to guarantee cheap and constant competition. Railroads owned or controlled by the government, the committee believed, would moderate private railroad rates wherever the government railroad ran.[50]

Here, however, the committee hesitated. While confident of the government's authority to regulate railroads and to make waterways navigable, the committee questioned the government's role in competing against private enterprises. Navigation improvement offered an acceptable and potentially successful solution to the transportation crisis, without such interference. Experience throughout the world, the committee insisted, had shown that waterways were the most economical way to ship heavy, bulky, or cheap commodities, and waterways, it proclaimed, were "the natural competitors and most effective regulators of railway-transportation." All the above considerations and the "remarkable physical adaptation of our country for cheap and ample water communications," the committee concluded, "point unerringly to the improvement of our great natural water-ways, and their connection by canals, or by short freight-railway portages under control of the government, as the obvious and certain solution of the problem of *cheap* transportation."[51]

Relying on the reports submitted by the Army Corps of Engineers, the committee remarked that the Mississippi River had received sporadic navigation improvements. No general plan had been developed or implemented. The committee recommended that Congress authorize surveys and prepare cost estimates as early as possible "in order to mature a plan for the radical improvement of the river, and of all its navigable tributaries."[52] The committee suggested the Corps establish a channel of 4½ to 6 feet for the upper Mississippi River from St. Anthony Falls to St. Louis. To create a channel of these depths, the committee acknowledged, meant constricting the river with wing dams and closing dams.[53]

The Windom report drew praise by some for its strong anti-railroad recommendations, and criticism from others for not going far enough.[54] The *St. Paul Daily Pioneer* proclaimed it "the strongest Grange and anti-monopoly tract which has yet appeared in print,..." The *St. Paul Daily Press* claimed that navigable rivers would "'emancipate the country from the chains of the railroad monopoly.'" The *Minneapolis Tribune* lauded the report for its detailed and masterful presentation. The *St. Paul Dispatch*, taking a conservative view of federal authority, questioned whether Congress had the power to implement the regulations proposed by Windom's committee. It did note, however, that the report was "in many respects considered one of the most important reports ever presented to Congress." Wanting more, the *St. Paul Anti-Monopolist* suggested that Windom was a railroad man and attempting to divert people from railroad regulation to "digging the mud out of the mouth of the Mississippi."[55]

Windom's report received a mixed national reaction. The *New York Times* and the *New York Tribune* praised the report for its thoroughness. But the *Chicago Tribune* and the *Chicago Times*, undoubtedly concerned about the threat to their city's status as a railroad hub, condemned the report for recommending an excessively expensive and utopian program. The *Times* labeled the report "a wild and reckless scheme of national canal digging...."[56]

On Windom's behalf, his biographer, Robert Salisbury, explains that Windom, "ever the nationalist," took the widest view of the government's authority to regulate commerce. To the senator, the federal government not only had the authority, it had the responsibility to facilitate commerce for the national good. And unlike many proposals before and after, Windom's report advocated a national program of internal improvement, not local or pork-barrel projects. Salisbury points out that the three Democrats on the committee dissented from the committee's interventionist stand. Salisbury presents this as evidence that the Democrats "remained mired in the shibboleths of negative government and states' rights."[57]

Most of Windom's critics failed to consider what was truly possible at the time. While getting over the issue of the federal government's authority to authorize and construct waterway projects, the country still questioned government control of private industry. Although threatening a dramatically intrusive plan, Windom deftly steered the committee's recommendations toward something acceptable to Congress and the president and that many midwestern farmers desired. Windom's report advocated a laissez-faire approach where possible and government regulation where necessary and feasible. Waterway projects preserved at least the appearance of a laissez-faire economy, and the minimal regulations suggested by the committee represented an important step toward more aggressive railroad regulation. If the committee delayed serious railroad regulation, it was because the country simply was not ready for it. Many genuinely believed or hoped that improving the Mississippi and other rivers for navigation would open a legitimate commercial route, increase competition, and reduce rates.[58]

The Urban Connection

Although never as organized as the Grangers, the river's commercial interests led the final push for a deeper and more reliable navigation channel. Between 1866 and 1878 they kept the issue before the people of the valley and Congress. They had held conventions at St. Louis in 1867 and 1873, at Prairie du Chien in 1868, and at New Orleans in 1869 and 1876. St. Paul hosted their meetings in 1875 and 1877. The 1877 convention culminated their drive for a new, radical navigation project. Although few, if any, farmers attended these conventions, urban navigation boosters used grain shipping in their arguments.[59]

River cities answered the call for a meeting at St. Paul on short notice. The St. Paul Chamber of Commerce sent out the invitation on September 18, 1877. It specifically asked that "editors and representative men" from the Mississippi River states gather in St. Paul to push for navigation improvements. In sending out its notice, the chamber declared that the "first duty of the general government" was to make the Mississippi River navigable. Building on the region's growing political strength and the Windom committee's report, the chamber hoped to generate a movement strong enough to secure immediate navigation improvements for the whole Mississippi River.[60]

Avoiding the stigma of the Anti-Monopoly parties and the

Grangers, the convention delegates in 1877 emphasized that they were "not a political organization." Their "members were practical business men" who came from boards of trade, chambers of commerce, and other organizations. They drew representatives from eighteen states and nearly every city from Louisiana to Minnesota. They resolved to petition Congress to deepen the Mississippi River and formed an executive committee to write a memorial to Congress. The committee included one representative each from St. Paul; Galena and Chester, Illinois; Dubuque; and New Orleans; and five from St. Louis.[61]

Sylvester Waterhouse, a professor at Washington University in St. Louis, became the executive committee's secretary and crafted the memorial to Congress. He also wrote a longer appendix, detailing the arguments for navigation improvement. Waterhouse had recently visited Minnesota and reported that it had taken him longer to make the 800-mile trip downriver to St. Louis than it had taken a friend of his to sail 4,000 miles from Ireland to St. Louis. At good stages, he said, steamboats hustled from St. Paul to St. Louis in four days; they had raced through round-trips in as little as seven days, including stops for passengers and freight. His trip had taken thirteen days, due in part to low water. The *Virginia* had taken only fifteen days on its second voyage in 1823. Such delays, Waterhouse complained, cost money, emphasizing that "in these days of rapid exchanges, nowhere is the truth of the adage that 'time is money' more sensibly felt than in the transactions of commerce." Low water and sandbars had cost hundreds of thousands of dollars in delays. An experienced steamboat captain informed Waterhouse that delays cost about $16 per hour.[62]

The committee outlined five arguments for why Congress should authorize and fund deepening the Mississippi River. First, they contended that the valley's extensive commerce "entitled" the region to the improvements. Taking a position echoed by many boosters during the next fifty years, they acknowledged that little commerce moved on the river but countered that "it is important to remember that *the rate by river determines the rate by rail.*"[63] The savings gained by having a competitive river, they asserted, would be national. "Practical steamboatmen," the second argument began, assured the committee that removing the river's obstructions would lower shipping costs by three-quarters. On an improved navigation channel, steamboats would suffer fewer delays and pay less insurance, and with deeper drafts, boats could carry more cargo and reap greater profit. On a truly navigable river, shippers could move grain to Liverpool, England, for eight to ten cents a bushel less than by way of New York. The country needed a navigable Mississippi River for national unity and defense, boosters offered as their third contention. Ignoring the drought of 1864, the river and its tributaries, they recounted, had served well during the Civil War and would help reintegrate the country. European countries had been undertaking navigation improvement for years, to their credit, and the United States should follow their example. As a fourth point, they complained that the government had overlooked the Mississippi River and had denied the river its share of federal funding. An unnavigable Mississippi, they contended, was a "national shame...."[64] Pointing out that government funds had flowed more liberally in recent years, they demanded something meaningful for the upper river.[65]

Finally, the executive committee urged Congress to authorize enough funding to complete work on the Mississippi quickly. Such work not only furthered national commerce and extended foreign trade, it saved the government money. Insufficient funds led to inadequate projects, which the Corps could not maintain. One large appropriation, they asserted, would do more good than a series of small ones. To support their point, they quoted General J. H. Simpson of the Corps, who headed the Mississippi River from the mouth of the Illinois River to the mouth of the Ohio River. Simpson reported that appropriating $1 million per year for seven years worked better than twenty appropriations of $500,000. If Congress appropriated only $200,000 a year, the Corps could just as well abandon the effort, he protested. Many future Corps commanders on the upper Mississippi would repeat his argument.[66]

The committee then presented its plan. They requested $617,000 for the river from St. Paul to the Des Moines Rapids, and $383,000 for the reach between the rapids and the Illinois River. From the Illinois to

New Orleans, they asked for $1 million. With this funding, they hoped the Corps could establish a 5-foot channel from St. Paul to St. Louis, an 8-foot channel from St. Louis to Cairo, Illinois, at the Ohio River's mouth, and a 10-foot channel between Cairo and New Orleans. "A river endowed with such vast capabilities of usefulness should be fitted for its grand destiny," they insisted. "But the Mississippi can never fulfill its grand office of commercial exchange," they warned, until it had been deepened permanently.[67] Hope for the "grand destiny" seemed brighter by the meeting's end. Summarizing the convention, the *St. Paul Pioneer Press* exclaimed that it had united the political power of the valley for navigation improvement.[68]

Waterhouse added to and bolstered these arguments in his appendix. In 1877, he said, the five upper river states produced 100 million bushels of wheat. Minnesota produced 30 million, of which 25 million could be exported. The corn crop was gaining recognition abroad for its value to people and animals. The amount exported had increased from 20 million bushels in 1875 to 50 million in 1876 and would exceed 70 million in 1877. Having extolled the advantages enjoyed by shipping on the Great Lakes, he argued that with proper navigation improvements, the Mississippi would surpass the lakes. Ice closed the river below Keokuk for two months or less per year, while ice often closed the lakes for four months. Fleets of river barges could haul larger cargoes than lake ships. On the river the current helped propel tows downstream, increasing the economy of shipping on the river. During good river stages, Waterhouse declared, tows could push eight to ten barges. Fully loaded, he maintained, these barges carried a volume equal to 384 to 480 railroad cars, respectively. Waterhouse believed that improving the river for navigation would establish "organized competition" and would lower the cost of shipping freight to Liverpool to 25 cents per bushel.[69] Given this evidence, he asked: "Is it not the duty of the Government to open the channel through which so full a tide of wealth would flow?" The high rates unfairly charged by railroads and the unimproved condition of the Mississippi River, he claimed, discouraged farmers from wanting to produce for the market.[70]

He even used a class-based argument in his essay and claimed that improving navigation would help relieve the economic depression. The government had spent millions on coastal improvements but little on interior rivers. "The ocean," he charged, "conveys to our shores the costly luxuries which embellish the residences of the rich; the river brings to the humble homes of the poor a cheaper means of livelihood. Which serves the first consideration of our Government?" If the Midwest's great agricultural wealth moved on the Mississippi River, farmers would have more to spend and would buy more from eastern manufacturers. Since labor was cheap, the government could put many people to work on navigation improvements, reducing the cost and relieving unemployment. The result, he believed, would help bring the country out of the depression that had begun in 1873. The federal government, he stressed, should build projects of such universal benefit.[71]

Waterhouse declared that an improved navigation channel would serve more than grain. The great iron and coal resources in the valley would make it "the great central machine-shop of the nation," he vowed. And, he reported, timber traffic had nearly surpassed the grain trade on the upper Mississippi River. The annual amount rafted averaged 1 billion board feet, valued at $15 million. Towns along the river used 900 million board feet, and the rest went to lumberyards in St. Louis. The lumber not used by the river towns traveled by rail to the west. According to "practical lumbermen," a permanent deep channel would lower the cost of shipping timber by one-third. The delays currently caused by low water, Waterhouse complained, embarrassed the region.[72]

On June 18, 1878, Congress responded to the first massive cry for navigation improvements and authorized the 4½-foot channel project. The people of the upper Mississippi River states had come together in the Granger movement, as boards of trade and chambers of commerce, and through their state governments to demand federal management of the river. From the outset they argued that only the federal government had the money and expertise to remake the Mississippi River into the commercial highway they dreamed it could be. The transportation demands generated by the region's dramatic population and agricultural growth between 1865 and 1878 made the river's inadequacies as a navigation route clear. Monopolistic practices by railroads underscored this. The region's growth also gave it the political strength to press for railroad regulation and navigation improvements. The Granger movement and the Anti-Monopoly parties brought the shipping crisis and the upper Mississippi's newfound strength to the nation's attention. Waterway boosters played off national protests against railroad abuses to gain support for their projects. Windom's committee showed the nation's unwillingness to seriously regulate railroads and how navigation improvements offered an easy and politically acceptable alternative.

The federal government's role in changing and managing the upper Mississippi River would become stronger and more permanent with the 4½-foot channel. To deepen the upper Mississippi and insure an adequate depth for navigation, Waterhouse, like the Windom committee, advocated channel constriction. He suggested that Congress should not think of the project as new construction. Viewing the river as most did during his day, he observed: "The bounty of Providence has freely provided the river for our commercial convenience. There is no cost of construction but only of improvement."[73] As navigation improvement proponents had begun arguing, meaningful improvement required large appropriations so projects could be completed quickly. During the 4½-foot project, this argument would be repeated constantly, and because it encompassed the entire upper river, the level of funding asked for would be beyond anything previously contemplated. Unlike any force outside nature, the 4½-foot project would begin physically and ecologically transforming the upper river.

CHAPTER 4

Making the Mississippi Over Again

When Captain Alexander Mackenzie took command of the Corps' Rock Island District in June 1879, the upper Mississippi River possessed most of its natural character. In 1896 he left a vastly different river. Congress, by authorizing the 4½-foot channel, directed the Corps to recast the upper Mississippi, to forge a permanent, uninterrupted navigation channel, 4½ feet deep at low water, for the river between St. Paul and the mouth of the Illinois River at Alton. This required dramatic changes in the Mississippi's physical and ecological character. It meant eliminating the wide shallows and sandbars and the innumerable little pools General Gouverneur K. Warren had wanted to preserve. The Engineers would have to alter how sand and silt moved along the river bottom. They would have to concentrate the river's current into one main channel and block off the scores of side channels that led to uncounted backwaters. The focus of the Corps' work between 1878 and 1906, the 4½-foot channel became the first systemwide, intensive navigation improvement project to transform the upper Mississippi River. It would be a monumental task, one many doubted the Corps, or anyone, could accomplish. Institutionally, the 4½-foot project would establish the Corps as the dominant actor on the upper Mississippi River.

Congress expanded the Corps' role in other ways during the 4½-foot channel era (1878–1906). It authorized the Corps to construct five dams at the Mississippi's headwaters to regulate downstream flow, and floodplain farmers temporarily pushed Congress and the Corps into building agricultural levees. When refuse from sawmills and garbage from cities obstructed navigation, Congress granted the Corps the authority to stop the dumping of pollutants into navigable waterways. Combined, the Corps' new roles made it the lead player on the upper river by the end of the nineteenth century, a role it has maintained.

Survey

Before the Engineers could begin remaking the Mississippi, they had to learn more about it. To begin, the Engineers needed up-to-date, detailed, and comprehensive maps. Warren and his successors had surveyed individual reaches and specific trouble spots, but they had not conducted a continuous, precise survey. During the winter of 1877–78, Major Francis U. Farquhar directed his engineers to synthesize all earlier maps into a general map from St. Anthony Falls to the mouth of the Illinois River. Farquhar, Mackenzie's immediate predecessor, had commanded the St. Paul District since 1873 and assumed command of the Rock Island District in November 1877. He headed both districts until 1879. Farquhar's map comprised twenty-six sheets.[1]

Farquhar rejected the map as a clumsy patchwork and asked the Chief of Engineers for $60,000 for a new survey. On July 8, 1878, the Chief approved his request, and between 1878 and 1879, Farquhar oversaw the first continuous and comprehensive survey of the upper Mississippi River. His engineers sounded the river to find the deepest and most unbroken channel. They calculated the drainage areas of the tributary rivers. They determined the Mississippi's elevation at low water and high water and the river's slope between towns.[2]

To illustrate the new map, Farquhar needed a talented draftsman. While commanding the St. Paul District, he had discovered such a person: Henry P. Bosse. Bosse joined the Corps in Chicago in 1874 to work on Great Lakes harbor improvements. But in 1875 he joined Farquhar and the Corps' U.S. River and Harbor Improvement Office in St. Paul. While at St. Paul, Bosse illustrated maps of the river above Minneapolis, specifically showing the use and effect of wing dams and closing dams. Knowing Bosse's skills, Farquhar probably convinced him to move to Rock Island in 1878.[3]

From Farquhar's new survey, Bosse and his assistant A. J. Stibolt completed an eighty-three-page map. They depicted the ideal navigation channel as a continuous dashed line, marking each river mile on it. In scientific fashion, they numbered the once innumerable islands. They showed all the bars and sloughs and chutes, where Pike, Schoolcraft, Featherstonaugh, and others had grounded or become lost. Their map demonstrates how Americans had occupied the land and the river with their names. It presents Deadman's Bar, Mechanic's Rock (for the boat that sank upon striking it), Horse Shoe Bend, Whiskey Chute, Dark Slough, and Demarais Bayou. Key landmarks along the river also appear, such as Chimney Rock and Eagle, Queens, Capoli, and Atchafalaya Bluffs. Most steamboat landings, such as Warner's, York's, Drury, Lone Tree, and War Eagle, appear on the map, as do ferry crossings. Bosse and Stibolt penned in every river and many creeks entering the big river. From their artistic rendering, one can see the bluffs close in on the river and the vast floodplains running away from it. Completed at a scale of 1 inch to the mile, their map would become the base map for the Corps' upper Mississippi River navigation charts until the 1930s. The Corps regularly updated the maps to show the shore protection, wing dams, and closing dams built in and along the river.[4]

Channel Constriction

His survey completed, Farquhar prepared to transform the upper Mississippi River, but the job went to Captain Alexander Mackenzie. Wherever he served, Mackenzie gained great respect. In 1860 he entered the U.S. Military Academy and graduated fifth in the class of 1864. Following a West Point tradition, Mackenzie and the other graduates attended dinner and then exited by twos and threes "to the thunderous accompaniment of the iron stools, as the undergraduates pounded out their parting salute." When Mackenzie left, "the din was something indescribable." After a brief stint in the Civil War, Mackenzie worked on the lower Mississippi's levees, on river and harbor projects in

Milwaukee, and on various western and midwestern rivers, including the Ohio. He led the Rock Island office for nearly sixteen years (1879–96), leaving the District as a lieutenant colonel. He then moved to Corps headquarters in Washington, D.C., and in 1904 became the Chief of Engineers. Upon his retirement as a major general in 1908, his staff presented him with a gold-headed cane to demonstrate their admiration. Mackenzie died in Washington, D.C., on February 23, 1921. He knew the river well, even before he arrived in Rock Island. Born near the Mississippi at Potosi, Wisconsin, on May 25, 1844, he attended grammar and high schools in the port city of Dubuque, Iowa. Through his work on the 4½-foot channel, Mackenzie earned his reputation as an engineer. The *Military Engineer* eulogized Mackenzie for having undertaken "the most successful example of river regulation known to engineers."[5]

Figure 10. Major General Alexander Mackenzie commanded the Rock Island District, U.S. Army Corps of Engineers, from 1879 to 1896 and was the principal architect of the 4½-foot channel project. Courtesy of the U.S. Army Corps of Engineers.

To achieve the 4½-foot channel, Mackenzie expanded on the channel constriction experiments begun by Durham and Meigs. By constricting or narrowing the river and increasing the main channel's volume and velocity, Mackenzie hoped to scour one uninterrupted navigation channel. He planned to use the wing dams to concentrate the river's flow, like tightening the nozzle on a garden hose, to cut through sandbars and connect the river's disjointed pockets of deep water.

The wing dams' success depended on the main channel's volume and velocity. During the late summer and early fall, the Mississippi usually became a shallow, slow-moving stream, and the wing dams lacked enough water to scour the main channel. (Imagine the garden hose nozzle as someone turns down the faucet.) Droughts had the same effect but could last an entire season. The river's many islands disbursed the little water available into side channels and sloughs. To deliver more

Figure 11. *Wing Dams below Nininger,* by Henry Bosse, shows the general pattern of channel constriction during the 4½-foot channel project. Courtesy of the St. Paul District, U.S. Army Corps of Engineers.

water to the main channel, the Corps built closing dams. These dams ran from the shore to an island or from one island to another. When high, the river passed over the closing dams, but for most of the year, the dams directed water into the main channel, denying flow to the river's side channels and backwaters.[6]

The river naturally eroded its banks, but channel constriction accelerated erosion. Wing dams forced the river away from one shore and against the other. To protect shores from naturally eroding or from being undercut by the constricted channel, the Corps armored hundreds of miles of shoreline with brush mats and rock.

Wing dams, closing dams, and shore protection required two simple materials: willow saplings and rock. Cut from the river's floodplain, contractors bound the saplings into long, narrow bundles. They quarried

Figure 12. *Closing Dam at Otter Chute*, by Henry Bosse, shows a typical closing dam. Otter Chute is above Burlington, Iowa. Courtesy of the St. Paul District, U.S. Army Corps of Engineers.

rock from the river's bluffs and loaded it evenly on a flat-topped barge. The Engineers or their contractors placed the rock and brush in layers until a dam rose above the water's surface to a level that would guarantee a minimum 4½-foot channel.[7]

Alberta Kirchner Hill spent nineteen summers (1898–1917) with her father's fleet as they built the dams for the government. Her father, Albert Kirchner, along with Jacob Richtman, both from Fountain City, Wisconsin, became leading contractors for the Corps. From the building boat, Alberta Kirchner recalled, "I could even smell the delightfully blended odor of the willows and of the creosoted marline twine with which the bundles were held together. It came to me strongly every time the men hoisted a swishing bundle of brush to their gunny-sack-protected shoulders...." Once laid in the water, the workers would sink the willow mats with rock. "No sooner had a barge of rocks been pulled up to the dam," Hill remembered, "than the symmetry of the load was destroyed as the men began the routine of sinking the mat.... From the quarterboats you could hear the big rocks hitting each other, like a rapid-fire rage.... as the mat went down under the load ... a splashing began. The sound grew in intensity as the mat sank lower and lower in the water."[8] After the mat sank, the workers added another layer if needed.

How much the Engineers narrowed the channel and how they arranged the dams determined how well the project worked. Although based on an established German model, the Mississippi forced the Engineers to learn on the job. Between Winona and La Crosse, the Corps reduced the channel's width to 800 feet. This width, Durham reported, was "not obtained from any hydraulic formulae, which are well-nigh impossible to apply to a river of such size and variety of conditions,..."[9] The width had been defined after years of experience. This held true for other reaches. Deciding how to arrange the dams evolved through experience also. For most of the 4½-foot project era, the Corps simply built a series of wing dams and closing dams and then waited to see what happened. Only toward the project's end did the Corps develop a rule. The plan became "to place them, in straight reaches, five-sevenths of the proposed channel width apart; in curved reaches, one-half on the concave sides and the full width on the convex sides."[10] Still, the river forced the Corps to adjust the formulas.

The 1903–5 edition of Bosse and Stibolt's map shows the river ribbed with wing dams, its side channels blocked with closing dams, and its shore lined with rock riprap. By 1905 the Corps had built 226 miles of wing dams and closing dams and had laid over 197 miles of shore protection. The Engineers did not build all the works depicted in one area at the same time. They built as many wing dams, closed as many side channels, and armored as much shoreline as needed to establish a $4\frac{1}{2}$-foot channel in a given reach. Then they moved to the next. In newly constricted reaches, the channel might be good for a season or two and then become difficult again, due to the river's natural tendencies or to

Figure 13. Wing dam construction. Workers formed the brush into mats and laid the mats in the water to form one layer of a wing dam. Photograph by Henry Bosse. Courtesy of the St. Paul District, U.S. Army Corps of Engineers.

the improvement works themselves. Where necessary, the Engineers returned and added more wing dams, closing dams, and shore protection. The density of channel constriction works and the degree to which they physically and ecologically changed the river increased gradually over the project's history.[11]

At times, no matter how many wing dams and closing dams the Corps built, the river fell too low. To ensure a more reliable flow, Congress authorized the Corps to construct six dams near the Mississippi's headwaters, in northern Minnesota. Warren first suggested the idea in his 1869 report, recommending a system of forty-one reservoirs for the St. Croix, Chippewa, Wisconsin, and Mississippi River basins. Subsequent engineers reduced the number to six. The Corps built five under

Figure 14. Wing dam construction. Workers threw rock onto a brush mat until it sank, and then they covered the rock with another layer of brush and piled rock on top of it. The builders repeated this process until the dam was high enough to direct the water to the main channel during low water. Photograph by Henry Bosse. Courtesy of the St. Paul District, U.S. Army Corps of Engineers.

the 4½-foot project. Millers at St. Anthony Falls especially pushed for reservoirs. One miller, William Washburn, went so far as to purchase land for one reservoir site, which he later gave to the government. The millers knew that releasing water from the reservoirs for navigation would increase the flow of water to their mills.

Congress initially balked at the project's pork-barrel appearance. In 1880, however, Congress authorized an experimental dam for Lake Winnibigoshish and approved the remaining dams shortly afterward. Under the headwaters project, the Corps built the Winnibigoshish dam in 1883–84 and then completed dams at Leech Lake (1884), Pokegama Falls (1884), Pine River (1886), Sandy Lake (1895), and (after the 4½-foot project) Gull Lake (1912). The dams became the first system of reservoirs built by the Corps in the country. In their 1895 annual report, the Engineers announced that releasing water from the headwaters reservoirs successfully raised the water level in the Twin Cities by 12 to 18 inches, helping navigation interests and the millers. Twenty-seven river miles downstream, at Hastings, the Corps recorded a rise of about 1 foot, and about 15 miles farther down, at Red Wing, about ½ foot. Given that the river had fallen to a record low, a ½ foot mattered. Below Red Wing, the effect of water released from the reservoirs disappeared.[12]

Planning for an Unpredictable River

Throughout the 4½-foot channel project, the Engineers on the upper Mississippi River refused to develop a predetermined plan for navigation improvements or to provide a detailed cost estimate for the overall project. Mackenzie established this position. He resisted developing a predetermined plan for two reasons. First, the river was too unpredictable. He did not know how it would respond to channel constriction or which reach would demand his attention in any given year. Second, Congress did not appropriate enough money to systematically develop the project. In 1882 Mackenzie explained his position to the Chief of Engineers: "The channel of the river changes materially during high stages, and the troublesome points cannot be predicted until the river falls sufficiently to develop them. It is therefore impossible, as a rule," he contended, "to lay out work long in advance, or to prepare satisfactory specifications as to locality and nature of work."[13]

For these reasons, Mackenzie insisted the Corps formulate a general plan each year. This plan would target the upper river's most difficult reaches but would be flexible enough to address trouble spots as they arose. While steamboat pilots and Corps surveyors knew the persistently bad reaches, they could not predict when those reaches would obstruct traffic. If the Corps established a rigid work schedule and Congress approved it, unexpected problems could interrupt commerce. Mackenzie stuck to this position throughout his tenure as the Rock Island District commander. In 1895, after working on the project for over fifteen years, he reported that "it does not now appear desirable or even practicable to prepare detailed plans for the whole river so long in advance of the time when it may be possible or necessary to carry out some of the work." It had become "the custom" under the project, he reported, "to select, when funds are available, such localities for improvement as may be at the time most detrimental to navigation." Mackenzie had made it the custom.[14]

Mackenzie also demanded flexibility because Congress appropriated little money for the project. Beginning with his first annual report to the Chief of Engineers in 1880, Mackenzie pleaded for more money. "The radical improvement of the Upper Mississippi River having been commenced," he urged, "it is of great importance that it should be actively continued." Throughout Mackenzie's tenure, Congress appropriated less than half the funding he requested. In his 1882 report, Mackenzie argued for at least $750,000 for the 1884 fiscal year; he got $250,000. Five years later, he asked for $1.5 million for the fiscal year ending June 30, 1889. Congress authorized $600,000. Noting that the Corps had to improve some 500 miles of the upper river, Mackenzie insisted that Congress liberally fund the work. Mackenzie often complained that funding shortages prevented the Corps from working on critical reaches. As boosters and Corps officers before him had, he argued that with greater funding the Corps could complete the project more quickly and economically.[15]

While he complained, Mackenzie used the situation to his advantage. By midsummer the river generally fell, and problem areas revealed themselves. Mackenzie hoarded his funds to work on the most serious reaches as they emerged. When Congress adequately financed the project, as it did in 1894 and 1895, he completed plans and contracts early and "vigorously" pursued channel constriction.[16]

Mackenzie insisted the Corps determine where to spend its funding. Generally, Congress appropriated a specific amount for work from St. Paul to the Illinois River and then directed that some of that funding go to special projects, such as harbor work. Mackenzie criticized the Rivers and Harbors Act of July 5, 1884, because it dictated where the Corps had to improve navigation. "The limited appropriation made for this work," Mackenzie contended, "renders it very desirable that the selection of places for improvement should be left to the Secretary of War, in order that the money may be properly apportioned and the work performed where most needed."[17] Traditionally, Congress left the allocation of funds to the secretary of war. "This," Mackenzie asserted,

> has resulted to the great advantage of the general improvement of the river, inasmuch as it has permitted work to be carried on at the points where it was most needed, which points, as a rule, are away from cities, and, while well known to those actually engaged in navigating the river, do not receive so great consideration from others as places near landings which are constantly under the eyes of the inhabitants.[18]

In other words, this method foiled pork-barrel influences. As long as Congress allowed the secretary of war to allocate the funds through the Chief of Engineers, Mackenzie and his successors could deviate from their general plan by requesting approval from the chief.

In 1896 Rock Island commander Lieutenant Colonel William R. King agreed. He reported that local interests had been clamoring for small allotments to improve the river at their cities. King maintained, however, that the Corps could not satisfy these demands and systematically improve navigation. The "diversion of the appropriations to local harbor improvements and for the reclamation of overflowed lands," he contended, "can only result in delaying—and perhaps defeating—the improvement of through navigation." The issue of reclamation arose when Congress authorized the Corps to begin working on the first two levee projects for the upper river.[19]

Mackenzie refused to develop a predetermined plan for the 4½-foot channel project, but his effort was not haphazard. In dealing with the worst reaches first and addressing emergencies as they arose, Mackenzie reported that "the good effects of work are spread over the entire stretch of river, and the improvement of the river, considered as a whole, is made progressive,..." Deepening the shallowest places first increased the ruling depth of the entire river. Every inch gained over the shallowest bar meant boats could draw a little more water and carry a little more cargo over the entire upper river.[20]

As the project evolved, Mackenzie and the other Engineers recognized that they could not "bull the Mississippi into right and reasonable conduct," as Mark Twain had criticized them for thinking they could do.[21] They had learned that if they used its natural tendencies, they could direct the river to meet their needs. In 1885 the rafting industry asked the Corps to make a side channel at Guttenberg, Iowa, into the main channel. Ten-Mile Island split the river at Guttenberg into two channels. One channel flowed past the town and the other along the Wisconsin bank. Mackenzie responded to the industry's request saying, "in this case, as in many others, it is necessary and proper to choose the right time for the work, a time when the river itself seems inclined to take the desired direction, and when it may be made to do a great part of the necessary work through its own volition, and by waiting for this opportunity much expense is saved." He added that "it would be impossible to indicate on the map a detailed project for improvement at this locality which would not be liable to perhaps a radical change within a few months, owing to the shifting nature of the channel...."[22] Subsequent District commanders agreed with Mackenzie. In 1900 Major Charles M. Townsend reported that the Corps' plan for the river "contemplates assisting the channel in its chosen course, as indicated by maps of recent

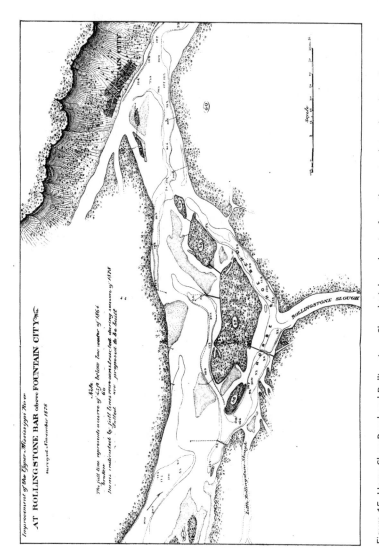

Figure 15. Horse Shoe Bend and Rollingstone Slough siphoned water from the main channel, making this reach one of the most troublesome on the upper Mississippi for the U.S. Army Corps of Engineers. *Annual Report, 1879.* Courtesy of the St. Paul District, U.S. Army Corps of Engineers.

surveys, following the natural curves as closely as possible, and building the dams over shoal places to retain bars already formed and augment those in the process of formation." Townsend promoted this method because, he said, "it avoids radical and violent changes and seeks to disturb existing conditions as little as possible consistent with the relief desired."[23] So, the Engineers used the river's own energy to transform it.

Navigation Improvement and Timber Shipping

Although timber shippers benefited more than industry or agriculture from channel constriction, they did not always agree with the Corps, forcing the Engineers to adapt their strategies. This was especially true between the Chippewa River and Winona. The Chippewa River flows into the Mississippi from Wisconsin and carried so much sand its delta formed a natural dam across the Mississippi, creating Lake Pepin above it. Downstream of the Chippewa's mouth, sand clogged the river with sandbars and helped spawn twenty-two islands, which divided the channel. The Corps scheduled some of the first channel constriction works for this troublesome reach.

The Chippewa River also delivered millions of board feet of timber into the Mississippi. Lumber companies floated loose logs down the Chippewa and gathered them at booming sites in the sloughs between the Chippewa and Winona. In Rollingstone and Beef Sloughs, and West Newton Chute, the companies formed their timber rafts for shipping downriver. During the 1880s and 1890s, this reach became the most important timber rafting area in the country.[24]

Near Island 57 the river crippled navigation most. The main channel flowed on the Wisconsin side of the island, but another channel, called Horse Shoe Bend, flowed on the Minnesota side. Midway through Horse Shoe Bend, Rollingstone Slough siphoned water from the bend into a backwater. Closing Horse Shoe Bend offered the simplest solution, but the rafters objected. They used the bend and slough for making rafts.

To force most of the water down the main channel, the Corps constructed two wing dams and two closing dams in 1878. One closing dam partially blocked Horse Shoe Bend, extending from Island 57 to the Minnesota shore. The Corps left, however, a 200-foot gap in the dam for rafters. Demonstrating the river's power, water poured through the gap so fast that it scoured a hole 54 feet deep behind the dam. The other closing dam cut off the gap between Island 57 and another island. The Engineers built the two wing dams near the opening to Horse Shoe Bend: one at the upstream entrance and one from the head of Island 57. They hoped that these dams would deflect the current away from the bend, sending most of the water into the main channel.[25]

In 1880 the closing dam in Horse Shoe Bend continued to create problems. It had settled so much that the depth over the dam had increased from 1½ feet at low water to 16 feet, making the dam worthless. To repair it, the Engineers tried sinking brush mats in the gap, but the current tore them apart. Consequently, they used mostly rock, making the job more expensive. They hoped that the improved closure and more wing dams would keep the main channel open, as the river here had been one of the most difficult for navigation for three consecutive seasons.[26]

Over the next several years, the Corps raised and extended more dams, protected more shoreline, and continued to complain about the gap in the closing dam in Horse Shoe Bend. In 1885 assistant engineer J. L. Gillespie reported that "the experiment of trying to keep openings in the dams at the head of Rollingstone Slough to permit the running logs into that slough by Winona parties, and at the same time maintain a good channel in the main river, was found to be an impossibility...." At low water, the current surged into the slough, draining water from the main channel. As a result, the Engineers again considered closing the head of the bend completely. They also built two more closing dams between nearby islands and the shore. They added 1,500 feet of shore protection to Islands 58 and 59 and armored 900 feet of the Wisconsin shore across from Island 59. Yet in 1887, Mackenzie reported that the bar near Rollingstone Slough persisted as one of the worst between the Des Moines Rapids and St. Paul. The Engineers built more wing dams to narrow the channel at the bar to 800 feet. Ten years later, Horse Shoe

Bend remained a problem. So much water escaped into the bend that the main channel became slack. William A. Thompson, the Corps' local engineer, reported that the river could not move the sand "to points of safety" downstream, and a massive bar had formed near the bend's opening.[27]

In 1898 the Engineers finally closed Horse Shoe Bend. The Wisconsin-based timber industry had collapsed, and rafting companies no longer needed the side channel. The Corps built ten more wing dams and a full closing dam. Demonstrating that other areas below the Chippewa River caused problems, the Corps added over thirty more dams to the 14-mile stretch above Winona by 1907.[28]

The Corps did not always accommodate the lumber interests but had to consider the consequences. In 1889 a sandbar blocked the head of Beef Slough, some 25 miles above Winona, where Frederick Weyer-haeuser's powerful Mississippi River Logging Company sorted and rafted its lumber. Weyerhaeuser played a pivotal role in the milling and rafting industries on the upper Mississippi River. Beginning in 1870, he, in cooperation with other lumber interests, consolidated control over the timber coming out of the Chippewa River basin. Weyerhaeuser's booming and rafting works below the Chippewa's mouth became the largest in the world during the 1880s and 1890s. Despite the company's strength, Mackenzie refused to dredge out the bar blocking Beef Slough. He paid for his decision. The company moved its rafting works to West Newton Chute, 10 miles downstream and on the Minnesota side of the river, meaning it had to float its logs across the river. In his 1889 report to Mackenzie, Durham declared that the running of loose logs had caused steamboats "much inconvenience, danger and delay."[29] An angry Mackenzie hoped the Mississippi River Logging Company would soon move. "If this running of loose logs is proper and permanently contin-ued," he warned, "it would appear questionable whether it is desirable for the government to continue its work of improvement between Read's Landing and Alma...."[30] With timber the river's only important commerce and all other steamboat traffic waning, Mackenzie could do little.[31]

Between 1878 and 1907, the Engineers remade much of the upper Mississippi River. They achieved a 4½-foot channel, during normal river stages, in the 14-mile stretch above Winona. Some one hundred wing dams pierced the river in this reach, and the Engineers had closed nearly all the old side channels. Much of the shoreline not studded with wing dams had been armored with stone. Few reaches troubled the Engineers like the one above Winona, but in most cases, they repeated the process of continually coming back to problem areas. By its work, the Corps created a much more reliable navigation route and changed the landscape and ecology of the upper river dramatically.

Reclamation

Aside from navigation interests and the Corps, floodplain farmers began transforming the upper Mississippi River and soundly established their stake in controlling it. The upper Mississippi River's agricultural, floodplain levee system originated largely as a result of private development. Some farmers erected levees before the Civil War. Soon after the war, they organized into levee districts and launched the first concerted effort to secure the river's floodplains for agriculture. They extended, raised, and connected the river's natural banks and their own feeble levees and then drained the lands behind them. In this way, to their minds, they reclaimed the river's floodplain from nature and put it to practical and economic uses. Whereas channel constriction altered the whole upper river, reclamation and levee building would transform the river most significantly below Rock Island.[32]

The Corps reluctantly entered flood control on the upper Mississippi River under its navigation improvement authority. Congress had conceded that navigation improvements had regional and national benefits but questioned the broader benefits of local flood control. During the 1880s farmers occupying the floodplain began pushing for federal help. As early as 1884 the Sny Island Drainage District—enclosing over 110,000 acres—south of Quincy, Illinois, asked the federal government to rebuild its 50-mile-long levee. The Corps reviewed the project and concluded that the levee did not help navigation and recommended against government support. But the levee district—the largest above the Ohio River—persisted, and from 1886 to 1896, Congress authorized navigation improvement funds to preserve portions of the Sny Island Levee. The Corps used this money to repair and riprap the levee and to build wing dams to throw the river's current away from it.[33]

Pressure continued from other levee districts, and in 1894 Congress instructed the Corps to survey the Mississippi River's west bank from Flint Creek, just north of Burlington, Iowa, to the Iowa River, and the river's east bank from Warsaw to Quincy, Illinois. Congress directed the Corps to determine how levees in these reaches could help navigation. Based on the Corps surveys, Congress, in 1895, authorized funding for both levees. In each case, Congress directed the Corps to improve navigation by protecting the levees and dredging. The Corps completed the nearly 50-mile Warsaw to Quincy Levee in 1896 and the 35-mile Flint Creek Levee in 1900. Joining the Sny Island Levee, these became the first federal flood control projects on the upper Mississippi River.[34]

By 1900 Congress had instructed the Corps to build or protect some of the most important agricultural levees on the upper Mississippi. But the Corps objected. From its perspective, levees contradicted the Corps' navigation constriction project. Levees, designed and built for high flows, scoured and placed sediment differently than did channel constriction works designed for low flows. In his 1898 report, Rock Island commander King complained that funding the levee projects took money from navigation improvement, the Corps' primary mission. To the Corps' satisfaction, Congress authorized no more levee work for the upper river until the 1917 Flood Control Act.[35]

Between 1878 and 1906 Mackenzie and the Corps embarked on the first intensive program to transform the upper Mississippi from a natural river into a modern commercial highway. By 1907 a new river coursed its way from the headwaters to St. Louis. Congress and navigation boosters had established the Corps as the dominant actor upon the upper river's landscape and environment. Five dams at the Mississippi's headwaters partially regulated how much water flowed downstream and when (the

Corps would complete the sixth in 1912). In May 1907 the St. Paul District completed the Meeker Island Lock and Dam between Minneapolis and St. Paul, extending the head of navigation to the mill city, and had nearly completed the lock for Lock and Dam No. 1 just downstream. In 1910 Congress approved revamping the project, calling for the removal of the Meeker Island project and turning Dam No. 1 into a high dam that would support navigation and allow hydroelectric power generation. The St. Paul District would finish the high dam in 1917.[36] From St. Paul to St. Louis, wing dams narrowed the river at low water and focused it into one channel. Closing dams ensured that the river spilled into fewer side channels and no longer wasted its energy, as shipping interests saw it, running around islands. Floodplain farmers briefly pushed Congress and the Corps into reclamation and levee building. Levees increasingly confined the river at high flows. At the Rock Island Rapids, the Engineers had chiseled and blasted a channel through the ancient rock. A new, artificial side channel flowed around the Des Moines Rapids. No one questioned that this work was for the good of the river, the region, and the country. The Mississippi was becoming the instrument of empire Midwesterners had dreamed it could be. If St. Paul could draw 1,500 steamboat dockings in 1858 on a river bristling with snags and teeming with sandbars, what could it attract on a clear and uninterrupted channel? Now that the Corps had established the 4½-foot channel, commerce was all that the river needed to achieve its glorious destiny.[37]

CHAPTER 5

Highway of Empire

By 1900 the upper Mississippi River appeared ready for its return as a great commercial thoroughfare. Under the 4½-foot channel project, the Corps had made the river more navigable than it had ever been. The national and regional economies had rebounded from the depression of the 1890s, and at times, farmers, merchants, and manufacturers offered more commodities than railroads could carry. Timber rafting still thrived, providing the foundation upon which a more diverse shipping industry could grow. But the end of riverboat commerce was rapidly approaching. Despite the Engineers' efforts to resculpt the upper Mississippi River, it remained too fickle for an economy more and more dependent on exports and railroads, on speed and reliability. Some thought Congress and the Corps should simply walk away. Others, however, refused to give up on a river they believed nature had designed for transportation.[1]

Opportunity Lost

Nothing more than the nation's tremendous agricultural production seemed to promise that the river would again become important for more than timber shipping. Since the Corps had begun work on the 4½-foot channel, agricultural production had undergone a revolution. Between the founding of Jamestown, in 1607, and 1870, farmers plowed up about 408 million acres of land. Between 1870 and 1900 they turned over another 431 million acres. While American farmers nearly doubled the land they cultivated during these thirty years, they increased their output of wheat, corn, cotton, and livestock by 130 to 150 percent, and they did it with relatively fewer farmers. During the 1860s the United States exported about 35 million bushels of wheat annually. By the 1880s it sent up to 120 million bushels abroad, and exports reached 200 million by the century's end.[2]

Midwestern farmers accounted for much of the nation's agricultural production. In 1870 they grew nearly 704 million bushels of wheat, corn, and oats. By 1900 their farms yielded over 3 billion bushels. In 1905, putting these statistics into perspective, Samuel Van Sant, a former raftboat pilot, former Minnesota governor, and avid navigation booster, claimed that Minnesota ground some 100 million bushels of wheat annually and exported 16 million barrels of flour each year. With this flour, he estimated, one could bake enough bread to encircle the earth. Minnesota also produced 76 million pounds of butter annually. This was enough, he figured, to butter all that bread.[3] If the river could capture a small portion of this output, it would easily surpass its heyday of the 1850s, especially if timber rafting held steady.

Timber shipping flourished during the nineteenth century's last decades, justifying to many the Corps' work. In 1886 the Corps reported that the total timber production of the upper river and its tributaries "if shipped by rail, would load 108,760 cars of 12,000 feet each (about 20 tons each), the amount generally accepted by lumbermen as a car-load." Using an average car length of 35 feet, they estimated that the timber "would load a train 721 miles in length, or 5,438 trains of 20 cars each."[4] By the early 1890s, twenty-four sawmilling centers, boasting over a hundred sawmills, operated on the river's main stem between Minneapolis and Hannibal, Missouri. In 1894 three centers accounted for over one-half of the 1.2 billion board feet of lumber produced: the mills at Minneapolis turned out 491.0 million board feet; those at Winona, 119.5 million; and those at Clinton, Iowa, 101.7 million. Together the other milling centers sawed 452.4 million board feet annually. Except for the timber consumed locally, most moved on the upper Mississippi River.[5]

Log and lumber rafts increased in size as the timber industry grew. Before 1860 large Mississippi River rafts contained 300,000 to 500,000 board feet of logs and lumber. By 1870 some rafts held 2 million board feet, and less than twenty years later, a few rafts totaled up to 3.5 million board feet. In 1895 one raft amassed 7 million feet of logs and lumber. While later rafts occasionally corralled up to 10 million board feet, the typical raft held less than 3.5 million board feet. A raft of 2.5 million board feet contained enough lumber to build 125 houses and covered 3 to 4 acres.[6]

Yet, despite timber's success, despite hundreds of wing dams and closing dams, despite the possibility of so much commerce, steamboats continued to lose freight and passenger traffic. Timber, largely because it floated, had remained the river's only important commodity, but it too would soon disappear. It seemed the more the Corps improved the river for navigation, the less shippers used it. As early as 1882 Mark Twain had remarked on this irony. During the heyday of the 1850s, he grumbled, "there wasn't a lantern from St. Paul to New Orleans, and the snags were thicker than bristles on a hog's back; and now, when there's three dozen steamboats and nary a barge or raft, government has snatched out all the snags, and lit up the shores like Broadway, and a boat's as safe on the river as she'd be in heaven."[7] Twain's comment, while off in its timing for the upper Mississippi, makes an important point. In 1882 the 4½-foot project was only four years old, and timber rafting on the upper river had just started to flourish. Packetboats, however, were rapidly disappearing.

Railroad expansion underlay the river's steady demise as a commercial highway. The railroads' phenomenal growth during the first decades after the Civil War continued through the end of the century. In 1870 Iowa tallied 2,600 miles of railroad lines, and in 1900 it had 8,700. South Dakota counted 65 miles in 1870, and 2,800 in 1900. North Dakota did not have to count its railroad miles in 1870; it did not have any. By 1900, the state reported it had 2,700 miles. Wisconsin had 1,900 in 1870, and 2,800 in 1900. From the 10 miles of track opened in 1862, Minnesota railways increased to 6,795 miles by 1900. Two transcontinental lines crossed Minnesota before 1900. By 1900 railroads had linked Minnesota to Chicago by several lines, provided two through routes to the Pacific, and offered service to Kansas City, Omaha, Los Angeles, Sault Sainte Marie, St. Louis, and Winnipeg.[8]

Railroads solidified their natural advantages over the river through aggressive measures. Steamboat owners could not match the tight organization and superior financing enjoyed by railroad companies. Where railroads competed directly with the river, they lowered rates below the profit margin and raised rates on lines not competing with the river to recapture the loss. Steamboat companies could not counter with a similar measure. Some railroads acquired steamboat lines only to dismantle them. As railroads expanded west of the Mississippi River, the grain they gathered flowed over the river rather than to it. Railways refused to build facilities to transfer goods between rail and river lines. Together with the natural advantages railroads held over river shipping, the railroads' tactics hurried the demise of the Mississippi's commerce. With navigation's failure, the region's dependence on railroads would become clearer.[9]

As railroads pulled shippers away, the river pushed them away. Railroad lines created a perfect model for what navigation boosters wanted the river to be. Although the Corps had completed much of the $4\frac{1}{2}$-foot channel by 1900, low water still plagued shipping. In contrast to the incomplete $4\frac{1}{2}$-foot channel, each new set of tracks created a smooth and uninterrupted link to regional, national, and world markets. The river was like a rail line with different gauges of track. Small boats, drawing little water, traveled above the Des Moines or Rock Island Rapids; larger boats ran below the rapids or below St. Louis. During droughts or in the late summer and fall, shippers partially loaded their boats. Railroads did not have to operate with half-full cars due to the condition of the track. Size constraints limited railcar capacity more than they did barges' or boats', and on this point lay the river's advantage. But nature bound the river more as a transportation route. Once laid, the tracks did not shift. The river shifted constantly. The Engineers had dramatically altered the river's natural landscape by 1900, but they had not engraved within the river's drifting sand and gravel a permanent, continuous trench $4\frac{1}{2}$ feet deep at low water. Only after the Engineers had transformed the river's ever moving bed into a stable and continuously deep passage for the entire navigation season and from one season to the next would shippers consider using the river. As most navigation boosters saw it, the Corps' challenge was to make the river like the railroad—less natural but more practical. A series of low-water years made this clear.

After Alexander Mackenzie took over the 4½-foot channel project in 1879, low water repeatedly hampered packets and raftboats. In 1880 he reported that from the beginning of August through the end of the season, steamboats struggled to navigate the river. "The large side-wheel packets were laid up and their places supplied by stern-wheel boats of very light draught, and most of these," he wrote, "could go no farther up the river than Red Wing. Even the small steamboats used for rafting," he remarked, "experienced great difficulty in reaching their destinations and some of these were compelled to lay up." At the foot of Cassville Slough, opposite Guttenberg, a bar forced raftboats to stop and wait for lighter boats to bring their rafts down to them. The following year, he reported, the larger boats had to stop at La Crosse, while the lighter ones only made it to Hastings.[10]

By the fall of 1883, Mackenzie believed that navigation improvements were making a difference. Even though the river fell near the 1864 low-water mark, steamboats of the Diamond Jo Line had been able to reach St. Paul. But in 1887 low water arrested shipping between Keokuk and St. Louis and, consequently, ended through traffic between St. Paul and the lower river. After flooding in the spring of 1888, the river fell to a low stage in June and remained unusually low until the season's end, and the regular Keokuk to St. Louis packet service quit running. Low water had suspended through commerce again.[11]

The navigation improvements did offer some hope but could not overcome extremely low water. In 1891 the river dropped once more below the 1864 low-water mark in many places. Yet the *General Barnard*, which, at 39 inches, had the second deepest draft of any boat on the upper river, made the trip from St. Louis to St. Paul. While the *Barnard* had a difficult time passing through natural areas, it steamed through constricted reaches easily. Those boats making it to Hastings in 1891,

Mackenzie remarked, paddled on to St. Paul with no problems, thanks to the navigation improvements. Still, raftboats lost money that year.[12] In 1894 the river rose to a good boating stage in the spring and remained safe until mid-June. By early August it had fallen so low that little traffic moved on the river, and those boats that operated did so at a loss. Two years later low water again forced raftboats to lay up early. And two years after that, during the 1898 season—twenty years into the 4½-foot channel project—some crossings had only 3 to 3½ feet of water over them, compelling the packets to stop running in September.[13]

Overall the Corps had successfully recast long reaches of the upper Mississippi. Only during low-water years did the river's worst bars have less than 4½ feet of water over them. But shippers needed more certainty. Extreme low-water years came too often. Before committing

Date	Bushels
1878	737,415
1879	2,192,642
1880	2,197,469
1881	1,154,092
1882	781,817
1883	729,174
1884	470,580
1885	776,432
1886	465,681
1887	366,432
1888	143,037
1889	381,559
1890	397,788
1894	83,650
1895	55,729
1900	6,902
1905	3,700
1906	24,835
1907	12,271

Figure 16. Grain traffic through the Des Moines Rapids Canal. *Source*: Frank Haigh Dixon, *A Traffic History of the Mississippi River System*, National Waterways Commission Document 11 (Washington, D.C.: U.S. Government Printing Office, 1909), 51.

Table 1. Classified Receipts at and Shipments from St. Louis via the Upper Mississippi River, 1876–1910

Article	Unit	1876	1880	1885	1895	1900	1906	1910
Flour	barrels	51,040	35,463	38,231	80,602	28,625	6,895	900
Wheat	bushels	641,952	780,923	300,051	282,337	172,829	239,420	168,782
Corn	bushels	305,830	960,086	226,175	139,900	58,235	40,150	24,965
Oats	bushels	704,424	596,986	758,167	50,287	12,535	28,295	4,335
Rye	bushels	23,035	58,209	86,078	7,428	2,660	1,512	54
Barley	bushels	401,414	156,042	47,393	nd	nd	nd	nd
Meat	pounds	626,000	1,653,707	560,678	84,129	nd	827,740	421,500
Lard	pounds	365,210	260,720	1,101,092	3,600	nd	260,400	22,900
Logs/lumber	mill. of ft.	165,890	229,561	135,517	87,196	57,900	839	nd
Unclassified	short tons	261,113	187,604	130,632	86,468	76,387	56,685	25,164

Source: Annual Report, 1911, 1934.

their crops or goods, potential shippers needed to know that the river would be open. Neither the river nor the Corps could guarantee this. Even had the Corps achieved the 4½-foot channel, commerce would have left the river. Shippers needed a deeper channel to compete with the increasing economies of scale offered by railroads.[14]

Records for grain traffic on the upper Mississippi River during the late nineteenth century illustrate the relentless decline of freight traffic due to railroad expansion and the inadequacy of the 4½-foot channel. In 1880 over 2 million bushels of grain passed through the Des Moines Rapids Canal, but only 400,000 bushels in 1890, and less than 6,900 bushels in 1900. Records of receipts and shipments from the upper Mississippi River at St. Louis between 1880 and 1900 further demonstrate the river's failure to attract grain or grain products. While St. Louis received and shipped 960,086 bushels of corn by water in 1880, it handled only 58,235 in 1900. It processed 596,986 bushels of oats in 1880, and 12,535 in 1900. And it moved 780,923 bushels of wheat in 1880, but only 172,829 bushels in 1900. While riverboats transported over 30 percent of the grain sent south from St. Louis in 1880, by 1900 they handled only about 6 percent. By 1903 grain shipments from St. Louis to New Orleans by river ended.[15]

Twain, during his 1882 voyage on the upper river, captured the demise of the steamboat grain trade as well as any statistics. Recounting what a clerk on the paddlewheel told him, he wrote:

> Boat used to land—captain on hurricane-roof—mighty stiff and straight—iron ramrod for a spine—kid gloves, plug tile, hair parted behind—man on shore takes off hat and says:
>
> "Got twenty-eight tons of wheat cap'n—be great favor if you can take them."
>
> Captain says:
>
> "I'll take two of them"—and don't even condescend to look at him.
>
> But nowadays the captain takes off his old slouch, and smiles all the way around to the back of his ears, and gets off a bow which he hasn't got any ramrod to interfere with, and says:

"Glad to see you, Smith, glad to see you—you're looking well—haven't seen you looking so well for years—what you got for us?"

"Nuthin'," says Smith; and keeps his hat on, and just turns his back and goes to talking with somebody else.[16]

For the moment, railroads, regardless of how much they charged or how much he might have complained about them, met Smith's needs.

Passenger traffic also left the river for trains. Nevertheless, hundreds of thousands of people still used ferries to move themselves, their animals, and other belongings across the river. Hundreds of thousands of people still boarded excursion boats to enjoy the river's scenery. When the Corps changed its method of keeping commercial statistics in 1903 to include ferried and excursion boat traffic, the total passenger traffic for the upper river tallied 1,408,593. Unlike freight traffic and lumber rafting, excursion and ferry traffic remained strong through the twentieth century's first three decades. By 1906 passenger traffic had exceeded 2 million, and it surpassed 3.5 million in 1920.[17]

As these figures show, railroads did not end passenger traffic, but ferries and excursion boats could not justify the millions of dollars needed for major navigation improvements. These boats made local trips and did not require a deep channel to contend with railroads. Railroads could not compete for the services these boats offered. Yet few navigation boosters would argue for greater funding for the 4½-foot channel or press for a new project for excursion and ferryboats. Once railroads laid tracks paralleling the river, they quickly took away the passenger traffic that mattered: the immigrants and travelers moving long distances between ports.[18]

When timber shipping began to falter, the demise of river commerce seemed inevitable. Timber shipping fell with the white pine forests of western Wisconsin and northern Minnesota. Initially the St. Croix, Black, and Chippewa Rivers of Wisconsin fed the largest quantities of logs and lumber into the upper Mississippi. By 1892, however, the quantity of lumber expelled from Wisconsin's tributaries began declining. From 718 million board feet of lumber milled along these tributaries in 1892, the amount produced dropped to 465 million feet in 1900, and to 193 million feet in 1906, the last year of the 4½-foot channel project.[19]

This decline was masked, however, as mills in the Twin Cities and above began contributing more logs and lumber to the upper Mississippi River. In 1887, the Corps noted, the large-scale rafting of logs on the Mississippi River above the mouth of the St. Croix had begun. Before the season's end, steamboats had guided twenty-seven rafts downriver from St. Paul. By 1897 sawmills in Minneapolis and above produced more than those on the Mississippi's Wisconsin tributaries. But lumber shipping from St. Paul peaked in 1904 at 387 million board feet. By 1906 it had fallen to 291 million board feet. Overall 1.6 to 2.1 billion feet of lumber moved into and on the upper Mississippi River each year between 1892 and 1900. After turning out 2.0 billion feet in 1901, lumber mills along the river steadily declined.[20]

Sawmills and raftboats faded with the industry. At its peak in the early 1890s, the lumber industry employed about one hundred raftboats and one hundred sawmills on the Mississippi River between Minneapolis and St. Louis. The number of raftboats plying the upper river fell to eighty-six in 1900, and to twenty in 1906. The number of sawmills dropped to eighty by 1900 and to thirty-six by 1903, and in 1906 the Corps did not report the number of sawmills, simply stating that the twenty remaining raftboats had delivered their timber to "various mills scattered along the river from Minneapolis to St. Louis."[21] In 1907, while still calling the lumber industry the most important business on the upper Mississippi River, the Corps reluctantly acknowledged the industry's decline.

Timber's demise revealed the upper Mississippi's inadequacies as a transportation route. During the last third of the nineteenth century and the early years of the twentieth, it had failed to attract other commodities. It had become a one-commodity river. As that commodity vanished, the river ceased to be a meaningful part of the Midwest's transportation network. Other commodities moved on the river but not in the volume or value needed to compete effectively with railroads, or

Table 2. Lumber Manufacture on the Upper Mississippi River, 1892–1909 (millions of board feet)

Date	Minneapolis	St. Paul to St. Louis	St. Croix River	Black River	Chippewa River	Above Minneapolis	Total
1892	489	932	176	241	299	nd	2,131
1893	409	812	165	175	292	nd	1,853
1894	491	674	170	158	282	nd	1,774
1895	479	713	230	173	302	213	2,110
1896	307	516	188	132	229	229	1,601
1897	460	687	210	168	275	294	2,092
1898	470	561	227	102	284	322	1,966
1899	594	504	247	85	252	438	2,120
1900	502	582	249	40	176	430	1,979
1901	625	460	252	157	27	472	1,992
1902	376	778	148	199	305	49	1,855
1903	43	340	256	23	142	558	1,761
1904	387	385	173	nd	97	544	1,586
1905	369	304	146	nd	174	524	1,517
1906	291	185	103	0	90	577	1,246
1907	200	156	106	0	70	514	1,044
1908	190	104	30	1	46	197	566
1909	88	87	88	nd	35	120	418

Source: *Annual Reports*, 1893–1910.

to bring meaningful employment to cities in the river valley, or to justify Corps work on the river.

Corps statistics collected between 1890 and 1906 demonstrate
how much the timber industry meant to river commerce and how the
river failed to attract other commodities, despite the 4½-foot channel
project. During this period the Corps simply estimated the gross and
freight tonnage of commodities hauled on the upper Mississippi. Exact
numbers are not needed to show the trends in river commerce. Gross
tonnage, which included all traffic, dropped from 4.2 million tons in
1890 to 1.9 million tons in 1902, paralleling the fall in timber milling.
In contrast, freight tonnage, which excluded rafted logs and lumber,
remained stable. Except for two years in which merchants shipped over
300,000 tons of freight on the river, freight tonnage varied between

Figure 17. Raftboats like the *W. J. Young* dominated shipping on the upper Mississippi
River during the late nineteenth and early twentieth centuries. Photograph by Henry
Bosse. Courtesy of the St. Paul District, U.S. Army Corps of Engineers.

Date	Gross Tonnage	Freight Tonnage
1890	4,200,000	338,023
1891	3,300,000	149,000
1892	3,750,000	195,036
1893	3,200,000	109,884
1894	2,975,000	128,452
1895	3,000,000	392,051
1896	2,250,000	120,973
1897	3,200,000	128,970
1898	2,800,000	147,399
1899	2,960,000	108,515
1900	2,400,000	135,000
1901	2,125,000	125,000
1902	1,900,000	139,000
1903	4,545,129	825,375
1904	4,534,539	1,144,932
1905	4,089,318	989,792
1906	3,847,319	1,001,867
1907	3,919,440	1,519,581
1908	2,581,857	1,437,205
1909	1,916,114	1,278,429
1910	1,836,035	1,313,146
1911	2,081,566	1,156,762
1912	1,830,294	1,265,589
1913	2,145,315	1,294,864
1914	1,426,970	1,132,574
1915	1,883,668	729,723
1916	499,531	499,531
1917	586,420	586,420
1918	696,503	696,503
1919	674,192	674,192
1920	630,951	630,951
1921	761,522	761,522
1922	818,509	818,509
1923	973,567	973,567
1924	769,139	769,139
1925	908,005	908,005
1926	691,637	691,637
1927	715,110	715,110
1928	1,034,972	1,034,972
1929	558,852	558,852
1930	527,487	527,487

Figure 18. Commerce on the upper Mississippi River, 1890–1930. *Source: Annual Reports, 1891–1931.*

100,000 and 200,000 tons between 1890 and 1902. These figures show that as timber shipping on the river began collapsing, no commodities emerged to replace it. They also show that by 1890 railroads had taken most of the freight traffic they would capture from the river. Freight commerce had held steady because the remaining traffic was mostly local.[22]

Corps statistics show a dramatic increase in gross and freight tonnage in 1903. A shift in the Corps' method of keeping data, rather than a surge in traffic, accounts for this increase. Beginning with its 1904 *Annual Report*, the Corps included "strictly local" or ferried commerce and government materials—materials used in building wing dams, closing dams, and shore protection—in its figures for gross and freight tonnage. These two new categories explain the increase. While the new accounting method showed traffic as much greater than in previous years, it could not obscure the timber industry's relentless decline or the fall in the gross tonnage carried on the river. Yet during this era, freight figures remained steady. Other than the 825,375 tons recorded for 1903, freight tonnage varied little. Without timber, river commerce would soon become insignificant, and navigation improvements difficult to justify.[23]

The 6-Foot Channel Movement

By 1900 some Midwesterners began thinking the river needed a new, more intensive, more modern project to challenge railroads. After all, the 4½-foot channel had been authorized a generation earlier. Railroads and the region had changed dramatically since the days of the Grangers and William Windom. Once timber rafting ended, river commerce would become a nostalgic memory. Railroad baron James J. Hill happily observed the steamboat's plight. In a 1902 speech in St. Paul, he charged that shipping on the upper Mississippi River had declined so much that the government was wasting money trying to make it navigable and should focus its efforts below St. Louis. Railroads, including his Great Northern Railway, he boasted, could handle all the traffic above the gateway city. Hill's speech backfired. He scared cities and business interests along the river and helped trigger the first movement focused specifically on improving the upper Mississippi River for navigation.[24]

Following Hill's speech, the Quincy, Illinois, Freight Bureau joined the city's chamber of commerce and summoned towns along the river to unite "to encourage the national government to protect and preserve" the river for commerce. They proposed a convention to examine the river's problems and plan for its revival. Upper river towns responded "unanimously." Quincy hosted the convention on November 12 and 13, 1902.[25]

Hill's comments alone did not lead to the Quincy convention. Lewis B. Boswell, chairman of the Joint Committee of the Quincy Freight Bureau and Chamber of Commerce, offered deeper motivations. The "inception of this cause," he observed, "lays purely in the fact that the Mississippi River, and the wide-spread interests served by it, for a great many years have been neglected on the part of the citizens of the numerous cities lying upon its banks."[26] The five upper river states, he complained, had not joined to push for navigation improvement for twenty-five years. Their failure had made Hill's comments possible. While railroads had been laying new tracks, leveling old grades, and increasing locomotive power and freight car size, the Corps had plodded along with inadequate funding and an outdated depth. Countering Hill, Boswell protested: "we regard the Mississippi River of such mighty value in our occupations and to our respective communities that we do not propose to have it slandered, or permit it to be neglected by the government, under whose charge this great stream is and should be."[27] Conventions had been held within the previous twenty-five years, but navigation boosters had mounted no sustained effort to redefine or intensify the Corps' navigation improvements. The Quincy convention would change that.[28]

Major Charles McDonald Townsend, the Rock Island District commander, made Boswell aware of their neglect and also helped initiate the movement. Boswell had gone to Townsend with a committee from Quincy to request that the Corps undertake local improvements. During the meeting Townsend asked them: "Do you know of any attempt having been made on the part of any Congressmen, to secure an appropriation for improvement of the upper river, or have the congressional delegations from the five states bordering on the upper river united in a request for such an appropriation?" Furthermore, he wondered, "Has any effort been made by the commercial organizations, or cities,

Figure 19. Lewis B. Boswell emerged as the key player in the push for a 6-foot channel. From *Proceedings of the Upper Mississippi River Improvement Association*, 1904.

along the river to influence Congress to this end?"[29] Boswell and his committee had not been thinking about the whole upper river. Townsend made it clear that local improvements meant nothing until the Corps rendered the entire upper river navigable. Boswell replied that he knew of no effort to influence Congress but would begin one immediately.[30]

With the 1902 convention, river towns organized to stop and reverse the decline of their local economies, which had been so tied to timber. Timber had supported sawmills, lumberyards, milling shops, and other industries. Timber's demise left business and financial leaders searching for ways to restore their prosperity. More intensive navigation improvements, they believed, would bring prosperity back to the river, and the river would bring its wealth to them.[31]

One hundred thirty-two delegates representing most cities on the upper river attended the 1902 Quincy convention. After acknowledging their neglect, they made deepening the upper river to 6 feet at low water their principal objective, and they boldly called for an appropriation of $15 million to carry it out quickly. A deeper channel, they argued, would bring commerce back. To push for the new project, they formed the Upper Mississippi River Improvement Association (UMRIA) and decided to meet annually.[32]

From the outset, navigation boosters recognized the Corps' importance and invited representatives from the Rock Island District to the Quincy convention and subsequent meetings. Noting that "his interests are yours and your interests are his," they seated Townsend as a member at the meeting. Following up on his earlier talk with Boswell, Townsend lectured the convention about the attitude in Washington, D.C. "The impression very generally prevails," he reported, "that money appropriated for our western rivers is money squandered.... This idea has entered into the minds of congressmen and permeates the committee on rivers and harbors."[33] Navigation proponents had to show they truly needed the money and would spend it well, that it was not for "'river and harbor steals.'..."[34]

Townsend encouraged the boosters to push for further navigation improvements. In the Rivers and Harbors Act for the current year, he said, Congress had provided only $475,000 for the upper Mississippi River. After deducting $75,000 for local projects, he pointed out, the Corps had about $500 per river mile for channel constriction. To complete the project in a reasonable time, he contended, the Corps needed $25,000 per mile. Railroads spent $1,000 per mile annually for maintenance alone, he claimed. The cost savings of shipping by water and the positive effect on rail rates, he insisted, made spending the money worthwhile.[35]

As Townsend had stressed, navigation boosters had to persuade a doubting Congress that deepening the upper Mississippi River to 6 feet at low water would bring commerce back. This would not be easy. The history of navigation on the upper Mississippi since the 1870s had been one of steady decline. Except for timber, railroads had successfully captured the flow of goods and products into and out of the upper Midwest. Only timber had justified the 4½-foot channel project, and timber shipping was rapidly dying. Given this history, what reason would Congress have to authorize and fund more work?

While they started with the vague argument that they had ignored the river for too long, they quickly articulated broader and more specific concerns. Excessive railroad rates became one focus, but the UMRIA emphasized other issues as well.[36] As during the 4½-foot channel movement, connecting to international markets became a central argument. Thus access to the Panama Canal emerged as a rallying cry. In October 1903, the United States supported Panama's withdrawal from Colombia. For that support, Panama agreed to let the United States build the canal. The canal promised to fulfill a need that had started growing when American settlers reached the West Coast and had intensified with the 1849 Gold Rush and the Alaska gold discoveries in the 1890s. Until the Americans finished the canal, shippers had to send their cargoes around South America's perilous Cape Horn or risk the jungles of the Panamanian isthmus. Railroads had made transcontinental travel much easier and quicker, but the cost of shipping bulk commodities remained high for such long distances. The Panama Canal offered a cheap and continuous water route from the Midwest to the West Coast and the Orient.[37]

The Panama Canal provided new reasons and a new urgency to make the upper Mississippi River navigable. In his 1905 banquet speech, UMRIA President Thomas Wilkinson explained this sentiment. "The building of the Panama Canal," he emphasized, "makes the improvement of the Mississippi and Ohio rivers imperative, as the natural trend of commerce will then be along these highways to the Gulf and thence to and from the markets of the world."[38] Even Chicago, he noted, sought to tie itself to the canal through the Mississippi River. Not only did Midwesterners need the canal, the canal needed goods from the Mississippi and Ohio Rivers to be successful. Colonel John L. Vance, president of the Ohio River Improvement Association, predicted that with the canal completed, "the products of the Ohio and Mississippi Valleys will control the markets of the world, . . ."[39]

On January 18, 1904, the UMRIA gained a hearing before the House Rivers and Harbors Committee and tried to convince its members that the Midwest needed the 6-foot channel to continue its economic growth. Captain Alonzo Bryson, of Davenport, said too many people viewed the Midwest as an agricultural region only, and stressed the region's trend toward manufacturing. Playing on the multiple-use mentality of the Progressive Era, he highlighted the Mississippi's potential waterpower and its use for manufacturing. Bryson, who had piloted raftboats on the river, defended his old industry. He criticized those who predicted the lumber industry's end. He claimed it was still thriving. Samuel Van Sant, governor of Minnesota and a former raftboat pilot, supported Bryson, adding that some people had forecast timber's imminent end twenty years earlier.[40]

Boswell, representing a new generation of navigation boosters, could listen no longer. He cut in and rebuked the preoccupation with lumber shipping. He asked the committee: "will you permit me . . . to disabuse your minds of the thought that the Mississippi is simply a highway for the transportation of lumber?" Too many people in Congress and across the country, he complained, thought of the river as a highway for lumber only. He admitted the lumber industry was dying. The river would have to turn to other commodities. In a statement that must have left Bryson and Van Sant with their mouths gaping, he declared: "I do not care if we float a log. We are not here to ask you to improve the Mississippi to float lumber on, but we want to float the products of manufacture, wheat and corn, and everything else of that kind. We are building for to-day and we are not estimating on the past. We are looking to the future. We may be pioneers, but we want you to be pioneers with us."[41] Bryson and Van Sant did not challenge him, at least not publicly.

Born in New Orleans, Boswell knew the river well. According to UMRIA President Wilkinson, he had spent his whole life near the Mississippi. In praising Boswell to the 1904 convention, Wilkinson lauded Boswell as one who "loves the river as a mother loves her first born child, . . ."[42] Boswell had helped organize the UMRIA, and while they elected Wilkinson president, Boswell emerged as the organization's strongest voice.

The UMRIA formally endorsed Boswell's shift away from timber. Doing so allowed them to focus on commodities that might justify a new federal project. It also let them criticize lumbering from a Progressive conservation perspective. Conservationists and some navigation boosters recognized that forests slowed the runoff of snowmelt and rainwater. On land denuded of forests, water flowed too quickly into streams and rivers. The streams and rivers rose too quickly, and they fell too quickly. With no further rain and without the slow but steady flow off the old forested lands, the streams and rivers fell earlier than normal, and they continued to fall to unnaturally low levels, making navigation difficult or impossible. Preserving the forests would slow runoff and even out the peak and low flows, providing a navigable depth for more of the year.

At the UMRIA's 1905 annual meeting Wilkinson called for the preservation of forests to conserve water for navigation. He praised Gifford Pinchot, the nation's chief forester, who was, he said, "fighting to preserve the Minnesota National Forest Reserve, which is being assailed by powerful interests bent upon its destruction for personal gain." Wilkinson then declared: "The preservation of this forest reserve is absolutely essential to the maintenance of navigation on the upper

Mississippi River."[43] In 1906 the UMRIA passed a resolution supporting the Department of Agriculture's Forestry Bureau "in effectively
guarding our forests from destruction and in the work of reforestation,
thereby subserving our natural resources and maintaining a continuing
water supply." They also resolved to support a bill before Congress
providing for education in forestry at the nation's colleges. How Bryson
and Van Sant reacted to these statements is not clear, but the UMRIA's
position represented a dramatic acknowledgment of Boswell's statements before the Rivers and Harbors Committee. Conceding timber's
demise, navigation boosters had to entice old and new commodities to
the river.[44]

As the timber industry failed and railroad rates climbed during the
1890s and early 1900s, Midwesterners became increasingly aware of
their dependence on railroads. While the Granger Laws had helped keep
rail rates down, the Supreme Court effectively ended state regulation in
1886, with its decision in *Wabash, St. Louis and Pacific Railroad v. Illinois.*
The court ruled that states did not have the power to regulate rates
on traffic moving into, out of, or through a state. This forced Congress
to deal with the problem. In response Congress established the Interstate Commerce Commission in 1887. Ideally, the five-person commission determined and set fare rates. The act also required the posting of
rates and ten days' advance notice of rate changes. But the courts again
did not support railroad regulation. During the commission's first
fifteen years, 90 percent of the cases for rate control went against the
commission. Then in 1896, the Supreme Court ruled in the *Maximum
Freight Rate Case* that the commission had the power only to prohibit
unreasonable rates, not to establish rates.[45]

Some UMRIA boosters pointed to increasing rail rates as the ori-
gin of their effort and the effort to improve navigation nationally. A. L.
Crocker, of Minneapolis, declared that by charging unreasonably high
rates railroads had rejuvenated the movement for Mississippi River navigation improvement and had given it "new life and national importance."[46] Navigation boosters lauded moves by Congress and President
Theodore Roosevelt in 1906 to strengthen the Interstate Commerce

Commission. Van Sant announced that these efforts "settled affirmatively the question whether the Government has the power to regulate commerce between the states."[47] And in 1907, Burton F. Peek, the president of the Moline Club, observed that for the last several years "a struggle has been going on over the system of transportation; a struggle between the carriers and the carried, between the railway companies, on the one hand, the shippers and passengers, on the other." Over the past year, he reported, the struggle had become bitter. "It has been marked," he observed, "by congressional enactments regulating interstate commerce and by similar legislative enactments which in most of the states have been challenged as confiscatory and unconstitutional." In some states, there had "been an open clash between the state and federal authorities." The struggle, Peek insisted, had been unnecessary. Navigation improvements, by providing effective competition, would have eliminated the need for federal regulation.[48]

Like navigation boosters before them, the new generation of boosters held the same visions for what the river was and could be. "By united and persistent effort," UMRIA President Wilkinson announced at the 1904 convention, "this association must succeed in having this mighty river made what nature intended it should be, the great artery through which the commerce of the people shall flow onward to the sea and to all the markets of the world forever." At the 1906 convention, Wilcomb D. Washburn, a powerful Minneapolis miller, confirmed Wilkinson's vision, as would many others. He proclaimed that "this great river here at our doors should be developed and improved, and it is our part to in our day and generation to do what we can to carry out what the Lord has evidently intended should be done."[49] If they carried out what should evidently be done to the upper Mississippi River, they would receive the praise of future generations.[50] Speaking before the UMRIA in 1907, Wilkinson reaffirmed what many boosters already knew: the Mississippi River was their "highway of empire...."[51]

UMRIA representatives hoped to sell this vision to the Rivers and Harbors Committee. At their first meeting with the committee, on January 18, 1904, they presented their case for a 6-foot channel. The

UMRIA's representatives returned pleased with their visit. They had met with the Speaker of the House, the chair of the Appropriations Committee, and about twenty-five other members of Congress. They had also visited General Alexander Mackenzie, now the Chief of Engineers. Certainly Mackenzie would support navigation improvements for the upper river. The highlight of their visit was the opportunity to present their case to President Theodore Roosevelt on January 20. Following these meetings, the committee concluded: "In so far as present efforts extend, all has been done that could be, . . . every end has been subserved."[52] Yet, they had overlooked something fundamental and essential.

Unaware of their oversight, their confidence rose further during the fall of 1904. At their presentation to the Rivers and Harbors Committee, the delegation had invited the committee to visit the upper Mississippi. The committee surprised the UMRIA and accepted the invitation in late July. On August 27, Chairman Theodore E. Burton and most of the committee members and their wives, along with Mackenzie, Major Charles S. Riche—the Rock Island District commander—and several members of Congress, boarded the Rock Island District's snagboat, the *Col. A. Mackenzie*, in St. Paul. Boswell reported that it was the "first time in the history of our country, a committee of Congress had made a formal inspection of the Upper Mississippi River. . . ." The committee disappointed some UMRIA members by hurrying through the trip. Still, Wilkinson believed, the UMRIA had achieved its goal. Burton and other committee members, assisted by Mackenzie and the Corps, had carefully examined the river. Mackenzie, as their guide, must have given the committee a thorough and convincing education.[53]

Then in December 1904, the UMRIA received news that it should immediately send a committee to Washington. The UMRIA did not have time to get a special committee together, so they sent Boswell. He arrived to find Congressman Burton too ill to meet. Instead, Boswell called on various Rivers and Harbors Committee members, who advised him not to push too hard for the 6-foot channel yet. Until Burton recovered, Boswell could do little but go home.[54]

He returned to Washington in February 1905. By the time he arrived, the Rivers and Harbors Committee had already drafted its bill and would soon put it before the House. Although the upper Mississippi River had received $1,011,543 for various projects, the bill contained only $300,000 for general improvements on the upper river. The rest went to the Headwaters Reservoirs, Locks and Dams 1 and 2 in the Twin Cities, and a project at Moline. When Boswell complained to the committee, they retorted that many other projects had received less. The whole bill, committee members emphasized, could not exceed $17 million.[55]

Now Boswell learned of the UMRIA's oversight. The Rivers and Harbors Committee, he protested, had completely ignored the "essence of our petition to Congress and the fundamental idea of our association, that is to say, securing a permanent depth of six feet at low water. . . ." The 1905 bill did not contain the 6-foot channel project for the upper Mississippi River. Alarmed, Boswell sought and won an interview with Chairman Burton. Burton pointed out that the UMRIA had neglected one of the most basic steps in the process. He explained that he had examined all his sources and could find no survey or estimate for the 6-foot channel project. The Rivers and Harbors Committee, he informed Boswell, needed to know the ultimate cost of the project, and the Corps had to approve the project before the committee would include it in a Rivers and Harbors bill. Boswell tried to convince Burton to add the 6-foot channel project anyway but acknowledged that the committee had to "keep within the limits of the rule laid down, . . ." He then persuaded Burton to put an amendment into the 1905 bill calling for the survey and estimate for the 6-foot channel project from St. Paul to the mouth of the Missouri River.[56] On March 3, 1905, the bill passed, and on March 14, 1905, the Corps assigned the survey to Riche. While disappointed, Boswell told the UMRIA that they should be happy with what they had accomplished in only three years. The results of the survey would make them even happier.[57]

CHAPTER 6

So Nearly Perfected by Nature

Even though 6-foot channel boosters had inserted their survey into the 1905 Rivers and Harbors Act, they faced a problem. They had not developed a broad base of support. Unlike the movement for the 4½-foot channel, farmers had not joined the 6-foot channel movement yet, nor had communities away from the river. So far, only towns along the river backed it. With these towns as their foundation, they hoped, as one booster urged them, to arouse interest from the Alleghenies to the Rockies and from north to south.[1] The new boosters, however, would soon learn they could hardly rouse their own members. If they hoped to succeed, forces outside their movement would have to favor them.

The 6-Foot Channel Survey

Major Charles S. Riche, the Rock Island District commander, directed Charles Durham to undertake the 6-foot channel survey and prepare a cost estimate. Durham had been working for the Corps on the upper river for thirty-five years. He had built the first experimental closing dam at Pig's Eye Island, just below St. Paul, in 1874, and had provided invaluable input to the 1875 Windom study for the 4½-foot channel project. Relying on reports from the assistant engineers and his own vast knowledge of the river, Durham submitted his report on June 30, 1906. Overall, he insisted, wing dams and closing dams had successfully deepened the upper river. He argued that the Corps could obtain a 6-foot channel by raising and extending existing dams and by building more of each. Durham prepared plans showing exactly where to place the additional wing dams and closing dams. The project also contemplated a lateral canal for the Rock Island Rapids and further excavation of the Des Moines Rapids canal. Durham estimated the 6-foot channel's cost at $20 million. Riche agreed with Durham's detailed plans and estimate but, acknowledging the river's complexity, qualified his approval with the understanding that the location of dams and shore protection would have to be modified as the river demanded. Riche noted that the Corps could improve navigation with locks and dams, but the cost would exceed $30 million.[2]

The UMRIA now had to get the Corps' Board of Engineers, the Chief of Engineers, and the secretary of war to accept Riche's report and convince the Rivers and Harbors Committee and Congress to approve it. Boosters had good reasons to believe that all would do so. The upper river region's political strength had continued to rise with its population and economic growth. At the UMRIA's 1905 meeting, Wisconsin Representative John J. Esch, of La Crosse, pointed out that the five upper river states had 72 members in the House and 10 in the Senate. Colonel John L. Vance, president of the Ohio River Improvement Association, went further, stressing that the upper Mississippi River system commanded 196 representatives and 40 senators. And Representative J. H. Davidson of Oshkosh, Wisconsin, a member of the Rivers and Harbors Committee, declared that all 17 members of the committee believed in waterway development.[3]

Davidson had come to the 1905 meeting to learn more about the UMRIA's reasons for wanting the 6-foot channel. He reported that the Rivers and Harbors Committee members had been traveling the country to find the most deserving projects. They made nonpartisan choices, based only on the evidence, he professed. He recommended that the UMRIA gather all the data it could on the upper river's shipping and on freight charges. He emphasized that it should calculate the potential for commerce. The UMRIA had to show how a 6-foot channel would bring traffic back to the river where a 4½-foot channel could not. He asked whether creating a deeper channel would lead to the building of more steamboats. Would it, he wanted to know, increase carrying capacity and reduce shipping costs? He stressed that the UMRIA had to show how the deeper channel would have a greater effect on rates than the present channel. He encouraged the UMRIA to pursue its goal. The Rivers and Harbors Committee, he informed them, would be looking for some new, large projects.[4]

The following year, Missouri representative and House Democratic Whip James T. Lloyd countered much of what Davidson had said. Lloyd delivered a frank lecture on the politics of the Rivers and Harbors Committee. Contradicting Davidson's praise of the committee as impartial, Lloyd charged that states represented on the committee secured the largest appropriations. If the UMRIA wanted major navigation improvements, he advised, they needed someone on the committee from a district bordering the river. Yes, he acknowledged, Minnesota, Wisconsin, and Illinois had representatives on the committee, but all three came from districts on the Great Lakes. Ohio, Michigan, and New York also had representatives from Great Lakes districts on the committee. So the Great Lakes had done well with the committee and Congress. The lower Mississippi had at least three members on the committee and had also done well for itself. Furthermore, he suggested, the UMRIA needed a full-time lobbyist in Washington. He urged them to create an Upper Mississippi River Commission or to get the existing Mississippi River Commission's jurisdiction extended to the upper river. He recommended the UMRIA unite with other waterway organizations, but in the end, he cautioned them, they had to pursue their own interests. The UMRIA applauded Lloyd's speech as the most informative ever delivered to them.[5]

When the UMRIA met in Minneapolis on October 10 and 11, 1906, the Corps had not yet transmitted Riche's report to the Speaker of the House; it would not do so until December 21. It did not matter. Congress did not produce a Rivers and Harbors bill that year.[6]

The UMRIA not only wanted their project authorized, they wanted Congress to appropriate $2 million annually, so they could finish it as quickly as possible. This desire ignored Congressman Lloyd's advice. He had warned the UMRIA that $2 million was too much to ask for. Too many others, he explained, wanted the funding. If the UMRIA received $800,000 per year, he said, they should consider themselves successful. He cautioned them not to do anything to scare the committee away, and asking for too much money would.[7]

Rivers and Harbors Committee member Joseph E. Ransdell, of Louisiana, explained the problem. Also speaking to the 1906 UMRIA convention, he reported that the committee had been getting an average of only $19.25 million per year over the past decade. Waterway boosters had projects pending before Congress totaling $500 million, and the Corps had already approved these projects. Consequently, he complained, "The work given to us is that of elimination, to cut off here, to slaughter there, to twist and to squirm around the difficulty and to do a little quarreling too."[8] But the problem, he insisted, was that Congress did not place the right priority on waterway development. Navigation projects, he argued, needed to be put on a par with other major programs such as the army, navy, post office, and pensions. Rather than the average $19.5 million, he called for an annual appropriation of $50 million.[9]

The National Context

If the UMRIA hoped to vie with hundreds of projects, totaling hundreds of millions of dollars, America's attitude toward river and harbor spending would have to change. The UMRIA could not do this on its own. Only a national movement could generate the support needed to make Congress and the American public alter their priorities. Two such movements were under way when Congress authorized the 6-foot channel survey. The first, a national waterways movement, focused specifically on navigation improvements. The second, the Progressive movement, was far broader and encompassed many aspects of American life, from business practices and urban government to the most efficient use of the country's natural resources. By calling for the preservation of forests, the UMRIA had already tapped into the Progressive movement. Both movements reflected new trends occurring in the nation's attitude toward waterway development.[10]

A change in how Congress and the president approached waterway projects underlay the national navigation movement. Before 1900, few presidents promoted federal spending on such projects, and none did so ardently. Between 1882 and 1889, Presidents Chester A. Arthur and Grover Cleveland generally opposed Rivers and Harbors bills. President Benjamin Harrison (1889–93) stressed that Congress should construct them more carefully and focus on completing projects already authorized before approving new ones. President William McKinley accepted the appropriation of March 3, 1899, but was shot on September 6, 1901, and died eight days later. His successor, Theodore Roosevelt, would become the strongest advocate of navigation improvements in the country's history.[11]

Political parties did not so clearly divide over internal improvements as they had previously. In their 1884 platform, the Democrats reversed their position, declaring their support for improving navigation on the Mississippi and other rivers. In each of the next four elections, they advocated national waterway development. As many Mississippi River levees had been destroyed during the Civil War and the damage made worse by flooding, Southerners, who were largely Democrats, needed a more liberal federal policy. The Republican party, however, after promoting a federal role in navigation improvements on the eve of the Civil War, would not officially endorse such improvements again until 1908. Nevertheless, many Republicans voted for internal improvements, especially those benefiting their constituents.[12]

After the Civil War and until at least 1883, unsound or questionable projects plagued Rivers and Harbors bills. Congress authorized and funded navigation projects even when opposed by the Corps. Rather than backing projects with enough money to complete them, Congress passed only piecemeal appropriations, yielding a large number of projects with little funding. As a result, few projects reached completion. The public believed that many projects benefited only local interests. Other problems arose after 1883 to make matters worse. Congress passed large appropriations and then divided and distributed the money to specific cities along a river. This prevented general navigation improvements from progressing and drew sharp criticism from the Corps. Mackenzie had repeatedly complained.[13]

To provide itself with a more reliable and rigorous review process, Congress established the Rivers and Harbors Committee on December 24, 1883. Ideally, all bills had to pass through the committee to be considered for authorization.[14] Ohio Representative Theodore Burton became the committee's chair in 1899 and remained its head until 1910. Burton led the assault on poorly conceived projects. More than any other individual, he brought credibility to the process. Even critics acknowledged the positive reforms he made. Under Burton's leadership, Congress ended the piecemeal funding of projects and began authorizing only those it could commit to finishing.[15] The Corps also began examining navigation projects more stringently. To winnow poor projects from appearing before the Rivers and Harbors Committee, Burton pushed for a review board in the Corps that would evaluate all projects before sending them to the secretary of war and on to his committee. So in 1902 Congress created the Board of Engineers for Rivers and Harbors.

As Burton and the Corps began scrutinizing navigation improvement projects, many waterway boosters considered them roadblocks to legitimate and badly needed public works. Yet, as Rivers and Harbors Committee member Ransdell had told UMRIA boosters in 1906, the Corps had approved more than $500 million worth of projects. Ransdell and other members of the Rivers and Harbors Committee had wanted to authorize more projects, Ransdell complained, but Congress had refused to provide the funding.[16]

The National Navigation Movement

Paralleling the new and more rigorous review of waterway legislation, America's attitude toward river and harbor projects changed between 1895 and 1912. Samuel Hays, who has written one of the most important studies of the debate over water resources, says that during the latter years of the nineteenth century and early years of the twentieth century, the United States "witnessed a new enthusiasm for the improvement of its navigable streams. Communities throughout the country seemed to catch a vision of the unlimited possibilities for local economic growth which cheaper transportation could create." Strongly supported by urban merchants and manufacturers, shippers fought to strengthen the Interstate Commerce Commission's power to regulate railroad rates and actively promoted inland navigation projects. Although not writing specifically about midwestern navigation boosters, Hays captures their sentiments well. "The interests of merchants and manufacturers," he contends, "soon became merged with the larger interests of the entire community, as local and regional waterway publicity groups and newspaper editors warned that the future growth of the community itself depended on cheaper transportation." Support for navigation improvement grew so intense, he says, that it became an issue of "local patriotism." Many politicians recognized a windfall and eagerly capitalized on this demand. One reason for the new attitude, Hays suggests, was that cheap transportation had become a critical issue, as low rail rates had begun rising.[17]

The new enthusiasm reached the Mississippi River. "A GREAT public movement has arisen in the Mississippi Valley," W. J. McGee proclaimed. Born in Dubuque County, Iowa, McGee would become a prominent voice on multiple resource water development. The national navigation movement had begun, McGee said, a decade or two before with the demise of the packetboat trade, which had been caused by unfair railroad competition. The problem had become worse with the increase in shipping costs and the decrease in shipping facilities for river traffic. As production from mines, factories, and farms mounted, the problem grew into a crisis. McGee contended that "the discontent has grown into a movement akin to revolt on the part of the millions of farmers, small manufacturers, and retail dealers in the interior." Placing the movement in a sectional context, McGee argued that the Midwest was now demanding "recognition of the rights of the interior as against those of the seaboard."[18]

McGee claimed that with support from the press, the national navigation movement had become so popular that "campaign jingles lodge in the minds of millions." Old jingles like "Remember the Alamo" and "Tippecanoe and Tyler Too" meant less in their day, he claimed, than "Fourteen feet through the valley" did at the present. A 14-foot channel was the goal of the Lakes-to-the-Gulf Deep Waterway Association. The deep channel would extend from Chicago, down the Illinois River, to the Mississippi and the Gulf of Mexico, connecting Chicago to the Panama Canal and the Pacific Ocean. Although he raised regional issues, McGee believed navigation improvements benefited the nation. "The end is the manifest destiny of North America," he insisted. "For not until seagoing craft enter into our great commercial artery, so nearly perfected by Nature, ply thence to all ports, and carry our products direct to the ends of the world—not until then will America come to its own."[19]

Another congressional inspection trip, this time on the Ohio River, provided the national waterway movement with the organization and structure needed to lobby Congress. Representative Burton and a dozen members of the Rivers and Harbors Committee traveled down the Ohio River in May 1905. During the trip, the Ohio River Improvement Association demonstrated the value and unrealized potential of river shipping. While the committee backed the Ohio River boosters' argument for a 9-foot channel, created by a lock and dam system, Congress, they pointed out, rejected annual bills or large appropriations. To fund a huge project on the Ohio would leave little money for other projects. Ransdell knew America's attitude toward waterway development had to change and called for a national meeting of waterway boosters. When the party stopped at Cincinnati, he delivered a speech calling for a national meeting of navigation improvement advocates. The purpose of the conference would be to begin planning for a large national waterway development program. Lewis B. Boswell and Thomas Wilkinson would go to the meeting.[20]

Despite the short notice, more than fifty waterway boosters from states between the Allegheny and Rocky Mountains attended the meeting in Cincinnati on June 29 and 30, 1905. They decided that the moribund National Rivers and Harbors Congress, which had been formed in Baltimore in 1901, should host a national convention. After forming in 1901 and pushing through the 1902 Rivers and Harbors bill, the Rivers and Harbors Congress had done little, but it agreed to take on the planning of the national convention.[21]

The Rivers and Harbors Congress hosted the gathering in Washington, D.C., on January 15 and 16, 1906. They quickly reorganized and elected Ransdell as their president. The UMRIA immediately joined the Rivers and Harbors Congress, paying a $100 fee, and Wilkinson accepted a seat on the board of directors. The organization's goal, he reported, was to teach people about the significance of waterways "and to create such a strong public sentiment, in favor of larger and more regular appropriations by Congress for river and harbors improvement, that will induce Congress to appropriate, at least, 50 million dollars annually for that object, instead of the beggarly amount now appropriated,..." Only a national organization, he declared, could secure the funding needed for waterway improvements. Over the next two years, the Rivers and Harbors Congress gained members from thirty-three states and a membership of some thirty thousand. Its supporters included "commercial, manufacturing, waterway and kindred associations, commercial firms and public spirited individual citizens." Farmers received no mention.[22]

Demonstrating the national waterway movement's political strength and popularity, members of Congress openly pushed for its rebirth. As Captain J. F. Ellison, secretary of the National Rivers and Harbors Congress, reported: "The re-organization of the National Rivers and Harbors Congress as it now exists, was by the direct request of more than a majority of the Rivers and Harbors Committee of the House of Representatives."[23] Chiefs of engineers, secretaries of war, and presidents of the United States would attend and speak at the organization's meetings. Representative Ransdell had become its president, and many other representatives and senators sat on its board. Of the 1906 Rivers and Harbors Congress meeting, McGee proclaimed: "It is safe to say that during the past quarter century no other body of delegates produced so deep an impression on the legislative and executive branches of the Government."[24]

The Rivers and Harbors Congress hoped to bind all waterway advocates together in changing Congress's attitude toward the nation's waterways. To ensure the broadest base of support, the Rivers and Harbors Congress declared that it would not back any particular project but all projects of merit, and that it would fight for full appropriations to construct all worthwhile projects, so the Corps could complete them as soon as possible.[25]

The Progressive Movement

The 6-foot channel project effort and national navigation movement occurred within the context of a far broader movement called the Progressive movement. Scholars disagree over the Progressive movement's character and impact, but they agree that between 1890 and 1920 something fundamental changed in American society, and Americans responded to that change in new and unique ways. Whether in the city slums or city halls, in the management of corporations or the management of the federal government, Americans sought to bring order to their rapidly changing lives through the application of scientific and technical rigor.[26]

Conservationists within the Progressive movement attempted to reshape how Americans approached their natural resources. Scholars also disagree over the national conservation movement's dominant themes. Some have seen it as an attempt by activists who sought to stop big businesses from selfishly taking the nation's natural resources. Samuel Hays, leading another school, suggests that "conservation, above all, was a scientific movement, ... Its essence was rational planning to promote efficient development and use of all natural resources." Progressive conservationists wanted professionally trained foresters, geologists, economists, and experts from other appropriate disciplines to determine how the nation used its public resources. They objected not to big businesses using the country's natural resources but to unplanned, inefficient, and wasteful destruction. So they initiated a broad campaign for the multiple use of natural resources, especially water resources. Some conservationists hoped to preserve untainted large parts of the nation's wild and scenic areas, but they represented a small minority. A growing realization that America's natural resources were finite motivated most conservationists.[27]

Through their efforts with irrigation, hydroelectric power, and forestry, conservationists recognized the need to think about how all the different uses of the nation's waterways, including navigation, could be planned to maximize the benefits to the American public. Given the growing popularity of the national waterways movement, Roosevelt conservationists hoped to capture the support of navigation boosters to make multiple-purpose water planning a reality. Recognizing that most navigation boosters cared only for their own projects, the conservationists began an effort to broaden those interests.[28]

McGee became one of the administration's most active proponents of a multiple-use program for the nation's waterways. He had helped found the Geological Society of America and the National Geographic Society, becoming its president from 1904 to 1905. The American Anthropological Society would elect him their president in 1911. McGee left the Bureau of Ethnology, in Washington, D.C., in 1903 to head up the anthropological exhibits for the St. Louis Exposition and became director of the St. Louis Public Museum. While in St. Louis, navigation improvement issues caught his attention.[29]

McGee laid out his multiple-use program for the nation's rivers, especially the Mississippi, in a 1907 article titled "Our Great River." After a resounding endorsement of navigation improvements, McGee pleaded with readers to consider more than navigation. Navigation interests had to help reduce the massive amounts of sediment flowing into the Mississippi and its tributaries. To reduce sediment, states within the watershed had to preserve their forests, and farmers had to practice soil conservation. In Italy, the Po River's bed, he said, had risen above the rooftops in the valley beside it, due to sedimentation. And before they began developing the Mississippi and its tributaries for navigation, they had to consider urban water supply, hydroelectric power development, irrigation, canals, and reclamation. The individual states and the federal government had to work together to develop a comprehensive plan. The plan would include all the related branches of science and treat the river as an interdependent system. While McGee's message did not resonate with most 6-foot channel boosters, together, the Progressive conservation and national navigation movements brought waterway issues into everyday life as never before. In this context, the 6-foot channel boosters waged their campaign for a deeper channel.[30]

The Fund-Raising Fiasco

Given the growing national fervor for waterway development, citizens of the upper Mississippi River, it seems, should have contributed freely to the 6-foot channel effort, but they did not. At the 1904 convention, Boswell reported that the UMRIA had raised $3,811.79 for the Rivers and Harbors Committee's trip on the upper river. St. Louis, St. Paul, and the Diamond Jo Line had each contributed $500. Nineteen other cities had chipped in from $5 to $300. While the convention's members favored contributing to such special efforts, they balked at regular donations.[31]

At the 1904 convention, the UMRIA's Ways and Means Commitee asked upper river cities to contribute a total of $1,710. Six cities— Minneapolis, St. Paul, Davenport, Dubuque, Quincy, and St. Louis— were assessed $100 each, and the others from $5 to $75. The committee's recommendation touched off a quarrel telling much about the UMRIA's breadth and depth.[32]

Wilkinson, Boswell, and other UMRIA members protested the trifling sum. The organization, they pressed, should aim for at least $5,000. Boswell demanded $10,000. Yet others objected to any amount. They feared some cities would quit the organization rather than be taxed, as they saw it, to belong to the UMRIA. They said cities along the river would financially support specific needs or events but not a general fund. Wilkinson, Boswell, and their backers countered that the growing organization needed a healthy treasury for education, lobbying, and operating expenses. When one member suggested that the Ways and Means Committee should go back and allocate $5,000 between the upper river's towns, M. J. McInery, of Moline, a committee member, responded that the committee had examined the issue carefully. He reported, "we should have brought in our report for $5,000, but we know that there is not that enthusiasm among the people on the river that they will go down in their pockets and get out the money." Clarifying just how little enthusiasm existed, he added: "If we get out and solicit nine out of ten men will say they get no direct benefit out of it."[33] To this, C. H. Williams, of Quincy, rejoined that $1,710 would not impress Congress. The UMRIA had to raise $5,000. It could not wait for an emergency, for, he contended, the emergency had arrived. The UMRIA, he observed, had reached a key turning point. Did it, he asked, want to forge ahead or not? The delegates failed to answer his question. Unable to resolve the issue, they left the matter to Wilkinson and a special advisory board. The board stayed with $1,710.[34]

Even this goal proved too high. Reporting for the Ways and Means Committee at the 1905 convention, F. G. Allen, of Moline, announced that the UMRIA had raised only half of the amount.[35] Allen implored the UMRIA to think bigger. To date, he observed, the UMRIA had been "a sentimental proposition." Its members had to recognize the UMRIA as a serious business enterprise, and they had to back it financially as such.[36] Allen, one of the largest manufacturers on the upper river, told the convention that he had not supported the project until the past year. Once he thought about the savings offered by reliable river navigation, he said, he appreciated the need to support the UMRIA. Allen urged the UMRIA to raise its target to $10,000. The UMRIA had started, he believed, to rouse the upper Mississippi valley. Every hamlet, he declared, could become a manufacturing center, every town a principal center, if the Corps established a 6-foot channel. So, they all had good reason to back the cause financially. Despite being unable to raise $1,710 the previous year, the delegates voted to collect $10,000. Each city received a minimum allotment, and each delegate agreed to pay a $5 membership fee.[37]

The higher goal only made the UMRIA's efforts look more feeble. At the 1906 convention, many cities still owed their dues from two years earlier. Of the $10,000 called for in 1905, the UMRIA had raised only $3,400. The Ways and Means Committee could not give an accurate account of which cities had paid and which had not. L. A. Hamill, of Keokuk, a committee member, admitted, "I was never in a position where we were more embarrassed than we were today."[38] Those cities that had paid did not want to pay again until the cities that had not paid did. The delegates resolved to defer a new assessment until Wilkinson and his advisory committee on collections had obtained as much as they could of the old assessments. To motivate the delegates, J. F. Diefenbach, of Red Wing, the new Ways and Means Committee chair, declared that "upon its finances rests very much the matter of success of this association." If that was true, the UMRIA was in trouble.[39]

The UMRIA had another problem. Although various congressmen from the Mississippi River valley touted the region's political strength, they did not necessarily back navigation improvements. Democratic Representative James Lloyd from Missouri spoke against the 6-foot channel's authorization. Lloyd had delivered the frank lecture to the 1906 UMRIA convention, for which they had praised him. Lloyd did not oppose navigation improvements for the upper river outright. He believed the whole Mississippi River should be approached as one system. He insisted that Congress should not authorize new projects for any part of it until the Corps had completed a comprehensive survey. Until then, he argued, the UMRIA had to accept funding for the 4½-foot channel. Pursuing the 4½-foot channel did the UMRIA little good; pouring more money into a project that had already failed made little sense. Fortunately for the UMRIA, national forces continued to favor them.[40]

Railroad Car Shortage and National Railroad Issues

Six-foot channel boosters received unexpected support for their crusade in 1906 when a railroad car shortage caused a nationwide shipping crisis. The crisis became a new rallying cry for the 6-foot channel project and other navigation projects before Congress. During the February 5, 1907, Rivers and Harbors Committee meeting, Congressman Ransdell quoted railroad barons to emphasize the seriousness of the crisis and the need for navigation improvement. James J. Hill, speaking to two members of the Interstate Commerce Commission the previous December, had pointed out that the country's business output had increased 110 percent between 1895 and 1905, while the facilities for handling freight had grown by only 20 percent. To catch up, railroads would have to build 73,333 miles of track at a cost of $5.5 billion. Hill had telegrammed Ransdell and, pointedly omitting the upper river, told him no subject before Congress in the past twenty years captured the Midwest's interest more than a deep waterway from St. Louis to the Gulf. Railroad congestion had created this interest. The Northern Pacific Railroad president likened the possibility of railroads carrying all the nation's freight to forcing a three-inch stream through a one-inch pipe.[41]

The rail car shortage hurt businesses throughout the United States. Farmers could not get their grain to market and had to borrow from merchants or grain elevator operators, who had to find enough capital to lend to them. Some farmers, merchants, and grain elevator operators were unable to deliver their products on time to meet contract deadlines. Because they could not ship the grain when they wanted to, some operators had to send their grain to markets at inopportune times. By the time one Chicago merchant could ship his grain to the East Coast, Argentina's crop had arrived, lowering the price and reducing his profit. Some farmers lost all their earnings, as their crops rotted in piles outside or in storage bins. The shortage affected more than grain. Arkansas Representative Joseph Taylor Robinson complained that it had hurt cotton farmers in his state. Like the grain producers, cotton farmers had been unable to get their harvest to market. As a result, many of them faced foreclosure. Robinson claimed that hundreds of thousands of Southerners had suffered from the cold when railroads could not deliver coal on time or in enough supply. Midwesterners, facing far colder temperatures, suffered through the fall and winter with "coal famines."[42] And lumber companies in the Northwest had been unable to fill orders, which limited their capital and delayed construction projects around the country.[43]

In response to the crisis, Ransdell, Robinson, Hill, and others called for navigation improvements. Robinson contended that it was his colleagues' "duty as Patriotic Representatives to conserve the public interest and relieve the present situation, to make impossible its recurrence."[44] The railroad crisis, more so than any effort by the UMRIA, made navigation improvements an immediate concern to the broader public and Congress.

The Final Push

Having learned some lessons about the legislative process, the UMRIA sent a committee to Washington on January 7, 1907, to monitor the Rivers and Harbors bill. They had missed an opportunity in 1905 and could not let the next bill pass without their project. After arriving, however, they heard that the Rivers and Harbors Committee did not plan to convene hearings on waterway projects, and they returned home on the fifteenth, after being assured that their project had been considered. Then some UMRIA representatives heard they should go back to Washington. Boswell and William A. Meese, of Moline, returned to the capital on February 2. Despite assurances to the contrary, the House had printed its version of the bill without the 6-foot channel project. How this could have happened is perplexing and a comment on the 6-foot channel's political significance. The committee knew that the UMRIA wanted the 6-foot channel project in the 1907 bill. Working quickly, the UMRIA convinced Burton to amend the bill, and on March 2, 1907, it became law. The act, however, provided only $500,000 per year for the project, one-quarter of what the UMRIA wanted. And as Major Charles McDonald Townsend had pointed out at the 1902 convention, this was not enough. The UMRIA made its new goal funding the project at $2.0 million per year.[45]

Despite the limited funding, UMRIA members celebrated. At their 1907 convention, Burton F. Peek, president of the Moline, Illinois, club, welcomed the delegates. "Well, Gentlemen," he praised them, "you have 'made good' and the people of the Upper Mississippi Valley owe to you an everlasting debt of gratitude." He knew of no other nonpolitical organization, he claimed, "which, within so short a time, has done so much to impress its purpose upon the people at large and to weave that purpose into the warp and woof of a national policy."[46] Peek was right and wrong. By itself, the UMRIA had failed to arouse much support, beyond the cities and towns of the upper Mississippi River valley, and that support was soft. As part of the national waterways movement, the UMRIA did not so much weave its specific vision and objectives into national policy as benefit from the overall movement's success at doing so.

Hindsights

Suffering from the loss of the lumber trade and grain and passenger traffic, cities along the river looked to it to revive their economies. They could not let the hope die that one day the river would be a commercial highway. To give up on that hope meant giving railroads control of the shipping of bulk commodities. It meant losing the advantage they held over inland towns and cities. Without at least the threat of river traffic, they became vulnerable to exorbitant railroad rates and greater competition from inland neighbors. For these reasons, Hill's call to end navigation improvements spurred river cities to push for a deeper channel.

Their problem was that they could not convince cities and farmers away from the river to join them, as they had done during the 1870s. During the early decades of the twentieth century, farmers enjoyed what some agricultural historians have called the golden age of American agriculture.[47] Although boosters insisted that farmers needed the 6-foot channel, few, if any, farmers participated in the UMRIA's meetings. As Minneapolis Mayor David Percy Jones told delegates at the 1906 convention, they were all "hard headed business men,…"[48] When the UMRIA finally ratified a constitution in 1907, Article III, Membership, stated: "The membership of this Association shall consist of Municipal, Civic and Commercial organizations of and from the cities, villages and towns on the Mississippi River and navigable tributaries thereof from

Minneapolis to St. Louis...."[49] Farmers received no specific mention. During the push for the 4½-foot channel, farmers had remained largely separate from the navigation conventions, but they had clearly made their concerns known through the Patrons of Husbandry and third parties. No such organizations formed to push for the 6-foot project. Overall the UMRIA generated little support outside the valley. The UMRIA succeeded because of a change in the nation's attitude toward river and harbor projects and because of the railroad car shortage rather than because the UMRIA raised local, regional, or national support for the 6-foot channel project.

While the UMRIA had little to do with the Progressive movement, it used the movement and in doing so, benefited from public support for projects that appeared to employ the nation's water resources to their fullest. Proponents of the Progressive conservation movement did not directly support the UMRIA. But the force of the waterway movement gained strength from the cumulative interest in multiple water resource uses. As conservationists began considering the multiple uses, they realized how much more the nation's waters had to offer industry and agriculture. In Progressive fashion, the UMRIA had advocated the preservation of forests. It members, however, did not care much for multiple-purpose water projects. They focused almost solely on navigation improvements and on the economic benefits they would reap from lower transportation costs.

The railroad car shortage of 1906–7 made many Americans aware that their maturing economy, an economy dependent on exports, had outstripped railroad capacity. As a result, they began thinking about a mature, multifaceted transportation system. To the extent that Progressive conservatism supported the development of a rational and efficient national transportation system, the UMRIA benefited from the movement's popularity.

The specific debate over the 6-foot channel focused on the availability of funds from Congress and on the potential for a deeper channel to truly restore commerce and lower rail rates. Whether the Midwest would get its project depended more, however, on the willingness of

Congress to authorize and fund major navigation projects in general than on its specific concern about a 6-foot channel for the upper Mississippi River. The Rivers and Harbors Congress failed to achieve its $50 million target, but it did convince Congress to pass the largest Rivers and Harbors act in the nation's history, at $37,108,083.[50] Had the bill been less, the UMRIA might have failed. In this context, the UMRIA's determined efforts led Congress, reluctantly, to authorize the 6-foot channel. No individual played a deciding role. Williamson, Boswell, and other members followed the process and had the growing political and economic clout of the region behind them, even if it was not wholehearted.

In hindsight, critics have decried the 6-foot channel, claiming that a small group of men backed the project and it was out of date before it began. The project, they contend, was a "futile and expensive attempt to artificially keep alive an older form of transportation whose decline was natural and inevitable."[51] Even some contemporaries questioned the 6-foot channel project. Lyman E. Cooley, a nationally known engineer, suggested the government should build a series of locks and dams in the upper Mississippi River to create a channel 9 to 12 feet deep, rather than pursuing further channel constriction. James J. Hill argued that a 6-foot channel could not compete with railroads, and Congress should reject it. Trying to eliminate any thought of navigation improvements on the upper river, Hill insisted that no channel less than 15 feet merited consideration.[52] Few boosters heeded Cooley or Hill. Maybe they realized that a $30-million lock and dam project (as estimated by Riche in 1906) had little chance of making it through Congress. Navigation boosters did not see anything natural or inevitable in the decline of river commerce. They saw a government that had given railroads huge subsidies but had done little to make the Mississippi navigable. They saw railroad magnates, like Hill, ready to capitalize on the end of river shipping. Granted, a small group pushed for the project, but they certainly did not think it was outdated. They could not have known that it was and would fail utterly. Still, over 80 million tons of commerce moves on the upper Mississippi River system each year now, so to suggest that the decline of river commerce was inevitable or natural overlooks this reality.

Some historians and contemporaries criticized the project's sponsors for thinking the river could really control rail rates. They even blamed navigation improvement efforts for causing the railroads' problems.[53] Boosters, however, sincerely believed that competition would reduce rail rates. In his 1906 annual report, Riche, stating a common understanding, stressed that as long as navigation on the upper Mississippi River was practicable and reasonably feasible, it should continue, even if little commerce moved on the river. The loss of the river as a navigation route, he contended, would cost the public several million dollars each year in increased rates. This expenditure, he estimated, would be higher than the cost of the work.[54] Furthermore, the issue had become one of capacity more than of rates. The 1906–7 railroad car shortage and the general agreement, even from railroad leaders, that the nation had exceeded railroad capacity led to national support for navigation development. This, more than the argument over rates, underlay the 6-foot channel project's authorization.

McGee and many others still believed that in the upper Mississippi River basin, Nature had laid out a nearly perfect transportation system, and that it would be wasteful not to complete it. Most Midwesterners believed the region's and the country's manifest destiny depended on finishing what Nature had begun. Up to the 6-foot channel's authorization, navigation boosters, the Corps, and most Midwesterners had operated under these visions. But as the UMRIA began its drive for a deeper channel, a small group with a new vision, a competing vision, emerged.[55]

CHAPTER 7

Cradle, Home, and Place of Sojourn

From the Midwest's beginnings, one vision guided the region's view of the upper Mississippi River. William Windom, Oliver Kelley, Lewis Boswell, W. J. McGee, Corps officers, and most Midwesterners subscribed to it. God, Divine Providence, or Nature had laid out America's rivers, especially the Mississippi, as an ideal transportation system. Not to use this gift amounted to blasphemy. An alternative vision was emerging, however, a vision that would challenge the navigation booster's worldview.[1]

In the early 1900s, as siltation, channel constriction, pollution, reclamation, and overuse degraded the river's environment, concern for its health grew. More and more Americans looked to rivers as recreational and aesthetic resources, and some questioned using rivers for sewers and navigation channels. In increasing numbers, they sought to preserve the natural resources of the upper Mississippi and other rivers. They did not think in ecosystem terms, but they prepared the way for such a view. Conservationists and preservationists, they would help define the upper Mississippi's physical and ecological future. Ecosystem issues today reflect their efforts.

The Changing Environment and Landscape

Channel Constriction

Channel constriction dramatically altered the upper Mississippi River's landscape and environment. Under the 4½- and 6-foot channel projects, channel constriction became the primary method of navigation improvement for over fifty years. During the 4½-foot channel's twenty-eight years, the Corps and its contractors built over 1,900 wing dams and closing dams. Laid end to end, the dams would have run for nearly 336 miles. During the same era, the Corps armored over 197 miles of shoreline with willow mats and rock. Under the 6-foot channel, the Corps intensified channel constriction, pinching the river's flow even more and for longer periods. They built new, higher wing dams and closing dams,

Figure 20. As Montgomery Meigs said, "The production and regulation of shores, then, is the proper designation of this kind of engineering, though its object is the regulation of the channel" (*Annual Report, 1875*). This image shows how much the shores had moved inward under the 6-foot channel project by 1933. Courtesy of the St. Paul District, U.S. Army Corps of Engineers.

they raised and extended the old ones, and they added miles more of riprap. By 1930, the Corps had built over 1,000 wing dams in the 140-mile reach between the Twin Cities and La Crosse alone and had closed many of the upper river's side channels.[2]

Wing dams and closing dams changed the river's normal processes. They maintained or accelerated the channel's velocity during low flows, when it would have been slowing down. Wing dams caused the shores between them to fill rapidly with silt. Closing dams denied water to the river's side channels, making them silt in, become stagnant, and dry out entirely or earlier than normal. In some cases, the Corps dredged sand out of the main channel and placed it in sloughs or side channels behind closing dams to plug them more permanently. In a 1917 article, Corps engineers William Thompson and H. M. Anderly proudly reviewed the accomplishments of channel constriction. They reported that in 1878, Dresbach Slough, just above La Crosse, had an abundant

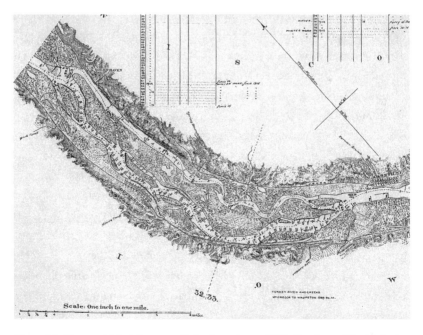

Figure 21. The constricted river near Guttenberg, Iowa, 1915. Courtesy of the St. Paul District, U.S. Army Corps of Engineers.

flow through it. In 1915, they pointed out, the slough was "partially filled up and in some places bars have formed with willow growths, making this arm nothing more than a shallow bayou." Addressing the "all-important question" of where the sand from the main channel went, they said most was "permanently put out of the way" between the dams, and the rest was in side channels and sloughs.[3]

Wing dams and closing dams helped cut away the river's banks, points, and islands, unless the Engineers protected them. In some places, the dams eroded a bank before the Engineers could shield it. At Dibble's Point, just below Hastings, the channel devoured 15 to 20 feet of shore in one year because a wing dam constructed just upstream at Prescott Island had forced the accelerated current against the bank. In other places the Engineers used wing dams to direct the river's flow at points or banks to deliberately carve them back.[4]

The Engineers also changed the pattern of island formation. They removed some troublesome islands. During the 1881 to 1882 season, the navigation channel above Winona threatened to go to the Wisconsin side of Argo Island, rendering the main channel shallow and unnavigable. To prevent this, the Engineers built a wing dam out from the Wisconsin shore, focusing the current at the island. Then they excavated the island down to the water level and dug a trench from one end to the other and removed all the trees, stumps, and roots. They also connected islands to the main shore or to other islands with closing dams, establishing bridges between them, allowing predators and other animals more frequent passage between them. The Engineers protected the heads of many islands with riprap to keep them from washing away and adding more sand and silt to the river. In doing so they preserved islands that might have eroded away naturally. They built wing dams over sandbars, helping the bars to collect sand and become either more stable islands or more firmly connected to the shore. Closing off side channels and chutes sometimes promoted reclamation, as farmers occupied the areas that dried out.[5]

The Corps also changed the river's forest habitat. In 1880, only two years after the Engineers began working on the 4½-foot channel project, they had denuded the floodplain of willow saplings in areas of intensive work. Under the 4½-foot channel project, the Engineers pulled back over 2,900 leaning trees and cut down over 90,000 trees. Under the 6-foot channel project, they removed more. Steamboats took uncounted numbers of trees from the river bottoms to feed their boilers.[6]

As the Engineers constricted the river, they succeeded in deepening it, maybe not enough for reliable navigation at extreme low water but enough to significantly change its average depth. By June 30, 1906, the Corps had established a minimum depth of 4½ feet or more for much of the upper river during normal low flows. Compared to the controlling depths of 16 to 24 inches between St. Paul and the Illinois Rivers originally present during low water, this represented a dramatic change. No longer did the pattern of sandbar formation that created Warren's small pools exist. Dredging further eliminated sandbars from the navigation channel. Sometimes vast mussel beds occupied these bars. Assistant Engineer J. D. DuShane reported on January 16, 1900, that between St. Paul and Winona the dredge had run into a bed of mussel shells so thick the cutter had trouble penetrating it.[7]

By 1930, at the end of the channel constriction era, the upper Mississippi River was profoundly different from what it had been in 1878, when the Corps had begun building wing dams and closing dams. In 1875 Montgomery Meigs said that "the production and regulation of shores, then, is the proper designation of this kind of engineering, though its object is the regulation of the channel...."[8] By 1930 his meaning was evident, especially at low water. Mature stands of trees grew from some wing dams. Between the dams the sediment had encroached well into the river, and plants had quickly followed. Under channel constriction, the river's opposing shores drew much closer together.

Pollution

While channel constriction changed the river's physical characteristics, pollution would most adversely affect the water itself, although the volume of pollutants could influence the river's physical character. Lumber mill refuse and urban garbage both disrupted navigation and degraded the Mississippi's water quality. As lumbermen clear-cut pine forests, they hastened runoff, promoted soil erosion, and added to the flow of silt into the Mississippi and its tributaries. As early as 1880, the mills spewed out "an estimated 1.5 million board feet of sawdust."[9] In 1883 a bar formed in the steamboat channel near Hastings, forcing the navigation channel to change course. When the Engineers dredged the bar, they found it contained at least 50 percent mill refuse. Water permeated with sawdust and pitch fouled steamboat boilers.[10]

Navigation interests complained, and when the St. Paul Chamber of Commerce protested to the secretary of war, the army referred them to Mackenzie. Although Mackenzie said he had no money to examine the problem, he was not disinterested. The mill refuse bar near Hastings was no anomaly. "As based upon general information and records of the office," Mackenzie commented, "I can say that at all points where improvements have been made above Lake Pepin, it is shown that many of the bars are largely composed of sawdust." His engineers had found sawdust deposits as far downstream as Winona. The "promiscuous depositing of sawdust in the river is a public evil," he charged. Mackenzie insisted that Congress or the states pass legislation to stop it.[11]

Sawmills were not the only culprits. St. Paul allowed garbage collectors to dump so much garbage on the ice during the winter, Mackenzie complained, that it was filling the harbor. In a letter to the Minnesota State River Commission on June 25, 1887, Mackenzie denounced the city's disposal policy, insisting that it injured navigation and turned the river into a sewer. The river, he declared, should be kept open for navigation. By the late 1880s, Minneapolis dumped 500 tons of garbage into the river each year, creating health problems and making navigation more difficult. Most other river cities sent their sewage and garbage into the river. In his annual reports, Mackenzie repeatedly criticized the disposing of sawdust and garbage into the river.[12]

Acting on complaints from the Corps and others, Congress included antipollution measures in the Rivers and Harbors Acts of 1890 and 1894, but the measures proved ineffective. Finally, in the 1899

Rivers and Harbors Act, Congress passed a stricter law. The refuse section "outlawed the casting of 'any refuse matter of any kind or description' into navigable waters (except with the special permission of the Secretary of War)."[13] This section also provided that refuse could not be placed on the banks of tributaries if it could wash into the main channel. Officials from the customs office and the Corps received the authority to arrest those who violated the act, although they rarely did. The Corps insisted that unless pollution hurt navigation, it was a state or local problem. Nevertheless, the 1899 Rivers and Harbors Act gave the Corps a management role in dealing with pollution on the upper Mississippi River, a role the Corps still retains under its permitting authority over dredge or fill material placed in navigable waters.[14]

Reclamation

Added to channel constriction and pollution, reclamation degraded the river's ecological character by removing large portions of the floodplain. After authorizing the Flint Creek and Warsaw to Quincy Levees in 1895, Congress had approved no further flood control or reclamation work for the upper river. This did not stop farmers from building levees and claiming more of the river's floodplain. In 1914 the Mississippi River Commission reported that fifty-two levee and drainage districts had formed between Cape Girardeau, Missouri, and Rock Island. Generally low and poorly constructed, these early levees defined the first major taking of the river's floodplains. The Mississippi River Commission's report came at the end of one of the strongest periods of levee district formation on the upper and middle (St. Louis to the Ohio River) Mississippi River. Seventeen—over half of Illinois's Mississippi River levee districts—formed between 1905 and 1916. Through their efforts, floodplain farmers below Rock Island established their stake in how the upper Mississippi River would be managed for flood control and floodplain development.[15]

Congress created the Mississippi River Commission in 1879 to develop plans for improving navigation, to prevent flooding, and to generally promote commerce. Its flood prevention authority extended only to planning, however. After the Mississippi River flood of 1882, the commission received authority to build levees, but this authority applied to the river below Cairo. In the 1913 Rivers and Harbors Act, Congress extended the commission's authority to Rock Island, which would eventually allow an intense program of federally supported reclamation on the upper river and become an essential factor in defining the river's future landscape and ecosystem issues.[16]

In a 1912 article on reclamation, Charles W. Durham, who had been the local engineer in charge of the Flint Creek Levee for the Corps, captured the significance of reclamation to many Midwesterners. He said:

> Aside from the pecuniary considerations, it is manifest that the conversion of a low, swampy and almost worthless tract into an aggregation of fertile farms with appropriate dwellings and farm buildings occupied by an industrious and prosperous population well provided with schools and good roads and reasonably insured against the inroad of malarious diseases, will be of great and lasting benefit to the public welfare and public health,...

Durham further contended that it had "become imperative to protect low lands from overflow by means of levees and to get rid of surface water, seepage, swamps, etc., by means of ditches and pumps" because good land was becoming scarce, and productive lands in the floodplain had to be preserved. "Thus the matter of conservation and improvement of the soil," he declared, "has become one of the most potent questions of the day and applies with force to the valleys of the Mississippi and its tributaries." Durham represented the mind-set of many Americans during this era. The river's floodplain represented a rich, untapped resource. It would be wasteful not to use it. A new vision would soon challenge this view.[17]

Responding in part to states along the Mississippi, Congress passed the country's first official flood control act in 1917. It allowed the Corps to work on levees from the Head of Passes, in Louisiana, to Rock Island, and on the Sacramento River, in California. This act marks the formal beginning of the Corps involvement in flood control on the upper Mississippi. Through the act, the federal government assumed an official role in securing the Mississippi's floodplains for agriculture. The act gave the Corps a new mission for managing the upper Mississippi River, a mission Congress would strengthen in the 1928 Flood Control Act. Under these acts, the Corps helped fortify levees in eleven levee and drainage districts, which enclosed over 260,000 acres of floodplain on the upper and middle Mississippi.[18]

A New Vision

As siltation, channel constriction, pollution, and reclamation increasingly threatened the upper Mississippi River's fish and wildlife and aesthetic character, conservationists began working to preserve them. They did not all share the same vision, but together they would establish a new way of looking at the river and try to carve out a part of it for themselves.

Fish Rescue

Soon after the Corps started improving the upper Mississippi River for navigation, state and national agencies began trying to improve it for recreational and commercial fishing. While conservation efforts on the Mississippi covered many areas, fish management provides a good example of the vision early conservationists held for the river and how their vision shaped it. Fish management began on the upper Mississippi River soon after Congress created the Office of the U.S. Commissioner of Fish and Fisheries in 1871. Congress established the commission "to solve the conservation problem, then acute, as it related to the diminishing supply of food and game fishes in our coastal and interior waters."[19] At first, Congress authorized the commission to study fishery problems, but in 1872 it expanded the commission's duties to include propagating and planting fish. Although the upper Mississippi River fishery was not in danger, the commission and the commercial and sport anglers it served wanted to make the river yield more of what they considered popular food and game species. So in 1872 the commission distributed about 25,000 shad below St. Anthony Falls, and from 1874 to

1884 placed some 1,340,000 shad in the river and tried introducing salmon. While neither the shad nor the salmon survived long, the commission successfully introduced carp (then believed to be a valuable commercial fish) and stocked the river with native fish, including catfish, buffalofish, and others. The fish for stocking came from controlled rearing ponds.[20]

Fish management on the upper Mississippi expanded in 1874 when Iowa, Minnesota, Missouri, and Wisconsin established their own fish commissions. Iowa's fish commission, under B. F. Shaw, its first commissioner, initiated the most influential program. Shaw liked the U.S. Fish Commission's strategy and saw fish propagation as a way to increase Iowa's game fish populations. Although Shaw initially focused on propagation, he soon turned to another source. Each spring when the Mississippi flooded, fish entered the river's backwaters to spawn. As the water receded, adult fish returned to the main river. Fingerlings—numbering in the hundreds of millions—remained and became trapped. As the shallowest pools evaporated, the fish died. Many pools that lasted through the summer and fall often froze to their bottoms in winter, killing more. In some pools that did not freeze solid, the fish became so concentrated they suffocated.[21]

Looking for a cheaper way to provide stocking fish, Shaw recognized the trapped fingerlings as a tremendous resource, a resource he believed nature wasted. During the early 1870s, he experimented with fish rescue; that is, he began catching the trapped fingerlings and placing them in the river. In 1876 he convinced Iowa's governor and legislature to fund fish rescue and sent crews into the field during September and October. Despite the short season, they captured over one million fingerlings.[22]

Other states and the federal government followed Iowa's lead. In the 1880s Missouri and Illinois began rescuing fish, and Wisconsin initiated its program in 1895. Recognizing the potential of fish rescue, the U.S. Fish Commission started rescue operations in 1889, which it continued after 1903 when it became the Bureau of Fisheries. That year it stationed a rescue crew at Bellevue, Iowa, and placed another at

Marquette, Iowa, in 1904. The bureau soon dominated fish rescue on the upper river.[23]

Congress increased the bureau's program for the upper Mississippi River in 1908, when it authorized the Fairport Biological Station at Fairport, Iowa. The station served several purposes. It raised fish for lakes and streams in the Midwest, developed fish culture techniques, and as an important part of its founding mission, engaged in mussel propagation research and planting. "For a period of about 20 years," fisheries historian Harriet Bell Carlander reports, "Fairport was probably the most important center of freshwater fish culture investigations."[24] For fish and mussels, Fairport became the center of the classic, scientific Progressive approach to natural resource management.

Between 1917 and 1923, the Bureau of Fisheries expanded its fish rescue program dramatically. In 1917 the bureau began sending rescue crews out from Fairport. It established ten stations in Minnesota, eight in Wisconsin, seven in Illinois, six in Iowa, and three in Missouri. By 1919 the bureau's program extended from Minnesota to Mississippi. Before 1922 the bureau funded fish rescue out of other programs, but that year Congress authorized money for the bureau to conduct fish rescue throughout the Mississippi River valley.[25]

Fish rescue became so important to the Bureau of Fisheries by the early 1920s that its chief ichthyologist declared the agency dependent on the Mississippi River for its national fingerling supply. In 1923, he reported, the bureau provided thirty-two states with fish from the Mississippi River. Overall the bureau rescued 100 to 176 million fish annually during the 1920s. The "importance of this work as a means of maintaining and increasing the food supply of the country," Clarence F. Culler, District Supervisor of the bureau's La Crosse office, asserted, "can hardly be equaled in any other field, when cost, results, and quick returns are considered."[26]

The Bureau of Fisheries placed all nongame species back in the river, but it sent some of the game species, especially black bass, to streams and lakes in states outside the valley. This angered some. Defending itself, the bureau maintained that it returned at least 50 percent of the game fish to their native waters. But the complaints had some merit. Records demonstrate that the bureau sometimes shipped up to 93 percent of bass away from the river.[27]

Fish rescue may have affected the river's ecosystems in unanticipated ways. During the 1916 season, rescuers from the Homer, Minnesota, station removed fish from "practically all the dead sloughs and pockets" in a 30-mile reach above La Crosse.[28] Removing the stranded fish took away food from birds and animals that preyed on the fingerlings. Culler, a strong proponent of fish rescue, reported that "predacious birds" often consumed the fingerlings before rescuers could save them. "The writer," Culler said, referring to himself, "has counted as many as 25 blue heron around a pool, feasting on young bass. One blue heron recently killed had 102 fish in its stomach. This is an example," he complained, "of the heron menace."[29] Fish rescue would affect the river's ecosystem in another important way.

Pearl Buttons, Mussel Propagation, and Fish Rescue

While fish rescue began as a way to restock the region's lakes and streams, it became important for another reason. During the last decade of the nineteenth century, freshwater mussels, used to make buttons, emerged as an important economic resource for the upper Mississippi River valley. Clam hunters quickly depleted the river's mussel populations. Since some mussel larvae spent their first weeks on the gills of fish, the millions of rescued fingerlings represented an opportunity to replenish the mussels.

The assault on the river's mussel populations began in 1891, when John F. Boepple, a German immigrant, convinced investors to support building a button factory in Muscatine, Iowa. Boepple had emigrated from near Hamburg, Germany, in 1887, where he had worked in button making. In 1890 he moved from central Illinois to the river town of Muscatine. Recognizing Boepple's genius, others soon established button factories in Muscatine and other cities on the river. Between 1897 and 1898, the number of button factories in Iowa and Illinois grew from 13 to 49, and by 1914 Iowa, Illinois, and Missouri together counted 121 button factories. During the late 1890s, button manufacturing replaced the faltering lumber industry as the principal business in some Iowa and Illinois river towns. Between 1912 and 1914, the Bureau of Fisheries estimated that the industry employed 9,746 mussel collectors. From 1898 to 1916, the industry's boom years, it expanded through much of the Mississippi River basin and to rivers around the country. Button manufacturers produced 11.4 million gross buttons in 1904, 21.7 million gross buttons in 1916, and 20.2 million gross buttons in 1929.[30] At its peak the industry extended from Minnesota to Mississippi.

By the early 1900s, it had become clear that the pearl button industry would exhaust the upper river's mussels. In the mid-1890s, clammers discovered a large mussel bed near New Boston, Illinois, that ran for about 1½ miles and spread up to 300 yards wide. In less than three years, mussel hunters gathered almost ten thousand tons of shells from the bed. By 1898 they had exterminated the mussels. Although certain species worked best for button making, clammers took all the mussels they could harvest. They did not want their competitors to get any mussels, regardless of size, and they hoped to find freshwater pearls. Consequently, the beds could not regenerate.[31]

Muscatine button manufacturers appealed to George M. Bowers, head of the U.S. Bureau of Fisheries, and to Iowa Congressman Albert F. Dawson to save their livelihood. With Dawson's support, Congress authorized the Fairport Biological Station in 1908. In 1912 biologists at the station began propagating mussels to help the pearl button industry. The bureau "infected" fish with mussel larvae and then released them into the Mississippi River. The larvae lived in the gills of the fish for several weeks and then dropped off. Using fish captured in the fish rescue operation, the bureau expanded its mussel infection program dramatically. During the 1922 season, the bureau rescued some 139 million fish and infected them with about 2 billion mussel larvae.[32]

The Bureau of Fisheries could not, however, stop the overkill or the devastating effects of pollution and siltation on the river's mussels and fishery. By 1921 the problems had become so bad that Commerce Secretary Herbert Hoover (a former Iowan) called for a national conference, which took place at Fairport Station in June 1921. The conferees included scientists, pearl button manufacturers, government administrators, and sport and commercial anglers. They focused on the causes of fish and shellfish depletion and potential remedies, preserving the river's wetlands and shores, and developing a scientific program to improve the river's health. Wetland drainage and the problems caused by pollution received special attention. The conference broadened public and professional awareness about habitat destruction.[33]

Trying to save mussel populations, Robert Coker, head of the Fairport Station, and his colleagues at the bureau worked for state regulations. Most upper river states placed some restrictions on the clamming industry by the early 1920s. They set size limits, prescribed gathering methods, and alternately opened and closed parts of the river.[34]

By the early 1920s, fish rescue had become the bureau's principal fish restocking source for the nation and its primary offense against mussel extinction. Fish rescue and mussel propagation demonstrated that the federal government's primary objective for the upper Mississippi River was to develop and use these resources like crops. Rather than address overuse and habitat loss, they focused on growing more. Some conservationists, however, had begun working to save the river and its resources for other purposes.

Park and Refuge

By the twentieth century's second decade, reclamation, pollution, siltation, channel constriction, and overuse threatened to decimate the river's fish and wildlife and ruin its scenery. As a result, those individuals interested in the river's biological and scenic qualities began organizing. They initiated two efforts to reserve and develop large parts of the upper Mississippi for native plants and animals and for recreation. First they tried to create a national park. Then they pushed for a national wildlife and fish refuge.

National Park

The movement for a national park began in Iowa. Started before 1900, it gained momentum early in the new century. In 1909 Iowa state representative George H. Schulte extolled the values of such a park in his county, near McGregor, in northeastern Iowa, to his fellow legislators in the Iowa General Assembly. He asked them to pass a resolution calling upon Congress to make the area around McGregor a national park. His call went unanswered.[35]

In 1916 a small and zealous group of Iowa conservationists initiated a more concerted effort. They had organized to fight against wildlife destruction, and for many years had been working to set aside scenic areas in Iowa, especially in northeastern Iowa, for state parks. They convinced Senator William S. Kenyon and Representative Gilbert Haugen, of Iowa, to introduce bills in Congress to establish a Mississippi Valley National Park in the area around Prairie du Chien and McGregor. Kenyon visited the area twice in 1915 and became enchanted with it. In 1916 Haugen sought $3,000 to study acquiring title to the land, but Congress granted only $1,000 for a general study of the area.[36]

To get support from the National Park Service, created the previous year, boosters convinced the new agency to send M. L. Dorr to inspect the area in 1917. According to George Bennett, a retired Episcopal minister from McGregor and a leading park advocate, "The inspector came, he saw and was conquered, his report being in complete and hearty unison with the contentions and efforts of the promoters."[37] But Dorr's report failed to persuade the National Park Service or Congress to establish the new park.[38]

Bennett and others called for the park to preserve scenic and natural areas being destroyed by industry and the growing population. "We are just beginning in our country to realize the fearful ravages we have been permitting for so long, ravages of wood, mountain and fen, ... of the beauty and grace of the hillside and dell...," Bennett lamented.[39] Many advocates argued that the park was necessary to save migratory birds and prevent the extinction of native plants and animals. The Midwest, another park proponent argued, did not have a national park and deserved one. When proponents tried to get Congress to create the park in 1917, New York Representative John Fitzgerald, who opposed spending federal funds for conservation, blocked the bill. World War I and opposition from anticonservation forces delayed the park bill for the next several years.[40]

At the 1918 Iowa Conservation Association meeting in McGregor, park supporters defined their strategy more clearly. Founded in 1901 by Drs. Louis Pammel and G. B. MacDonald of Iowa State College, and Bohumil Shimek and Thomas MacBride of the State University of Iowa, the Iowa Conservation Association promoted conservation and worked to establish a system of parks in Iowa. At the meeting, Bennett, Edgar R. Harlan, who was the curator of the Iowa Department of History and Archives, and others decided to promote the park idea by publicizing the scenic beauty of the region and by promoting the area for conventions. To do this, the association, aided by local residents and the Permanent Wild Life Protection Fund, initiated a series of lectures and nature hikes on conservation, natural history, archaeology, and history during the summer of 1919. They also established a "Win the Park Board," which Iowa's Governor W. L. Harding agreed to head. At one of the meeting's suppers, they toasted to the national park, "which everyone was sure would soon be established."[41]

From the 1919 meeting and excitement about the park emerged the American School of Wild Life Protection. The first of its kind, the school provided a national model. The school met annually during the summer up to World War II. It brought key figures and students of all ages together from across the country "for two weeks of birding, nature hikes, and lectures on ornithology, geology, botany, ichthyology, entomology, astronomy, forestry, and archaeology."[42] Most teachers came from Iowa's colleges, and its advisory board included Dr. William T. Hornaday, chairman of the Permanent Wild Life Protection Fund and an employee of the National Museum of Natural History, and Dr. T. Gilbert Pearson, president of the National Association of Audubon Societies. Iowa's inner circle of conservationists—Shimek, MacBride, MacDonald, and Pammel—often taught classes and led field trips. Other notable conservationists, such as Dr. Harry Oberholser of the U.S. Biological Survey in Washington, D.C., and Dr. Melvin Gilmore, who taught Native American history at the University of North Dakota and later at the University of Michigan, lectured at the school.[43]

The school succeeded in drawing attention to the area, but park proponents could not convince Congress to create a national park. Park advocates submitted their bill in 1921, 1923, and 1924, but each time it failed. In part it failed because Congress had traditionally created parks from federal lands, and the proposed park would require purchasing lots of private land. It also failed because supporters had been unable to create national backing for the project; it appeared to be a local or regional boon. The park effort, however, publicized the natural and scenic qualities of the upper river, increased awareness of the river's importance as a fish and wildlife reserve, and in doing so, prepared the way for a new movement.[44]

Fish and Wildlife Refuge

With the national park stalled, upper river conservationists initiated a new movement, one that would exceed the park movement in vision and accomplishment. Ignoring the park movement's repeated failures, Will Dilg—one of the Izaak Walton League's founders and president—brazenly suggested that Congress establish a 260-mile-long national fish and wildlife refuge, extending from Wabasha to Rock Island. Dilg and fifty-three other men had formed the Izaak Walton League in Chicago in January 1922. That summer, Dilg and his assistant Merton S. Heiss traveled through the upper Mississippi River valley, promoting the league. At Wabasha, Dilg paused to go fishing. Heiss recalled that he and Dilg had been catching bass off a wing dam when, "Suddenly, Will said, 'We can do it, we can make this whole cockeyed territory into a fish and game refuge.' There was no more fishing; there was no more organizing of chapters." Dilg hurried back to Chicago to "start making history."[45] The movement Dilg initiated for the refuge spurred and shaped the conservation vision for the upper Mississippi River.

If Dilg and the Izaak Walton League hoped to establish the refuge, they needed support from outside the upper Mississippi River valley. As

Figure 22. Will Dilg cofounded the Izaak Walton League and championed the Upper Mississippi River Wildlife and Fish Refuge. Courtesy of the Izaak Walton League of America.

early navigation boosters had done, they needed to create a ground-swell that Congress could not ignore. Playing on the effects of siltation, pollution, channel constriction, and especially reclamation, refuge proponents argued that the upper Mississippi River valley faced an environmental crisis. If Congress did not create the refuge immediately, the nation would lose one of its greatest fish and wildlife reserves, important commercial food and fur resources, the best recreation area in the central United States, and spectacular scenery. H. C. Oberholser, speaking for the Biological Survey, asserted that "we must, if we are to keep up the supply of our wild life, do something before it is too late; and it is rapidly becoming too late." To Oberholser, Dilg, and other conservationists, the proposed refuge represented the "last stand" for fish, wildlife, and other resources in the Mississippi River valley.[46]

The draining of wetlands along the river precipitated the crisis, according to refuge proponents. Reclamation destroyed feeding, breeding, and resting grounds for millions of migratory birds, the spawning beds for the black bass and other fish, and the habitat of muskrats and other furbearing animals. Upland agriculture dumped tons of silt into the river, and use of the river's bottomlands would add even more. Farmers, the conservation boosters contended, did not need the land, as the country already faced a farm crisis due to overproduction and low prices (the golden age of farm prices had come to an end shortly after World War I). Creating more farmland, they contended, made little sense. Congress still had time to preserve some of the river's best wetlands, but it had to act quickly.

Under Dilg's leadership, conservationists used the reclamation issue to push for the refuge. In 1923 landowners in an area called Winneshiek Bottoms proposed to drain much of this 30-mile-long wetland for agriculture. The bottoms comprised about 13,000 acres below Lansing, Iowa, on the Wisconsin shore, and about 15,000 acres above Lansing on the Iowa side. Dotted with lakes, ponds, sloughs, and inlets, the bottoms comprised one of the key wildlife areas in the proposed refuge.

On August 10, 1923, at the request of the Chief of the Biological Survey, Oberholser inspected the area to assess the drainage project's merits and its potential biological impacts. Drainage advocates, according to Oberholser, planned to dredge the main channel, erect levees along its borders, and reclaim the land up to the bluffs. After surveying the bottoms, he reported that "at the present time this whole area is an excellent resort for waterfowl of all kinds, particularly during the spring and fall...." Wood ducks, mallards, "and water birds of less economic importance" populated its waters. Muskrats abounded, and their pelts brought significant income to trappers. Even more important, the Bureau of Fisheries collected some 23,607,000 fingerlings from the backwater sloughs, lakes, and ponds during 1921. All this would be lost, Oberholser warned, if the drainage project took place. Local anglers and hunters, the Iowa State Game Warden, Culler, and the Chief of Fish Culture for the Bureau of Fisheries opposed it. Oberholser concluded that "it is strongly recommended that the proposal for the drainage of the bottoms be abandoned."[47]

Oberholser added a sense of urgency. Under Wisconsin state law, if a majority of landowners in a proposed reclamation project supported it, they could call for a commission to begin the process. The main proponent had gained his majority, and he sat on the commission. As required by federal law, the Corps had also reviewed the project, and the local engineer favored it. Neither the commission nor the Corps had approved the project yet. Before they could, conservationists felt they had to do something.[48]

Winneshiek Bottoms became the rallying cry for refuge supporters. In February 1924, Dilg presented one expert after another to hearings on the refuge before the House Agriculture Committee and the Senate Commerce Committee. Most witnesses criticized drainage in general and the Winneshiek project in particular. To show the dangers of reclamation, some reported on a project that had failed near La Crosse. The project had drained over 7,000 acres at the confluence of the Trempealeau and Mississippi Rivers. A. A. Holmes, the county's conservation warden, claimed that this area had been "one of the finest hunting grounds" and "one of the finest places for fish and for raising fish" in the region.[49] After the drainage project, ducks, fish, and furbearing animals abandoned the area. To compound this loss, Holmes emphasized, the land proved worthless for agriculture. In a letter to Henry C. Wallace, the secretary of agriculture, Dilg condemned the project, as it "resulted in abomination and desolation and," he warned, "proves the dread and ruinous result which would come should drainage go further in this region."[50] To conservationists, Winneshiek Bottoms and other floodplain wetlands faced the same fate if Congress did not create the refuge soon. The *Saturday Evening Post*, adding to the growing support from outside the valley, joined the call for the refuge, arguing, "It is time for America to wake up and to call a halt on waste and our haste to develop every resource regardless of conditions. These great swamps . . . may conceivably be a better national asset in their natural state than under cultivation."[51]

In their push for the refuge and in their many writings, conservationists detailed what losing the Winneshiek Bottoms and other wetlands would mean not only to the region but to the country. Between June 1923 and July 1924, the Izaak Walton League published some two dozen articles on the refuge in its magazine *Outdoor America*. Dilg touted the proposed refuge as the greatest black bass fishery in the country, and Americans, he said, favored black bass over all other fish. Black bass tackle, he claimed, accounted for 90 percent of fishing tackle made in the United States. Dilg predicted bass would become extinct in the upper Mississippi River unless Congress established the refuge soon.[52]

Anglers from well outside the valley worried as well. E. C. Kemper, secretary of the Potomac Angler's Association, Washington, D.C., testified that his organization unanimously favored the refuge bill. They believed losing the Mississippi River bass hatchery would jeopardize bass fishing in the East. While the East did not receive many black bass from the Mississippi River, much of the central United States did. They feared that as the country's center lost its bass fishery, pressure would mount on eastern fisheries.[53]

To some refuge proponents, losing the river's fisheries went beyond simple recreation; it affected the country's moral character. Representative Harry B. Hawes argued that "we are going to make mollycoddles of our kids if they don't know how to use a fishing rod and a gun. We are going to lose the best American traditions if we do not have a place for our boys to play." The refuge, he added, would be a place for kids from all over the country. E. W. Nelson, chief of the Bureau of Biological Survey, contended that "a large part of the mental and physical vigor of the Americans is due to our out-of-door habits." As the growing assault on the country's natural areas took away places to recreate, he asserted, the American character would suffer.[54]

Refuge supporters insisted that reclamation threatened all the upper Mississippi River's fish, endangering the fish rescue program. Diking and draining backwaters eliminated the overflow lands and the pools from which federal and state agencies rescued fish. Compounding this problem, removing the backwaters would force all the river's water down one narrow channel, increasing its velocity at high water, as wing and closing dams did at low water. During the annual spring flood, conservationists predicted, the current would sweep spawning fish down the main channel. Exaggerating, G. C. Leach, from the Bureau of Fisheries, imagined the river carrying fish from the upper Mississippi into the cotton fields and sugar plantations of the South. Frances E. Whitley, chair of the Conservation Division, General Federation of Women's Clubs, suggested that a faster-flowing river would prevent mussel larvae from attaching to host fish, threatening mussel populations already endangered by pollution, silt, and overcollecting. Strengthening this argument, Stephen A. Forbes, a fisheries expert from Illinois, reported to the Agriculture Committee that "a stream flowing down between its banks, without any extensive overflow is a barren stream and necessarily so, . . ."[55]

Conservationists warned that destroying the upper Mississippi's wetlands would have national consequences, for the river's floodplain comprised one of North America's most important flyways. W. T. Cox, Minnesota's State Forester, characterized the upper river as "a great geographical funnel through which the water-loving birds pour in their flight southward and from which they emerge on their northern migration."[56] Reclamation, he contended, imperiled the flyway, and to preserve it, Congress had to establish the refuge. F. Gilbert Pearson, the

National Audubon Society's president, agreed and added another reason for protecting the flyway. As ducks and geese began their migration down the flyway, he reported, "hunters lie behind every bush and every point, and the ducks and geese have no large open waters on which they can rest. As a result of that they are driven continuously, pell-mell, from every foot of ground or water on which they light, until they are simply driven down to the mouth of the Mississippi River, into the great marshes of Louisiana." Consequently, they reached their wintering ground too soon, consumed their food supply too early, and were starving when they returned north.[57]

Barrington Moore, secretary of the Ecological Society of America, spoke to the Agriculture Committee for organizations represented by the Council on National Parks, Forests, and Wild Life. The organization included his and at least twenty-five others. Demonstrating the organization's breadth, the council included the Sierra Club, Boone and Crocket Club, American Automobile Association, Architectural League of New York, Camp Fire Club of America, National Arts Club, Save the Redwoods League, American Society for Landscape Architects, American Museum of Natural History, Field Museum of Natural History, National Association of Audubon Societies, General Federation of Women's Clubs, and National Geographic Society. While acknowledging that he did not have petitions from each, he declared, "they unanimously, to a member, approve this legislation."[58] Focusing on the Winneshiek Bottoms, Moore asserted, "We have here … an area which is rapidly being destroyed and very soon we won't have any more that remarkable assemblage of plants, fishes, birds and other animals." The Ecological Society had been working to establish reserves around the country as outdoor laboratories. To the Society, losing areas like Winneshiek Bottoms meant losing the opportunity to study how nature worked. "To drain that area, even though it were valuable for agriculture, which it is not," Moore argued, "would be the same as destroying a library which contained manuscripts of which there were no other copies." How could biologists learn to control pests like the boll weevil, he asked the committee, without such laboratories?[59]

Overall, refuge advocates contended, eliminating the upper Mississippi River's wetlands threatened the Midwest's economy. Because commercial and game fish used backwater pools to spawn, draining these pools would eliminate an important food source. The great quantity of fish taken from the upper river on a Sunday, Culler speculated, affected "the Monday income of every butcher" between Wabasha and Rock Island.[60] Without these fish resources, Midwesterners would have to import fish at a much higher cost. Federal and state agencies would have to build rearing ponds throughout the region to stock rivers and lakes in the central United States, which would cost much more than fish rescue. Conservationists warned that the loss of host fish for mussel larvae would decimate the pearl button industry, an industry worth $5 to $6 million annually and employing some five thousand people. Recreation income for the region, they added, would disappear with its fish and wildlife.[61]

Emboldened by his mounting success, Dilg wrote to Henry C. Wallace, secretary of agriculture, on October 25, 1923. He reminded Wallace of their recent meeting in Washington, D.C., at which Dilg had stressed the need for two important surveys. To persuade Congress to pass the refuge bill, which Dilg said they planned to submit in the coming session, they needed to show the economic, biological, and social values of the Winneshiek Bottoms and how worthless floodplain agriculture in the refuge would be. He needed Wallace to push the Biological Survey to complete agricultural and wildlife studies. Commerce Secretary Hoover had already directed the Bureau of Fisheries to study food and game fish. Showing his impatience, Dilg announced that he was ready to unleash a juggernaut for the refuge. People in the Mississippi River valley and throughout the country, he asserted, wanted the surveys completed. Two million members of the General Federation of Women's Clubs backed the refuge. "Every Chapter of these Women's Clubs," he intimated, "will appeal to its Congressmen and Senator," and he announced that "the machinery to bring this about has already been launched." Ten U.S. senators and over sixty representatives had declared their support. And the Izaak Walton League had not yet turned its members on their congressional delegations. "It will now be the duty of the hundreds of Izaak Walton League Chapters to appeal to their Congressmen throughout the nation. It is not extravagant to say that an avalanche of public opinion is back of our measure...." Dilg informed Wallace that Congress would authorize the refuge in the next session.[62]

He was right. It took one try for Congress to pass the refuge bill. But in June, after both houses had passed the bill and only two days remained in the session, Dilg learned from the Bureau of Biological Survey that the bill contained a fatal flaw. Knowing only President Coolidge could get Congress to pass it again quickly enough, and knowing that only Secretary of Commerce Hoover could get him in to see the president, Dilg hurried over to the secretary's office. As told by Senator Harry Hawes, the bill's sponsor, Dilg burst into Hoover's office and said, "Mr. Hoover, for God's sake put on your hat and coat, quick, and come with me to see the President. Your must ask him, and beg him if necessary to ask Congress to repass our Mississippi River Refuge bill—before Congress adjourns, day after tomorrow. If he will not do it, our bill is dead!" Hoover agreed, and they caught a cab and rushed to the White House. Coolidge interrupted his schedule, met with them, and said he would help. "Its second passage," Dilg modestly told Hawes, "was wholly due to what President Coolidge did, in response to the appeal of Secretary Hoover."[63]

On June 7, 1924, President Coolidge signed the bill creating the Upper Mississippi River Wildlife and Fish Refuge, and Congress appropriated $1.5 million for purchasing land between Rock Island and Wabasha. Although Congress had created refuges in nearly half the states, this was the first time it had appropriated funding for one in the original act. The amount of the initial appropriation, the size of the refuge, and the direction to preserve fish, birds, and other wildlife were unprecedented. By 1929 the federal government had bought over 100,000 acres for the refuge. The refuge would grow to 233,000 acres, including marshes, wooded islands, and backwaters. Conservationists had successfully established a new vision for the river, and they now had something to protect and foster. They had also successfully established another federal presence on the river. In doing so, they deepened the federal government's management role on the Mississippi.[64]

Dilg and the Izaak Walton League succeeded for three primary reasons. First, they campaigned for the refuge in a favorable context. Second, they mounted an effort unmatched in its financing, political acumen, and grassroots appeal. Third, professional biologists in the Bureaus of Fisheries and Biological Survey fought to preserve Winneshiek Bottoms and other floodplain wetlands and raised the issue to the secretaries of commerce and agriculture. The Izaak Walton League, concludes historian Phillip Scarpino, "did not create a preservationist sentiment in an unwilling population. Instead, when they shook their fists at the worshipers of materialism and spoke of obligation to the land, beauty, recreation, and closeness to God, they preached to a congregation already prepared to believe."[65] By the early 1920s, the effects of pollution, siltation, navigation improvements, overfishing, and excessive mussel harvesting alarmed many residents of the upper Mississippi River valley and the nation. They believed the river faced a crisis, and the crisis required that they view the river differently. Locally, the national park movement had played an important role in preparing the way for the refuge.[66]

Americans had more time for and greater access to the river as the twentieth century progressed. They worked shorter hours and had more vacation time. They had automobiles and a rapidly expanding road system. Railroads offered quick and convenient passenger service. Outboard motors made the river more accessible. Each year tens of thousands of passengers boarded excursion boats to recapture a piece of the river's romantic past—a past some believed should be left to history. As they used the river more, they valued it more—not for the navigation it was supposed to provide but for the recreational enjoyment they readily and frequently experienced.[67]

Politically, the Izaak Walton League conducted a masterful crusade. It was, Scarpino asserts, "the first modern environmental campaign."[68] Four states bordered on the proposed refuge and provided a political constituency upon which to build a national campaign. To lobby Congress and the executive branch directly, Dilg moved his head-quarters to Washington, D.C. From there, he coordinated the procession of scientists and professionals who appeared before the House and Senate hearings on the refuge bill. With the Izaak Walton League's magazine, *Outdoor America*, and the nationally recognized authors he convinced to write for it, Dilg reached across the country for support.[69] Arguing to preserve the upper Mississippi River valley as a refuge proved to be a good strategy. In contrast to the national park proposal, which many in Congress viewed as simply a regional boon, the refuge idea gained national attention and support. While critics could challenge the region's beauty as compared to other areas, they could not contest the region's importance as a flyway and fishery.

The park and refuge movements redefined conservation in the upper Mississippi River valley. Through fish rescue and mussel propagation, professional biologists had pursued conservation in the classic Progressive tradition. They had tried to keep ahead of depletion by artificially regenerating the river's resources for commercial and recreational interests. In their scientific research, they focused on the commercially valuable species, hoping to plant, grow, and harvest them like crops. Where artificial propagation failed, they moved toward regulation as a way to slow the destruction, but with the same goals in mind. Increasingly, they recognized that drainage, pollution, siltation, and navigation works were undermining their programs and the river's natural resources. Regionally and nationally, fish rescue anchored the Bureau of Fisheries restocking program, and the program demanded healthy floodplain wetlands. From local fish rescue stations to the bureau chief, they called for the preservation of Winneshiek Bottoms and other floodplain wetlands. Dilg's refuge was exactly what they needed, and they let Secretary of Commerce Hoover know.

Habitat preservation became more important to nonprofessionals as well. Preservationists, those who wanted the valley's natural resources and scenic beauty preserved unchanged, joined the park and refuge movement. Not all were anglers and hunters. Some advocated preserving the river as a natural area for aesthetic reasons. Frances E. Whitley, chair of the Conservation Division of the General Federation of Women's Clubs, testified that her federation did not support the refuge as a hunting or fishing reserve; they were not, she stressed, sportsmen. Rather, they backed the refuge because it stood "for one of the things that we have been working for ever since this division was organized in 1894, which is to try to conserve for the future some of the resources of this country both for the material prosperity and for the natural beauty that we believe is just as great a heritage which we ought to pass on to our children."[70] Critical of the hunters, the Audubon Society's president had condemned the slaughter of migratory waterfowl as they passed through the upper Mississippi flyway.[71] Yet these preservationists recognized the larger goal of saving the river's habitat and willingly joined Dilg and others who had a different agenda. Pulling together these diverse groups of conservationists, Dilg succeeded where other conservationists had failed.[72]

Some refuge boosters questioned the Progressive, multiple-use approach. The river, they claimed, demanded higher commercial and noncommercial purposes. They denounced using the river as a sewer, challenged reclamation, and criticized channel constriction and overuse. In a short time, they would confront a new, major navigation project.

How faithfully and how far conservationists, especially those along the upper Mississippi River, had come toward a new vision for the river would soon be revealed. Despite the apparent conflict between the refuge and channel constriction, the War Department did not oppose the refuge. Rather, the secretary of war placed an amendment in the bill stipulating that the refuge would not eliminate "any portion of the Mississippi River from provisions of federal law for the improvement, preservation, and protection of navigable waters...."[73] The Corps would soon implement this provision. A new navigation improvement movement was getting under way just as Congress established the refuge. The new movement would far exceed any previous navigation improvement effort on the upper river.

Dilg and the Izaak Walton League had accomplished a remarkable feat. Their success has defined the upper Mississippi River's landscape and ecology. By establishing the refuge, they removed much of the floodplain above Rock Island from drainage and levee construction. While refuge advocates thought reclamation worthless, many floodplain farmers did not. Below Rock Island, they continued forming levee districts, building and raising levees, and draining the land. Below Rock Island, floodplain farmers would successfully lobby for federal help for decades to come. They would continue removing more floodplain from the river. Above Rock Island, the refuge prevented this. The upper river's landscape today above and below Rock Island is defined by this difference. Many ecosystem issues facing the upper river today are defined by it. How the new navigation project would reshape the river above and below Rock Island would be defined by it. The fact that refuge proponents had successfully offered a different vision represented a landmark change. No longer could navigation boosters assume their dreams were the only dreams for the river and the region. Future navigation improvement efforts would take place in a very different context.

CHAPTER 8

A Marooned Interior

Conservationists won a piece of the Upper Mississippi River valley as navigation seemed to be fading away for good. Soon, it appeared, conservationists would have the river to themselves. By 1918 no through commerce moved on the upper river; no packets or raftboats made the trip from St. Louis to St. Paul. Nearly every city on the upper river had abandoned its riverfront, and few had facilities for loading and unloading barges. But in 1924, the same year Congress authorized the Upper Mississippi Wildlife and Fish Refuge, a new navigation movement began to stir. The movement would exceed any previous movement in economic and political strength. It would result in a new approach to restoring commerce to the river, an approach that today defines the upper river's landscape and ecosystems.[1]

By the mid-1920s, many midwestern business interests and farmers believed that the Midwest faced a transportation crisis. As the region's need for a multifaceted bulk transportation system had grown, its shipping options had declined. The crisis had been building for forty years. Its origins lay in channel constriction's failure to make the upper Mississippi River a competitive transportation route. Other factors contributed. More railroad car shortages, the Panama Canal's opening, and an Interstate Commerce Commission decision that declared the Midwest landlocked erected what Midwesterners called an "economic barrier" around their region.

The UMRIA's Final Efforts

The UMRIA's struggle did not end with the 6-foot channel's authorization. The association planned to complete the project in ten years and needed to convince shippers to use the river. Hoping to keep its momentum, the UMRIA sent a delegation to Washington in 1908 to lobby for full and immediate funding. But the economy had turned down in 1907, and Congress did not pass a Rivers and Harbors bill in 1908. On January 13, 1909, the UMRIA persuaded Representative James A. Tawney, chairman of the House Committee on Appropriations, to introduce a bill to get the 6-foot channel completed within ten years. Tawney, a Republican from Winona, had represented the state's first district in southeastern Minnesota since 1892. Congress did not act on the bill, but the UMRIA persisted, and on December 14, 1909, Tawney submitted his bill again.[2]

The UMRIA sent a committee to Washington, D.C., to work with Tawney. While there, the committee attended the Rivers and Harbors Congress meeting. The organization's strength had continued to grow following the 6-foot channel's authorization in 1907. In presenting the Rivers and Harbors bill to the U.S. Congress, Representative D. S. Alexander of New York, chair of the Rivers and Harbors Committee, noted that during the previous three to four years, Washington had "witnessed the presence of a great river and harbor congress, representing the friends of river and harbor improvements from nearly every state in the Union." The organization, he added, had "had a decided leavening effect" on the Rivers and Harbors Committee.[3] Benefiting from this "leavening effect," Tawney's bill passed with the Rivers and Harbors Act of 1910, and Congress appropriated $1 million for the project. By this point, the completion date for the 6-foot channel had been extended from ten to twelve years.[4]

Passage of the act did not guarantee that Congress would appropriate all the funding needed to build the project. The association had to persuade Congress to continue its support. This would become harder and harder, unless traffic increased. The UMRIA had hoped that as the Corps began deepening the river to 6 feet at low water, commerce would return, and Congress would keep supporting the project.[5]

At their 1910 convention the UMRIA's stalwarts made clear the relationship between restoring traffic to the river and funding from Congress. Former Minnesota Governor Samuel Van Sant knew how reluctant Congress had become to support navigation improvements on the upper river. When Van Sant appeared before Congress to request money, Congress wanted to know why it should fund the project when so little traffic used the river. W. A. Meese, chair of the resolutions committee, reported that the region's representatives in Washington had always asked him and the rest of the committee to show that shippers employed the river. When they could do this, the representatives told them, they would get more funding. Captain Alonzo Bryson put it more bluntly. He complained in 1910 that only three through packets and several short packets operated on the upper river. "I warn you," he declared,

> that if this river is only going to be used by the above transportation and a fleet of pleasure, motor and house boats, and no effort made by those interested to put on the bosom of this beautiful river modern means of transportation, that we will never see the fruition of our hopes in a six-foot channel, because, the government will withhold the appropriations until some show of interest and results are shown by the people of the Mississippi Valley.[6]

In response, delegates at the 1910 convention passed a resolution urging cities to encourage shippers to use the river, no matter what size the cargo.[7]

To demonstrate its sincerity to Congress and to encourage river traffic, the UMRIA resolved to make the improvement of river terminals and waterfronts a principal focus. No aspect of its effort reveals how greatly cities had abandoned navigation and how far the UMRIA had to go to restore commerce. At the 1910 convention, the association began its push. They wanted cities to clean up their riverfronts, provide adequate storage facilities, build modern terminals, with loading and unloading equipment, and connect these to railroads. President Wilkinson lectured the association that "the river fronts should be made the most attractive part of every community, and not, as now in many places, a dumping ground and storage place for old junk and local crafts, . . ."[8] Beautifying the riverfronts alone, however, would not bring commerce back.

To gauge the extent of the task before it, the UMRIA asked each city to report on its wharves during the 1911 convention. Only St. Paul, Rock Island, and St. Louis had facilities that could begin to meet modern shipping demands. Alton's representative, confirming Wilkinson's description of what riverfronts had become, reported: "If the average man has any junk that he is not in particular need for, he dumps it on the levee."[9] Some cities had been improving their riverfronts, but for parks rather than for terminal facilities. As the roll call proceeded, it became increasingly clear that most river towns had turned away from navigation and the river.[10]

Some cities reported that they had kept control of their riverfronts and could develop them, but they had no reason to. The La Crosse delegate announced that his city planned to build wharves and docks, adding, "That would be a great thing if we had the boats to land there." The Burlington representative admitted that his city's levee had deteriorated but said it did not matter. Shippers, he confessed, had little reason to use the levee, because they "all enjoy side-track facilities and it is rather a hard matter for them to haul their freight from the levee on account of the extra work in handling and hauling from the levee." Wabasha had no docks or landings and little terminal equipment. Draymen had to move cargoes to and from the boats, its representative complained. Galena's delegate noted that his city had enough riverfront and a levee, but it lacked machinery for loading and unloading. This did not matter, however, since no traffic demanded such facilities. Muscatine, too, still owned some of its riverfront and hoped to develop terminal facilities. But, its representative said, summarizing what many other cities were experiencing, "It is pretty hard to get any one interested in the river at that place." Fort Madison, one of the few cities still receiving lumber rafts in 1911, presented a telling report. While the city hoped to develop modern terminal facilities, it did not have them at the time. Despite its success as a milling center, Fort Madison had abandoned its terminal facilities for other types of river traffic.[11]

Major Charles Keller, the Rock Island District commander, learned firsthand how poor river terminals had become. In 1910 he traveled on the river from Rock Island to St. Paul to attend the UMRIA convention. Getting supplies from the towns at which he stopped proved more challenging than the river. "Unless supplies are forthcoming with more promptness and in larger quantities than we find them today," he warned, "terminals and deep water will not do much for steamboats."[12]

Even their old nemesis James J. Hill chided river cities for the state of their terminals. At the 1911 convention, Wilkinson read part of a paper Hill presented at a National Millers' Association meeting in Minneapolis. Hill had criticized river cities for their poor terminal facilities and had berated river ports for using manual labor to move freight to and from the levees. "It is a deplorable fact," he charged, "that in no branch of commercial activity, has there been so great a lack of development and progress, as in river transportation and river terminals. The whole system stands today just about where it stood fifty years ago."[13] Wilkinson quoted Hill because he knew how right the railroad magnate was.

In 1911 Keller reported that the Rock Island District had undertaken a study of terminals at Wilkinson's request. Keller met with an eastern engineer in St. Louis on the subject just before coming to the convention and promised the UMRIA a report on waterway terminals worldwide. Despite the UMRIA's studies and exhortations, few cities made progress. In 1917 Wilkinson still pleaded for modern terminals.[14]

The Final Fall of Commerce

The 6-foot channel could not proceed fast enough, either for the UMRIA or to bring commerce back to the river. Timber continued its plummet due to the unrelenting devastation of the region's forests. From the twenty raftboats plying the river on the eve of the 6-foot channel project, the number had fallen to four by 1912. By 1913 only one sawmill remained to serve the river trade, the one at Fort Madison. In

Table 3. Average Miles: Upper Mississippi River, 1903–15

	Logs		
Date	Tons	Ton miles	Average haul (mi)
1903	3,110,271	808,670,460	260
1904	2,833,405	796,685,300	281
1905	2,683,517	697,714,420	260
1906	2,525,390	636,601,400	252
1907	1,928,133	481,433,250	250
1908	721,659	180,414,750	250
1909	389,430	97,357,500	250
1910	231,849	80,936,152	349
1911	294,801	117,920,400	400
1912	82,476	37,214,964	451
1913	64,489	30,245,340	469
1914	nd	nd	nd
1915	nd	nd	nd

	Rafted lumber, etc.		
Date	Tons	Ton miles	Average haul (mi)
1903	363,458	145,989,957	402
1904	267,736	110,063,790	411
1905	105,298	41,294,704	392
1906	104,751	39,866,185	381
1907	74,928	30,137,625	402
1908	40,473	16,028,375	396
1909	29,621	10,230,710	345
1910	15,348	5,540,740	361
1911	26,109	9,967,260	382
1912	10,918	3,718,643	341
1913	13,570	4,400,147	324
1914	13,211	4,482,868	339
1915	7,612	3,434,700	451

Miscellaneous freight			
Date	Tons	Ton miles	Average haul (mi)
1903	825,375	22,478,556	27
1904	1,144,932	33,538,789	29
1905	989,792	23,443,102	24
1906	1,001,867	20,072,604	20
1907	1,519,581	19,021,959	13
1908	1,437,205	28,656,909	20
1909	1,278,429	21,277,535	17
1910	1,313,146	16,992,543	13
1911	1,156,762	16,420,151	14
1912	1,265,589	13,469,619	11
1913	1,294,864	12,229,310	9
1914	1,132,574	15,472,577	14
1915	1,247,981	23,535,175	19

Government materials			
Date	Tons	Ton miles	Average haul (mi)
1903	246,025	2,812,928	11
1904	288,466	3,663,572	13
1905	261,889	2,567,010	10
1906	215,311	1,491,652	7
1907	396,798	2,306,388	6
1908	382,520	2,661,321	7
1909	218,634	2,424,876	11
1910	275,692	2,569,825	9
1911	603,894	4,844,015	8
1912	471,311	3,506,680	7
1913	772,392	9,445,576	12
1914	281,185	2,115,662	8
1915	628,075	6,590,415	10

Source: *Annual Reports,* 1904–16.

Table 4. Classified Freight Traffic, Upper Mississippi River, 1910–25 (in tons)

Date	Flour	Corn	Wheat	Oats	Coal	Lumber	Gravel	Rock	Sand	Misc.	Freight	Gross
1910	nd	1,504	4,341	22	18,315	71,742	305,209	248,151	379,952	344,292	1,313,146	1,836,035
1911	473	9,284	1,646	20	20,091	41,488	122,204	552,996	175,559	270,393	1,156,762	2,081,566
1912	nd	3,595	221	38	20,868	23,156	200,830	418,710	511,324	118,567	1,265,589	1,830,294
1913	nd	3,463	382	55	26,236	31,491	398,179	708,066	562,040	71,042	1,294,864	2,145,315
1914	nd	4,797	1,936	959	18,678	30,855	178,017	261,805	599,558	77,615	1,132,574	1,426,970
1915	nd	3,633	2,573	421	27,803	20,571	471,070	407,051	430,391	209,052	729,723	1,883,668
1916	nd	3,409	2,685	1,364	31,207	10,967	217,040	303,440	462,871	272,245	499,531	499,531
1917	nd	342	730	14	24,089	2,085	187,903	24,026	178,827	83,266	586,420	586,420
1918	nd	962	3,710	75	18,735	2,155	nd	nd	nd	72,925	696,503	696,503
1919	196	566	6,017	443	12,503	2,162	225,867	33,704	279,386	20,276	674,192	674,192
1920	291	610	2,507	188	10,882	5,865	211,193	56,046	212,270	12,749	630,951	630,951
1921	74	812	3,251	191	17,535	1,192	334,042	43,940	289,515	2,801	761,522	761,522
1922	321	412	5,078	51	11,530	1,911	259,738	70,188	356,252	10,507	818,509	818,509
1923	477	1,810	5,530	42	10,642	3,113	421,239	88,383	305,036	10,738	973,567	973,567
1924	547	605	1,181	nd	14,488	12,345	396,067	15,706	181,396	nd	769,139	769,139
1925	331	1,111	1,313	36	5,885	2,891	312,163	9,119	492,550	nd	908,005	908,005

Source: Annual Reports, 1911–26.

1915 the *Ottumwa Belle* guided the last lumber raft down the St. Croix and Mississippi Rivers from Hudson, Wisconsin, to Fort Madison. From 1903 to 1915, the quantity of logs and lumber rafted on the river dropped from 3,473,729 tons to 7,612 tons. While barges carried logs and lumber after 1915, the tonnage moved was small. But as Lewis B. Boswell had stressed, the 6-foot channel was not intended for timber.[15]

Other river freight either fell or failed to increase, however. From the 4.5 million tons recorded in 1903, gross tonnage dropped during the next twelve years to 1.9 million tons. (Remember, at this time, the Corps recorded gross tonnage as all commerce, including strictly local or ferried commerce and government materials—materials used in building wing dams and shore protection. Freight tonnage excluded these.) The figures for freight tonnage remained steady. Other than the 825,375 tons recorded for 1903, the figures for the period 1903 to 1915 varied between 1 million and just over 1.5 million tons. Despite work on the 6-foot channel, freight traffic did not grow.[16]

The Corps introduced another method of keeping commercial statistics in 1916. The new method excluded strictly local traffic and government materials from the gross tonnage figures. As a result, the gross tonnage dropped from the 1.9 million tons recorded in 1915 to 0.5 million tons in 1916. Overall, between 1916 and 1934, river commerce figures remained steady. This was largely because the lumber industry had bottomed out and did not continue to carry gross tonnage down with it. As in previous periods, however, freight tonnage failed to increase. Except for 1928, freight tonnage figures remained below 1 million tons annually until 1934. As the lumber industry declined and other commercial interests failed to take its place, transportation on the river stagnated.[17]

Beginning in 1910 the Corps published a "Classified Freight Statement." This statement itemized products shipped on the river, and it reveals the extent of commercial stagnation. Rock, sand, and gravel surpassed other commodities in gross tonnage carried on the river from 1910 through 1925 and did little to add new life to river commerce. In the first classified freight statement, these commodities accounted for

Table 5. Key commodities, 1910–1925

		Coal	
Date	Valuation	Tons	Value per ton
1910	65,221	18,315	3.56
1911	68,843	20,091	3.43
1912	59,607	20,868	2.86
1913	90,400	26,236	3.45
1914	62,271	18,678	3.33
1915	90,283	27,803	3.25
1916	127,637	31,207	4.09
1917	102,942	24,089	4.27
1918	83,588	18,735	4.46
1919	70,143	12,503	5.61
1920	67,699	10,882	6.22
1921	102,632	17,535	5.85
1922	79,436	11,530	6.89
1923	46,616	10,638	4.38
1924	90,387	14,488	6.24
1925	49,055	5,885	8.34

		Corn	
Date	Valuation	Tons	Value per ton
1910	20,935	1,504	13.92
1911	163,395	9,284	17.6
1912	59,215	3,595	16.47
1913	77,431	3,463	22.36
1914	113,070	4,797	23.57
1915	70,325	3,633	19.36
1916	109,764	3,409	32.2
1917	11,447	342	33.47
1918	36,617	962	38.06
1919	28,447	566	50.26
1920	16,723	610	27.41
1921	10,202	738	13.82
1922	6,670	412	16.19
1923	20,485	1,810	11.32
1924	12,282	605	20.3
1925	19,155	1,111	17.24

	Logs		
Date	Valuation	Tons	Value per ton
1910	1,420,952	267,379	5.31
1911	2,341,065	329,906	7.1
1912	550,831	118,101	4.66
1913	463,631	98,268	4.72
1914	64,296	8,853	7.26
1915	56,458	9,820	5.75
1916	196,171	35,493	5.53
1917	119,629	18,441	6.49
1918	117,059	18,508	6.32
1919	106,400	14,198	7.49
1920	162,024	24,811	6.53
1921	112,180	19,647	5.71
1922	364,560	16,826	21.67
1923	1,313,209	37,130	35.37
1924	5,314,968	73,819	72
1925	531,194	9,612	55.26

	Lumber		
Date	Valuation	Tons	Value per ton
1910	434,430	70,425	6
1911	603,017	39,109	15
1912	340,650	22,703	15
1913	467,775	30,408	15
1914	419,625	28,247	15
1915	224,590	18,624	12
1916	198,675	10,868	18
1917	46,986	2,059	23
1918	45,652	2,155	21
1919	66,348	2,027	33
1920	163,159	5,831	28
1921	71,420	1,583	45
1922	71,307	1,909	37
1923	34,350	1,793	19
1924	740,700	12,345	60
1925	158,990	2,891	55

	Oats		
Date	Valuation	Tons	Value per ton
1910	1,031	22	46.86
1911	840	20	42
1912	1,780	38	46.84
1913	1,775	55	32.27
1914	85,490	959	89.14
1915	11,421	421	27.13
1916	50,261	1,364	36.85
1917	516	14	36.86
1918	2,999	75	39.99
1919	24,954	443	56.33
1920	7,102	188	37.78
1921	5,449	191	28.53
1922	1,420	51	27.84
1923	1,100	42	26.19
1924	nd	nd	nd
1925	900	36	25

	Wheat		
Date	Valuation	Tons	Value per ton
1910	125,987	4,341	29.02
1911	46,543	1,646	28.28
1912	7,300	221	33.03
1913	12,347	382	32.32
1914	65,272	1,936	33.71
1915	98,148	2,573	38.15
1916	169,221	2,685	63.02
1917	50,068	730	68.59
1918	251,470	3,710	67.78
1919	529,832	6,017	88.06
1920	146,280	2,507	58.35
1921	113,030	3,251	34.77
1922	169,362	5,078	33.35
1923	184,322	5,530	33.33
1924	40,196	1,181	34.04
1925	54,620	1,313	41.6

Source: *Annual Reports*, 1911–26.

over 50 percent of the gross tonnage, and 71 percent of the freight tonnage. For the next fifteen years, they comprised between 60 and 90 percent of all tonnage. Hoping for something to replace timber, the Corps argued that rock, sand, and gravel were important to river traffic and that their value would continue to increase.[18]

Rock, sand, and gravel could not revive river traffic. Their weaknesses lay in their low value and the short distances barges moved them. While they comprised from 60 to 90 percent of the freight tonnage, they generally accounted for less than 5 percent of the total value of products carried on the river, and barges hauled them an average of only 10 miles.[19]

Boswell and the UMRIA had hoped the 6-foot channel would attract grain, coal, and other more valuable commodities. Farmers did

Table 6. Average Ton-miles Transported by Commodity, Upper Mississippi River, 1910–25

Date	Corn	Wheat	Oats	Coal	Logs	Lumber	Total average
1910	2.8	36.7	1	8.9	305	109.3	57.7
1911	6.2	11.1	6.5	8.2	360.4	240.8	71.7
1912	2.3	8.6	2.3	12.9	322	167.4	31.6
1913	6.4	7.9	1	13.5	316.2	138	26.2
1914	4.7	2.5	1.4	11.8	22.5	160	15.5
1915	7	3.6	2.9	13.8	20	325.6	17.8
1916	2.8	31.9	1.4	18.5	29.2	7.7	14.3
1917	24	48.3	32.5	92.3	22.9	23.5	35.8
1918	11.7	55.8	23	140.9	33.1	32.6	59.6
1919	26.9	46.4	53.8	54.5	25.6	31.6	18.3
1920	52.3	82.5	84.9	13.2	40	22.2	20.8
1921	60.4	100	322.5	18	34.6	69.2	73.3
1922	28.8	60.8	62.5	37	59.9	74.9	31
1923	197.1	73.4	26.7	61.6	51.7	49.2	29.8
1924	25.7	42	nd	75.4	10.2	26.8	31.6
1925	58	60	100	18.4	68.3	96.8	72.5

Source: Annual Reports, 1911–26.

ship corn, wheat, and oats on the river, and these crops counted among its most valuable commodities. Between 1910 and 1925, the average value per ton of corn was $21.07; of wheat, $47.89; and of oats, $50.28. But agricultural interests used the river sparingly. Between 1910 and 1925 these crops comprised less than 1 percent of either the gross or the freight tonnage and rarely moved more than 75 miles between ports. Railroads still made the long hauls.

Coal consistently ranked among the leading commodities shipped on the river. From 1910 to 1918 tows moved from 18 to 31 thousand tons of coal annually. But after 1918, the tonnage fell, and over the next five years coal interests shipped only from 10 to 20 thousand tons annually (Table 4). If the initial tonnage figures for coal had encouraged river boosters, the ton-mileage data must have dismayed them. Except for 1918, when barges carried coal an average of 141 miles, they rarely averaged more than 60 miles between 1910 and 1925.[20]

Spurred by high rail costs, some companies turned to the Corps to help them demonstrate the value of shipping on the river. In 1917, in what the Corps called a "new departure in long-distance traffic," private investors used barges from the federal government to ship their products.[21] The John Deere Company of Moline, Illinois, sent 360 tons of plows on four government barges from Moline to Minneapolis. With adequate terminal facilities, the company's transportation manager believed that he could save at least 40 percent on shipping costs. In 1917 other tows carried 2,118 tons of coal from St. Louis to St. Paul. And tows moving downstream pushed 3,030 tons of iron ore from St. Paul to St. Louis. While admitting that some of these efforts had failed financially, the Corps said that they "demonstrated that with suitable towboats, barges, and terminals and proper management, certain coarse freight could be carried at a cost much less than the railroad tariff."[22] Despite these demonstrations, boosters failed to reinvigorate river traffic. In 1918 no packetboats or barges carried freight between St. Paul and St. Louis. All the traffic was local, and local traffic could not justify navigation improvements for the upper Mississippi over its entire length.

Railroad Car Shortages

As the steamboat trade waned, Midwesterners relied almost exclusively on railroads. A number of railroad car shortages in the early twentieth century demonstrated the region's growing dependence on railroads. The shortages caused acute, short-term transportation crises. To some Midwesterners, "it looked as though the demands for transportation had permanently outrun the capacity of the railroads to satisfy them. . . ."[23] The first shortage, from 1906 to 1907, had helped spur the 6-foot channel's authorization. The second occurred during World War I. As the nation shifted cars to the war effort, railroads had fewer cars for commercial shipping. Transportation analyst William H. Clark defended the railroads. He contended that a lack of ocean-going freighters left loaded cars sitting idly in rail yards. Whatever its cause, the shortage was real. As it had after the earlier shortage, the government established a task force to study the use of inland waterways. Called the Committee on Inland Transportation and chaired by the Chief of Engineers, the task force examined how water transportation could relieve railroads. But the car shortage ended with the war, and while the war revived river transportation on the lower Mississippi River, interest on the upper river waned.[24]

In 1921 another railroad car shortage crippled the Midwest. This shortage occurred, according to C. H. Markham, president of the Illinois Central Railroad, just as the United States economy began rebounding. And, he admitted, demand outpaced the ability of railroads to carry all the commerce offered to them, which threatened to stifle the recovery. This situation was not new. Each time it had occurred, he said, it had cost the United States greatly, and each shortage had occurred at a business peak and had been remedied by a period of depression that "lulled the country into forgetfulness."[25]

Except for unusual circumstances, railroads appeared capable of handling the freight offered to them. Nevertheless, the shortages caused short-term crises that crippled the Midwest and awakened Midwesterners to their dependency on a single transportation mode and to the vulnerable position that that placed them in. Each crisis reminded

Midwesterners that the upper Mississippi River had once been an important commercial artery and made them wonder why it had failed and if it could be restored.[26]

The Panama Canal

For many Midwesterners, the Panama Canal's opening in 1914 became the event that aroused their interest in navigation improvement. Six-foot channel boosters had looked forward to the canal's opening, but now they feared it would siphon from them the prosperity it was supposed to bring. The canal's opening changed the nature of the Midwest's transportation problem. Even if railroads had been able to meet midwestern demands at reasonable rates, the region still had to compete against businesses that enjoyed ready access to the Panama Canal. While the railroad car shortages hurt the Midwest, they occurred infrequently. The canal created a problem that promised to grow steadily worse.[27]

Herbert Hoover and other proponents of navigation improvement defined the problem by saying that economically the Panama Canal placed the East and West Coasts closer to each other while moving the Midwest farther away from both coasts. It became cheaper to ship goods from New York to San Francisco through the Panama Canal than to ship the same goods from the Midwest to San Francisco by rail. These rate changes, Midwesterners complained, formed an economic barrier around the Midwest, ruined its markets on both coasts, discouraged businesses and industries from locating in the Midwest, and caused other businesses and industries to move away.[28]

Midwesterners often repeated Hoover's argument, adding that their taxes had helped build the canal. Why, they asked, should they suffer from its operation? The federal government, they argued, should improve the upper Mississippi River for navigation so that the Midwest could take advantage of the canal. In addition, they protested, the canal placed other agricultural producers closer to major markets on the coasts, in South America, and in Europe. With the end of World War I, European markets for agricultural products declined. This stemmed from the return of European domestic production and from strong nationalistic trade barriers. Nevertheless, Midwesterners asserted, if the United States hoped to develop new markets in South America and the Orient, it would have to provide Midwest farmers with access to New Orleans and the Panama Canal.[29] But as a decade passed, the crisis deepened, and navigation on the upper Mississippi River continued to fade.

The Indiana Rate Case

The transportation crisis climaxed with the Interstate Commerce Commission's (I.C.C.) decision in the Indiana Rate Case of 1922 and the subsequent decisions that upheld it. On October 22, 1921, the Public Service Commission of Indiana and others challenged the railroad rate structure in the Midwest. For unfair reasons, the Indiana Commission argued, railroads operating out of Illinois and cities along the west bank of the Mississippi River in Missouri and Iowa could charge lower rates than railroads operating out of Indiana. These railroads charged lower rates because in a 1909 decision the I.C.C. found that these railroads faced competition from the Mississippi. In the Indiana Rate Case, the I.C.C. reversed this decision because, it stated, "Water competition on the Mississippi River north of St. Louis is no longer recognized as a controlling force but is little more than potential."[30] Consequently, the I.C.C. ordered, on February 14, 1922, that "the defendants will be expected to establish rates and exceptions to the official in conformity with the conclusions above stated, on or before July 1, 1922."[31] In other words, the I.C.C. directed railroads in the Midwest to raise their rates dramatically. Appeals by the defendants and waterway advocates delayed the decision's implementation until June 1, 1925.

The Indiana Rate Case officially declared what had been evident to many for decades: the upper Mississippi River was no longer a viable shipping route. The decision genuinely frightened midwestern business and farm interests. The Midwest's development, they believed, had been premised on cheap transportation rates—either with the river as the primary means of transportation or as a regulator of railroad rates. Without the river to restrain railroad charges, they believed their region could not compete in national or international markets. For this reason, they argued, the Midwest would stagnate: its booming cities would become prairie towns, and its economy would never mature. To the region's merchants, it meant that competitors in Chicago and cities outside the Midwest could take away their trade territory. Despite over sixty years of work by the Corps to make the upper Mississippi River a highway to the world, the Indiana Rate Case decision pronounced the Midwest landlocked.

The Farm Crisis

An already bleak farm situation in the Midwest threatened to become worse with the Indiana Rate Case ruling. Most of the country suffered from a postwar depression that lasted from 1920 to 1922. While many segments of the economy began recovering in 1922 to enjoy the Roaring Twenties, the farm sector did not. Just when farmers needed to ship their crops to foreign and domestic markets cheaply, their transportation options declined and became more costly.

Farmers had prospered for the first two decades of the twentieth century.[32] While the rate of agricultural expansion slowed after 1900, the growing urban population demanded increasing quantities of agricultural produce, and with this increased demand, farmers received more for their crops. Farm prices rose over 89 percent from 1899 to 1910.[33] Whereas a bushel of wheat sold for 62 cents in 1900, it sold for $1.43 by 1916, and had jumped to $2.58 by 1920. Demand from European countries increased during World War I and continued for almost a year after the war ended, as Europe and Russia struggled to resume production and rebuild their transportation systems.[34] Because agricultural commodity prices increased faster than the cost of industrial goods, the purchasing power of farmers grew.[35] This prosperity explains why farmers felt no need to back the 6-foot channel project.

Prosperity turned to depression in 1920. During the summer, agricultural prices plummeted. From its $2.58 price per bushel in June of 1920, wheat fell to $1.43 per bushel by December 1, and by the next June prices had collapsed to $1.00 per bushel. Agricultural historian Gilbert C. Fite puts the falling prices in perspective. "Considering the farm price index in 1913 as equaling 100," he says, "by 1921 corn had dropped to 59, wheat to 78 and cotton to 48. The purchasing power of several basic farm products in 1921 was only 67 per cent of what it had been in 1913."[36] While farm commodity prices fell, production costs remained high, further reducing the purchasing power of farmers. High operating costs, heavy debt burdens, and low returns plagued farmers throughout the 1920s, leading to farm foreclosures and the flight of farmers to cities.[37]

Two interrelated factors caused the farm crisis: overproduction and the failure to capture foreign markets. Surplus production arose from a number of factors. One was that agricultural output grew faster than demand. Between 1913 and 1920 farmers expanded their gross production by 15 percent. Some of this growth resulted from the American farm effort to meet European demands during the war and the farmers' inability to adjust to the lower postwar demand. Between 1919 and 1929 farm production rose another 20 percent, though crop acreage had changed little and the population had increased only 16 percent.[38]

More efficient farm machinery and scientific farming methods accounted for much of the rise in American agricultural production, especially in the Great Plains states. Technological innovations reduced the human and animal labor needed to produce crops. From 1920 to 1929 the number of tractors used in farming rose from 246,083 to 852,989. New threshers and harvesting equipment made wheat and corn production more efficient. Scientific seed selection increased the durability of some crops, allowing farmers to grow them in previously unproductive lands and boosting the yield per acre.[39]

While American agricultural production soared, the nation's consumption lagged behind. In part this occurred because the use of agricultural products is inelastic. People can consume only so much wheat, corn, or beef, regardless of how low the price might be. Other factors curtailed American demand during the 1920s. Changes in dietary concerns, conservation measures encouraged during World War I, a decline in the birthrate, immigration restriction, and the change in the status of the United States from a debtor nation to a creditor nation also limited

American consumption. From 1922 to 1927 the per capita use of grain decreased by more than 20 percent, and the per capita consumption of corn fell by over 60 percent.[40]

The second key factor behind the agricultural depression was that foreign markets absorbed less as the American surplus increased. Foreign markets were critical because the quantity of agricultural products sold abroad determined the extent of overproduction and the domestic price of American farm products. Following World War I, however, the purchasing power of European nations declined. Some countries established tariffs and other barriers to American agricultural products. And after World War I, Americans faced growing competition from farmers in Canada, Australia, Argentina, and Brazil. American farmers could not compete well in foreign markets against these countries with their lower production and shipping costs. This was especially true for midwestern farmers after the Panama Canal opened. Farmers had some hope. The Far East, Japan, and China, in particular, represented a great new market that the Midwest hoped to enter. High transportation costs, however, threatened to keep them out.[41]

Farmers could not regulate their output, putting them at a disadvantage against other producers. Farmers could neither influence the price of their commodities by regulating output as industries could, nor bargain over the price they paid for industrial goods or the price they received at the market for their crop. Because of their individual character—each farm family acting as a single company—farmers did not successfully organize to regulate their production and had only limited success dealing with merchants who bought their products.[42]

Shortly after the Indiana Rate Case decision, two of the largest and one of the oldest manufacturing institutions in Minneapolis decided to leave the region.[43] Farmers, however, could not take their farms to other regions; they had to stay and solve their problems or go bankrupt trying. As one solution to their crisis, they would begin supporting efforts to revitalize navigation on the upper Mississippi River. They joined businesses throughout the river valley that wanted to or had to stay.

The Midwest's transportation crisis was born in the upper Mississippi River's failure to keep pace with modern transportation demands, exacerbated by periodic railroad car shortages, accelerated by the opening of the Panama Canal, and made intolerable by the Indiana Rate Case and the farm crisis. Together these events spurred the new push by Midwesterners for a viable navigation channel on the upper Mississippi River.

CHAPTER 9

Straining at the Chains

Midwesterners had reached a turning point by 1925. Would they give up on the river as a commercial highway, or would they fight to restore navigation? More than one critic of navigation improvements suggested the Corps should end its work, that any further efforts were misguided nostalgia. But many Midwesterners, especially farmers and business interests along the upper Mississippi River, feared railroads would soon monopolize bulk shipping. They still hoped to develop a diverse transportation system so they could compete successfully in domestic and foreign markets. They no longer trusted the Interstate Commerce Commission. With the commission's approval, railroads had steadily increased their rates since World War I. To many Midwesterners, the Indiana Rate Case confirmed their suspicion that railroads controlled the commission. Those Midwesterners still believed that the region's manifest destiny depended on restoring navigation. So they had to find a way to revitalize navigation and reverse the relentless decline in river commerce. They had to find a project that would entice shippers to use the upper Mississippi River, where no other project had. Where the UMRIA had failed, they would have to gain regional and national attention.

A growing discontent over transportation prices offered navigation boosters the opportunity to build a new movement. High shipping costs had hurt North Dakota, South Dakota, Nebraska, and Montana as well as those states located in the upper Mississippi River valley. Transportation rates in most of these areas would increase when the Indiana Rate Case decision took effect on June 1, 1925. Before navigation boosters could make the upper river a viable part of a diverse transportation system, however, someone or some group had to organize and focus the discontent. It would not be the UMRIA, for it disbanded after 1917.[1]

During the first weeks of 1925, the Minneapolis Real Estate Board seized this role, initiating a movement that spread quickly throughout the upper Mississippi River valley. The movement would draw support from the largest and smallest businesses in the valley, from nearly all its cities, from the Midwest's principal farm organizations, and from the major political parties, including Democratic and Republican presidents. Loyalty to the movement would lead some supporters to question their party loyalty. The movement's supporters would have to win over two important government agencies: the Army Corps of Engineers and the Inland Waterways Corporation (IWC). The Corps had become skeptical of the upper river's commercial potential. Also located in the War Department, the IWC possessed the means to jump-start navigation on the upper river, for it managed a government fleet of barges and tows on the lower Mississippi River.

Founded in 1887, the Minneapolis Real Estate Board recognized that property values depended on commercial and industrial growth. To assess the city's ability to attract new industries and retain those it had, the board studied the city's business environment during the early fall of 1924. "Like those industries who plan for twenty and twenty-five years ahead," the board's magazine, *The Realtor*, explained, "so Minneapolis must diagnose its merits, its present state of health and then with this knowledge Minneapolis can be sold to the industrial world."[2] High freight rates, the board suspected, threatened the city's economic health. The final report confirmed their suspicion. The realtors feared that if they did not solve this problem soon, the real estate market in the Twin Cities would collapse. They quickly decided that to lower transportation rates, they had to revive shipping on the upper Mississippi River.[3]

The realtors knew they had to get farmers, business leaders, and key politicians throughout the region to back their effort. So they began, during the first weeks of January 1925, by calling several meetings to assess how much support yet another effort to revive river commerce could muster. By mid-January over two hundred manufacturers and shippers voiced their interest in restoring navigation. From this group, the Real Estate Board created a fifty-member shippers committee to develop plans.[4]

Hoping to convince shippers and manufacturers that commercial boats could navigate the upper river, the Real Estate Board asked the River Transit Company to bring two barges to the Twin Cities. The company had quietly begun operating in 1922. While it claimed to operate on the whole upper river, it carried mostly local traffic between Winona and La Crosse. Transporting high-class package freight and charging 75 to 80 percent of rail rates, the line began earning a profit after several years. In 1925 the company shipped 4,000 tons of high-class freight but refused several thousand tons of bulk freight that it did not have the equipment to handle. With the River Transit Company's barges, the Real Estate Board planned to announce the return of commerce to the upper Mississippi River.

On May 4, 1925, the company sent a towboat and two barges to Minneapolis. The towboat and barges cruised upriver without event, despite the river being 5 feet below normal. One barge, loaded at Alton, Illinois, carried 3,500,000 rounds of sportsmen's ammunition from the Western Cartridge Company for delivery to the Hall Hardware Company, of Minneapolis. The other barge held 108 tons of farm machinery manufactured at the John Deere plant in Moline, Illinois, for the Deere-Webber Company, of Minneapolis. The barges returned downriver filled with road machinery manufactured by the Russell Grader Company, of Minneapolis, and Cream of Wheat. The barges also transported the first Fords manufactured at the company's new plant in St. Paul. Challenging the Indiana Rate Case decision, *The Realtor* proclaimed navigation possible and profitable and that Minneapolis stood as the head of navigation. The River Transit Company, however, did not possess the quantity or kind of tows and barges needed to reestablish large-scale bulk shipping. The new navigation boosters would have to build their own equipment or get it from somewhere else, and they would have to generate far more support for their cause than the UMRIA had for the 6-foot channel.[5]

To create enthusiasm, the Real Estate Board called prominent navigation boosters to Minneapolis. Halleck W. Seaman, one of these boosters, had been promoting transportation most of his life. A lawyer and civil engineer, Seaman presided over seven railroad companies by 1911. He was also vice president of the City National Bank of Clinton, Iowa. Most important to navigation boosters, Seaman supervised the newly created Upper Mississippi River division of the IWC. Unfortunately, the division had no equipment; still, the IWC had created a division for the upper river, and someone who cared about developing traffic oversaw it.[6]

The IWC managed the Federal Barge Line Service. Built to relieve railroads overburdened by the war effort in 1918, the barge fleet was placed by Congress under the Railroad Administration. The Federal Barge Line worked on the lower Mississippi River system and Warrior River system, the latter running from Birmingham to Mobile, Alabama. In 1920 Congress transferred the fleet's management to the Inland and Coastwise Waterways Service, putting it under the secretary of war's direction. Then, in 1924, Congress placed the barge fleet's twenty-five tows and sixty-nine barges under the IWC.[7]

Congress established the IWC for a variety of reasons. Since Congress had created the fleet, it had to do something with it. As railroads had destroyed waterway competition, Congress believed it could not give the line away or sell it to private investors. The railroad car shortages during World War I and in 1921 led many in Congress to question the railroads' ability to handle America's transportation needs, and convinced them that river transportation should be reevaluated. The barge fleet would let Congress determine whether waterway transport was feasible or profitable on important American rivers. Why, Congress wanted to know, had European countries been able to develop successful waterway systems? So Congress created the IWC as an experiment, hoping to promote, encourage, and develop private investment in river transportation.[8]

Seaman's concern for Iowa and his business operations in the region motivated his desire for improving navigation on the upper Mississippi River. In a *Waterways Journal* article titled "What's the Matter with Iowa?" Seaman blamed Chicago's "trade ambitions" and railroads for arresting Iowa's development. "With the Mississippi restored to its rightful function as a modernized carrier of commerce," Seaman contended, Iowa's river towns would begin booming. "Iowa can then boast of the big towns on the river," he predicted, but "now," he lamented, "she apologizes for them as the runts in the litter."[9]

Seaman recognized the need to secure popular support. On May 27 and 28, 1925, he addressed the fifty-member shippers committee and the Real Estate Board. "By persistent effort," he encouraged them, "we will put the whole Mississippi Valley into a good big blaze of enthusiasm for the return of river navigation on a large scale." The "ultimate growth and development of Minneapolis," he warned the shippers and realtors, "depended primarily upon the extent to which river facilities were developed."[10] Seaman did not mention that the UMRIA had failed to accomplish this.

Two prominent figures arrived in the Twin Cities in August to push for navigation improvements. Cornish Bailey, field representative for the still active National Rivers and Harbors Congress was one. Lachlan Macleay, secretary of the newly formed Mississippi Valley Association was the other. For the next several months both men joined the Real Estate Board and other Twin Cities organizations to help awaken interest in river commerce. Minneapolis should not forget, Bailey asserted, that the "supremacy in commerce is not merely coincident with, but is consequent upon, economy of transportation, and the cheapest of all transportation is water; . . ." He warned them that "it behooves the citizens of the Twin Cities to take up this matter of developing and using the upper Mississippi River, and consider it their most vital and important work; either this or make up your minds to consider your grain and milling industrial growth as a thing of the past."[11] He pointed out that while the Twin Cities had solved its production problem, it had failed to address distribution.[12]

As enthusiasm grew, the Real Estate Board and other navigation improvement advocates explored ways to restore navigation. Seaman offered one possibility. He suggested that the IWC extend its Federal Barge Line Service to the Twin Cities. While the IWC had created an upper river division, it had no equipment and no immediate plans to begin operating on the upper river. Yet the possibility that it might expand its service excited navigation boosters. This solution seemed wonderfully obvious and simple. The Federal Barge Line could restore commerce and do it at federal expense. Navigation supporters thought their effort fit the IWC's mission perfectly. Here was a chance to test a major branch of the nation's inland waterway system, and the 1924 act specifically allowed the Federal Barge Line Service to operate on the upper river. Since the War Department managed the IWC and the Corps, boosters assumed they could easily convince the IWC. Secretary of War Dwight F. Davis oversaw the corporation and delegated his duties to the chair of a six-person advisory board. The chair, Brigadier General T. Q. Ashburn, served as the corporation's president and principal administrative officer. Navigation boosters believed that if they could convince Ashburn and his advisory board that the upper Mississippi was navigable, then the secretary of war would extend service to the upper river.[13]

So the boosters invited Ashburn to the Twin Cities for a meeting in the summer of 1925. Ashburn knew his position well. He had been selected to head the Inland and Coastwise Waterways Service when Congress created it in 1920. In 1924, with the Inland Waterways Corporation Act, he became the IWC's president and chairman, and the army promoted him from colonel to brigadier general. Ashburn had prepared many of the recommendations on which Congress acted in creating and defining the IWC. While he governed the IWC with the advisory board, he dominated. A study of the corporation's history in 1935 revealed that the advisory board rarely challenged Ashburn, and its recommendations had "no chance of prevailing against the opposition of the Chairman-President and the Governor-Secretary of War." River boosters had to secure Ashburn's support.[14]

Ashburn arrived in the Twin Cities on August 22, 1925, to begin negotiating the extension of barge line service to the upper river. Ashburn suggested that the committee create a new subcommittee with seven to nine representatives. This subcommittee would develop detailed plans for restoring commercial navigation with the IWC. On August 24, following his suggestion, the shippers committee created the Upper Mississippi River Cities, Barge Line Committee, or River Cities Committee.[15]

Before the River Cities Committee could begin negotiating with the IWC, however, the committee had to convince the Corps that boosters seriously wanted to restore navigation. The Corps had grown skeptical, since so little commerce used the river. For decades boosters had been pleading for improvements, for decades they had promised navigation would come back, and for decades the Corps had poured federal dollars into making the river navigable. Yet, commerce had declined. Major General Harry Taylor, the Chief of Engineers, revealed the Corps' frustration to boosters in St. Paul shortly before Ashburn's arrival. When asked about the upper river's condition and whether traffic could be revived, Taylor responded that the river had sustained a 4½-foot channel or better throughout the year, despite a drought. He declared the river was more navigable in 1925 than it had been during the steamboat heyday. Nevertheless, he complained, little commerce moved on the river. The Corps, he chided them, "had developed a very nearly perfect channel" and was "rather dissatisfied" that the people of the region had failed to use it. He concluded that the Corps was wasting money on navigation improvements for the upper Mississippi River.[16]

On September 14, the River Cities Committee completed its plan for reviving river commerce and sent it to the IWC. In part, the plan called for building six barges and a towboat that could operate on a 4½-foot channel. A private corporation, named the Upper Mississippi Barge Line Company, would raise the necessary capital for the equipment and operate the fleet, with the guarantee that the IWC would someday purchase it.[17]

By October 1 the IWC responded with its own proposal, and Ashburn announced that he was coming to the Twin Cities on October 14 to present it. Soon, navigation boosters hoped, the Federal Barge Line's towboats and barges would be running on the upper river. Quickly, the River Cities Committee issued a public notice of the meeting. It called for representatives from "diversified businesses, especially jobbing and manufacturing interests," to attend the meeting. "The fact that the Interstate Commerce Commission have ruled that the Twin Cities are rated as prairie towns and not entitled to water and rail rates," the notice ended, "makes this a very important situation."[18]

The meeting disappointed navigation boosters. Ashburn informed them that the IWC would extend its service to the upper river only if it could win a legal fight that had tied up a fleet of four towboats and nineteen barges. Although built to relieve overburdened midwestern railroads during World War I, the fleet's draft had been too deep for the upper Mississippi River. After the war, retired Colonel Edward R. Goltra leased the fleet from the army, and the IWC wanted it back, claiming that Goltra had failed to comply with the terms of his lease. If the IWC succeeded, Ashburn promised the IWC would release equipment from other rivers for use on the upper Mississippi. Ashburn advised navigation advocates to secure private capital and get barges for the next season, in case the government did not resolve the Goltra conflict soon. He suggested that they buy the River Transit Company and more barges to establish a fleet large enough for regular shipping on the upper river. The IWC, he added, might be able to lease them one or two barges. "It is essential and extremely important," he stressed to them, "that a barge line be in operation by the next season in order to protect the upper Mississippi River cities and the Northwest from being classed as prairie towns in rate decision cases."[19] Ashburn could not free the Goltra fleet from its legal moorings, and the IWC refused to provide the upper river with barges or tows. Once again navigation boosters had to confront the burdens and risks of developing and financing a fleet by themselves.[20]

Despite this setback, the boosters could be optimistic. At the

October 14 meeting with Ashburn, the St. Paul District Engineer, Major Charles F. Williams, reported that only 39 miles of the 675 miles between St. Louis and Minneapolis had less than a 6-foot depth at low water. Nearly the entire channel had a depth of at least 4 feet, he claimed. In short, he had declared the channel navigable and opened the way for the IWC to extend barge line service. Navigation backers could be optimistic also because their movement had grown dramatically, and they had secured the support of Minnesota's leading politicians. At the October 14 meeting, Governor Theodore Christianson, Senator Henrik Shipstead, and Representative Walter Newton had pledged their support for navigation improvement.

Before winning the governorship in 1924, Christianson, a lawyer, had been editor of the *Dawson Sentinel*, a rural Minnesota newspaper. He entered politics as a liberal Republican, supporting Wisconsin's radical Republican Senator Robert M. La Follette. While Christianson had become more moderate, his agrarian background influenced his decisions. His two principal goals as governor were to reduce taxes and limit government spending. He adhered to these goals so strictly that some opponents accused him of ignoring basic human needs. Yet Christianson recognized the benefits to agriculture and industry that a navigable river could bring. Considering "the fact that there was no single factor as important in the development of the entire Northwest," he pledged to do whatever he could to acquire the $10 million needed to complete the 6-foot channel and restore navigation.[21]

Senator Shipstead shared Christianson's rural heritage and concern for farmers, but he represented Minnesota's Farmer-Labor Party (which did not join the Democratic Party until 1944). A dentist and once mayor of Glenwood, in western Minnesota, Shipstead grew up steeped in Populist distrust for railroad companies and eastern businesses. Backed by the Nonpartisan League, a liberal farm organization that accounted for the Farmer portion of the Farmer-Labor party, Shipstead won election to the U.S. Senate in 1922, 1928, and 1934. At the October 14 meeting with Ashburn, he told boosters he was pleased that the Midwest had awakened to the transportation crisis, and that he would do whatever he could to help. Shipstead would become the navigation boosters' champion in the Senate.[22]

Walter H. Newton, a Republican, represented Minnesota's fifth district in Congress from 1919 to 1929 and would serve as President Herbert Hoover's personal secretary from 1929 to 1933. Newton became the president's primary liaison with the upper Mississippi River navigation boosters. At the October 14 meeting, Newton reminded boosters that he had consistently backed navigation improvement for the upper river and would continue to do so. While Newton supported river commerce, he stood by the administration's position, a position that navigation proponents would increasingly renounce.[23]

While Twin Cities business leaders still dominated the movement, other cities and businesses were becoming more active. The movement's leaders recognized the need to geographically broaden their effort. The River Cities Committee represented the growing base of support. Half the committee's ten members came from the Twin Cities. Samuel S. Thorpe, a leading Minneapolis realtor and member of the Real Estate Board, became the committee's chair. Edgar J. Ellertson represented the Russell Grader Company, a manufacturer of roadway equipment. William Hamm, the son of brewer Theodore Hamm, was president of a real estate company. Richmond P. Warner was vice president of Griggs, Cooper & Company of St. Paul, a wholesale grocery company. And Willard W. Morse of Minneapolis was president of the Security Warehouse, the city's first commercial warehouse. The other five committee members came from other cities in the upper Mississippi River valley and, like their fellow members from the Twin Cities, represented a wide variety of businesses. A. W. Chittenden, of the Chittenden and Eastman Company, a furniture manufacturer, came from Burlington, Iowa. A. R. Ebi was the John Deere Company's traffic expert, from Moline, Illinois. P. S. Fawkes came from Dubuque, Iowa, and represented the H. B. Glover Company. L. E. Luth, of Winona, Minnesota, represented the Traffic Bureau, Association of Commerce, Incorporated. Finally, F. W. Sisson was from La Crosse, Wisconsin, and co-owner of Sisson-Scielstad-Hougen Company. The variety of businesses represented showed the diversity of commercial interests supporting the movement and the movement's growing geographic base.[24]

When the Mississippi Valley Association held its first annual meeting in St. Louis, on November 23 and 24, 1925, cities from the upper river sent the largest delegation, with fifty-four delegates. The new association promoted inland waterways development in the entire Mississippi River basin. The upper river delegation had gone to the meeting, *The Waterways Journal* reported, to demonstrate that the region "was fully awake to the importance of river navigation" and to gain support from the Mississippi Valley Association.[25]

The number and prominence of businessmen and politicians who traveled to St. Louis demonstrated just how awake the upper Mississippi Valley had become. While Governor Christianson, Mayor George C. Leach, and St. Paul Mayor Arthur Nelson led the delegation, representatives from Cedar Rapids, Clinton, Davenport, and Dubuque, Iowa; Moline, Rock Island, and Quincy, Illinois; and La Crosse, Wisconsin, including the city's mayor, attended the meeting. The Twin Cities still dominated the organization, with fifteen delegates from Minneapolis and nine from St. Paul. Minnesota's remaining delegates came from Stillwater and Winona. The delegates from Minneapolis and St. Paul included representatives from the Rotary Club, the Minnesota Sugar Company, the investment firm of Lane, Piper and Jaffray, the Kiwanis Club, the Crail Coal Company, the Builder's Exchange, the Marquette National Bank, the city councils, the Federal Land Bank, the Waldorf Paper Products Company, and the North West Fuel Company. Between June and November 1925, the movement to restore commerce on the upper Mississippi River began gaining regional significance and continued attracting a wide range of businesses.[26]

On the first day of the Mississippi Valley Association conference, delegates to the convention initiated their plan to renew commercial navigation by incorporating the Upper Mississippi Barge Line Company and electing Samuel Thorpe chairman. Thorpe had been serving as chair of the River Cities Committee. He represented one of the Twin Cities' oldest real estate firms, serving as the board's seventh president from 1904 to 1905. In 1908, he helped found the National Real Estate Association, becoming its third president in 1911. Early on, Thorpe recognized the implications of the Midwest's transportation crisis for the real estate business and for the region's general economic prosperity.[27]

Following the conference, twenty delegates stayed in St. Louis to meet with the IWC's board of advisors and implement the next phase of their plan. Rather than wait for the Goltra fleet, they hoped to convince the IWC to lease the equipment that the Upper Mississippi Barge Line Company planned to build. Although the advisory board questioned whether the IWC could agree, it promised to lease the equipment, if legal and if Ashburn and Secretary Davis consented. The River Cities Committee wanted to lease its equipment to the IWC for several reasons. They believed that the IWC had the organization and experience to make the barge line succeed. As a branch of the federal government, the IWC, they thought, could convince railroads to accept joint rates more easily than a private company. And as the secretary of war commanded both the IWC and the Corps, boosters assumed he would want the agencies to work together to make commercial navigation succeed. Encouraged by the St. Louis meeting, representatives of the Upper Mississippi Barge Line Company headed to Washington. Legal problems still threatened to obstruct an accord, however. Barge Line Committee representatives had not convinced Ashburn that the IWC had the authority to lease equipment from the Barge Line Company until the army had resolved the Goltra fleet issue.[28]

On December 1, Arne C. Wiprud, secretary and counsel for the Barge Line Company, met with Ashburn and the advisory board and argued that the IWC had failed to fulfill its responsibility to operate on the upper Mississippi River. Wiprud had been an attorney for Lane, Piper and Jaffray, a Twin Cities investment firm. While at the Mississippi Valley Association meeting in November, he read the Inland Waterways Corporation Act and determined that no provision of the act required the corporation to wait until the Goltra fleet issue had been settled before extending service to the upper river. Wiprud's insights so impressed the fellow boosters that they asked the investment firm if it would loan him to the navigation movement, to which the firm agreed. Wiprud did not, however, impress the advisory board enough to change its position, and on December 2, the board forwarded the matter to the IWC's general counsel for review. On December 15 the general counsel declared that the IWC did not have the legal authority to lease equipment from the Barge Line Company. Congressman Newton and George C. Lambert, a lawyer and member of the Barge Line Company, immediately filed a brief challenging the IWC.[29]

Lambert had been supporting waterway development for more than two decades, and the plight of farmers worried him. Early in the twentieth century, he recognized that the upper Mississippi valley was becoming landlocked, and lobbied for the 6-foot channel. In 1923 Lambert became the secretary-treasurer and general counsel of the Minnesota Farmers Union, which had taken over the Equity Cooperative Exchange that year. Organized in 1908, the Equity's goal had been to secure better prices for farmers by establishing grain terminals, cutting out large grain elevators in Minneapolis and other cities. In 1916 the Equity built a grain terminal on the St. Paul riverfront that was "reputedly the first cooperative terminal grain marketing agency of account in the United States, . . ."[30] Lambert believed that the success of this terminal and the Farmers Union depended on river transportation. Therefore, he hoped to convince the IWC that it should operate on the upper river.[31]

Legal arguments, however, did not win the IWC's support. River boosters had to initiate an intense political campaign directed at Republican President Calvin Coolidge and several cabinet members. Coolidge had been Warren G. Harding's vice president, and when Harding died of a cerebral embolism on August 2, 1923, Coolidge became president. He then won the 1924 presidential election. Coolidge believed that the government should not interfere with business and sought to reduce taxes and cut government spending. Yet upper Mississippi River navigation boosters wanted Coolidge to expand federal involvement and expenditures on the river.[32]

Shortly after arriving in Washington, representatives of the Barge Line Company met with George Akerson, a correspondent for the

Minneapolis Tribune and a friend of Commerce Secretary Herbert Hoover. Once they convinced Akerman of the project's importance, he arranged for them to meet with Hoover, and Hoover then scheduled a meeting with Coolidge. On December 10, Wiprud wired Thorpe to tell him that the meeting with the president had gone well. Barge Line Company representatives had given Coolidge a memorandum explaining their view of the Midwest's plight. The memo cited the Indiana Rate Case decision as the principal cause of the region's transportation crisis. This decision, the representatives argued, had allowed railroads to raise rates on goods shipped from Chicago to the Twin Cities while lowering rates on goods sent to the Twin Cities' retail hinterland. Rate changes, the memo's authors complained, were destroying the Twin Cities' wholesale business by taking away its trade territory. New first-class rates, for example, created a 31-cent advantage for Chicago in shipping goods to Crookston, Minnesota, and shipping costs, at all rates, had increased from St. Louis to the Twin Cities. Only by reviving navigation, Twin City boosters argued, could they save the Twin Cities' status as a manufacturing and distributing center.[33]

Knowing that President Coolidge could override Ashburn and Secretary Davis, the upper river delegates tried to convince the president that Congress had intended to extend government barge service to the upper river when it created the IWC. They argued that the "very life" of upper-river cities was "dependent upon immediately carrying out the intent of Congress as so expressed." And besides saving the commercial life of upper-river cities, they asserted, the IWC fleet would relieve the agricultural crisis in Wisconsin, Minnesota, the Dakotas, Montana, and Iowa. Farmers would save 10 cents per bushel over railroad transportation of grain. Potato growers in Minnesota, North Dakota, and Wisconsin could ship their crop south at about one-half the cost of railroad transportation. Farmers could get sisal fiber—used for binder twine—from the Yucatan more cheaply. Sugar, rice, coffee, California canned goods, and hardwood timber could also be imported to the Midwest cheaper than by rail. And canneries in Minnesota and Wisconsin could export their products more economically. With barge line operation on the upper river, the Midwest could take advantage of the Panama Canal. The savings and profits achieved by shipping goods on the river would increase the purchasing power of businesses and farmers. This, in turn, would improve the economy of the Midwest, from which even the railroads would profit.[34]

President Coolidge apparently accepted the Barge Line Committee's arguments. "We feel that he now understands the situation in an entirely different light than before," Wiprud confidently reported. Wiprud believed that Secretary Hoover, Agriculture Secretary Frank B. Kellogg, and possibly the war secretary also supported the delegation's request. Wiprud's optimism was premature. The secretary of war remained uncertain and requested more briefs.[35]

On December 11 Wiprud asked Thorpe to organize an "avalanche of telegrams" from prominent individuals and organizations. These telegrams, he hoped, would convince the president that the Barge Line Company needed to resolve the conflict with the IWC favorably and quickly to begin service in the upcoming season. Wiprud stressed that the telegrams should show individuality and be sent that night.[36] Demonstrating how much the Barge Line Company's political organization had matured and how its base of support had grown, Thorpe replied the next day that key people and organizations had sent telegrams. He boasted that he could "easily get thousands of such telegrams if time permitted."[37]

The telegrams and intense lobbying of the War Department, the commerce secretary, and the president succeeded. When the Barge Line's Washington representatives returned to the Twin Cities near Christmas, Thorpe held a meeting to hear their reports. "President Coolidge," they informed Thorpe, "very forcefully announced his willingness to sanction a program for development of the Midwestern waterway system as an emergency measure of transportation relief to that part of the country."[38] On January 8, 1926, the IWC's general counsel reversed his opinion. He now said that the IWC could lease equipment from the Barge Line Company. Soon after, the president and his cabinet approved the deal.[39]

On January 20, 1926, the IWC signed an agreement to lease vessels from the Barge Line Company and to maintain regular service between St. Louis and Minneapolis. The company promised to build a fleet that cost at least $600,000 and build it in accordance with specifications approved by the secretary of war. They consented to provide weekly service, in both directions, to cities between Minneapolis and St. Louis. The company planned to lease the equipment to the IWC for $30,000 per year. The IWC agreed to maintain and operate the barge fleet for five years. They also agreed to buy the company after two years, though not later than five years, if the company wanted to sell. Despite navigation's long history of failure on the upper river, the Barge Line Company was making a huge financial commitment.[40]

Navigation boosters had won the first round in reestablishing shipping on the upper river, but it was only the first round. By fighting for the Upper Mississippi Barge Line Company and the extension of barge line service to the upper river, they had established the foundation upon which they could fight future battles. A small group, mostly from the Twin Cities, had led the effort, but through the conflict with the IWC, they had broadened their base of support. The had a long way to go, however. They needed a project radically different from the 6-foot channel project, and they needed the support to persuade Congress to authorize and fund such a project.[41]

CHAPTER 10

An Inland Empire's Need

Navigation boosters entered the fall of 1928 pleased with themselves and confident that they could restore commerce to the upper Mississippi River. They had won their battles with the Coolidge administration, and they had made shipping on the river a regional concern. The 1928 election and efforts to solve the farm crisis would give navigation improvement national attention. Problems still remained, problems that could ensure the river's failure as a transportation route, despite the boosters' efforts. Over the coming year, the boosters' satisfaction would turn to anger and frustration, but their confidence and determination would grow.

The Farm Crisis and Waterway Development

Farmers, in particular, looked forward to the 1928 election, hoping to get a president more concerned with their plight. Neither Harding nor Coolidge believed the government should manipulate the nation's economy to solve the farmers' problems. Coolidge knew little about the Midwest, "cared even less, and thought the farm depression was unimportant politically."[1] While Secretary of Commerce Herbert Hoover knew the Midwest well (he had spent most of his boyhood in West Branch, Iowa) and cared about the region's crisis, he also believed that the government should leave the economy alone.[2]

Farmers fared little better with Congress. In 1921 a group of senators and representatives sympathetic to agriculture formed a coalition called the farm bloc and made the farm crisis a leading issue on Capitol Hill. While the farm bloc raised the nation's awareness of the farm crisis, Congress failed to pass legislation that successfully addressed agricultural overproduction and the price gap between agricultural and industrial products.[3]

Despairing of federal leadership, farm interests developed their own plans. In 1921 two executives from the Moline Plow Company, Hugh S. Johnson and George N. Peek, devised the plan farmers most enthusiastically supported. They suggested that the federal government buy the country's surplus grain at the domestic price and sell it to foreign countries at the world market price, which was less than the domestic price. In other words, the government would lose money. Farmers, however, would pay a tax to reimburse the government for the difference between the world market price and the domestic price. Farmers could afford the tax if the federal government established a "ratio price" for farm products sold in America. The ratio price would bring the domestic price of key farm products up to or in parity with prices enjoyed by farmers between 1905 and 1914—a price much higher than the world market price. Combined with effective tariffs, their plan, they claimed, "would give farmers a 'fair exchange value'" on their products as compared to industry.[4] From 1922 to 1923 Peek and Johnson actively pushed their plan, and by late 1923 it had gained a large rural following and significant congressional support. By 1926 parity supporters had built "the most powerful agricultural lobby in the nation's history."[5] The national debate over the parity plan raised the visibility of the farm crisis and, with it, the issue of waterway development.

Harding and Coolidge vehemently opposed the parity plan, or the McNary-Haugen bill, as it became known once Senator Charles L. McNary and Representative Gilbert Haugen sponsored legislation for it. Both presidents heeded Commerce Secretary Hoover's warnings against government tampering with domestic prices and that foreign countries would retaliate against high tariffs. Hoover also warned that artificially raising agricultural prices would inflate food prices and cause labor to demand higher wages, that large agricultural producers would benefit more than small farmers, and that other industries would request similar help. Overall, he feared, the plan would politicize the economy and undermine U.S. economic self-sufficiency.[6]

While Hoover and like-minded opponents of the McNary-Haugen bill played a large role in defeating it, southern cotton farmers initially rejected it as well. In 1926, however, a compromise with the cotton growers led many southern congressmen to support the bill, enabling its passage. Coolidge, with strong backing from Hoover, vetoed it. Proponents then changed the bill, attempting to mollify Coolidge and Hoover, and Congress passed it again in May 1928. The new version satisfied neither man, and the president vetoed it again.[7]

Rejecting government manipulation of the farm economy, Secretary Hoover and the Republican party sought other ways to aid farmers. They offered to help them establish voluntary associations to control their marketing, distribution, and output. These measures received mixed approval. While Republicans raised tariffs on some agricultural products, they neither compensated farmers for high production costs nor addressed the critical problem of surplus production.

Throughout his tenure as Commerce Secretary, Hoover offered, instead, inland waterway development as a solution to the farm crisis. Waterway improvements became one of his most important alternatives to McNary-Haugenism and deflected some of the Midwest's anger with the administration over their opposition to the McNary-Haugen bill. An inadequate distribution system, Hoover declared, underlay the farm crisis, and he believed reducing distribution costs was one of his principal roles as the secretary of commerce.[8]

Hoover identified the causes behind the distribution problem early in his tenure as commerce secretary and frequently listed them in his speeches on the agricultural crisis. Railroad rate hikes had devoured what little profits farmers earned and had made it impossible for them to compete in foreign markets. Hoover condoned these increases because railroads had faced labor and material cost increases following the war. Therefore, farmers and Midwest businesses could not look to rate reductions. Furthermore, Hoover believed that American production had exceeded railroad capacity, and population growth expected over the next decade threatened to widen the gap unless the country developed some other form of bulk transportation. Hoover pointed to the Panama Canal's effect on the Midwest's transportation costs. These factors, he concluded, had erected a "row of tollgates" around the Midwest.[9]

Figure 23. Secretary of Commerce and President Herbert Hoover. Underwood and Underwood, Washington, D.C., Library of Congress, Prints and Photographs Division.

Hoover stressed that while transportation rates in the Midwest had risen, ocean rates had remained the same. Consequently, it had become relatively cheaper for foreign countries to ship their agricultural produce to other countries and to the major markets on the East Coast of the United States than it was for Midwesterners to reach the same markets. Farmers in Argentina, Australia, and Canada had all begun to undersell American farmers. While midwestern businesses had begun moving to the coasts, farmers, unable to move, endured a prolonged depression. A fully developed inland waterway system, Hoover argued, would alleviate these problems.

In a speech in the Twin Cities on July 20, 1926, Hoover emphasized that in waterway improvement lay "the most practical exit from our national transportation dilemma."[10] He promoted improving America's waterways as the best long-term solution to the farm crisis. Hoover listed three factors that made waterway improvements reasonable: the economic plight of the Midwest due to railway rate increases, the advances of science and engineering in deepening waterways and improving craft, and the country's growing prosperity.[11]

Hoover insisted that the United States had to approach waterway improvements systematically. In his acceptance speech for the Republican nomination in August 1928, Hoover emphasized that "this development of our waters requires more definite national policies in the systematic co-ordination of those different works upon each drainage area. We have," he continued, "wasted scores of millions by projects undertaken not as part of a whole but as the consequence of purely local demands. We cannot" he concluded, "develop modernized water transportation by isolated projects." If approached systematically, he predicted, the entire Mississippi River navigation system could be completed in five years.[12]

To Hoover, the Progressive and the engineer, public works represented a scientific solution not only to the Midwest's problems but to national problems. The country needed a multifaceted transportation system to operate efficiently. Making transportation more efficient reduced costs to consumers and producers.[13] In contrast to

McNary-Haugenism, government spending on "reproductive" public works, Hoover asserted, did not require manipulating the economy to favor one economic group or region. Comprehensive public works transcended local or regional pork-barrel projects to become a national benefit.[14]

As the 1928 presidential election approached, supporters of the parity plan hoped the new administration would support it. While several issues dominated the campaign—Prohibition and Alfred E. Smith's Catholicism especially—farm relief emerged as a central issue. Navigation improvement gained momentum in the presidential campaign as one solution to the agricultural crisis.

Republican party candidate Hoover called the farm crisis "the most urgent economic problem in our nation today...," and added that "the working out of agricultural relief constitutes the most important obligation of the next Administration."[15] Despite this emphasis, the Republican platform on agriculture offered the familiar proposals and policies of the Harding and Coolidge presidencies. It called for the creation of a Federal Farm Board to promote farmer cooperatives that would control and prevent surpluses, with the caveat of keeping the government out of business. The Republicans also called for strong tariffs to protect important farm products, as well as zealous efforts to expand foreign markets. Finally they promised to seek for farmers economic equality with laborers in other industries.[16] In addition to these measures, Hoover continued to push inland waterway development. The "modernization" of the nation's inland waterways, he stated, would "comprise a most substantial contribution to midwest farm relief and to the development of twenty of our interior states."[17]

Alfred E. Smith and the Democrats also sought the farm vote, and the farm crisis figured prominently in Smith's campaign. Smith attacked the Republicans' failure to solve the crisis during their eight years in power. He criticized them for suggesting that farmers limit production and for supporting business over agriculture. The Republican inability to solve the farm crisis presented the Democrats with an opportunity to capture the South and Midwest. But the Democratic platform on agriculture differed little from that of the Republicans. They proposed to provide government aid to cooperatives, create a Federal Farm Board to assist farmers and stock raisers in marketing their products, and reduce the disparity between what farmers received for their produce and what consumers paid for it. They promised to consider the farmers' plight in government financial and tax measures. While Smith agreed that surplus agricultural production was the key problem facing farmers, to avoid alienating eastern voters, he did not openly support the McNary-Haugen bill.[18]

The Democrats also backed navigation improvements. Trying to discount Hoover's claim to the issue, they declared that no political party opposed waterway development. They called such improvements essential and noted that the Mississippi River, in particular, needed navigation improvements. The Democrats criticized Hoover, however, for placing too much emphasis on waterway development. Such development, they insisted, would take too long; farmers needed more immediate solutions.[19]

Hoover won the election, not for his stand on navigation but because Prohibition, Smith's Catholicism, and the general good health of the economy prevailed over the farm crisis.[20] Yet, throughout the election and the battle over an agricultural parity plan, waterway improvement gained national visibility and support. To advocates of channel improvement, the farmers' plight fit ideally into their drive to reestablish navigation on the upper Mississippi River. Not since the Granger movement had the combination of urban and rural forces offered such a strong base for navigation improvements.

A Nine-Foot Channel

Added to the growing base of support, boosters now had a president who backed systematic navigation improvements. But a serious problem remained. They knew that the Mississippi remained too shallow and unpredictable to reliably carry the bulk commodities needed to meaningfully reduce transportation costs and ensure a profitable barge line service. They knew well the causes behind the decline of river commerce, and they knew that even with a completed 6-foot channel, the river would be too shallow to compete with railroads. As early as the Mississippi Valley Association meeting in St. Louis in November 1925, some had called for a 9-foot channel. By 1927, the 9-foot channel had become a key element in the program of the Mississippi Valley Association's Northern Division. Supporters recognized that only a 9-foot channel would allow the economies of scale required to permanently restore river commerce, encourage private investment, and compete with railroads.[21]

Upper river navigation boosters moved slowly in demanding a deep channel. Their first objective had been to restore commerce. Once they established barge line service, they began actively pushing for a 9-foot channel. They expected that the 9-foot channel would come without much effort. Responding to their demands, Congress authorized the "Preliminary Examination of Mississippi River between Missouri River and Minneapolis with a view to securing a channel depth of 9 feet with suitable widths," on January 21, 1927.[22] The survey, navigation boosters expected, would demonstrate the project's need.[23]

Inflating the boosters' confidence, Congress also authorized Lock and Dam No. 2 at Hastings in the 1927 act. How could the Corps support a brand new lock and dam and not approve a full system of locks and dams for the upper river? As of 1925 the Mississippi River between St. Paul and Hastings remained the most troublesome for navigation. Responding to navigation boosters, Congress had authorized a survey of the river from St. Paul to the head of Lake Pepin in the Rivers and Harbors Act of March 3, 1925. Congress directed the Corps to determine if locks and dams were needed to make the river navigable above the lake. The Corps' report showed that the reach between St. Paul and Hastings remained as difficult as it had been when Byron Merrick steamed through it during the 1850s. The report also revealed how far river commerce had fallen.[24]

The Corps' report, known as House Document 583, detailed where river commerce stood in 1925. Twenty-three railroads, grouped into nine systems, including five lines to Chicago, four to Duluth, four to the

Pacific Coast, and six to the South, served the Twin Cities. Railroads, the Corps flatly stated, met the Twin Cities' needs and would for a long time. "An increase in river transportation," the Engineers determined, "must come from competition with well-organized railway service or from new business which cheaper transportation will bring to the territory."[25] Except for a few excursion boats, the River Transit Company provided the only commercial navigation on the upper river, and it offered irregular service.[26]

In its preliminary examination and survey, the Corps broke the river into three reaches. The first ran for about 7.5 miles from Lock and Dam No. 1 to downtown St. Paul. Here, the Engineers reported that they had nearly completed the 6-foot channel. The controlling depth in 1925, however, was only 3.7 feet. The Corps maintained it could have dredged the river to a 5-foot depth, but it did not need to since no traffic used this reach. A second reach extended from Hastings to the head of Lake Pepin. Here the Corps decided that it could easily establish the 6-foot channel by channel constriction and dredging. But in the middle reach, from St. Paul to Hastings, the Engineers were not anywhere near completing the 6-foot channel and recognized that it would be impossible to do so with wing dams, closing dams, and dredging.[27]

Since Congress had authorized the 6-foot project in 1907, the Corps had undertaken little work in this reach. In fact, nearly all the constriction works had been built before 1896. Still, the Engineers reported, it contained about three hundred wing dams and closing dams. They estimated that there was "an average of 10 per mile," and declared that the river between St. Paul and Hastings was "probably the most completely regulated stretch of river in the country." Despite all the channel constriction works, the river remained extremely shallow. The Corps did not dredge the river above Hastings during the 1925 season. At the season's end, the low-water depth measured only 3 feet. Normal dredging, the Engineers insisted, could have increased the depth to 4 feet, still 2 feet below the required 6-foot channel.[28]

On the basis of its experience and the growing demand for a navigable channel, the Corps recommended a lock and dam for Hastings, at an estimated cost of $3,780,310. The new structure, the Engineers suggested, should be considered part of the 6-foot channel project, already authorized. Since channel constriction and dredging could not establish a 6-foot channel, the Engineers concluded that only by damming the river could they create the 6-foot channel. As the major metropolis on the upper river above St. Louis, the Twin Cities provided the justification for all navigation improvements on the upper Mississippi River; all the work below the cities meant nothing if the navigable channel ended 30 miles downstream.[29]

Accepting the Corps' arguments and pressure from navigation boosters, Congress authorized Lock and Dam No. 2 for Hastings in the 1927 Rivers and Harbors Act. It did not, however, immediately authorize funding for the project. Consequently, the Upper Mississippi Barge Line Company loaned $30,000 to the Corps to undertake the preliminary surveys, design work, and borings. Finally, on May 22, 1928, Congress ordered the Corps to begin construction. Because Congress had authorized Lock and Dam No. 2's construction and the survey for the 9-foot channel, navigation boosters believed their goal of establishing a deep channel for the upper river was near. They were wrong.[30]

The 9-Foot Channel Survey
The Corps charged Major Charles L. Hall, the Rock Island District commander, with the 9-foot channel survey and directed the District Engineers from the St. Paul and St. Louis Districts to evaluate their reaches of the river. Now navigation boosters would learn how disillusioned some within the Corps had become about navigation on the upper river. The boosters had some inkling that the Corps might not support their effort when Hall refused to accept their tonnage figures for river commerce. Still, they remained confident that Hall would submit a favorable report; the Corps had always supported navigation improvements on the upper Mississippi.[31]

Hall shocked 9-foot channel advocates on August 25, 1928, by submitting a negative report to the Chief of Engineers. Hall, citing the thirty-year decline of river traffic, concluded: "the maximum savings per ton mile due to transportation on a 9 ft. depth over those due to transportation on a 6 ft. depth multiplied by the potential ton mileage are entirely insufficient to repay the minimum cost of the proposed improvement."[32] While navigation boosters had had their differences with the IWC and President Coolidge, they expected the Corps to support them. Hall's decision threatened all that the boosters had fought for; their successes to date meant nothing without a deep channel.[33]

Boosters responded swiftly to Hall's report. Their organization and support were well in place. Within two days the Upper Mississippi Barge Line Company sent a letter of protest to the Chief of Engineers. The Mississippi Valley Association endorsed the 9-foot channel project and telegrammed cities along the river to write protest letters to the War Department. Responding to this barrage, the Chief of Engineers informed the Mississippi Barge Line on August 28 that the Board of Engineers for Rivers and Harbors would contact them soon to set a hearing. Two days later, the Barge Line Company, the Upper Mississippi

Figure 24. Major Charles L. Hall (Rock Island District Engineer, 1927–30) repeatedly rejected the 9-foot channel project. Courtesy of the Rock Island District, U.S. Army Corps of Engineers.

and St. Croix River Improvement Commission of Minnesota, and the Mississippi Valley Association called a meeting of navigation proponents for September 14 to discuss their appeal to the board. Five days after Hall submitted his report, A. C. Wiprud declared that "the unfavorable report by Major Hall on the proposed 9′ foot project ... has resulted in a volume of protest which is without parallel in this movement."[34]

Representatives from river cities from New Orleans to the Twin Cities attended the meeting. They adopted a resolution requesting the Chief of Engineers to conduct a hearing on Hall's report. They established an executive committee to prepare and present their case before the Board of Engineers and before Congress. And they secured financial support from a number of organizations to combat Hall's report.[35]

According to the Corps' standard procedure for unfavorable reports, those objecting had thirty days to submit a request to appeal before the Board of Engineers. Once the board acted on the appeal, the matter went to the House Rivers and Harbors Committee and then to the Senate Commerce Committee. While 9-foot channel proponents wanted a meeting as soon as possible, the Chief of Engineers doubted that one could be held before December. But pressure from 9-foot channel advocates became too great. By October 6, breaking with its normal procedure, the Corps ordered Hall to reassess his report and accept documentation from groups favoring the 9-foot channel. In this way the Corps avoided hearings before the board and the two congressional committees.[36]

Navigation boosters demanded a public meeting to confront Hall, but Hall and the Coolidge administration refused. (Hoover would not take office until January 1929.) As a compromise, the Corps offered to hold a private meeting in St. Paul with key boosters. The boosters agreed when the Corps assured them that the survey would proceed quickly after the meeting. On November 16, 1928, they presented their arguments to Hall. To supporters, "it appeared ... that the evidence was so overwhelmingly in favor of the adoption of the nine-foot channel that nothing less than a favorable report was anticipated from Major Hall...."[37] Hall did not find the evidence so convincing.[38]

He surprised 9-foot channel advocates again by calling for a public meeting to be held on January 16, 1929, to decide whether the Corps
should continue its survey. Again boosters felt betrayed. They had
agreed to the private meeting at the War Department's request, "with
the understanding that Major Hall's reconsideration and report would
be expedited."[39] Not only was the government delaying the report, but,
boosters realized, the November meeting had not persuaded Hall of the
project's merit.[40]

Deep-channel advocates opposed the meeting. They believed that
Hall had already made up his mind to submit another adverse report and
that he wanted to have a public meeting before announcing his decision.
They argued that the Corps had all the data needed to justify the project, and, one advocate argued, "the people of the valley should not be
further drawn into army red tape...."[41] On its behalf, the administration
argued that some groups had not participated in the private conference,
and wanted their say. Navigation proponents had no choice but to mar-
shal their arguments another time.[42]

As they feared, Hall still opposed the project. On February 27,
1929, he delivered a second negative report. While this report did not
surprise 9-foot channel supporters, it angered them as much as the first.
The Minnesota State Legislature immediately issued a resolution to the
president, the secretary of war, and Congress, urging them to back the
9-foot channel project. The state offered three arguments. First, it contended that a trade outlet to the ocean had "been claimed and recognized
as an economic right by all nations," and that the Midwest (a region
"greater in area, in population, and in resources than a dozen European
nations") had the same right. Second, it claimed that the Midwest had a
"special right to demand that its balanced trade relations," ruined by the
Panama Canal, "be speedily restored" by extending the benefits of the
canal to the Midwest. Third, the state stressed that farmers needed the
project.[43] The following day, the St. Paul City Council sent a similar
resolution to Congress, adding that St. Paul and other cities had built
expensive, modern terminals believing the government would create an
adequate channel.[44]

To rebut Hall and influence Congress and the Corps, newspapers throughout the upper valley campaigned for the project. Even the *Minneapolis Tribune*, which one river booster called a conservative paper for its regular opposition to federal spending on internal improvements, argued for the project. In an editorial the *Tribune* contended that the Minnesota legislature knew nothing about engineering. However, the paper noted, the report rejected the 9-foot channel on economic grounds, and the paper considered the region's business interests more than capable of refuting Hall in this arena.[45]

Newspapers focused the boosters' anger and frustration on Hall. Congressman Newton, now a secretary to President Hoover, finally scolded 9-foot channel supporters for attacking Hall. On March 12, 1929, A. G. Godward, executive engineer for the Mississippi Valley Association, apologized and informed Newton that navigation boosters were "endeavoring to avoid all unfriendliness which will tend to antagonize the Army Engineers and insofar as the Twin Cities situation is concerned have been quite successful." At a meeting in Chicago the previous week, they had agreed to "discontinue the policy of fighting this matter in the press and to get down to business in the matter of the presentation of the appeal." Hall had completed an extensive report, Godward acknowledged, and they had to criticize the report's economic conclusions, not Hall.[46]

The 9-foot channel advocates' last recourse was to appeal to the Board of Engineers. The Mississippi Valley Association presented the case for the entire Mississippi valley. The association carefully planned its appeal, assigning experts to study channel regulation with wing dams versus canalization with locks and dams; competitive markets and the relationship of Minneapolis and St. Paul to other ports on the river to the twin ports of Duluth-Superior; and the shipping of lumber, coal, iron ore, oil, grain, and other commodities. The association wanted the briefs by the first week of April.[47]

Despite this preparation, project proponents feared that the Board of Engineers would agree with Hall on the economics of the 9-foot channel project, and they focused their defense on a technicality. They planned to argue that Hall had not completed the survey as directed by Congress on January 21, 1927: he had not assessed the project's technical feasibility and, therefore, the cost of a deep channel. Hall had decided against the 9-foot channel because he believed the river could not draw meaningful commerce. While project proponents thought they could rebut Hall's economic analysis, they believed his failure to evaluate the project's technical aspects would determine the outcome. They hoped to convince Newton and the secretary of war of their position. The secretary might agree with them, they surmised, because he "would undoubtedly ... have in mind the rather awkward position the Engineers are in *from a practical business standpoint*, in that they have determined the unworthiness of a great project without taking the trouble to ascertain its cost." By ordering the survey completed before a congressional hearing, channel proponents thought, the secretary could avoid embarrassment.[48]

On April 23 and 24, 1929, the Mississippi Valley Association presented the boosters' arguments to the Board of Engineers. Their strategy worked. They convinced the board on the technicality that Hall, by not examining the project's engineering details thoroughly, had mistakenly found those costs too high. On May 29, 1929, George C. Lambert, as chairman of the Mississippi and St. Croix River Improvement Association, wrote to Minnesota Congressman Frank Clague that there was "great rejoicing along the upper river valley when the news was received that the U.S. Board of Engineers had overruled Major Hall and recommended a survey." He noted to Clague, however, that they were "not yet out of the woods...."[49]

Time was becoming critical. The 1930 Rivers and Harbors bill was expected to be the last for several years. Nine-foot channel supporters worried that if they did not get their project in this bill, they might never obtain a deep channel. Boosters expected eastern projects to pack the 1930 bill and feared that once the easterners had their work, they would not support a bill with a 9-foot channel for the Midwest. Furthermore, Congress opened again in December 1929. It was nearly June, and the Corps still had to complete an acceptable survey report.

As 6-foot channel boosters had belatedly learned, Congress would not adopt a project without a report detailing the economic and engineering requirements. If a district engineer delayed the survey now, he could prevent Congress from considering the 9-foot channel. To ensure that this did not happen, deep-channel advocates needed the president, the secretary of war, and the Chief of Engineers to press for a quick survey.[50]

This time the Corps established a special board of engineers to conduct the survey. The board's members included Brigadier General Thomas H. Jackson, president of the Mississippi River Commission and head of the Corps' Western Division; Louisville District Engineer, Lieutenant Colonel George R. Spalding; St. Paul District Engineer, Lieutenant Colonel Wildurr Willing; and St. Louis District Engineer, Major John C. Gotwals. Despite Hall's opposition, the Corps put him on the board. To have the survey ready for the December opening of Congress, the special board had to determine how many dams to build, study the foundations at potential dam sites, define the relationship between flowage and pool elevation for each site, develop preliminary plans and estimates, and write the report. The acting secretary of war had instructed the board "to expedite action in every way."[51]

On August 23 Jackson provided the Mississippi Valley Association a progress report. The board, he said, had met on June 27 and August 7, 1929. The board had gathered topographic and hydrographic information before the first meeting, and the engineers had begun a geological study of the entire riverbed. They were combining surveys completed in 1883 and 1927 into a new map and studying trouble spots. They were preparing profiles of the river at high and low water and of the river's bottom. Willing was examining water supply, sanitation, and other conditions at the Twin Cities. Gotwals was completing a traffic study of the upper river. Hall and Spalding were analyzing canalization methods. In addition Hall was studying Mississippi River discharges and had the survey's administrative work. The board also directed Hall to evaluate the project's effects on the river's fish and wildlife and water quality; these would give Hall new grounds to oppose the project.[52]

Notwithstanding the War Department's assurances, 9-foot channel boosters worried that the project would not make it into the Rivers and Harbors bill. They expressed their fears to Secretary of War James W. Good when he visited the Twin Cities in August 1929. They believed eastern interests were plotting to kill the 9-foot channel project. These interests had already pushed to pass the bill in a special session of Congress the previous spring, when it had few projects. Deep-channel advocates also knew that other duties distracted board members from their work on the upper river survey. Hall's presence on the board troubled 9-foot channel advocates. Finally, the special board had expanded its study to include the effects of the project on the environment, including fish and wildlife and sanitation, and was collecting more traffic data. As only four months remained before Congress opened, navigation boosters wanted the Corps to narrow the survey's scope, set a deadline for its completion, and use commercial statistics already gathered.[53]

Confirming the navigation boosters' worries, Hall continued criticizing the project and its supporters. In a speech before the School of Wild Life Protection in McGregor, Iowa, Hall warned that the project would magnify pollution problems and destroy the upper river's flora and fauna. Burton F. Peek, of Deere and Company, in Moline, Illinois, heard that Hall considered support for river transportation a temporary phenomenon, that Hall thought the survey would take at least three years to complete, and that Hall believed interest in the river would wane by then. Navigation boosters, Hall charged, were interested in improving the upper Mississippi River only as a way of lowering freight rates, not as a legitimate transportation route. Peek rejected Hall's view of navigation boosters, announcing that his company planned to ship five hundred carloads of implements from Moline by the end of the 1929 season. Because of Hall's outspoken opposition and increasing objections from navigation boosters, the Corps removed him from the special board on October 14. They let him complete his tenure as the Rock Island district commander, which ended on December 12, 1929.[54]

Despite efforts to hurry the survey, Congress opened its December session and accepted the Rivers and Harbors bill without the 9-foot channel project. The special board sent the completed survey to the

Board of Engineers on December 16, 1929, and the board forwarded it to the Chief of Engineers on January 22, 1930.[55] On January 27, Charles Webber reported to Walter Newton, secretary to the president, that the Corps still had the survey. He warned Newton that enemies of the 9-foot channel "will not be inactive. They will try in various ways to put it off or compromise and do something to prevent its authorization by Congress, but now is our time." They could not let anything prevent it from being authorized in the current session of Congress. "It is the greatest move for the relief of the northwest and Upper Mississippi River agriculture that could be imagined," he stressed, playing on the impact of the early Great Depression. He did not yet conceive that the Hoover administration might become one of the enemies.[56]

Not until February 15, 1930, did Congress receive the report from the secretary of war, and he insisted that it was only an interim report. It held information to bolster project opponents and encourage project supporters. The first part outlined the problems and potentials that navigation proponents had been discussing for years, in some ways more clearly. It reaffirmed the value of deep channels in allowing greater economies of scale. "As the size and draft of the barges or tows become greater," the report stated, "the net cargo carried increases at a more rapid rate than the capital and operating expenditures, consequently these charges are distributed over a greater pay load and the cost of transportation per load is decreased." The Midwest, the report observed, lacked competitive markets for its grain. Railroads, through their rate structures, had coerced farmers to market their grain through them, preventing farmers from taking advantage of the Great Lakes route. As a result, no competition existed between the grain markets of Minneapolis and Duluth, forcing farmers to sell at one price. High transportation costs had prevented industrial development in the Midwest. The special board pointed out that the 6-foot channel had been "designed for types of river traffic that have become obsolete," and that the project was "certainly inadequate for present needs." The board noted how the Upper Mississippi Barge Line Company and the IWC had increased commerce on the upper river but said that inadequate barge size limited shipping. Large, deep-drafted barges used on the river below St. Louis could not operate on the upper river. As in the early days of navigation, shippers had to break bulk at St. Louis. Barge line operation had convinced shippers that a deep channel would guarantee lower costs and a successful revitalization of river commerce. The Mississippi and Missouri Rivers, the board observed, had been passed over. In its rush westward, the country had not paused to modernize them. Their time had come. The report also examined the products that would move on a 9-foot channel, the value of deep channels on European and American rivers, and the technical needs of such a project on the upper Mississippi River. All the statistics and findings seemed favorable for the 9-foot channel. Despite its positive remarks, the special board's conclusions exasperated the boosters. The board suggested that Congress partially authorize the 9-foot channel project and provide $50 million to continue improving the 6-foot channel.[57]

The Board of Engineers took a more rigid, and to navigation boosters more disheartening, stand. In submitting the report to the Chief of Engineers, Major General Lytle Brown, it stated: "This is a very important project, justifying most careful and detailed study. From the information available the Board of Engineers for Rivers and Harbors is unable to determine upon a satisfactory plan, either for betterment of the existing project or for the provision of a 9-foot depth." The board recommended waiting for the final survey, due in December 1931, and continuing work on the 6-foot channel. Charles C. Webber, president of the Upper Mississippi Barge Line Company, informed Wiprud that the special board had favored the project, but the Board of Engineers had rejected it outright. Brown, Webber had heard, recognized the politics involved and had tempered the Board of Engineers' language.[58]

Even before Congress received the interim report, navigation boosters began formulating a strategy to get their project into the Rivers and Harbors bill. They focused their efforts on representatives from the Mississippi valley, the Corps, and the president. They had already formed a committee to monitor the project in Congress. On February 10, five days before the interim report reached the House, boosters met with about twenty-five midwestern representatives in Washington. Most of the Congressmen had agreed with a compromise plan suggested by Brown. Brown, Wiprud informed them, had assured Senator Shipstead and himself that the survey would be good enough for Congress to include it in the bill. At a meeting the next day, however, Brown undermined Wiprud. The chief told the representatives that the report was inadequate and not to authorize the 9-foot channel project yet. He suggested that Congress approve work compatible with a 9-foot channel. The meeting convinced many of the Congressmen to support the compromise plan, but the boosters wanted all or nothing.[59]

Having failed with the Chief of Engineers, they turned to President Hoover. They had, after all, forced Brigadier General T. Q. Ashburn to reverse his position regarding the IWC's responsibilities to expand its operations. The president, they hoped, would also direct the chief to reverse his position. Hoover had advocated navigation projects as long as they had, and he strongly supported them during his presidential campaign. On March 6, 1930, R. P. Warner, vice president of the Mississippi Valley Association, wrote to President Hoover seeking his support for the project. "People of the central west want this nine foot channel," he pleaded, "and are voicing their demand by editorials and group meetings of shippers and farmers and service clubs from all parts of the valley. It is my prediction and my earnest belief," he added, "that when you and all others look back ten years from now that the Mississippi system as outlined will not only be a completed reality but that it will be considered as one of the greatest contributions that any administration has ever given to the people." Finally, Warner tried to persuade Hoover to influence Brown to change his mind.[60]

Shortly after meeting with Brown, Wiprud and other navigation boosters called on the president. They "were astonished" to learn that the president opposed the project's authorization.[61] Hoover did not reject the 9-foot channel project itself. Rather, he found the timing bad. The Great Depression had begun less than five months earlier, and he believed the country too weak financially to fund a project then estimated at $98 million. Nine-foot channel advocates responded that they only wanted the project authorized; they could wait for funding. An authorized project, they insisted, would demonstrate to the Midwest that it could invest in river terminals and barge line transportation. Rather than viewing the Great Depression as a barrier to the project's authorization, project proponents contended that it could be a helpful relief measure.[62]

Regardless of the depression, the administration and other opponents declared the interim report inadequate. Nine-foot channel advocates responded that Congress had authorized projects based on reports less well researched. The interim report, they asserted, demonstrated the economic need for the project and its general technical feasibility. They argued that the Corps could work out the engineering details in the final report.[63]

To appease the boosters, opponents suggested that Congress authorize two 9-foot channel dams and that the Corps continue work on the 6-foot channel in other places. Proponents dismissed this argument, pointing out that the interim report declared channel constriction worthless. Such a piecemeal approach, they argued, contradicted the Corps' own findings and Hoover's progressive approach to navigation improvements. The Ohio River 9-foot channel had taken nineteen years to complete because, they contended, Congress had not authorized all the work at once. Given the objections of "official Washington," navigation boosters intensified their effort.[64]

With the executive branch firmly against full authorization for the 9-foot channel project, proponents hoped to convince the House Rivers and Harbors Committee to include it in the bill. In hearings before the committee on March 18 and 27, 1930, key supporters presented their arguments. The entire Minnesota congressional delegation appeared before the second hearing to endorse the project, as did congressmen from Iowa and Illinois. But New York Congressman S. Wallace Dempsey, the committee chairman, insisted that the interim report was deficient. He stressed that the committee and the Corps had exceeded normal procedures to accommodate project proponents.[65] "And I will say to you frankly," he lectured the boosters, that it was because the Chief of Engineers shares the sentiment which you have uttered here that he has gone away beyond the ordinary practice in making this which is really an advance report. It is something that never had been done up to this time, and it was done just simply because of the realization that your project is an important project.... There has never been such a report come before us before in the history of this committee, in my 15 years' experience.[66]

Dempsey was clearly trying to soothe them. Another committee member, Congressman William E. Hull, from Illinois, also sympathized with the boosters but encouraged them "not to crowd the thing too hard, any more than to get before the public that you are to have a 9-foot channel, and to have an understanding with the Chief of Engineers and with the Secretary of the War that that is the understanding." Chairman Dempsey encouraged the boosters not to go back to their people thinking that they had lost.[67]

Dempsey offered another reason why the House did not want the 9-foot channel project in the 1930 Rivers and Harbors bill. He complained that Congress had not had a Rivers and Harbors bill for several years. As a result, the bill before his committee had too many projects. In a debate before the full House, Dempsey warned that he might lose the entire bill if it contained the upper Mississippi River 9-foot channel project, because President Hoover would veto it. The president, it appears, had decided to limit the bill by excluding the 9-foot channel project.[68]

Nine-foot channel advocates remained determined to get their project into the bill before it left the House. Representative Melvin J. Maas, from Minnesota, again pointed out that immediate authorization would provide relief from the depression by encouraging economic development. His colleague from Minnesota, Representative Godfrey G. Goodwin, rebuffed the chairman's call for patience and gratitude. "I see no reason why," he objected, "this action can not now be taken by this committee and give to the project an established and recognized status as part of the navigation program." He thanked the committee for its concern but retorted "we need assurance and action and not sympathy."[69] Sympathy was all the committee had to offer.

Giving up on the House, business and agricultural leaders again turned to President Hoover. On April 4, 1930, the Farmers Elevator Association of Minnesota, representing about fifty thousand farmers, wired the president that it unanimously supported the project's full authorization, even if Congress could not fund the entire project. The Elevator Association added that the state associations of North and South Dakota, representing about a hundred thousand farmers, had endorsed the project also. The association and the Cooperative Farmers Northwest Grain Corporation argued that a 9-foot channel would give midwestern grain producers two markets—Duluth and Minneapolis—through which to market their crops. Deflecting responsibility away from the president, George Akerson, one of Hoover's personal secretaries from 1923 to 1931, replied to the Cooperative Farmers Northwest Grain Corporation that the House could not include the 9-foot channel project until the Corps had completed its survey.[70]

At a meeting held on April 14, cities and business interests from the upper Mississippi composed a telegram appealing to Hoover to support full authorization of the 9-foot channel project. High transportation costs were throttling midwestern agriculture and industry, they argued. An "emergency" existed that required "immediate action." The governors of Minnesota, North Dakota, and Iowa; the Upper Mississippi and St. Croix River Improvement Commission; the Dubuque Dock Commission; the mayors of Minneapolis, St. Paul, Stillwater, Dubuque, and Burlington; the Mississippi Valley Association; the Upper Mississippi Barge Line Company; and the Associations of Commerce from Winona, St. Paul, and Stillwater signed the telegram.[71]

In response to the Midwest's increasing pressure for a 9-foot channel, former Congressman Newton restated the president's stance. In a letter to Webber, he stressed that the president had chosen the best man he could for the job of Chief of Engineers—Lytle Brown—and "the best river man to head up the work on the Upper Mississippi," Spalding. Both engineers opposed authorizing the project without the detailed survey. Such an expensive project, Newton contended, required a more accurate survey. He charged that the Ohio River 9-foot channel project had cost much more than it should have because it did not have a comprehensive survey when started. The Rivers and Harbors Committee, Newton reported, felt that it should listen to the advice of its experts, the Corps, and the Corps opposed full authorization.[72]

Webber, in responding for upper Mississippi River valley navigation boosters, revealed much about their sentiment. While he appreciated the value of a detailed survey, he argued that the administration could not blame them for being impatient. The 9-foot channel, he claimed, should have been included as a part of the act authorizing the Panama Canal, and the Midwest had "patiently suffered ever since." He reported that "public opinion in the valley is united for immediate authorization in spite of attempts to divide it," and that "it is too late now to stem the tide and solidarity of public opinion on this subject." The valley still hoped that the president would save their project, but they were unwilling to quit or compromise if he did not. Nine-foot channel proponents knew that their project had little chance of being authorized in another Rivers and Harbors bill. "There is a time," Webber concluded, "when patience ceases to be a virtue."[73]

Supporters of the deep channel lost their patience as chances for their project dimmed. The Rivers and Harbors Committee sent the bill to the full House without recommending authorization of the 9-foot channel project, and on April 25 the House passed the bill. The Corps, the House, and the president had rejected their call for a 9-foot channel. Their last chance was for the Senate Commerce Committee to add the project to their version before sending it to the full Senate.

Throughout the fight for the 9-foot channel project, some Midwesterners sensed their Manifest Destiny slipping away. The Midwest had established its agricultural base, its cities were growing, it had abundant natural resources, it had all the elements needed to make it a commercial and industrial region except ready access to the ocean. On the eve of the House vote on the 1930 Rivers and Harbors bill, John Kerper, chairman of the Maritime Committee for the Dubuque Chamber of

Commerce, wrote that "the entire middle west is at the threshold of a critical period in its history. The future industrial development of the states along the Upper Mississippi River will be vitally affected by legislation which is now pending in Congress." The 9-foot channel, he emphasized, was "imperative" for upper river states "to assume the position in the Nation to which they are logically entitled."[74] In its editorial "An Inland Empire's Need," the *St. Paul Pioneer Press*, echoing the mood of the region, declared that a landlocked Midwest could not realize its potential for commercial growth and, therefore, could not achieve its noble destiny.[75] Yet to a growing number of Midwesterners, the river claimed a different and more noble destiny. Their efforts would complicate the 9-foot channel's path through Congress and, for the first time, challenge a major navigation project.

CHAPTER 11

This Noble River

As navigation boosters tried to hurry the 9-foot channel survey ahead, conservationists realized that a threat, possibly far greater than any the river had faced, was gaining momentum. The effect of slack-water reservoirs on the Upper Mississippi River Wildlife and Fish Refuge especially worried the Izaak Walton League. The league cherished the refuge as its "first born and probably greatest accomplishment."[1] Commenting on pollution, Judson Wicks, president of the Minnesota Izaak Walton League, captured the league's sentiment well and evinced a radically different vision for the river. "There is something shocking and scandalous," he bristled, "in the thought that this noble river, designed by nature to serve as a means of health and vigor for the body and mind of man as well as an inspiration for his soul, should be obliged to abdicate this high role and function to assume the low and menial office of scavenger of his liquid wastes."[2] This unseemly office would play a critical role in how conservationists viewed the 9-foot channel project and, along with other stresses degrading the river, would divide them.

Despite the league's power, demonstrated in winning the Upper Mississippi Wildlife and Fish Refuge, the Corps might have ignored them, but professional biologists in the Bureaus of Fisheries and Biological Survey also questioned the project. Their agencies, the Departments of Commerce and Agriculture, had spent $600,000 to acquire land for the refuge and planned to spend more. They wanted to know how the

9-foot channel might change the refuge and affect not only their investment but the reserve's fish and wildlife. The secretaries of both departments wrote to the secretary of war, relaying the concerns expressed
by their scientists. Working with the Izaak Walton League, the Departments of Agriculture and Commerce helped convince the Corps to evaluate the 9-foot channel project's environmental effects.

Railroads belatedly protested against the project as well. They had
rid themselves of serious river competition over forty years before. The
Indiana Rate Case had announced the death of commercial river traffic
and the railroads' final triumph. Now shipping on the upper Mississippi
River threatened to rise again, not as a ghost of the steamboat days but
as a strong and substantial competitor. Like conservationists, railroads
began a campaign to modify or stop the project.

The Biological Backlash

By November 1929, the Department of Agriculture officially recognized
the potential impact of the 9-foot channel project on the refuge. In a
November 22, 1929, letter to the secretary of war, R. Dunlap, the acting
secretary of agriculture, worried that flooding the refuge with reservoirs
or lowering the water table by extensive dredging would destroy the
land's habitat value, land the federal government had recently purchased.
He also pointed out that Congress had established the refuge to comply
with the Migratory Bird Act signed with Great Britain. Patrick J. Hurley,
the acting secretary of war, replied to the secretary of agriculture on
December 4. He assured the secretary that the Chief of Engineers and
the Board of Engineers would examine the biological impacts carefully before sending their report to Congress. He also promised to coor-
dinate fully with the Agriculture Department.[3]

The Izaak Walton League remained skeptical. Henry Baldwin
Ward, the league's president, wrote to President Hoover on December
6. Ward charged that "the proposed nine-foot channel from St. Paul to
St. Louis will radically modify the biological conditions in the Upper
Mississippi Wild Life Refuge...." Damaging the refuge, he warned,
could violate the compacts the United States had signed with the four

states along the refuge. Ward appealed to the president to let the secretaries of the interior and commerce appoint experts to help with the survey. Then the Corps could design the project appropriately. Because navigation boosters were hurrying the War Department to complete the survey, Ward needed the president to act soon. The league and biologists from the two bureaus had started late and faced a well-seasoned campaign for navigation improvements.[4]

In January 1930 the two bureaus began discussing how they could jointly comment on the project. Together they drafted a letter from the president to the war secretary, responding to the Izaak Walton League. The president did not send the letter, but on March 19, Arthur W. Hyde, the secretary of agriculture, did. The letter addressed the concerns of the Departments of Agriculture and Commerce and hinted that they did not object to the project overall and even found it might benefit fish, wildlife, and aquatic plants.[5]

On February 15, 1930, the secretary of war submitted the 9-foot channel survey to Congress, without input from the Departments of Agriculture and Commerce. The Izaak Walton League passed a resolution at its eighth national convention in 1930 objecting. The league resolved that "if a nine (9) foot channel will be of benefit to commercial traffic, it shall be so constructed so not to operate to the detriment of the wild life, . . ." More boldly, they resolved that the War Department let the Bureaus of Biological Survey and Fisheries determine the method used in creating the 9-foot channel to minimize impacts to the refuge.[6]

Reflecting a growing consensus in the two bureaus, Secretary Hyde believed that the refuge's fish, wildlife, and aquatic plants would suffer for a short time and then flourish, as long as the Corps used low dams and did not fluctuate the pools too much. Excessive fluctuation, he warned, would negate any positive effects. Pollution, he conceded, would become worse near large cities, but that was their problem. Hyde thought reaches away from large point sources might improve. He stressed that the federal government had already recognized the region's concerns for fish and wildlife by creating and investing in the refuge. Finally, he doubted the war secretary's comment that the Chief of Engineers and

Board of Engineers would consider fish and wildlife issues. Although the Corps had submitted its report to Congress, he still wanted some influence on the final design. "Because of the probable far-reaching effects of new channel developments in the upper Mississippi on the animal and plant life," he argued, "it appears to me that this subject is of sufficient importance to warrant your engineers in the field seeking the advice of experts from the Bureaus of Biological Survey and Fisheries" to avoid adverse impacts.[7]

On April 19, F. Trubee Davison, the secretary of war, replied to Hyde. He discounted the project's potential negative effects, saying that no dam would raise the water level more than 10 feet and that along the banks it would not exceed 5 feet. He acknowledged the conservationists' concern about dropping the water levels behind the dams after the navigation season, but insisted this was necessary to deal with ice. "To alter the plans so as to provide for no draining of pools during the winter season would," he argued, "greatly increase the total cost of the project." The Corps could, he offered, drain the pools slowly and not fluctuate them much other than for the winter drawdown. Furthermore, the Corps would remove all large trees from the pools to avoid forests of dead trees after the dams closed. And the Corps' special board of engineers, he mentioned, was willing to talk "about plans for preservation of wild life as an incidental to improvement of the river in the interests of navigation." The special board wanted information on the depth of water biologists considered adverse. At the end, he suggested that representatives from the two bureaus be designated to meet with the special board on May 6, 1930, in St. Louis. Six days after Trubee wrote his letter, the House passed the Rivers and Harbors bill without the 9-foot channel project and sent it to the Senate. If conservationists felt relieved, they would not enjoy the feeling for long.[8]

The Corps hosted the May 6 meeting at its division office in St. Louis. Lieutenant Colonel George Spalding chaired the meeting, and the Corps' special board that conducted the 9-foot channel survey attended. Dr. M. M. Ellis and E. W. Surber from the Bureau of Fisheries joined Frances M. Uhler from the Bureau of Biological Survey, who provided a detailed report on the meeting to his superiors. The Corps and the two bureaus quickly agreed that low dams would do the least harm to fish, wildlife, and aquatic plants. The Corps gave away nothing on this, as it had to keep the dams low to reduce damages to roads, railroads, and other property.

Overall, the Corps impressed Uhler. He found they genuinely wanted to understand how the project would harm the river's environment, but they had a fundamental disagreement. The Corps had moved well along on a dam design that would let them draw the reservoirs down in the late fall and winter. Lowering the pools at this time, Uhler, Ellis, and Surber contended, would eliminate the new reservoirs' potential positive effects. The Engineers asked whether either bureau had conducted biological studies of Lake Cooper, the 65-mile-long reservoir created by the Keokuk and Hamilton Power Company's dam near Keokuk, Iowa, completed in 1913. The Corps thought Lake Cooper might indicate what effect the 9-foot channel reservoirs would have on the river. Spalding even offered to pay for the studies and the use of a Corps boat. The Corps also asked what the "monetary" cost to biological resources would be of fluctuating the pools. They wanted to compare the cost of potential damages to the refuge to the cost of using dams capable of maintaining a stable water level. Uhler replied he could provide only rough estimates. This satisfied the Corps, but the Engineers stressed that they needed the information by October 1 to use in the hearings on funding. Now, it appeared, the conservationists might have a chance to influence the project, especially since the Senate still had the Rivers and Harbors bill, and the House and the president opposed its full authorization.[9]

The appearance quickly changed. Navigation boosters had turned to the Senate for their last stand to get the 9-foot channel project authorized. Senator Shipstead led the fight. In the Senate the boosters hoped to have more strength. The Mississippi River valley alone counted twenty senators. By May 13, to the boosters' delight, Senator Shipstead convinced twenty-one of his colleagues to sign a petition favoring the project. On May 21, Wiprud wired George Lambert that the Commerce

Committee had voted fifteen to four to include the 9-foot channel project in the bill and had suggested initial expenditures of $7.5 million.
Only a veto of the Rivers and Harbors bill could kill the project now.
While Hoover may have threatened to veto the whole bill, he could not.
It held too many projects, benefiting too many states, and the Great
Depression had started. On June 16 the full Senate passed the bill,
and by June 24 the House accepted the Senate's version. On July 3,
1930, President Hoover signed it. Nine-foot channel advocates still had
to get funding, and they could not overlook supporters of the Upper
Mississippi Wildlife and Fish Refuge, but they had accomplished their
long-sought goal.[10]

The Biological Survey

Even though Congress had authorized the 9-foot channel project, conservationists still had an opportunity to influence how the Corps would
build it. An interim report, House Document 290, left important issues
undefined. The Corps had to decide where to place the dams, how high
to build them, and whether to make them fixed or movable. Major
Charles L. Hall's persistent objections and growing protests by conservationists had forced the Corps to consider environmental issues. Out of
the May 6 meeting, the Corps had requested the two bureaus to study
Lake Cooper, "with an eye toward mitigating the impact of the nine-
foot channel on fish and wildlife."[11] The Bureau of Fisheries placed Ellis,
a nationally recognized expert on water quality, mussels, and the effect
of impoundment on streams, in charge of its study. The Biological Survey chose Uhler, who had been conducting studies on the upper Mississippi since at least 1926. For the first time, it appeared, conservationists
might provide substantive input to a navigation project.[12]

  The Bureau of Fisheries report on Lake Cooper affirmed conservationists' worst fears and portended a dismal future for the river if
dammed. Silt, mixed with undecomposed organic pollutants, covered
the lake's downstream bottom to depths of 3 to 6 feet. As the matter rotted, it stole the lake's dissolved oxygen needed by fish, mussels, and other
aquatic life. The soft silt smothered the lake's plants and mussels. Only

Figure 25. Minnesota Senator Henrik Shipstead became the champion of the 9-foot channel project. Photograph by Lee Brothers; courtesy of the Minnesota Historical Society.

commercially unimportant mussels, like the papershell, Ellis remarked, survived. Only organisms that could tolerate little oxygen lived on the bottom, organisms that typified badly polluted streams. Levees, railroad beds, and roads, combined with agricultural drainage and channel constriction, had eliminated much of the lake's shoreline wetlands and backwaters. These areas had been the principal breeding grounds for plankton and the primary spawning beds for popular game fish. Without these areas, fish had few places to spawn, and fingerlings had little to eat. Consequently, Lake Cooper's game fishery had deteriorated, yielding mostly rough fish.[13]

In August 1930, after they had nearly finished the Lake Cooper study, the Corps and the Bureau of Fisheries decided to expand their research to include an undammed portion of the refuge and Lake Pepin. Broadening the survey to Lake Pepin allowed the bureau to examine another large river lake, one that had existed for thousands of years. And by looking at an open reach in the refuge, Ellis hoped to determine the potential effect of impoundment on the refuge overall.[14]

A much healthier river ran through the refuge than through Lake Cooper, reaffirming the Keokuk dam's negative effect. The open river produced far more game fish and carried cleaner water. Large, undisturbed shallows along the shore and the many backwaters accounted for the greater number of game fish. Even though the Corps had cut off many chutes and sloughs, the river's backwaters produced abundant plankton and fish. Farmers had not leveed and drained the floodplain wetlands in the refuge. Furthermore, due to the narrower, faster-flowing channel, no large or deep deposits of fine, pollution-laden silt covered the channel bottom, and, as a result, the river bottom fauna proclaimed a healthier river. Nevertheless, silt and channel constriction posed important problems for the refuge. "Wherever wing dams, closing dams, and other obstructions had been placed in the river," the bureau reported, "silting-in was proceeding at a rapid rate." If placed near a mussel bed, wing dams could quickly bury the mussels in silt. Yet, the wing dams kept the main channel flowing fast enough to prevent silt and pollution from accumulating. In Lake Cooper silt had amassed all across the riverbed.[15]

Lake Pepin displayed many problems found in Lake Cooper. But the lake provided evidence that the 9-foot channel project might not harm the river's fish and wildlife as badly as the Lake Cooper study suggested. Also smothered by pollution-laden silt, Lake Pepin's bottom fostered the same fauna or unhealthy indicators found in its artificial counterpart. Like Lake Cooper, silt buried mussel beds throughout Lake Pepin. Unlike Lake Cooper, Lake Pepin retained its shoreline marshes and shallows and could potentially support abundant plankton and game fish populations.[16]

Based on Ellis's findings in all three areas, the Bureau of Fisheries concluded that in and of itself the 9-foot channel would not adversely affect the river's fisheries. As long as the government preserved side-channel sloughs, backwaters, and marshes, plankton and fish would be as abundant in the dammed river as under channel constriction. The bureau strongly recommended, however, that the Corps build fixed dams. Fixed dams would guarantee a constant minimum depth and prevent fish from becoming stranded, and provide habitat for plankton. If farmers and federal, state, and local groups worked to reduce soil erosion and pollution, the bureau believed that fish and wildlife might even thrive in the new reservoirs. To some conservationists the Bureau of Fisheries study shortchanged the river's environment; yet, the Biological Survey's findings would confuse them much more.[17]

Uhler examined a 90-mile reach of the upper river from Hogback Island, below LaGrange, Missouri, and Benton Island, above Oquawka, Illinois, for the Biological Survey. He also relied on previous reports covering the river from Diamond Bluff, Wisconsin, just above Red Wing, into Arkansas. His task was to determine "the character, distribution and abundance of aquatic and moist-soil vegetation...." Whether reflecting his association with the Department of Agriculture or his own views of conservation, Uhler cared more for creating habitat for waterfowl than preserving or restoring the river's natural character.[18]

Throughout the 90-mile reach, Uhler found little to satisfy his criteria of "true aquatic or marsh vegetation." The right plants appear to have been those liked by ducks and geese, and, less so, by furbearers, like the muskrat. Uhler found the southern two-thirds of Lake Cooper too deep and open to support waterfowl habitat, but he criticized the natural river above and below Lake Cooper as much. Little or no aquatic plants or marsh vegetation grew in these reaches because, he concluded, the river flowed too swiftly and fluctuated too much. Lake Cooper had reduced the fluctuation through its reach from 20 feet to 6, and Uhler thought it could be reduced even more, if the dam operators properly managed the gates. Below the reservoir, tributary streams brought in floodwaters that caused the main stem to rise too quickly. Uhler preferred slack-water impoundments, since they had little current and produced a more stable water level. Finally, he preferred Lake Cooper over the Des Moines Rapids, which the lake had replaced. A rapids, he professed, offered little opportunity for waterfowl habitat. Only in Lake Cooper's upper third, which most imitated a 9-foot channel reservoir, did his true aquatic plants and marsh vegetation thrive. Therefore, he concluded, "It is very probable that considerable portions of the Upper Mississippi River Wild Life and Fish Refuge would be benefited by the construction of low dams...."[19] This would only be true, he pointed out, if the Corps held the water levels constant and the dams raised the water level over the bottomlands by less than 5 feet. Uhler acknowledged that "an entirely different type of Refuge" would emerge from the 9-foot channel, "but following re-adjustment and reestablishment of the aquatic vegetation, the refuge should be an improved place for waterfowl and also for muskrats."[20] Uhler's conclusions not only differed with the Bureau of Fisheries' but with those of the Izaak Walton League and others more concerned about preserving and restoring the river's natural character.[21]

Two Big Meetings

On February 20, 1931, the Izaak Walton League's Minnesota division issued a notice about "Two Big Meetings."[22] The Corps was hosting the first in Wabasha in six days, and the Izaak Walton League had called the second for Winona on March 7. At these meetings, differences between the government's biologists and the league would become clearer and more complicated. These divisions prevented conservationists from presenting a concerted effort. The river's condition and how the 9-foot channel might make it better or worse in part caused the dissension. As some conservationists today are warning about an ecosystem collapse, many conservationists in the early 1930s thought the river was dying.

Lock and Dam No. 4, planned for Alma, Wisconsin, sparked the first meeting. Alma lies about 7½ river miles downstream from Wabasha. The reservoir created by the dam threatened to permanently inundate low-lying areas at and around Wabasha, which lay at the upper end of the refuge. The city, the Izaak Walton League, railroads, private citizens, and highway departments from Minnesota and Wisconsin raised concerns about the new dam. Not everyone who appeared at the meeting opposed the project, although it seemed that way to some project supporters. J. J. Gleason, representing the Alma Commercial Club, defended the project, which, he declared, Alma overwhelmingly supported. Surprised by the controversy, he commented that he had not planned to attend "a funeral procession...."[23]

A 3-foot difference in the reservoir level behind Lock and Dam No. 4 became the critical issue, but the league and a few other conservationists questioned the entire 9-foot channel project. Wabasha feared that it would have to rebuild the town's water supply and sewer systems, that the reservoir would flood low-lying private and public lands, and that the river's "scenic beauty and recreation values" around Wabasha would be destroyed if the Engineers set the pool or reservoir at 670 mean sea level (m.s.l.). The city wanted the Corps to move the dam site about 4 miles upstream, to the foot of Lake Pepin. Otherwise, they insisted that the Corps lower the proposed elevation to 667 m.s.l., to eliminate most of the city's problems. Representatives from the Chicago, Burlington and Quincy Railroad Company and the Chicago, Milwaukee, St. Paul and Pacific Railroad Company wanted to know how the reservoir might damage their rail lines. They did not raise serious objections but expected the government to pay for all damages. The Wisconsin State Highway Department and the Highway Commission of Buffalo County, in which Alma lies, took the same position.[24]

The Izaak Walton League's state divisions in Minnesota and Wisconsin were not as accommodating. They objected to the Alma dam and to the whole 9-foot channel project. Pollution, erosion, water-level management, and the 9-foot channel's potential effect on the Upper Mississippi River Wildlife and Fish Refuge worried them. W. H. Pugh, president of the league's Wisconsin division, could not attend the meeting but detailed the league's stand in a letter to the St. Paul District commander, Lieutenant Colonel Wildurr Willing, dated February 23. Pugh insisted that the river's maladies had to be resolved before the Corps built any dams. Pollution, the river's most serious affliction, would become worse, he warned, with the new dams. Echoing Ellis's findings in Lakes Pepin and Cooper, he predicted that the dams would trap organic pollution, and the rotting mass would steal the river's oxygen, killing the river's aquatic life. The stagnant cesspools created by the dams would threaten human health as well. Pugh demanded that the appropriate state and federal agencies reduce pollution and siltation before the Corps began construction.

Pugh also listed the Wisconsin Izaak Walton League's demands if the Corps built the project. Because fluctuating water levels caused problems for the river's fishery, the Corps had to guarantee stable water levels behind the dams. Pugh worried that the Corps would release water from the pools to aid navigation at St. Louis and below during the winter, just as the Corps opened the headwaters reservoirs to aid navigation from the Twin Cities on down. He was disturbed that the Corps might flush the pools, as it did at Lock and Dam No. 1, to get rid of the waste and sediment that accumulated behind the dams. Such fluctuations, Pugh feared, would kill fish and furbearing animals. And the dams, Pugh exhorted, had to have fishways, so fish could migrate from pool to pool. Finally, the effects of the 9-foot channel on the refuge "deeply concerned" the Wisconsin league. Pugh questioned the project's economic merits and insisted the Corps put it on hold until proven economically justified. Only then, and after all the conservation issues had been resolved, should the Corps build the project. At the Wabasha hearing, the Minnesota Izaak Walton League "heartily" endorsed Wisconsin's position.[25]

The league's La Crosse chapter joined the two state divisions in questioning the project. In a set of resolutions sent to Willing on February 25, the La Crosse chapter defined its position. It objected to flushing the pools, and it argued for fixed-crest dams so the Corps could not lower the pools beyond a guaranteed minimum depth. It opposed constructing any dams until pollution had been reduced; otherwise, it claimed, public health and conservation problems might become insurmountable and irreversible. The La Crosse chapter also demanded that the Bureau of Fisheries be allowed to design fishways for the dams and wanted the cost added to the overall appropriation.[26]

Other conservationists voiced their concerns too. Julius Haun, a dean at St. Mary's College in Winona and secretary to the diocese of Winona, delivered the most emotional plea. "A cry for Beauty amidst a clamor for dollars stands little chance of being heard," he preached. "But when the hard-headed practical and economic reasons have had a hearing to show the proposed nine-foot channel to be a costly and fruitless experiment, destined to be a vast liability, ending with both its own ruin and the undoing of all beauty on the upper river for several generations after its ultimate wrecking," he concluded, "then let the piping voice of Beauty sound clear." Haun objected to the project because he thought silt would fill the pools and the costs of dredging would rise continually. He believed the project would be available only five months of the year, which, he, contended, made the investment unjustified. All the cities below the Twin Cities would suffer, he argued, for a project only those two cities wanted. It was an "economic absurdity," he railed, to build "a snail-pace carrier for a high-speed age." And even if the new waterway somehow succeeded in lowering rail rates, doing so, he asserted, would ruin already faltering railroads.[27] Less emotional but equally concerned, the Wisconsin Conservation Commission advised the Corps not to begin with the idea of restoring fish life if the reservoirs proved harmful. "Late remedial measures will be too late and ineffective," it protested.[28]

W. C. Henderson, acting chief of the Bureau of Biological Survey, did not see the meeting as controversial.[29] He reported that the Corps

had made a tremendous concession. Demonstrating that conservationists had had an important impact on the Corps, Willing stated "that
at first it was contemplated to construct a series of dams which were to
be opened each fall permitting the pools to be drained, but that on
account of the effect this draining of the pools would have upon wild life,
including fish, the plans had been modified and it was now proposed
to maintain the pools at stabilized levels."[30] Sticking to the bureau's official position, Henderson told the audience that the Biological Survey
thought the pools would "ultimately prove beneficial" to wildlife if the
Corps held the levels held steady.[31] He acknowledged that the project
would transform the refuge's character, since "the value of this Refuge
for waterfowl and fur bearers may be either entirely destroyed or decid-
edly benefited, depending on the policy which the Government adopts
in the construction and maintenance of the proposed nine-foot channel,..."[32] Henderson admitted the reservoirs would flood nearly all of
the lands within the refuge, destroying much of the bottomland timber.
Conservationists could expect a period of adverse conditions, "but following the re-adjustment and re-establishment of the aquatic and marsh
vegetation," he assured them, "the Refuge should be an improved place
for waterfowl and probably also for muskrats."[33]

The only potential controversy, Henderson thought, came from
within the federal government. Suggesting some disagreement between
the Bureaus of Fisheries and Biological Survey, Henderson confided to
his bureau's chief that Clarence Culler had delivered a statement "at
variance with statements found in published reports of the Bureau of
Fisheries."[34] As proof, he attached Culler's comments to his report. Culler
testified that his bureau had grave concerns about the project. He
declared that given the extent of pollution and siltation in the river, the
new pools might eliminate the river's fishery and mussels, if Lakes Cooper
and Pepin provided an accurate indication. Henderson questioned Culler
after the meeting, and as a result, Henderson reported, Culler's "position at the hearing held by the Izaak Walton League at Winona seemed
to me to be considerably less antagonistic to the nine-foot channel project."[35] The Izaak Walton League was not so restrained at Winona.

The league's meeting at Winona, the *Winona Republican Herald* proclaimed, made preserving the refuge a national issue. The meeting did get the national Izaak Walton League's attention and demonstrated the league's regional solidarity. The league had called the meeting to formulate its stand on the 9-foot channel project. At the outset, M. K. Record, of Chicago, the league's general manager, reported that "the national organization is open minded on this matter, . . . and desires to find out what is be[s]t for conservation in regard to the proposed nine foot channel." A ten-member executive committee planned to review the issue after the meeting and report to the national convention. Judson Wicks, president of the league's Minnesota division and the national vice president, and Frank Warren, a member of the national executive board, also attended the meeting. Pollution, erosion, water levels, the river's scenic value, and the project's effect on the refuge again became the critical issues.[36]

The league's state divisions from Illinois, Iowa, Wisconsin, and Minnesota attended the Winona meeting. The Minnesota and Wisconsin divisions had made their objections known at Wabasha. At Winona, the Illinois and Iowa divisions joined them. The Illinois league's president, Dr. Pliny Belitz, "declared the Walton league should oppose it vigorously." He claimed it would "make a treeless swamp" of Winneshiek Bottoms.[37] "This whole project," he announced, "is another example of the great American pork barrel."[38] In a separate heading, the *Winona Republican Herald* announced: "Iowans Oppose Project." A representative from Elkader, Iowa, claimed everyone along the river in Iowa opposed the project. Still hoping to create a national park, he complained that the reservoirs would mar the river's scenic landscape. A. L. Baumgardner, secretary of the league's Iowa division, asserted that controlling pollution and erosion outweighed navigation improvements and that recreation was more valuable than navigation. Heeding the protests from league members, Record vowed that the national league would back the state chapters and make the 9-foot channel project "paramount" at the national convention in Chicago in April.[39]

To counter the league's arguments, the Corps relied on testimony from the Bureaus of Fisheries and Biological Survey. Henderson, Uhler, and Raymond Steele of the Bureau of Biological Survey, and Ellis, Culler, and H. L. Canfield of the Bureau of Fisheries attended one or both meetings. According to the Corps, they "stated as their definite opinion that the canalization plan proposed would be advantageous to the refuge and to fish and game."[40] Each, however, had substantially qualified his support.

Henderson restated the Biological Survey's position given at Wabasha. He did admit that controlling the pollution and holding the river levels stable would most likely benefit fish life, "although it is possible that if there were very little current, as a result of the construction of these dams, small-mouthed bass might disappear from this part of the river."[41] Steele, the refuge's superintendent, strengthened the bureau's overall stand; however, he concluded that the new reservoirs would benefit the refuge in the end.[42]

The Bureau of Fisheries recognized the potential impacts from the dams but did not fault the 9-foot channel project. Although taming his remarks at Winona, Culler detailed the dangers of impounding the river before pollution and erosion had been dealt with. Due to the accumulation of organic pollutants, oxygen levels in Lake Cooper had plummeted, causing a dramatic drop in the lake's fish populations. A similar fate, he warned, loomed for Lake Pepin. The oxygen content in Lake Pepin had fallen to 1.12 parts per million, nearly three points below the "danger point" for fish, Culler emphasized. Agreeing with nearly all conservationists, he stressed the need to keep the reservoirs stable and for the Corps to build fishways.[43]

Ellis backed Culler. He testified that silt and pollution were killing the river's fish and mussels and questioned the merits of building the locks and dams until pollution and siltation had been addressed. But he did not blame the dams, saying that they were "going to put the condition into existence in which the War Department officials themselves are not responsible."[44] At Keokuk, he acknowledged, "The critical situation ... is not a condition of the Dam creation, but roads and railroad building and cottages, etc are responsible for the source of supply in the Keokuk situation."[45] Speaking at the Winona meeting, Dr. Thaddeous

Surber, a fisheries expert from the Minnesota State Game and Fish Commission, voiced his approval for maintaining stable water levels.[46] Taking a more trusting perspective than the Izaak Walton League, Bureau of Fisheries Superintendent Canfield told conservationists at Winona that "'if everybody does what they claim they will do the project will not be as destructive as first presented.'"[47]

Fish passage became a key issue. Most conservationists who spoke had insisted that the Corps add fish passages and that Congress fund them as part of the project's cost. Willing, however, told the gathering at Wabasha that "our Board is of the opinion that no fish-way will be necessary."[48] The final report, he pointed out, said the government would build fishways if shown necessary. However, the Corps believed that the dams' movable gates would allow fish to pass, and building fishways would unnecessarily add to the project's cost. Willing said that the roller gates would allow water to flow under them, and fish could then migrate through. Ellis, and other conservationists, disagreed.[49]

The Final Report

On December 9, 1931, one and one-half years after Congress passed the 1930 Rivers and Harbors Act, the Corps sent its final report, House Document 137, to Congress. Throughout the document the Corps examined the many factors that influenced the project's design, including environmental concerns. The Corps took special note of the refuge, specifically identifying it as one of the factors determining the selection of low-head dams. But the Corps chose low dams primarily because they would minimize the damage to roads, railroad beds, levees, farmlands, and towns. While conservationists had hoped for fixed dams to prevent the Corps from lowering the pools too much, the Corps chose dams with movable gates. Movable gates would give the Corps greater control over the river level and, the Corps insisted, would better serve fish and wildlife by enabling the agency to maintain a higher water level throughout the winter. The combination of low-head dams and movable gates would especially benefit fish, Corps engineers thought. The strong current running through the gate openings would oxygenate the water, attracting fish. The fish could then pass through these openings and move upstream more easily, the Engineers believed, than through fishways. Acknowledging the concerns of conservationists, the Engineers agreed to add fishways if their assumptions proved wrong.[50]

The Corps selected dam sites based on a variety of criteria, partially considering the environmental and social impacts. Potential flowage damages—to the refuge as well as to roads, railways, cities, and farms—and the river's profile determined the general location. However, "The final locations and pool elevations were determined only after the detail surveys of sites indicated that the requirements of navigation had been fully met." The requirements of navigation included straight approaches, adequate foundation conditions, and the difficulty of construction at the site.[51]

The Corps also had to address the fear that pollution would turn the reservoirs into cesspools. The Engineers concluded, however, that pollution was not their problem. Furthermore, pollution did not bother shipping in Lakes Pepin or Cooper. Urban water supply, recreation, ice harvesting (for refrigeration), and the river's fishery had been spoiled by pollution. As the human population along its banks grew, the river would become more and more important as a water source, the Engineers predicted. Demand for clean water from this growing population would lead the cities to build wastewater treatment plants, especially as the dams held the pollution close to the offending cities. In this regard, the Corps and the Bureau of Fisheries agreed. With the issues of pollution, siltation, and habitat integrity unresolved, some conservationists refused to give up.[52]

Sacred Obligation

As during the refuge campaign, the Izaak Walton League relied on its publication *Outdoor America* to mobilize its members. In its August–September 1932 issue, Judge George W. Wood published an editorial that left no doubt about his position. Wood criticized the 9-foot channel as government-subsidized and outdated. Citing Lake Cooper, he predicted the reservoirs would become polluted, oxygen-sucking cesspools.

"We now believe that the attempt being made to induce Congress to appropriate five hundred million dollars to construct a series of dams along the Mississippi River, in order to provide a nine foot channel is," he charged, *"destructive and dangerous."* Like many Waltonians, he valued the refuge as a retreat from urban life. Raising the battle cry of Winneshiek Bottoms, he warned that the 9-foot channel would flood the refuge. At the refuge, he preached, "the flow of the mighty river has stopped the wave of civilization which seems to have broken at the crest of the hills above these bottoms. Among the trees overhanging these sloughs," he proclaimed, "is the *last stand of our picturesque, native beauty in the middle West."*[53] George Catlin's splendid juggernaut, he insisted, had jumped over the Mississippi.

William Aberg, chairman of the league's national executive board, continued the assault. Aberg declared the refuge "the League's first born and probably greatest accomplishment." To protect its beloved child, the league, he pressed, had to "scrutinize fearlessly and carefully any effort which may destroy it or so change its character as to make of it something entirely different from what Will Dilg and his disciples visioned in the days of its making."[54] Aberg then put the significance of the league's opposition in perspective. The league, he admitted, had to work with industries, like paper mills, that polluted rivers. The league could have called for the enforcement of public statutes against the mills but had remained silent, recognizing the number of jobs at stake. The league was not withholding criticism of the 9-foot channel. Although he initially used the correct estimate of $124 million for the project's cost, he later claimed that Wood's estimate of $500 million might be conservative. Like the covered wagon, he declared, rivers had outlived their usefulness for transportation. The 6-foot channel, he pointed out, had not restored river commerce, and he doubted that a much more expensive project could. The league's "sacred obligation," Aberg preached, was to preserve the refuge.[55]

Despite this rhetoric, *Outdoor America*'s summary of the league's 1932 national convention suggests a more temperate approach by the national assembly. In its summary, the magazine reported that chapters along the refuge and the national league had been studying the potential effects of the 9-foot channel on the refuge carefully over the previous year. *Outdoor America* clearly recognized the possible damage that the project could cause. Emphasizing the effects on fishing and hunting, it stressed that the dams would flood much of the refuge, destroying "its game preserve qualities." And, the magazine predicted, the reservoirs would disrupt side-channel and backwater spawning areas and, by permanently flooding some backwaters, allow more pollution into them. But the national convention did not condemn the project.[56]

The league passed two resolutions concerning the 9-foot channel project at the convention. They resolved to continue their efforts to ensure that whatever method the Corps used, it would "be that type least destructive to the game, fish, and other natural resources of the Upper Mississippi River Wild-Life and Fish Refuge." Showing their special concern for the Winneshiek Bottoms, the league resolved to "utilize every means within its power to preserve that area of the Mississippi River known as the Winneshiek Bottoms from excessive damages by the proposed construction of a nine-foot channel."[57] In an analysis of the league's resolutions for his boss, Rudolph Dieffenbach, head of land acquisition for the Biological Survey, captured the essence of the league's position. "It appears this resolution ... does not oppose the proposed developments of the War Department," he reported, "but it does emphasize the necessity for the League to be alert to prevent the destruction of its usefulness as a wild life and fish sanctuary."[58]

Several factors may explain the league's softer tone. *Outdoor America* acknowledged that the refuge's authorizing legislation had explicitly stated that nothing in the act could be used against navigation improvements. Like others concerned about the project, the national league resolved that five key issues had to be addressed. These included pollution, erosion, stable water levels, fishways, and locating the dams to minimize adverse impacts to the refuge. Like the Bureau of Fisheries, the magazine observed that pollution and siltation would have to be solved with or without the dams and cautiously offered that fish and game might thrive if the Corps held the water levels steady.[59]

Strong, individual conservationists continued the fight. Northeastern Iowa had produced the most ardent proponents of the national park and of the refuge. Not surprisingly, it produced some of the most fervent opponents to the 9-foot channel project. Congressman Frederick Biermann, representing Iowa's fifth district, emerged as one of the project's most vocal adversaries. The fifth district included the river around McGregor and Guttenberg, Iowa. Biermann championed the crusade against the project in the House. Three times during the 1930s, he unsuccessfully introduced legislation to repeal the project. During the House Rivers and Harbors Committee hearings between May 2 and 5, 1933, he tried to cut off the project's funding. Echoing the fears of his constituents, he charged that the project would ruin the river's natural beauty and destroy the growing tourist trade that the refuge had been attracting. Biermann contended that the project, if successful, would take traffic from railroads paralleling the river. These railroads paid more taxes in his district and other districts along the river than most other businesses.[60] He reminded Congress that the 4-foot (he probably meant 4½-foot) and 6-foot channels had failed, and predicted the 9-foot channel would fail as well. "The idea along the Mississippi River, and I think that is almost without exception," Biermann advanced, "is that it is almost physically impossible to handle this upper Mississippi River in such a way as to promote commerce by water."[61] And "There appears to be," he asserted, "a disposition of the Almighty to make it impossible to provide commercial navigation for the Upper Mississippi River."[62] This undoubtedly rankled navigation boosters, who had considered the nation's rivers a gift for transportation from the Almighty.

Admitting the hearing had caught him unprepared, Biermann quickly acquired seven telegrams from project opponents, which he introduced on May 3. All came from railroad interests or representatives of northeastern Iowa. One spoke for the railroad brotherhoods, and another proclaimed himself a "railroad man" from Mason City, Iowa. The Postville Commercial Club and the Northeastern Iowa Press Association, headquartered in Postville, decried the undertaking. The press association, its telegram said, unanimously opposed the project "because of the destruction such a project will make to natural beauty and ruinous effect on efforts already made for preservation of our wild life."[63] The editor of the *Allamakee Journal* in Lansing, Iowa, worried about the project's effect on the river's scenic beauty too and added concerns about the flooding of agricultural lands. The Lansing Kiwanis Club joined the others to go on record against the locks and dams. While Biermann secured the telegrams on short notice, they demonstrate how weak organized opposition to the 9-foot channel was. Other than railroads, most dissenters came from a small area. It centered in southeastern Minnesota, southwestern Wisconsin, and northeastern Iowa, where the national park movement had been strongest.[64]

A. C. Willford, another U.S. representative from Iowa, also rejected the navigation project and appeared at the 1933 Rivers and Harbors Committee hearings. A national Izaak Walton League director and the Iowa state director, Willford stressed the league's role in establishing the refuge. Only the previous Sunday, the league, he reported, had unanimously resolved to stand against the 9-foot channel project at its national convention in Chicago. This represented a change in the national league's position or simply Willford's interpretation. Since 1930, the league had not rejected the project outright but insisted that the Corps build it in a way that did not harm the refuge.[65]

Willford objected to the project for a variety of reasons. The refuge, he asserted, was invaluable to the region, because it was "the only outdoor park" in the central United States.[66] Furthermore, he testified, the reservoirs would inundate Winneshiek Bottoms. Willford concurred with Biermann that silt would fill the river, making the dams useless, and pollution would destroy the river's fish and wildlife. The project, which he concluded had no chance of succeeding, would destroy an invaluable and irreplaceable natural resource. The 9-foot channel project, Willford contended, was "merely a dream . . . an engineer's dream."[67] Based on the history of commerce and navigation improvement, he had good reason to doubt the project's potential for success.[68]

A third Iowa representative, Edward C. Eicher, raised objections to the project at the 1933 hearings but for different reasons. He represented a group of landowners (the Upper Mississippi Valley Drainage Association), who held about 400,000 acres of land. They feared that seepage from the 9-foot channel reservoirs would come through their levees and flood their fields. Four levee and drainage districts had sent telegrams challenging the project. The levee districts worried that their land values would plummet. While the levee districts expanded the geographical size of the opposition, they did not increase its numbers much. Overall, the levee districts were responding more from a lack of understanding than from fact. The Deputy Chief of Engineers, Brigadier General George B. Pillsbury, told the Rivers and Harbors Committee that the dams would not raise the river enough to put water constantly against any levee. The dams, he admitted, would increase the water level and therefore the hydraulic pressure near some levees, which could lead to increased seepage. Pillsbury, however, assured the Rivers and Harbors Committee that existing pumps could handle the change, although they would have to work harder.[69]

Like Dilg and other refuge proponents, 9-foot channel opponents emphasized the refuge's recreational values, which in turn had economic and social values. Recreation brought tourism and tourism dollars, and people needed recreation. Wicks lectured his readers: "let no man decry or minimize the value of recreation in modern life. *Recreation is no longer a luxury. Recreation is a necessity.*" People, he argued, had to look back to the root meaning of the word recreation: to re-create. Given the stresses of urban life, people needed to rebuild or re-create themselves. "If the human race is to adjust itself to these radically and speedily changed conditions, it can not dispense with this process of re-building which we call recreation." To Wicks and the Izaak Walton League, the refuge offered a place for the human race to re-create itself; people came from all over the United States and the world to see the Mississippi and be reborn in its presence.[70]

Railroad Opposition

Railroads mounted the most threatening attack on the 9-foot channel project. On November 21, 1931, Judge Ferdinand A. Geiger, representing the U.S. Western Wisconsin District Court in Madison, granted a temporary injunction stopping land condemnation for Lock and Dam No. 4 at Alma. On January 13, 1932, the court issued a permanent injunction. The Chicago Burlington and Quincy Railroad (CB&Q) sought the injunction, arguing that the Corps had raised the project's pool elevation between the interim and final reports without proper authority. Although Corps officers at the February 26, 1931, hearing in Wabasha had recommended the 667 elevation, the Corps settled on 670 in House Document 137. The CB&Q protested that at the new elevation the reservoir would flood $5 million worth of track. In making his decision, Judge Geiger declared that the Corps had to build the project as defined by the original authorization, which had been based on the interim report, unless Congress approved the changes. Since Congress had not authorized the project based on the final report, the Corps could not proceed with anything not in House Document 290, if Geiger's ruling stood. The decision threatened to paralyze the entire project.[71] Senator Shipstead quickly countered. He introduced a resolution to Congress on February 2, 1932, that allowed the chief to construct the 9-foot channel as called for in House Document 137. Congress passed the resolution on February 24.

Since the court challenge had failed, the railroads appeared at the 1933 hearings looking for other ways to fight the 9-foot channel and other navigation projects.[72] On May 2, 1933, the first day of the Rivers and Harbors Committee hearing, Arthur J. Lovell, Vice President and National Legislative Representative for the Brotherhood of Locomotive Firemen and Engineermen, appeared before the committee representing twenty-one associated organizations for the railroad industry. He emphasized that they opposed the 9-foot channel project and all inland waterway projects. The depression, he emphasized, had idled 40 to 60 percent of the railroad rolling stock. Clearly, the number of idle cars might grow if waterways became viable competitors.[73]

To 9-foot channel boosters, the most alarming proposals came from the Association of Railway Executives and four individual railroads, on May 5, the last day of the hearing. Represented by attorney

Bruce Dwinell, the railroads, taking a different tack than Lovell, insisted from the outset that they did not oppose the 9-foot channel specifically. Instead, they presented several amendments to the funding bill before the Rivers and Harbors Committee that would make all navigation projects more acceptable to them. Railroads, Dwinell said, would not object to waterway projects if Congress agreed to the amendments. First, in calculating the price or economic viability of a navigation project, Dwinell proposed that the Corps include all damages and all operation and maintenance costs in the project estimate. The Corps, the railroads argued, was not. Although the Corps measured the expense of direct damages and the operation and maintenance costs for the navigation project, it did not tally all related costs. Railroads wanted any new operation and maintenance costs to the railroads figured as part of the navigation project's costs. If the expense of maintaining a railroad bed went up due to the navigation project, railroads wanted the cost measured and included in the overall project figure. They wanted these costs measured for all property owners affected by the project, whether private, local government, or state and wanted the costs added to the project's overall expense too. Only by including these costs, Dwinell and the railroads argued, could Congress determine the real price of a navigation project.[74]

The second suggested amendment followed directly from the first. The railroads proposed that if the government still found a project economically feasible and went ahead with construction, then the government had to pay all related costs. Dwinell insisted that it was unfair for the government to create a transportation system that took traffic away from railroads and expected railroads to pay the costs of modifying tracks and bridges affected by the waterway project.[75]

If the waterway projects survived the first two amendments, Dwinell and his clients offered a third to sink them. Once the Corps completed any project, railroads wanted waterway users to pay a tax or toll. Dwinell contended that since the government was helping a private industry with federal funds, that industry should reimburse the government. He offered an amendment that would require a toll on freight traffic and commercial passenger traffic to the extent needed to make waterways "self-supporting and self-liquidating."[76] As soon as Dwinell finished, the committee began grilling him on the proposals, which one of its members called "revolutionary."[77]

This time the navigation boosters had been caught unprepared. Clearly taken aback, Arne Wiprud, general counsel for the Upper Mississippi Waterway Association (which had succeeded the Upper Mississippi Barge Line Company in 1932), asked for a short break, so he could prepare responses to the proposed amendments. After reconvening, Wiprud protested that the Supreme Court had already decided that the federal government was not liable for secondary costs or what the court had called "consequential and remote damages." The government's right to develop the nation's waterways for internal commerce, Wiprud exclaimed, "is paramount, that is fundamental."[78] And, Wiprud reported, the government did not have to pay for damages below the ordinary high-water mark, which was where most of the damages mentioned by the railroads occurred. Once the government had declared a stream navigable, it could flood anything built below the ordinary high-water mark without compensating the owner. The government even had the right to make the owner remove obstructions—at the owner's expense—if they were below the high-water mark. As to the government including all the secondary costs into the total estimate for a project's cost, Wiprud believed the Supreme Court would declare it unconstitutional. To dismiss the third proposal, the waterway user tax, Wiprud fell back on the argument that waterway transport had been declared free to all since the country's early history. Europe, he said, had tried charging tolls and had learned it did not work. At this point, the Rivers and Harbors Committee entered a long argument about the subsidies railroads had received versus waterways.[79]

Wiprud and other 9-foot channel boosters grew increasingly upset during the 1933 hearings. The project had been authorized. Why, they wanted to know, was Congress rehashing its merits? Wiprud pointed out that twenty-three congressmen from the upper Mississippi River valley supported the project; project opponents could secure only six. On

May 5, acknowledging concern about the hearings, Chairman Joseph J. Mansfield remarked that the committee had received numerous telegrams that day, all favoring the project. The telegrams demonstrated how much more support 9-foot channel boosters had versus Biermann and other opponents. The telegrams came from the mayors of Dubuque, Muscatine, Minneapolis, Stillwater, and Winona; the Muscatine Chamber of Commerce and the Minneapolis Junior Association of Commerce; the Stillwater Association of Public and Business Affairs and the city's Chamber of Commerce; the Moline Association of Commerce; the chairman of Winona's Traffic Bureau; the Minnesota Federation of Labor; the Minnesota and Iowa Farm Bureau Federations, the Farmers Union Terminal Association, and the *Farmers Union Herald*. The telegrams objected to the hearings' focus, insisting that the project had been authorized and no one should question it now. They wanted the project funded and built as soon as possible. The telegrams and testimony from 9-foot channel backers overwhelmed those opposed to the project. In response, Chairman Mansfield included $11 million for the project in the upcoming Rivers and Harbors bill. Congress, however, withdrew the funding because of President Franklin Roosevelt's flurry of spending proposals during his first one hundred days in office.[80]

The Conservation Divide

The determination by the Bureaus of Fisheries and Biological Survey that the locks and dams would not harm the wildlife refuge perplexed Willford and Biermann and made the Izaak Walton League's arguments against the project less convincing. When, at the 1933 hearings, Biermann criticized the 9-foot channel because it would destroy the refuge, Wiprud pounced. Ray Steele, the refuge manager, Wiprud retorted, had authorized him to say that the project "would make a better wildlife refuge than exists today."[81] When Representative Clause V. Parsons, of Illinois, referred to Ellis's study, questioning Willford's fears, Willford replied that Ellis "solved the problem before he gets to the point where it starts."[82] Willford's comment captures the issue dividing conservationists. Ellis, Culler, and like-minded conservationists viewed the project from how it would improve or worsen existing conditions. Willford, Biermann, some in the Izaak Walton League, and their supporters wanted a much cleaner and healthier river before considering whether to add the locks and dams. Conservationists, then, split over the project largely due to the river's condition by 1930 and how the 9-foot channel would interact with that condition.

On the eve of the 9-foot channel project, many conservationists believed the river was dying. As logging companies and settlers stripped the upper Mississippi valley of its timber and farmers plowed ever increasing acres of land, erosion delivered greater and greater quantities of sediment to the river. Culler complained that thick, muddy water brought by spring freshets into the backwaters made them unsuitable for spawning. To deal with the added silt, the Corps had built more and more wing dams and closing dams. By 1930 the Corps had closed nearly every side channel between St. Louis and St. Paul and had ribbed the river with wing dams. Below Rock Island, floodplain farmers had built more levees and were reinforcing those already in place, with, in some cases, federal help. As they did, they reduced riverine habitat and flood storage capacity.[83]

Cities and industries along the upper river had dumped and were still dumping so much sewage and garbage into the river that fish and mussels were dying at an alarming rate. The river from the Twin Cities to Hastings had become one of the most polluted reaches. It gave Wicks and other Izaak Walton League members cause to fear the 9-foot channel locks and dams. Above Lock and Dam No. 1, all but one of Minneapolis's sewers and thirteen of St. Paul's emptied into the river, yielding some 65 million gallons of sewage daily. Since 1917, when the Corps had completed the dam, sludge had accumulated to a depth of 12 feet upstream. Gas bubbles boiled to the surface during the summer. There was no dissolved oxygen at the dam, and the bacteria counts grew astronomically. Wicks estimated that the Twin Cities' 1,100 and 1,200 miles of sewers put 144 million gallons of sewage into the river each day. When these sewers flowed full and the river fell to its low-water stage, 5.8 gallons of water had to dilute 1 gallon of sewage. Just below St. Paul, stockyards and meat packing plants accounted for nearly a quarter of the pollution leaving the metropolitan area. Publishing his findings in 1930, Wicks noted that the Corps had just completed Lock and Dam No. 2 at Hastings. He feared the worst. Even without the dam, the oxygen content of the river from St. Paul to Hastings dropped to zero during the summer. Wicks found game fishing poor from St. Paul to Wabasha, and he reported that the commercial catch of fish between Wabasha and Winona had declined 75 percent between 1922 and 1929.[84]

Also writing in 1930, Culler emphasized that pollution was "the most destructive of the menaces" facing the river. From the Twin Cities to La Crosse, the river was becoming uninhabitable to fish, mussels, wildlife, and humans. Great quantities "of acids, oils, dyes, tannins and other commercial wastes, and some organic sewerage originating in the Twin Cities, as well as in all other communities along the river," he lamented, "[are] constantly pouring into the Mississippi River."[85] And no cities along the river had waste treatment plants. Culler stressed that above Lake Pepin, the river's oxygen content had fallen so low that it could not support fish life. During the winter of 1929 to 1930, the oxygen content of Lake Pepin plummeted, threatening to suffocate the lake's fish. Culler learned in only one year what pollution did behind the new dam at Hastings. People traveling on trains along the new reservoir, he reported in 1931, were confronted by "very offensive odors, . . ." At times, he added, he could not breathe naturally when near it, having to bury his nose in his coat. But the pollution was becoming more than a nuisance. A sixteen-year-old boy, Culler wrote in *The Minnesota Waltonian*, had died after swimming in the river at La Crosse that summer.[86]

Habitat destruction menaced the upper river's fisheries and endangered the fish rescue program. In 1926 Culler warned that fishing on the river would be "only a memory," unless pollution, erosion, and drainage problems were corrected.[87] As the river's fisheries died, the issue would become of more immediate concern than stocking lakes and rivers away from the Mississippi. "The time is not far distant," he cautioned, "when the Bureau of Fisheries and the Conservation Departments of the various states bordering this vast Mid-west playground will have to establish a program of co-operation for the restocking of the river." Natural reproduction, he concluded, would provide adequate stock for sport and commercial fishing on the upper Mississippi only if the states and the federal government confronted the problems degrading the river.[88]

Mussels faced a more immediate demise. By 1930 the Bureau of Fisheries admitted that due to overuse and habitat destruction, its mussel-raising efforts had failed. Giving up, the bureau urged the states on the upper river to revoke their laws and let the industry take the remaining mussels before the silt buried them or pollution poisoned them.[89]

To Culler and many others, the 9-foot channel project offered a reprieve from, if not a solution to, the river's maladies. So Culler, like Ellis and Steele, concluded that the "plan to construct a nine foot channel undertakes another project favorable to the battle against pollution along the river."[90] Cities putting out the most pollution, Culler believed, would have it "under their own noses and it will no longer be a matter of fish life, but a problem of public health."[91] Although he worried that the new reservoirs would flood many spawning beds and feeding areas, he hoped the locks and dams would capture sediment near the dams and leave the upper parts of the reservoirs clearer. Still ignorant of the ecological role played by fluctuating water levels, he hoped that by holding the river up during the late summer and fall, the 9-foot channel would allow millions of fingerlings to escape the river's backwaters. Like Culler, when considering whether to support or oppose the project, conservationists had to weigh the river's current state against what the locks and dams might do to it. The decision was not easy or straightforward. Consequently, they split in their response to it.[92]

Yet because the 9-foot channel project threatened to reshape the upper Mississippi, and because they had found their voice, most conservationists questioned the new project. They relentlessly warned the Corps, Congress, and the public of the consequences for the river if they did not solve the myriad problems facing it. The conservationists' efforts mark a revolution in the relationship between conservation and navigation and in the vision Midwesterners held for the upper Mississippi

River. From the 1860s to the 1920s, conservation and navigation had grown along separate paths. Few people questioned the environmental effects of navigation projects. With the 9-foot channel project, conservationists forced navigation boosters and the Corps to consider the river's fish and wildlife and scenic qualities. As a result, conservationists, for or against the 9-foot channel, lobbied the Corps and Congress to evaluate and reduce the project's impacts on the river's resources.

One Dream Fulfilled

No serious threats to the 9-foot channel project arose after the 1933 congressional hearings, but the Corps still needed most of the project's funding. The Corps had received $7.5 million in the 1930 Rivers and Harbors Act and had $6.3 million left from the 6-foot channel project, for a total of $13.8 million. In early 1931, this funding allowed the Corps to begin surveying the project sites, buying the land and flowage easements, and working on the first three dams. After the 1932 hearings, Congress appropriated just over $4 million and added another $3.2 million from the $30 million Emergency Relief and Construction Act of 1932. While the Corps now had about $20 million for the project, it needed much more if it hoped to complete the project anytime soon.[93]

The 1933 Rivers and Harbors bill, which the White House had put on hold during the early New Deal, provided the next opportunity for significant funding. In the National Industrial Recovery Act of June 16, 1933, however, Congress authorized $51 million for the 9-foot channel through the Public Works Administration (PWA). To oversee how the PWA allocated its funds, President Roosevelt established an advisory board headed by Secretary of the Interior Harold Ickes. On July 28, 1933, when Ickes balked at releasing money for the 9-foot channel, the president ordered him to approve the funds at the board's next meeting. In the afternoon, the president held a news conference and invited Senator Shipstead. "On that July afternoon, he came out of President Roosevelt's office with a broad grin on his face. The waiting reporters asked Shipstead the reason for the broad grin. The grin grew broader, but Shipstead said nothing. A few minutes later the President announced that work on the 9-foot channel in the upper Mississippi was to be carried on with all haste."[94] The next day, the *Minneapolis Star* proclaimed, "The announcement marks the end of a splendid fight for the revival of shipping on the Upper River, a fight which seemed hopeless when it was begun...."[95]

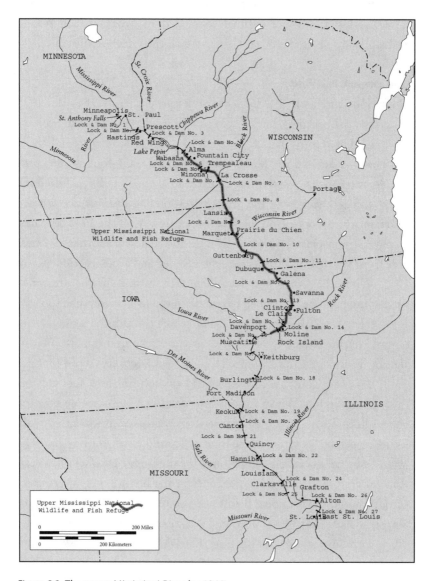

Figure 26. The upper Mississippi River by 1940

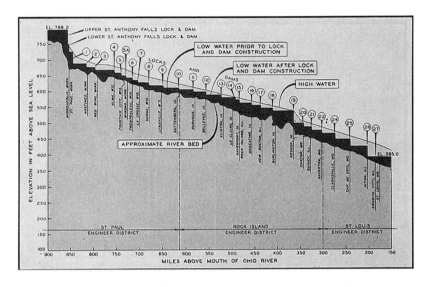

Figure 27. The design selected by the U.S. Army Corps of Engineers would transform the gently sloping river into an aquatic staircase for boats to climb or step down. Courtesy of the U.S. Army Corps of Engineers.

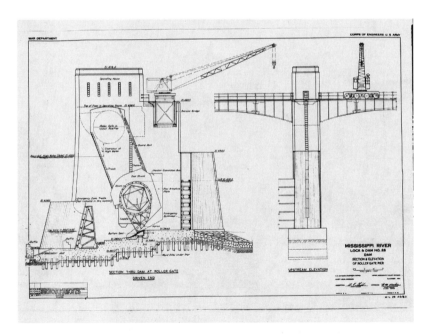

Figure 28. Diagram of roller gate assembly and pier. Lock and Dam No. 26, Alton, Illinois. Library of Congress, Historic American Engineering Record (Photograph No. M-L 26 40/3, December 1934, HAER, ILL, 60-ALT, 3-72, by John P. Herr, John Herr Photography, October 1988).

Shipstead continued to champion the drive for full funding. As Roosevelt had promised, the money followed quickly. The PWA provided $11.5 million in early August 1933 and delivered another $20 million in September. With the new money, the Corps completed as much in 1934 as it had in the previous three years. In August 1934, under the Public Works Administration Emergency Appropriations Act, the 9-foot channel received $20 million, and the Emergency Relief Act of 1935 added another $25 million. By June 30, 1935, the Corps had finished about one-third of the project. In May 1936 the project received $27 million under the War Department Appropriation Act and $28.6 million from the War Department Civil Appropriation Act of July 1937. This completed the major funding. The large appropriations allowed the Corps to put thousands of people to work, and construction of the

Figure 29. Roller gate construction at Lock and Dam No. 26, Alton, Illinois. The government acquired the patent rights to use the cylindrical gates from the Krupp and M.A.N. Corporations in Germany. Library of Congress, Historic American Engineering Record (Photograph No. 1463, HAER, ILL, 60-ALT, 3-54, by John P. Herr, John Herr Photography, October 1988).

Figure 30. Lock and Dam No. 7 under construction. This photograph shows old wing dams as rows of brush on the right side, the floodplain cleared of timber on the upper left, and the dam under construction. Courtesy of the St. Paul District, U.S. Army Corps of Engineers.

Figure 31. The 9-foot channel begins. Lock and Dam No. 6, Trempealeau, Wisconsin, looking downstream prior to inundation. Courtesy of the U.S. Army Corps of Engineers.

dams moved rapidly. On March 12, 1940, the Corps opened Lock and Dam No. 24 at Clarksville, Missouri, the last of the twenty-three new locks and dams (Locks and Dams 3 through 26) authorized under the 1930 Rivers and Harbors Act. As of 1940, the final construction costs came to over $170 million. Including Locks and Dams No. 1, at St. Paul, No. 2, at Hastings, and No. 19, at Keokuk, locks and dams now controlled the river for navigation from Minneapolis to Alton, Illinois, just above St. Louis. The river of dreams for navigation boosters had been built; only commerce was needed to make it real, commerce that had failed to come for all the previous projects.[96]

Fourth River

A new Mississippi River coursed its way from Minneapolis to St. Louis in 1940. As the last roller gates and tainter gates dropped into the river, they gave rise to a third era in the river's physical and ecological evolution. The natural river was already gone. For sixty years wing dams and closing dams had transformed the upper Mississippi, but the channel constriction works vanished beneath the waters of the new reservoirs and from the minds of most Midwesterners. The constricted, fast-flowing, and clearly defined main channel gave way to a broad, often slow-moving river in which the navigation channel is difficult to identify, unless you can read navigation buoys.

In 1940 no one knew what would become of the Mississippi. Would the hopes of a commercial revival or the warnings of an ecological calamity come true? In some ways both have, which has led to the current dilemma. History does not repeat itself, but Midwesterners and the nation are facing issues similar to those that confronted them on the eve of the 9-foot channel project. As navigation interests push for a better shipping lane, conservationists warn that the river is dying, its ecosystem collapsing. As the dammed river ages, it is evolving into a new river, a fourth river, something qualitatively different from what it was naturally, under channel constriction, or shortly after the Corps completed the locks and dams. The physical and ecological character of that river will depend on the actions of the current generation.

Commercial Rebirth

Every time navigation boosters prophesied the return of river commerce with a new project, their prophesies went unfulfilled, but under the 9-foot channel, commerce has far exceeded their most extravagant predictions. Traffic had all but died on the upper river by the 1920s. In 1940, 2.4 million tons of goods moved on the upper river. By 1960 this number had multiplied by more than ten, to over 27 million tons, and by 1970 the total had doubled to about 54 million tons. In 1980 towboats pushed just over 76 million tons on the upper river. Although commerce declined during the mid-1980s, by 2000 shipping had jumped to more than 83 million tons.[1]

Figure 32. Navigating the Mississippi River near Lansing, Iowa, the heart of Winneshiek Bottoms. An Environmental Management Program structure, regulating the flow to a backwater, lies immediately below the tow. Courtesy of the U.S. Army Corps of Engineers.

Grain returned slowly to the river but would eventually dominate. Wheat, corn, and soybeans accounted for less than 10 percent of the total commerce shipped on the upper river until 1958, when these crops reached 14 percent. Leading the resurgence of river commerce, grain comprised 30 percent of the total tonnage shipped by 1964, remaining at this level until 1972, when grain exports began booming. Between 1986 and 1995, grain shipping averaged 42.9 million tons, or about 52 percent of the total annual tonnage. Corn and soybeans are the two principal crops moved on the upper river.[2]

Although no other commodities approach the quantity of grain shipped, barges carry significant amounts of other commodities. Coal and petroleum products are the next most important. Between 1986 and 1995, barges carried an average of 9.8 million tons of coal, or about 12 percent of the total. Petroleum products trailed just behind at an average of 9.2 million tons (11 percent of the total) for the same period. Non-metallic minerals and metals, and industrial and agricultural chemicals accounted for most of the remaining tonnage. Towboats shoved 7.2 million tons of nonmetallic minerals (9 percent) and 3.8 million tons of metals (5 percent) on the river during the decade. And they guided barges holding 3.8 million tons of industrial chemicals and the same amount of agricultural chemicals (fertilizers) over the ten-year span (about 5 percent).[3] At 3.8 million tons and only 5 percent of total tonnage, industrial chemicals still exceeded total shipping on the river in 1940 by 1.5 million tons. Despite their seemingly inflated predictions, these numbers would stun Samuel Thorpe, George Lambert, Arne Wiprud, Henrik Shipstead, and other 9-foot channel navigation boosters.

Commerce has increased so dramatically that a new generation of navigation boosters is calling for more work. The boosters are complaining that demand for shipping on the river has exceeded the ability of the lock and dam system to carry it all. They have cited eight of the twenty-nine upper river locks as among the twenty worst for delays in the country. These delays, they contend, cost shippers as much as $35 million per year. A fifteen-barge tow—the standard size for the upper river—costs about $250 per hour to operate. It carries the equivalent of

870 semitrailers or 250 railroad cars. Glen Moeller, an Iowa corn farmer, reported that a three-day traffic jam on the upper river cost him five cents per bushel. Such delays hurt farmers, the barge industry, and, in the end, the consumer, the boosters contend.[4]

These delays cannot continue, they warn, since the United States is in an "intense battle" with other grain-producing nations. The boosters are especially worried about South America—Argentina and Brazil. Both countries, the boosters point out, are investing hundreds of millions of dollars to make their waterways more navigable. Farmers in Argentina have had low production costs, but their shipping costs have been high. On the basis of a 1996 study, the barge industry found that Iowa farmers paid an average of $2.33 a bushel to grow and harvest corn. Argentine farmers, they reported, paid $1.22. Iowa farmers, however, regained the advantage in shipping costs. By the time their grain reached a port, it cost $3.01, while the Argentine farmers' cost had increased to $3.21. Transportation costs accounted for most of the difference. Navigation boosters warn that delays at the locks and dams could easily consume the twenty-cent or so advantage Moeller and other midwestern farmers enjoy. As South American countries improve their rivers for navigation, the midwestern farmers' advantage will shrink. Unless the United States improves the locks and dams, the boosters predict, the advantage will disappear. As they exist today, the locks and dams on the upper river are "stop signs" or tollbooths on the route to the world's markets, according to grain shippers.[5]

Making matters worse, boosters argue, competition among railroads is weakening, and producers have again exceeded rail capacity. They say that several large railroads are dominating. Some states have only one major railroad. The boosters are not calling for more railroads; the competition, they point out, does not have to come from other railroads but from alternative transportation systems. As so many navigation boosters before them, they assert that just having an alternative provides competition and keeps shipping prices down.[6]

To navigation boosters, therefore, the Midwest's economic future lies with increasing the number of barges traveling up and down the river. The best solution, they insist, is to extend Locks 20 to 25 by 600 feet. Since a fifteen-barge tow is nearly 1,200 feet long, it has to break in half to go through the existing 600-foot locks. This can take from an hour and one-half to more than two hours. It is a problem reminiscent of the old days when steamboats had to break bulk to travel above St. Louis or the Des Moines Rapids. While the Corps is also examining small-scale measures such as helper boats, mooring cells, and extended guide walls, navigation boosters insist these are not enough. They assert that major improvements are the only solution. Environmentalists retort that even without further navigation improvements, the locks and dams have inflicted a potential deathblow to the river's native ecosystem.[7]

Ecosystem Change

In 1940 conservationists had little choice but to wait and see how the river's ecosystem would respond to the 9-foot channel project. Soon after the Corps completed the locks and dams, some favorable reports came in. They indicated that the river's fish and wildlife were thriving, as refuge manager Ray Steele had predicted. The new reservoirs created so much new aquatic habitat that waterfowl numbers had increased dramatically by 1953. The muskrats and other furbearing animals also multiplied, although other small mammals did not. Focusing on hunting and fishing, a 1954 study sponsored by the Upper Mississippi River Conservation Committee (UMRCC) found that the 9-foot channel had made the river more productive than on the eve of the project. The UMRCC formed in 1943 to study the upper river's fish and wildlife resources. Its twenty-two original members came largely from state and federal conservation offices of the five upper river states. The river's commercial fishery especially concerned them. Worry about drawdowns during World War II, pollution, and differing regulations among the five states led them to work together. Since the UMRCC's initial studies, biologists have recognized that some of the early benefits were temporary. In fact, the UMRCC issued the first warning of an ecosystem collapse on the upper river in 1993. In 2000, they released a report titled "A River That Works and a Working River: A Strategy for the Natural

Resources of the Upper Mississippi River System," in which they propose how to restore and preserve the river's ecosystem. Overall the effects of the locks and dams have been mixed. While some of the conservationists' greatest fears have not been realized, problems are occurring that they did not anticipate, and they have changed their minds about the nature of at least one problem.[8]

The worst fear of the Izaak Walton League, the Bureau of Fisheries, and other conservationists did not materialize. The new reservoirs did not become rank cesspools of organic pollution. As C. F. Culler and others had forecast, pollution combined with the new reservoirs led the Twin Cities and other towns along the upper river to build sewage treatment plants. St. Louis did not have to worry about dams holding back its pollution. So not only did the city continue dumping untreated sewage into the Mississippi, it decided to grind its garbage and send it down the river too.[9]

While organic pollutants have declined, other pollutants are threatening the river's water quality. Farmers applied twenty times more fertilizer to their crops in 1985 than they did in 1945, primarily phosphorus and nitrogen. As these nutrients run off the land and into the river, they cause widespread algae blooms, primarily in the still backwaters and side channels, reducing the river's oxygen levels. Between 1985 and 1998, the upper Mississippi River basin contributed 31 percent of the total nitrogen reaching the Gulf of Mexico, despite representing only 15 percent of the land area of the Mississippi River basin. Fertilizer runoff from the upper Mississippi is adding to the growth of the Gulf of Mexico's "deadzone." Pesticides and herbicides are also reaching the river in alarming quantities. "Although it drains just 22 percent of the total Mississippi River drainage basin, the upper Mississippi drainage contributes about 40 percent of the atrazine, and 50 percent of other pesticides," according to the *Mississippi Monitor*, a monthly newspaper published by the environmental organization American Rivers.[10] As more and more factory farms for hogs and cattle are established, animal feedlot runoff is flowing into the Mississippi's tributaries and into the main stem, killing thousands of fish. DDT and other hazardous chemicals remain embedded in the river's sediment and can escape when the sediment is stirred.[11]

Silt is still an issue, but in ways more complex than anyone anticipated. Frederick Biermann and A. C. Willford feared that the reservoirs would fill with silt. Their fears were being realized during the first decade and one-half after the Corps built the 9-foot channel project. The amount of silt entering the upper Mississippi River has decreased since the mid-1950s, however. Combined with the effects caused by the locks and dams, silt or the lack of silt are having a great impact on how the upper river is developing physically and ecologically. Some effects are occurring within the individual reservoirs, and some across the system.[12]

A variety of factors account for the decrease in the river's sediment load. Farmers have implemented soil conservation measures, the Corps and others have built dams on the upper river's tributaries, and the Corps has changed its dredging practices. Upland reservoirs have played an especially important role. Rather than flowing down the tributaries and into the Mississippi, the sediment is being trapped by the reservoirs. Together with improved farming practices, the tributary reservoirs have helped reduce the tributary sediment supply by about 45 percent since the building of the 9-foot channel. Although still needed, the demand for dredging has declined throughout much of the upper river.[13]

To reduce sediment from the Chippewa River, the Corps built a sediment trap at the river's mouth in 1984. The trap has cut the amount of silt entering the Mississippi from the Chippewa River by about 40 percent. As a result, the need for dredging in Pools 5 through 9 has declined. But the reduced sediment flow is affecting the river's geomorphic processes, its physical development. So much less sediment is coming into the river that the Chippewa's delta is not growing as fast as it had historically. The declining sediment load has decreased the sediment that helped build islands in the river below the Chippewa, where Pike, Long, Schoolcraft, and steamboat pilots became lost among the multiple channels.[14]

Key sedimentation and ecosystem issues are different above and below Rock Island. In general, the size of the reservoirs decreases as one moves downstream. This is largely due to the agricultural levees that line the river below Rock Island. Between Rock Island and St. Louis farmers have captured about 53 percent of the river's floodplain. The river is no longer able to meander through its floodplain. As a result, moving downstream the river has fewer landform features and, consequently, is less diverse. By separating the main channel from its floodplain, the levees prevent the flow of water, nutrients, fish, and wildlife across the valley floor, reducing habitat and species diversity. Levees have limited the area into which floodwater can spill, raising the flood profile, and the areas into which the river can deposit its sediment. The sediment has to be deposited along the main channel or in what side channels and backwaters exist, further reducing the available aquatic habitat. Above Rock Island only about 3 percent of the floodplain has been lost, owing largely to the Upper Mississippi River National Wildlife and Fish Refuge, and the river is still connected to most of its floodplain.[15]

As levees and the refuge define the Mississippi's boundaries, the river's natural features defined many aspects of its physical character after impoundment. Some high points that had once been seasonal islands became permanent islands. Side channels that had once dried out as the river fell acquired a continuous flow. Seasonally inundated floodplains became permanently flooded, forming permanent lakes and ponds. The greatest effects of impoundment occur in the lower part of each pool, where more of the historic floodplain has been permanently inundated. Within each pool, the downstream end has more open water. Moving up a pool, the depth over the floodplain becomes less, and more islands, braided channels, and shallow marshes exist. In the upper end of each pool (generally above Pool 13), the river retains its braided channels and is closest in appearance to what it was like before the locks and dams at moderate and high flows.[16]

In general, sediment is filling the deeper channels. The river's bottom at the downstream ends of the reservoirs and in the backwaters is becoming more uniform, taking away the variation in depth required by some fish and other aquatic species. Where areas of seasonally inundated floodplain have become permanently flooded, the continually saturated soils support fewer tree species, leaving the floodplain forest more vulnerable to disease. Due to the constantly moist conditions, the floodplain trees do not develop strong root systems, and strong winds push them over more easily, quickening shoreline erosion.[17]

Water-level management remains an issue but not in the way conservationists had feared on the eve of the 9-foot channel. The Bureau of Fisheries and the Izaak Walton League had insisted that the Corps hold the river level steady. Now biologists realize that one of the greatest adverse environmental effects of the locks and dams is the loss of the river's natural low-water cycle. The dams allow the river to rise to natural high-water elevations. Once the river reaches a certain high point, the Corps lifts the roller gates and tainter gates out of the water and the river runs free. As the river falls, the Corps lowers the gates to maintain the 9-foot channel. Without the river dropping to its natural low level, the backwaters and channel borders cannot dry out, the sediment cannot compact, the natural vegetation cycle cannot occur, and the fish, birds, and other animals that rely on aquatic plants lose something critical to their ecosystem. Even though a pool approaches the appearance of the natural river at the upstream end, it is still high enough to maintain a 9-foot channel during low water and never falls as low as it might have before the Corps built the dam.[18]

Fish passage became a critical issue to conservationists during the debates over building the 9-foot channel. Corps engineers believed that the gates in the dams would allow fish to pass through. The locks and dams, however, obstruct fish migration to various degrees. Conservationists are again raising the issue of fish passage. The upper Mississippi River supports about 143 native fish species. At least 25 species migrated historically. Some made long-distance migrations, including the lake sturgeon, paddlefish, American eel, Alabama shad, skipjack herring, blue sucker, blue catfish, northern pike, white bass, walleye, and sauger. Many of these fish migrated to and from spawning grounds.[19]

Connectivity—the uninterrupted connection between the main channel, secondary channels, floodplain water bodies, and tributaries—

is critical to the movement of fish and other species between and within the navigation pools. Connectivity can be longitudinal (up and down the river) and lateral (from the main channel to side channels and backwaters). Fish evolved migration patterns to take advantage of the seasonal availability of different habitats up and down the river and along it. The dams have primarily disrupted longitudinal connectivity, and the levees below Rock Island have obstructed lateral connectivity. Sedimentation associated with the dams and levees has interrupted lateral connectivity as well.[20]

Locks and Dams 1 and 19 present the greatest barriers to fish movement on the upper Mississippi River. Lock and Dam No. 1, however, does not pose a serious problem. St. Anthony Falls is only 6 miles above the lock and dam and may have created a natural barrier historically to fish migration. Lock and Dam No. 19, at just over 38 feet, has the second highest lift on the river and bars the river for over 480 miles above. The skipjack has disappeared from above Lock and Dam No. 19, along with the ebony mussel, whose larvae use the skipjack as a host. Lake sturgeon, paddlefish, blue sucker, and blue catfish are rare above Lock and Dam No. 19. During the annual spring snowmelt, Locks and Dams 3, 5A, 9, 10, 12, 16, 17, and 20 through 26 usually lift their gates, and the river flows freely. These dams present an opportunity for fish to migrate upstream most years. Locks and Dams 2, 5, 11, 14, and 15 do not lift their gates out as often, and obstruct fish migration in most years.[21] Some fish, however, may not be able to take advantage of the gates being open during high water, since their migration may not coincide with high water. The swimming abilities of different species vary and also determine the conditions under which they migrate. It is more difficult for fish to migrate during periods of low flow, since the head, or difference between the pool above and the one below, is too great and the velocity through the gates too strong. Because they cannot migrate, some fish species lose access to seasonal habitat needed for foraging, wintering over, or cool-water retreats in the summer.[22]

Other factors affect connectivity. By disconnecting the river from its floodplain, levees bar fish from their natural spawning grounds, where the young fingerlings once found plankton abundant. Levees also eliminate the isolated floodplain pools essential to many invertebrates, reptiles, amphibians, and birds. Levees, by reducing the area the river can place sediment and forcing it to deposit more sediment in the main and secondary channels, accelerate habitat loss and fragmentation.[23]

New problems threatening the river have little to do with the locks and dams. Although related to the development of America's waterways for navigation (in this case the Great Lakes), exotic species have entered the Mississippi River, and others may arrive soon. In 1848 Chicago completed the Illinois and Michigan Canal, connecting the Great Lakes and Mississippi River basin. The canal connected the Chicago River, which flowed into Lake Michigan, with the Des Plaines River, a tributary of the Illinois River. In 1871, Chicago reversed the flow of the Chicago River to send its sewage and animal packing plant wastes into the Illinois River. This connection and the opening of the Great Lakes to ocean-going freighters made possible the interbasin transfer of exotic species. In 1959 the St. Lawrence Seaway opened allowing ocean-going freighters into the Great Lakes. Most invaders have entered through ballast tanks of these ships. The zebra mussel and the sea lamprey are probably the best known. The zebra mussel moved into the Illinois River in 1991. The small mussel attaches to practically anything and multiplies like a coral reef in fast motion. Now all 297 freshwater mussel species in the Mississippi River are threatened with extinction. The Chinese mitten crab and the round goby have infested the Great Lakes and are poised to enter the Illinois and Mississippi Rivers. The crab is a host for a fluke called the Oriental lung, which can attack humans. The round goby, a fish from the Caspian Sea, is already pushing native fish out of their habitat in Lake Superior. It soon may invade the Mississippi River. Zooplankton found in the waters of Africa, India, and Australia have been discovered in the Illinois River. The plankton has spines that make it difficult for fish to swallow.[24]

The 9-foot channel project and other natural and human-made forces are clearly changing the upper Mississippi River. As the above discussion shows, determining the overall impact of the 9-foot channel system on the river's ecosystem is complex, far more complex even than presented here. The river's ecosystem is evolving into something much different from what it had been before American settlement. Yet there is continuity. Some of the changes have been detrimental to some species and beneficial to others. Some parts of the upper Mississippi River are losing one type of habitat faster than others. If left unaddressed, some habitat types and the species that depend on them may disappear from parts of the upper river.

The Power Structure

Just as historical developments have defined the river's physical and ecological character, they have formed the power structure that governs the river today. The power structure was well grounded by 1940. The federal government dominated. At the request of navigation interests and floodplain farmers and through the Corps of Engineers, the government had transformed the river for navigation and floodplain development. For conservationists and through the precursors of the Fish and Wildlife Service, it had carved out a large part of the upper Mississippi River valley for a fish and wildlife refuge, which it manages. As of 1940, navigation interests, farmers, and others who sought to develop the river and its floodplains clearly prevailed and would for many more years.

In 1940 navigation was still the primary use, and the Corps the dominant agency. Neither might have been true without the 9-foot channel project. On the eve of the 9-foot channel, all the Corps' efforts and millions of the nation's dollars had failed to keep or bring commerce to the river. Navigation opponents could argue, with good cause, that a new project and more money would not work either. Some Corps officers agreed and wanted to walk away. The 9-foot channel reversed this. Not only did commerce return, the Corps remained the leading entity. Its flood-control mission strengthened this position.[25]

What role the government should play in protecting floodplain occupants had been established by 1940. Farmers had convinced the federal government to reinforce their investment in the river's floodplains.

With the flood-control acts authorized for the upper Mississippi River between 1917 and 1928, Congress approved the first major federal efforts to fortify the upper and middle Mississippi River's agricultural levees. Floodplain farmers have come to expect the federal government, through the Corps, to defend them and their property, largely at federal expense. After 1928, Congress and the Corps—at the insistence of floodplain occupants—expanded flood control to include urban areas, reservoir projects, and the river's tributaries. The greatest changes in the upper Mississippi River basin after 1940 would occur in the river's tributaries and uplands.[26]

The debate over 9-foot channel project ended navigation's singular hold on the river. No longer could navigation boosters assume that the region would unite behind their dreams. In creating the Upper Mississippi River National Wildlife and Fish Refuge, Will Dilg and the Izaak Walton League challenged agricultural and commercial interests as to the primary values of the river and its floodplains. And during the final stages of the 9-foot channel's approval, the league and other conservationists demonstrated that they planned to stay and to have their say about the river. The compromises they won under the 9-foot channel project—even if minor—signaled a new framework for managing the upper Mississippi River.

The river's improving health has spurred recreational use. Millions of visitors come to the upper Mississippi River each year. Recreation—boating, swimming, fishing, birding, or simply enjoying the scenery—generates more than $1.2 billion annually for the states of the upper Mississippi River and has created 18,000 jobs nationwide. Recognizing the connection between tourism, economic prosperity, and the river's history, President Bill Clinton declared the upper Mississippi River a national heritage river in 1998. People who recreate on the river are increasingly concerned for its ecological and scenic qualities and have added to the constituency worried about the effects of further navigation improvements. At the same time, many of the large recreational boats could not operate on the river without the locks and dams.

The River Divided

Since 1940, the hopes of navigation boosters have been realized, and the fears of conservationists have come to pass, if not exactly as they predicted. This history has led to the present debate over the need to expand the navigation system again and the need to preserve and restore the river's ecosystem. How does the nation balance the needs for navigation against the river's ecosystem needs? Is balance possible? Some environmental historians suggest it is not. For the Columbia River, Richard White argues that sharing the pie between various users "has not worked and will not work."[27] Salmon and huge hydroelectric dams cannot coexist. Another environmental historian, Donald Worster, believes he knows why. He sees the West locked in a "hydraulic trap."[28] The great water systems built by the Bureau of Reclamation and others for urban water supply, irrigation, flood control, and hydroelectric power have created a snare from which the West cannot escape to develop solutions that are economically and ecologically sustainable. Within Worster's framework, the upper Mississippi River locks and dams and the agricultural levee system below Rock Island form such a trap.[29]

Yet, on the upper Mississippi, Congress has directed the parties to divide the pie. In 1986, Congress pronounced the upper Mississippi River a "nationally significant ecosystem and a nationally significant commercial navigation system." To this end, Congress declared: "The system shall be administered and regulated in recognition of its several purposes."[30] The battles, negotiations, meetings, and summits going on now are about dividing the pie. Navigation boosters are trying to hold on to the piece they have, and, if possible, get more. Environmentalists are calling for a bigger piece. Supporters of both sides predict dire consequences if their needs are not met.

Trying to balance navigation and ecosystem protection, Congress established the Environmental Management Program (EMP) in 1986. The EMP emerged from the largest battle between navigation interests and environmental organizations in the upper river's history. The program demonstrates how much stronger conservationists have become since Dilg won the refuge. Congress authorized the EMP to compensate for the potential ecological effects that adding a second lock at Lock and Dam No. 26, at Alton, Illinois, would have. The principal impacts were expected from increased traffic. The program has five key components: habitat rehabilitation and enhancement projects, long-term resource monitoring, recreation projects, an economic impacts of recreation study, and navigation monitoring. The Corps oversees the program with help from the Department of the Interior, the Upper Mississippi River Basin Association, and the five states of the upper river. The public also provides input.[31]

Under the EMP, federal and state agencies are cooperating on dozens of habitat restoration and enhancement projects. These efforts include dredging to remove sediment from backwaters and side channels, and building dikes and levees to keep silt out of backwaters and to regulate flow to the backwaters to increase dissolved oxygen during low flow. Regulating the water level helps re-create the river's natural cycles and maximize aquatic plant growth. Under the EMP, the Corps is building and protecting islands in the lower portions of some pools, where the large reservoirs have caused many to erode away. Made of dredged material, the new islands stop waves from stirring up sediment, so plants can get the light they need to grow. The Corps is also notching wing dams near the shore to restore main channel habitat. EMP participants recognize that they cannot truly re-create the natural river, but they hope to retard the worst ecosystem effects and restore some of the river's natural functions. Critics of the EMP contend that its solutions are too local and too insignificant to make much difference. They see it as coming from within the trap, and therefore limited in scope and effect.

Separate from the EMP, conservationists are working with the Corps to manage the navigation pools to re-create or mimic the river's natural cycle. The Corps has lowered the reservoir levels behind a number of dams, exposing side channel mud flats. This has promoted the resurgence of aquatic plants that supply food to migratory waterfowl. Whether these measures will be enough is still in question. The success or failure of these measures and of the EMP will tell whether dividing the pie in this way can work.

The UMRCC has developed a nine-point program to address the problems discussed above. They too hope to restore the river's natural processes and to preserve those that still exist, within the framework of locks and dams and levees. The UMRCC sees its effort as a test of whether the pie can be divided. If its program yields measures that are successful, says the UMRCC, the results "could have the added benefit of showing that it is possible to maintain and manage a large floodplain river for both navigation system and ecosystem benefits." If the river's ecosystem continues to decline under the 9-foot channel project, the UMRCC warns, it will become "increasingly difficult for resource managers and the public who benefit from the natural resources of the river to support continued operation and maintenance activities for commercial navigation."[32] In this respect, the upper Mississippi River is in a time of testing. The success or failure of the various environmental restoration programs will determine whether the pie can be divided and whether the upper Mississippi is locked in a hydraulic trap. How long the testing will occur is not clear.

If the upper Mississippi River is locked in a trap and can only be released by removing the locks and dams and levees, what does this mean? To address this question, we have to consider the consequences of removing the infrastructure of the upper Mississippi's hydraulic system. The implications are not as clear for the Mississippi as they are for the West. The West's economic and political existence is based on controlling water. Los Angeles, San Francisco, and many other cities could not survive as they do without the huge dams, tunnels, pipes, and canals that bring them water and electricity. The Imperial Valley and other normally arid lands would revert to desert without irrigation.

The upper Mississippi is not the same as the Colorado, Columbia, or other western rivers, and it is used differently. It may not be locked as tightly in Worster's hydraulic trap. Controlling the Mississippi does not underlie the Midwest's economic and political character as the control of western rivers does the West's. Therefore, the possibilities for change may be greater for the Midwest and the Mississippi. Taking out the locks and dams would not cause the economic collapse of the Midwest. Grain and other bulk commodities would have to move by rail or truck. This would have profound consequences for midwestern agriculture, but agriculture would continue. Other commodities would have to move on other modes as well, and their costs would increase. Eliminating the river's agricultural floodplain levees would hurt specific areas and businesses but would not undermine the Midwest's economy. Of course, many cities and businesses along the river have become dependent on the reservoirs for a variety of uses from drinking water to cooling power plants. Taking out the dams would have effects far beyond navigation and agriculture.

Yet, would an ecosystem collapse on the upper Mississippi fundamentally alter the Midwest's economy and society? Biodiversity would decline. Different, "less desirable," or invasive species would replace preferred species. Severely diminishing the upper Mississippi as a flyway would reverberate internationally, from South America to Canada. Fewer ducks, geese, and neotropical songbirds would travel the Mississippi corridor. Hunting, fishing, and bird-watching would change, and the economic benefits gained from recreation that depends on such activities would fall. The extended ramifications of an ecosystem collapse on the upper Mississippi are difficult, if not impossible, to determine.

Is the Midwest or the nation willing to accept either the demise of the Mississippi River's ecosystem or the loss of navigation? To many people, the river is a place that has escaped, or at least slowed, George Catlin's splendid juggernaut. Running from Lake Itasca to the Gulf of Mexico, it is the biggest piece of nature in the central United States. As the third largest of such large floodplain rivers in the world, it is an especially unique piece of nature. For too long it has suffered from our focus on what we can extract from it. Trapped or not, the upper Mississippi is defined more by the visions that made it a navigation channel than by its own natural character. Yet, today, popular grassroots support for the river is behind protecting its scenic and ecological qualities.

Would the Midwest react differently than Samuel Thorpe and other

9-foot channel boosters to a modern-day Indiana Rate Case that declared the region landlocked? Historically, the Mississippi River has been a symbol of connection between regions and to the world. For two centuries Midwesterners and the nation have thought of and used the Mississippi as a highway. Zebulon Pike made clear the potential and problems for navigation on the upper river, and the locks and dams have realized that potential and have overcome those problems. However, the navigation interests have lost the grassroots appeal they had up through the 9-foot channel movement. Large agricultural corporations and the towing industry dominate the current movement. Today, the public is largely unaware that the Mississippi River is part of the Midwest's transportation system.

Apparently, Americans are unwilling to accept either the loss of the river's ecosystem or the loss of the river as a transportation artery, since Congress has mandated that it be managed for both. Again, we are in a time of testing to see if both can be accomplished. The fourth upper Mississippi River is coming; what it looks like and how it functions will depend on the outcome of this testing.

The questions raised and speculations offered here demonstrate the complexity and weight of decisions before the Midwest and the nation. No side has the inherently right answers. We have to make choices about what we value most. My goal has been to get people interested in the debate over the river's future so they can enter that debate with some knowledge of its depth and breadth, and so the decisions they make are informed. This book has been about how the values, dreams, and desires held by Midwesterners have shaped the river physically and ecologically. Today, we are making choices, or avoiding choices, that will define the river's ecosystem and the Midwest's economy. As the river wrought by our predecessors has led us into the current dilemma, whatever we decide will become manifest in the river and the economy we leave to the future generations.

Notes

Introduction

1. "Two-Big-Meetings," February 20, 1931, papers of the Izaak Walton League of America-Minnesota Division, 151.F.17.13B, Minnesota Historical Society, St. Paul.

2. I define the upper Mississippi River as the reach between Minneapolis, Minnesota, and St. Louis, Missouri. Throughout the history of navigation improvements, Congress and the Corps have approached this reach, or most of it, with the same projects. The middle Mississippi runs down to the mouth of the Ohio River, and the lower Mississippi from there to the mouth. Some divide the river into two segments, with the Ohio River the divide between the upper and lower.

3. Upper Mississippi River Conservation Committee (Rock Island, Ill.), "Facing the Threat: An Ecosystem Management Strategy for the Upper Mississippi River, A Call for Action from the Upper Mississippi River Conservation Committee," December 1993; Steve Johnson, "The Mississippi River: A Great Ecosystem in Decline," Presentation, April 6, 1994, Minnesota Department of Natural Resources, Division of Waters; "Position Statement, Management of the Upper Mississippi River Ecosystem (Minneapolis, Minnesota, to Cairo, Illinois)" (St. Paul: Minnesota Department of Natural Resources, January 1995); Ann Robinson and Mark Robbins, "Restoring the Big River: A Clean Water Act Blueprint for the Mississippi," (Izaak Walton League of America and Natural Resources Defense Council, February 1994), 1, 7, 12, 14, 15.

4. Richard White, *The Organic Machine: The Remaking of the Columbia River* (New York: Hill and Wang, 1995), 112; White adds that "dividing the

Columbia up among users has not worked and will not work. Nor can a solution be found by reducing uses to dollars and selecting the most valuable ones" (112).

5. Upper Mississippi River Basin Association, "Forging a New Framework for the Future: A Report to the Governors on State and Federal Management of the Upper Mississippi River" (St. Paul: Upper Mississippi River Basin Association, August 1995).

1. Innumerable

1. G. C. Beltrami, *A Pilgrimage in America, Leading to the Discovery of the Sources of the Mississippi and Bloody Rivers; with a Description of the Whole Course of the Former, and of the Ohio* (1828; Chicago: Quadrangle Books, 1962), 127.

2. Beltrami, *Pilgrimage*, 127–28; Walter Havighurst, *Voices on the River: The Story of the Mississippi Waterways* (New York: Macmillan Company, 1964), 110, says the Virginia's draft was 5 feet, as opposed to Beltrami, who says 6.

3. Mildred Hartsough, *From Canoe to Steel Barge* (Minneapolis: University of Minnesota Press, 1934), 29–32, 48–49, 52, 67; Erik F. Haites, James Mak, and Gary M. Walton, *Western River Transportation: The Era of Early Internal Development, 1810–1860* (Baltimore: The Johns Hopkins University Press, 1975), 15–17; Roald D. Tweet, *History of Transportation on the Upper Mississippi and Illinois Rivers* (U.S. Army Water Resources Support Center, Institute for Water Resources, 1983), 14–15; Roald Tweet, "A History of Navigation Improvements on the Rock Island Rapids: The Background of Locks and Dam 15" (Rock Island District: U.S. Army, Corps of Engineers, April 1980), 1–3.

4. David A. Lanegran and Anne Mosher-Sheridan, "The European Settlement of the Upper Mississippi River Valley: Cairo, Illinois, to Lake Itasca, Minnesota–1540 to 1860," in *Historic Lifestyles in the Upper Mississippi River Valley*, ed. John S. Wozniak (Lanham, Md.: University Press of America, 1983), 23–25; Roald Tweet, *A History of the Rock Island District, U.S. Army Corps of Engineers, 1866–1983* (Washington, D.C.: U.S. Government Printing Office, 1984), 39; William J. Petersen, *Steamboating on the Upper Mississippi* (Iowa City: State Historical Society of Iowa, 1968), 206–9, 246; William J. Petersen, "Captains and Cargoes of Early Upper Mississippi Steamboats," *Wisconsin Magazine of History* 13 (1929-30): 227–32; Hartsough, *Canoe*, 65–66; Tweet, "Rapids," 2. John O. Jensen, "Gently Down the Stream: An Inquiry into the History of Transportation on the Northern Mississippi River and the Potential for Submerged Cultural Resources," *Wisconsin Archeologist* 73: 1–2 (March–June 1992): 71, says that only about twenty boats were operating above Galena before 1847.

Military supplies and furs dominated the much smaller steamboat trade above Galena.

5. George Byron Merrick, Appendix B, "Opening of Navigation at St. Paul, 1844–1862," in *Old Times on the Upper Mississippi: The Recollections of a Steamboat Pilot from 1854 to 1863* (St. Paul: Minnesota Historical Society Press, 1987), 295. Merrick lists the number of arrivals and the number of boats at St. Paul for each of these years. His figures for arrivals differ slightly from those of Dixon in Table 1.1. He lists 99 boats as accounting for 965 arrivals in 1857, and 62 boats as accounting for 1,090 arrivals in 1858; see Frank Haigh Dixon, *A Traffic History of the Mississippi River System*, National Waterways Commission, Document No. 11 (Washington, D.C.: U.S. Government Printing Office, 1909), 20–24. Hartsough, *Canoe*, 57, 100–103; Tweet, "Rapids," 2.

6. Hartsough, *Canoe*, 103.

7. Hartsough, *Canoe*, 101–2; Merrick, *Old Times*, 162, says that "from 1852 to 1857 there were not boats enough to carry the people who were flocking into the newly-opened farmers' and lumbermans' paradise."

8. Tweet, *Transportation*, 22.

9. Tweet, *Transportation*, 21–22; Petersen, "Captains and Cargoes," 228, 234–38; Hartsough, *Canoe*, 74–75, 106–7; Walter Havighurst, *Upper Mississippi, A Wilderness Saga* (New York: Farrar and Rinehart, 1937; New York: J. J. Little and Ives Company, 1944), 166; Frederick J. Dobney, *River Engineers of the Middle Mississippi: A History of the St. Louis District, U.S. Army Corps of Engineers* (Washington, D.C.: U.S. Government Printing Office, 1978), 33; Donald B. Dodd and Wynelle S. Dodd, *Historical Statistics of the United States, 1790–1970*, vol. 2, *The Midwest* (University: University of Alabama Press, 1973), 2, 10, 22, 46.

10. Dixon, *Traffic History*, 29–30; Frederic L. Paxson, "Railroads of the Old Northwest, before the Civil War," *Transactions of the Wisconsin Academy of Sciences, Arts, and Letters* 17 (1914): 257–60, 269–71. William Cronon, *Nature's Metropolis: Chicago and the Great West* (New York: W. W. Norton and Company, 1991), 296, says that the first railroad to reach the Mississippi River was the Chicago, Alton and St. Louis in 1852–53. However, Paxson, whom he cites, shows that the railroad completed tracks from Alton to Springfield, Illinois, in 1852, and then from Springfield to Chicago, via a roundabout route, in 1853, but did not have the line in operation until 1854. Gary F. Browne, "The Railroads: Terminals and Nexus Points in the Upper Mississippi Valley," in *Historic Lifestyles in the Upper Mississippi River Valley*, ed. John S. Wozniak (Lanham, Md.: University Press of America, 1983), 84, says the first railroad reached the

Mississippi River at Rock Island on February 22, 1854. Petersen, *Steamboating*, 298, also recognizes the railroad at Rock Island as the first to reach the river.

11. Dodd and Dodd, *Historical Statistics*, 2, 12, 24, 48.

12. Hartsough, *Canoe*, 103, 116–17; she notes that barge shipping—as opposed to steamboat shipping—grew rapidly in the 1860s and 1870s.

13. Robert F. Fries, *Empire in Pine: The Story of Lumbering in Wisconsin, 1830–1900* (Madison: State Historical Society of Wisconsin, 1951), 20; Cronon, *Nature's Metropolis*, 152; William G. Rector, "A Concise History of the Lumber Industry in the Upper Mississippi River Valley," in *Historic Lifestyles in the Upper Mississippi River Valley*, ed. John S. Wozniak (Lanham, Md.: University Press of America, 1983), 413–15; Cronon, *Nature's Metropolis*, 153–54; Fries, *Empire*, 78.

14. Fries, *Empire*, 55; Havighurst, *Upper Mississippi*, 246–47; Rector, "Concise History," 430–32.

15. Hartsough, *Canoe*, 54, 104, 119; Rector, "Concise History," 436.

16. Haites, *Western River Transportation*, 26, contends that only economic crises and the unimproved rivers slowed the rise of navigation on western rivers before the Civil War. Cronon, *Nature's Metropolis*, 296–305, shows how railroads helped Chicago begin undermining St. Louis as the major metropolis of the central United States, and how river boosters in St. Louis still believed the river would overcome any competition offered by railroads. He does not, however, challenge the river's growing significance as a transportation route in the antebellum era, and he does not argue that railroads sent the river into decline at this time. This happened after the war.

17. Todd Shallat, *Structures in the Stream: Water, Science, and the Rise of the U.S. Army Corps of Engineers* (Austin: University of Texas, 1994), 141.

18. Zebulon Pike, *The Expeditions of Zebulon Montgomery Pike*, ed. Elliott Coues, vol. 1 (1895; reprint, New York: Dover Publications, 1987), viii–ix.

19. Pike, *Expeditions*, 7–8, 12. Hartsough, *Canoe*, 29, says that the average keelboat had a draft of 20 to 30 inches.

20. Pike, *Expeditions*, 1, 287–93; the discussion of timber is from chap. 7, "Geography of the Mississippi." River miles are based on the U.S. Army Corps of Engineers, Upper Mississippi River Navigation Charts (1989).

21. Henry Rowe Schoolcraft, *Schoolcraft's Narrative Journal of Travels: Through the Northwestern Regions of the United States Extending from Detroit through the Great Chain of American Lakes to the Sources of the Mississippi River, in the Year 1820*, ed. Mentor L. Williams (East Lansing: Michigan State University Press, 1953, 1992), 232.

22. Jonathan Carver, *The Journals of Jonathan Carver and Related Documents, 1766–1770*, ed. John Parker (St. Paul: Minnesota Historical Society Press, 1976), 89.

23. Beltrami, *Pilgrimage*, 131–32.

24. Beltrami, *Pilgrimage*, 176–78. Writing in the 1850s, Henry Lewis, *The Valley of the Mississippi Illustrated*, ed. Bertha L. Heilbron, trans. A. Hermina Poatgieter (St. Paul: Minnesota Historical Society, 1967), 156, says that the prairie fires had two purposes: to make it easier to kill game, and to remove the old grass and allow new shoots to come up for cattle. He also notes that the fires prevented trees from growing.

25. Louis Hennepin, *Father Louis Hennepin's Description of Louisiana, Newly Discovered to the Southwest of New France by Order of the King* (Minneapolis: University of Minnesota Press, 1938), 93–94, 104–5; William Watts Folwell, *A History of Minnesota*, vol. 1 (St. Paul: Minnesota Historical Society Press, 1956), 27–29.

26. Schoolcraft, *Narrative Journal*, 232.

27. Pike, *Expeditions*, 49.

28. Ibid., 244; see also 4, 292.

29. Schoolcraft, *Narrative Journal*, Appendix F, "The Journal and Letters of James Duane Doty," 435.

30. George W. Featherstonhaugh, *A Canoe Voyage up the Minnay Sotor*, vol. 1 (1847; reprint; St. Paul: Minnesota Historical Society, 1970), 220.

31. Havighurst, *Upper Mississippi*, 249; Merrick, *Old Times*, 232.

32. Featherstonhaugh, *Canoe Voyage*, 224.

33. Pike, *Expeditions*, 212.

34. William H. Keating, *Narrative of an Expedition to the Source of the St. Peter's River, Lake Winnepeek, Lake of the Woods, & c., Performed in the Year 1823 by the Order of Hon. J. C. Calhoun, Secretary of War, under the Command of Stephen H. Long, U.S.T.E.* (Minneapolis: Ross and Haines, 1959), 296.

35. Ibid., 303.

36. Pike, *Expeditions*, 13–15; Stephen H. Long, *The Northern Expeditions of Stephen H. Long, The Journals of 1817 and 1823 and Related Documents*, ed. Lucile M. Kane, June D. Holmquist, and Carolyn Gilman (St. Paul: Minnesota Historical Society Press, 1978), 104.

37. Pike, *Expeditions*, 24–25.

38. Beltrami, *Pilgrimage*, 149, 159–60; Tweet, "Rapids," 1–3; John B. Appleton, "The Declining Significance of the Mississippi as a Commercial

Highway in the Middle of the Nineteenth Century," *Geographical Society of Philadelphia Bulletin* 28 (January–October 1930): 267–68.

39. Merrick, *Old Times*, 295, presents a table of the opening dates for navigation between 1844 and 1862.

40. U.S. Army Corps of Engineers, *Annual Reports of the Chief of Engineers* (Washington, D.C.: U.S. Government Printing Office, 1876–present), 1872, 309. The U.S. government began printing the *Annual Report of the Chief of Engineers* in 1867. It was usually published at the end of the fiscal year, which has varied over time. For most of the era covered by this book, the fiscal year began on July 1. All subsequent references to these reports are shortened to *Annual Report*, with the date of the fiscal year. *Annual Report*, 1877, 528–29; *Annual Report*, 1881, 2746; U.S. Congress, House, "Mississippi River between Missouri River and St. Paul, Minn.," House Document No. 341, 59th Congress, 2d sess., 3.

41. Pike, *Expeditions*, 4–5, 13, 287–90. Contrary to his journal entry that the river above the Des Moines Rapids was full of sandbars, Pike later wrote that above the rapids "the navigation is by no means difficult" (291).

42. Long, *Northern Expeditions*, 78, 81, 96.

43. Schoolcraft, *Narrative Journal*, 216–17; Appendix G, "The Journal and Letters of Charles Christopher Trowbridge, Expedition of 1820," 494.

44. Merrick, *Old Times*, 15, 18–19, 29–30.

45. Ibid., 35.

46. Ibid., xii–xiii, 35, 80, 83, 240.

47. Ibid., 93.

48. Merrick, *Old Times*, 100; Havighurst, *Upper Mississippi*, 158–59.

49. Merrick, *Old Times*, 224.

50. Lewis, *Mississippi Illustrated*, 51.

51. Capt. "Nate" [Nathan] Daly, *Tracks and Trails: Incidents in the Life of a Minnesota Pioneer* (Walker, Minn.: Cass County Pioneer, 1931), 18.

52. Havighurst, *Upper Mississippi*, 161.

53. Hennepin, *Louisiana*, 93, 118–21; Keating, *Narrative*, 302.

54. Pike, *Expeditions*, 6; George Catlin, *Letters and Notes on the Manners, Customs, and Conditions of North American Indians*, vol. 2 (1844; reprint, New York: Dover Publications, 1973), 143–44; Keating, *Narrative*, 285, 323.

55. Pike, *Expeditions*, 5; Schoolcraft, *Narrative Journal*, 215; Keating, *Narrative*, 295; Hennepin, *Louisiana*, 120.

56. "The Log of Capt. R. [Robert] A. McCabe," Typed manuscript, Manuscript Notebooks, yP2111, Minnesota Historical Society Collections, 1.

57. Long, *Northern Expeditions*, 82, 84; Schoolcraft, *Narrative Journal*, 213; Beltrami, *Pilgrimage*, 160, 186; Keating, *Narrative*, 279, 296.

58. John Lauritz Larson, "'Bind the Republic Together': The National Union and the Struggle for a System of Internal Improvements," *Journal of American History* 74, 2 (September 1987): 363–87; Shallat, *Structures*, chaps. 4 and 5, quote from 118–19; Tweet, *Rock Island District*, 35; John R. Howe, *From the Revolution through the Age of Jackson: Innocence and Empire in the Young Republic* (Englewood Cliffs, N.J.: Prentice-Hall, 1973), 84.

59. Shallat, *Structures*, chap. 4. Shallat does not dispel the overall argument that the federal government did not support a large, sustained program of internal improvements; he does not try to. He demonstrates that federal support went through phases, and he strengthens a theme that much of what the Corps is today emerged before the Civil War. No matter how extensive, he argues, the Corps' work before the war "created a vast civil-works jurisdiction for the Corps … " (118). Edward L. Pross, "A History of Rivers and Harbors Bills, 1866–1933" (Ph.D. diss., Ohio State University, 1938), chap. 1, argues that Congress funded almost no work before 1866, and it had little impact.

60. Shallat, *Structures*, 126–27; Dobney, *River Engineers*, 20; Pross, "Bills," 13–15.

61. Dobney, *River Engineers*, 21–23; Louis C. Hunter, *Steamboats on Western Rivers: An Economic and Technological History* (Boston: Harvard University Press, 1949; reprint, New York: Octagon Books, 1969), chap. 2; Jon Gjerde, "Historical Evaluation, St. Paul District Locks and Dams on the Mississippi River and Two Structures of St. Anthony Falls," unpublished report, St. Paul District, U.S. Army Corps of Engineers, St. Paul, September 1983, 56, 58–59; Shallat, *Structures*, 146, 151; Howe, *Age of Jackson*, 189, notes that both the Whig and Democratic Parties contained internal contradictions. Despite his public opposition to federal backing for internal improvements, Jackson approved the spending of more money than all his predecessors combined. Isaac Lippincott, "A History of River Improvement," *Journal of Political Economy* 22 (Chicago: University of Chicago Press, 1914): 632, contends that presidents from Monroe to Buchanan supported internal improvements, but they believed that the constitution prohibited federal spending on such projects.

62. Shallat, *Structures*, 153. St. Louis finally completed the project in 1856; see Dobney, *River Engineers*, 28–29, 31.

63. Dobney, *River Engineers*, 26–28; Tweet, *Rock Island District*, 38–47.

64. Shallat, *Structures*, 153; Pross, "Bills," 24.

65. Tweet, *Rock Island District*, 49; Howe, *Age of Jackson*, 187; Pross, "Bills," 25–33.

66. Combined with a high tariff on imports and a strong central bank, internal improvements comprised the elements of Clay's American System. See Shallat, *Structures*, 123.

67. Shallat, *Structures*, 125.

68. Shallat, *Structures*, 142, 171, 174; Pross, "Bills," 33–35.

69. Shallat, *Structures*, 178.

70. Shallat, *Structures*, 153, 177, 184; Dobney, *River Engineers*, 32; Tweet, *Transportation*, 46; Tweet, *Rock Island District*, 52–61; Tweet, "Rapids," 1–3; Lippincott, "River Improvement," 633–34; Pross, "Bills," 33–40.

2. This Splendid Juggernaut

1. George Catlin, *Letters and Notes*, 1835, vol. 2, 156.

2. Ibid., 155–59.

3. Edward L. Pross, "A History of Rivers and Harbors Bills, 1866–1933" (Ph.D. diss., Ohio State University, 1938), 44; Roald Tweet, *A History of the Rock Island District, U.S. Army Corps of Engineers, 1866–1983* (Washington, D.C.: U.S. Government Printing Office, 1984), 64; Todd Shallat, *Structures in the Stream, Water, Science, and the Rise of the U.S. Army Corps of Engineers* (Austin: University of Texas, 1994), 189.

4. *Annual Report*, 1892, 1760.

5. Isaac Lippincott, "A History of River Improvement," *Journal of Political Economy* 22 (Chicago: University of Chicago Press, 1914): 631; Tweet, *Rock Island District*, 66; William Cronon, *Nature's Metropolis: Chicago and the Great West* (New York: W. W. Norton and Company, 1991), 299; Pross, "Bills," 51.

6. Lester Shippee, "Steamboating on the Upper Mississippi after the Civil War: A Mississippi Magnate," *Mississippi Valley Historical Review* 6: 4 (March 1920): 496; Frank Haigh Dixon, *A Traffic History of the Mississippi River System, National Waterways Commission, Document No. 11* (Washington, D.C.: U.S. Government Printing Office, 1909), 49; Mildred Hartsough, *From Canoe to Steel Barge* (Minneapolis: University of Minnesota Press, 1934), 84–85, 91, 196–97, 199, 203; Roald D. Tweet, *History of Transportation on the Upper Mississippi and Illinois Rivers* (U.S. Army Water Resources Support Center, Institute for Water Resources, 1983), 38-39.

7. Tweet, *Transportation*, 25, 28, suggests that shippers formed the "habit" of shipping goods along the east-west route during the Civil War. Hartsough,

Canoe, 195-96, contends that the Civil War "accentuated and hastened" a trend already under way. John B. Appleton, "The Declining Significance of the Mississippi as a Commercial Highway in the Middle of the Nineteenth Century," *Geographical Society of Philadelphia Bulletin* 28 (January–October 1930) argues that "after 1847 the volume of trade on the Mississippi represented a rapidly decreasing proportion of the commerce of the Upper Mississippi Region owing to the advantages offered by the less hazardous, more direct East-West Route" (64); see also 47–64.

8. Cronon, *Nature's Metropolis*, provides the most in-depth analysis of the shift in the region's flow of commerce away from the Mississippi River. For an extended discussion of how railroads captured the region's trade for Chicago, see chap. 2 and 295–309.

9. Ibid., 112. Cronon declares that the invention of the steam-powered grain elevator was "the most important yet least acknowledged in the history of American agriculture ..." (111).

10. Ibid., 112–13. Sacks of grain had to pay an overhead cost of six to eight cents per bushel, and the sacks cost two to four cents each. "The economic benefits" of transferring grain from elevators to railcars or lake freighters, Cronon argues, "were so great that moving a bushel of grain from railroad car to lake vessel cost only half a cent, giving Chicago a more than tenfold advantage over St. Louis"; see 113–14.

11. Tweet, *Rock Island District*, 59, 64–65, 87; Lippincott, "River Improvement," 651–52, see 651 n. 4; Marquis W. Childs, *Mighty Mississippi: Biography of a River* (New Haven, Conn.: Ticknor and Fields, 1982), 98–99.

12. *Proceedings of the Mississippi River Improvement Convention Held at Dubuque, Iowa, February 14th and 15th, 1866* (Dubuque, Iowa: Daily Times Steamboat Press, 1866), Minnesota Historical Society (MHS) Collections, 4.

13. Ibid., 11. Robb, of the Dubuque Producers Exchange, who provided these statistics, recognized that farmers would not necessarily reap high profits simply by cheaper transportation. Once the shipping costs fell and farmers could get their produce to the East more cheaply, more grain would flood the eastern markets and the prices there would fall. Nevertheless, he insisted, prices in the East would still be higher. Tweet, *Rock Island District*, 64–66.

14. *Convention at Dubuque*, 10, 32, and 27; see also 12 and 31.

15. Ibid., 23.

16. Ibid., 14, 30.

17. Ibid., 30.

18. U.S. Senate, "Memorial of the State of Wisconsin," approved February 16, 1866, Misc. Doc. No. 65, 39th Cong., 1st sess.

19. *Convention at Dubuque*, 29; Tweet, *Rock Island District*, 65–66; *Laws of the United States relating to the Improvement of Rivers and Harbors*, vol. 1 (Washington, D.C.: U.S. Government Printing Office, 1913), 152–53.

20. Ibid., vol. 1, 152–53, 156.

21. *U.S. Statutes at Large* 14 (1866), 39th Cong., sess. 1, chap. 138, 74.

22. Raymond H. Merritt, *Creativity, Conflict, and Controversy: A History of the St. Paul District, U.S. Army Corps of Engineers* (Washington, D.C.: U.S. Government Printing Office, 1984), 33, 37; Tweet, *Rock Island District*, 67–68. Duties for the middle Mississippi stayed with the Office of Western Improvements in Cincinnati until 1873, when St. Louis became the new office for the middle river. See Frederick J. Dobney, *River Engineers of the Middle Mississippi: A History of the St. Louis District, U.S. Army Corps of Engineers* (Washington, D.C.: U.S. Government Printing Office, 1978), 44–45. Minnesota Senator Alexander Ramsey in particular, spurred by lumber interests and other shippers, advocated the 4-foot channel. Ramsey had inserted the words "economizing the water" by establishing a 4-foot channel into the 1866 Rivers and Harbors bill. Alexander Ramsey, "Cheap transportation obtained by improved water routes and railways," Speech of Hon. Alexander Ramsey, of Minnesota, in the United States Senate, March 6, 1874, MHS Collections.

23. Emerson Gifford Taylor, *Gouverneur Kemble Warren: The Life of an American Soldier, 1830–1882* (New York: Houghton Mifflin Company, 1932), 8–10, chaps. 6 and 7; Tweet, *Rock Island District*, 54–55; Frank N. Schubert, "Warren: Explorer and Civil War Tactician," *Crosscurrents* (August 1982): 4 (*Crosscurrents* is the St. Paul District's monthly newsletter); Shallat, *Structures*, 174–76.

24. Tweet, *Rock Island District*, 67–68, 111, 361–63.

25. U.S. Congress, House, "Survey of Upper Mississippi River," Exec. Doc. No. 58, 39th Cong., 2d sess., 18.

26. *Annual Report*, 1867, 262; House Exec. Doc. No. 58, 17–18.

27. *Annual Report*, 1875, Appendix CC, "Reports on Transportation Routes to the Seaboard," CC 3, "Part of the Third Subdivision Mississippi Transportation Route, Which Comprises the Improvement Necessary to Give a Navigation of 4½ to 6 Feet from Falls of Saint Anthony to Saint Louis, Report of Col. J. N. Macomb, Corps of Engineers," 455.

28. Lucile M. Kane, *The Falls of St. Anthony: The Waterfall That Built Minneapolis* (St. Paul: Minnesota Historical Society Press, 1987), 77.

29. House Exec. Doc. No. 58, 5.

30. John O. Anfinson, "The Secret History of the Mississippi's Earliest Locks and Dams," *Minnesota History* 54: 6 (summer 1995): 254–67; *Annual Report*, 1867, 260.

31. Office of History, Headquarters, U.S. Army Corps of Engineers, *The History of the US Army Corps of Engineers*, 2d ed. (Alexandria, Va.: 1998), 42.

32. Office of History, *Corps*, 26–27, 25; House Exec. Doc. No. 58, 25–26.

33. Ibid., 19. Warren feared, probably on the basis of his experience with timber rafters, that some local interests might object to their side channel being closed off.

34. Ibid., 25.

35. Ibid., 25.

36. Ibid., 27.

37. *Annual Report*, 1867, 262.

38. *Annual Report*, 1875, Appendix CC, 463; *Annual Report*, 1877, 527–28; *Annual Report*, 1885, 1664.

39. *Annual Report*, 1875, 453.

40. *Annual Report*, 1869, 237; U.S. Congress, House, "Survey of the Upper Mississippi," Exec. Doc. No. 247, 40th Cong., 2d sess., 2, 6.

41. *Annual Report*, 1872, 280, 309; *Annual Report*, 1871, 260. Colonel Macomb had taken over the improvement of the upper Mississippi River from Warren on June 1, 1870. Then on October 1, 1870, Macomb succeeded the Rock Island District commander, Colonel Wilson. Macomb headed both St. Paul and Rock Island Districts until April 26, 1873, when Francis Farquhar became the new St. Paul District chief. Macomb would remain chief of the Rock Island District until November 15, 1877. Macomb had graduated from the U.S. Military Academy in 1832 and had become the Chief Topographical Engineer for the Army of the Potomac under Major General George McClellan when the Civil War began. After the Civil War, the Chief of Engineers made Macomb the Superintendent of Western Rivers at the Corps office in Cincinnati, a position he held until replacing Warren. See Tweet, *Rock Island District*, 9, 363–64; Merritt, *Creativity*, 437; *Annual Report*, 1875, 453.

42. *Annual Report*, 1872, 309–10. To make the channel more navigable, they dredged out an island that was 120 feet long and 20 feet wide. It had been in a narrow part of the river and in the way of rafts. *Annual Report*, 1875, 302. The *Caffrey* may have done some work with closing dams earlier. In his report for the 1871 season, Captain Wm. Hillhouse stated that the *Caffrey*'s work had

included 1,600 feet of wing dams. He does not provide a location for this work, and there is no mention of it in later reports. See *Annual Report*, 1872, 310.

43. *Annual Report*, 1874, 301.

44. *Annual Report*, 1875, Appendix CC, 454.

45. Tweet, *Rock Island District*, 357–58, 399–400.

46. *Annual Report*, 1875, Appendix CC, 456–57.

47. Ibid., 457.

48. Ibid., 459, 460.

49. Ibid., 459, 462, 466. To limit the amount of sediment entering the river and to protect against the accelerated current created by channel constriction, Meigs also recommended using rock and brush to armor the river's banks.

50. *Annual Report*, 1875, "Preliminary Report," sent from Col. J. N. Macomb to Brig. Gen. A. A. Humphreys, Chief of Engineers, Jan. 12, 1875, transmitting "Report of Mr. Montgomery Meigs," Assistant Engineer, Rock Island, Jan. 6, 1875, 467, 453–54, 467–68.

51. Roald Tweet, "A History of Navigation Improvements on the Rock Island Rapids: The Background of Locks and Dam 15" (Rock Island District: U.S. Army, Corps of Engineers, April 1980), 2-8; Tweet, *Rock Island District*, 35-38.

52. Tweet, *Rock Island District*, 40-44; for a more detailed history of the Corps' work at the two rapids, see 75–105, and Tweet, "Rapids," 1-15.

53. House Exec. Doc. No. 58, 11.

54. Ibid., 17.

55. "The Memorial of the Legislature of the State of Minnesota," House Exec. Doc. No. 58, 47.

56. *Annual Report*, 1877, 528–29.

3. The Bounty of Providence

1. Gilbert C. Fite, *The Farmers' Frontier, 1865–1900* (Chicago: Holt, Rinehart and Winston, 1966), 2.

2. Fite, *Farmers' Frontier*, 35–37; Donald B. Dodd and Wynelle S. Dodd, *Historical Statistics of the United States, 1790–1970*, vol. 2, *The Midwest* (University: University of Alabama Press, 1973), 10–11, 14–15, 22–23, 30–31, 34–35, 42–43, 46–47, 50–51.

3. Dodd and Dodd, *Historical Statistics*, 12–13, 16–17, 24–25, 32–33, 36–37, 44–45, 52–53; Solon J. Buck, *Granger Movement: A Study of Agricultural Organization and Its Political, Economic, and Social Manifestations, 1870–1880* (Cambridge: Harvard University Press, 1933), 28–34.

4. Frederic L. Paxson, *History of the American Frontier, 1763–1893* (Chicago: Riverside Press, 1924), 500, 517; Fite, *Farmers' Frontier*, 31, 35, 37–38; Frank Haigh Dixon, *A Traffic History of the Mississippi River System, National Waterways Commission, Document No. 11* (Washington, D.C.: U.S. Government Printing Office, 1909), 48; Patrick Brunet, "The Corps of Engineers and Navigation Improvements on the Channel of Upper Mississippi River to 1939" (master's thesis, University of Texas, Austin, 1977), 46.

5. Dixon, *Traffic History*, 49; quote on 48.

6. Fite, *Farmers' Frontier*, 55–62; chap. 4 is about the calamities faced by frontier farmers on the plains during the 1860s and 1870s. *St. Paul Anti-Monopolist*, July 16, 1873.

7. Harold B. Schonberger, *Transportation to the Seaboard: The Communication Revolution and American Foreign Policy, 1860–1900* (Westport, Conn.: Greenwood Publishing Corporation, 1971), 22–23. Buck, *Granger Movement*, 8, 20–21, 34. Buck, an agricultural historian, blames farmers for expecting to make a profit from wheat, suggesting that railroads, banks, and others became their scapegoats (7–8).

8. Buck, *Granger Movement*, 11–14; Thomas A. Woods, *Knights of the Plow: Oliver Kelley and the Origins of the Grange in Republican Ideology* (Ames: Iowa State University Press, 1991), 79–80; Schonberger, *Transportation*, 57.

9. William Cronon, *Nature's Metropolis: Chicago and the Great West* (New York: W. W. Norton and Company, 1991), 135–36.

10. Ibid., 132–35.

11. Ibid., 136–37.

12. Buck, *Granger Movement*, 40–42; William D. Barns, "Oliver Hudson Kelley and the Genesis of the Grange: A Reappraisal," *Agricultural History* 41 (July 1967): 229–30; Woods, *Knights*, chaps. 7 and 8, supports and greatly expands on Barns's argument that Kelley actively pushed economic and political solutions or tacitly approved while others did so.

13. Buck, *Granger Movement*, 46, 50, 52; Woods, *Knights*, 111–12.

14. Buck, *Granger Movement*, 53–56, Map 1, opposite Buck, 61, 62, 66; Woods, *Knights*, 163.

15. Buck, *Granger Movement*, 108, 109.

16. Ibid., 9.

17. Woods, *Knights*, 99, 106, 108, 111, 124, 131, 135; Buck, *Granger Movement*, 52.

18. *St. Louis Democrat*, May 5, 1873.

19. Buck, *Granger Movement*, 52, 90–100, 111, 123; Woods, *Knights*, 147.

20. Cronon, *Nature's Metropolis*, 137–38. For a background on the origins of the Board of Trade, see 114–16. Schonberger, *Transportation*, 42, also raises questions about the Grangers' role in railroad legislation. See also Buck, *Granger Movement*, 82–84.

21. Buck, *Granger Movement*, 85.

22. Buck, *Granger Movement*, 85–89; Cronon, *Nature's Metropolis*, 142, says that the real enforcement came with the 1877 decision in the case of *Munn v. Illinois*. This Supreme Court decision established the principle that grain elevators were of public interest and "could not escape state regulation."

23. Woods, *Knights*, 141; Buck, *Granger Movement*, 160–61.

24. Woods, *Knights*, 153–56; Buck, *Granger Movement*, 160–64.

25. Buck, *Granger Movement*, 166–94; Schonberger, *Transportation*, 43–46, 56–59.

26. Buck, *Granger Movement*, 215–16, 224–27; Schonberger, *Transportation*, 41; Cronon, *Nature's Metropolis*, 139; Louis M. Hacker and Benjamin B. Kendrick, *The United States since 1865* (New York: F. S. Crofts, 1939), 271–73. Regional voting, Hacker and Kendrick demonstrate, shows the Midwest and East/Southeast were still at odds and shows how the Midwest had become strong enough in the House to outweigh opposition in the East.

27. Buck, *Granger Movement*, 9; Buck largely defines the shipping crisis as a railroad problem, examining the Grangers' waterway improvement efforts as an aside. Schonberger, *Transportation*, 37 and 42 specifically, and chap. 2 in general, stresses that the Grangers actively pursued navigation improvement and had a clear effect on federal legislation.

28. Henry Eames, "The Advantage of Transporting the Products of Minnesota to Europe via New Orleans," *Minnesota Monthly* 3 (March 1869): 92. On the *Minnesota Monthly* becoming Kelley's voice, see Woods, *Knights*, 119–22.

29. "How Every Man Who Owns a Farm in Minnesota Will Soon Be Made Rich by a Reduction of the Cost of Transportation of His Surplus to Market," *Minnesota Monthly* 4 (April 1869): 117, 116.

30. "Patrons of Husbandry: State Grange of Minnesota," *Minnesota Monthly* 7 (July 1869): 250.

31. Ibid.; Woods, *Knights*, 124.

32. Woods, *Knights*, 138–139.

33. Buck, *Granger Movement*, 112. Buck calls the 1874 meeting "the most

representative gathering of farmers which had ever taken place in the United States" (63). Schonberger, *Transportation*, 55–56, 59.

34. Schonberger, *Transportation*, 21–22.

35. *St. Louis Democrat*, May 14 and 15, 1873.

36. Buck, *Granger Movement*, 218–20.

37. Woods, *Knights*, 141; Theodore C. Blegen, *Minnesota: A History of the State* (Minneapolis: University of Minnesota Press, 1963), 290.

38. Blegen, *Minnesota*, 293.

39. Woods, *Knights*, 148, 151–52, 155; Schonberger, *Transportation*, ix–xix, 3–30; Robert S. Salisbury, *William Windom: Apostle of Positive Government* (New York: University Press of America, 1993), 123–24.

40. Salisbury, *Windom*, 113.

41. U.S. Congress, Senate, *Senate Report of the Select Committee on Transportation–Routes to the Seaboard*, Report 307, Part 1, 43d Cong., 1st sess. (Washington, D.C.: U.S. Government Printing Office, April 24, 1874), 7; Schonberger, *Transportation*, 29.

42. Windom, *Routes*, 80.

43. Ibid., 79–108.

44. Ibid., 109–22; quote on 122.

45. Ibid., 140, 122–40.

46. Ibid., 140–61.

47. Ibid., 161; see 161–240 for a discussion of the four routes.

48. Windom, *Routes*, 45–47, 187–88, 193–201; Schonberger, *Transportation*, 23.

49. Windom, *Routes*, 240–41; quote on 241.

50. Ibid., 242; quote on 242.

51. Ibid., 242–43; quotes on 243.

52. Ibid., 213.

53. Ibid., 211, 243; the Select Committee recommended a depth of 5 feet at low water for St. Paul to St. Louis, 213.

54. Salisbury, *Windom*, 121–23.

55. *St. Paul Daily Pioneer*, April 28, 1874; Salisbury, *Windom*, 121; *St. Paul Dispatch*, April 28, 1874, 2; Salisbury, *Windom*, 121–22; *St. Paul Anti-Monopolist*, July 16, 1874; Salisbury, *Windom*, 122.

56. Salisbury, *Windom*, 122, 123, 125.

57. Ibid., 124.

58. Partially rebutting the critics, Buck commended the report as "the

first comprehensive plan for the regulation by the federal government of interstate traffic on railroads" (*Granger Movement*, 221).

59. Roald D. Tweet, *History of Transportation on the Upper Mississippi and Illinois Rivers* (U.S. Army Water Resources Support Center, Institute for Water Resources, 1983), 52.

60. *St. Paul Pioneer Press*, October 12, 1877.

61. "Memorial to Secure an Adequate Appropriation and Thorough Improvement of the Mississippi River," with an Appendix by Sylvester Waterhouse, of Washington University (St. Louis: John J. Daly and Co., 1877), 1, 3.

62. Ibid., 11–13; quote on 12. Although Waterhouse says the upper Mississippi was about 800 miles long, it was closer to 730 miles at this time.

63. Ibid., 5, italics in original.

64. *St. Paul Pioneer Press*, October 11, 1877.

65. "Memorial," 4–7, Waterhouse, Appendix, 15–16. Edward L. Pross, "A History of Rivers and Harbors Bills, 1866–1933" (Ph.D. diss., Ohio State University, 1938), 61, says that President Johnson had approved the Rivers and Harbors bill of 1866 and subsequent bills in 1867 and 1868 with no comment. He notes, that Grant would approve bills from 1869 to 1876 with generally favorable comments, although Grant grew more critical of the increasingly local nature of many projects (61–63).

66. "Memorial," 7–8; *St. Paul Pioneer Press*, October 12, 1877.

67. "Memorial," 8–9; quote on 8.

68. *St. Paul Pioneer Press*, October 12, 1877; *St. Paul Pioneer Press*, October 13, 1877.

69. "Memorial," 16, 23–25.

70. Ibid., 15, 21–23; quote on 25.

71. Ibid., 33–34, 38; quote on 28.

72. Ibid., 32–33, 25.

73. Ibid., 39, 16.

4. Making the Mississippi Over Again

1. Roald Tweet, *A History of the Rock Island District, U.S. Army Corps of Engineers, 1866–1983* (Washington, D.C.: U.S. Government Printing Office, 1984), 9–10, 119.

2. *Annual Report*, 1880, 1514–25.

3. Edward North, "Wing Dams in the Mississippi River above the Falls of St. Anthony," *Transactions of the American Society of Civil Engineers*, 1877, 268–76.

4. H. Bosse and A. J. Stibolt, *Map of the Mississippi River from the Falls of St. Anthony to the Junction of the Missouri River, in twenty-seven sheets, 1903–1905*, St. Paul District records. While the Corps completed the initial survey in 1878–79, it would not publish the first maps until 1887–88. Bosse did more than illustrate maps, however. He photographed the river between 1883 and 1893, capturing the upper Mississippi River as the Corps transformed it from a natural river into a modern commercial highway. See John O. Anfinson, "Portraits of Old Man River" *Minnesota Volunteer* (November–December 1991): 32–49; Anfinson, *Henry Bosse's Views of the Upper Mississippi River*, St. Paul District, St. Paul, Minn., March 1996; Mark Neuzil, *Views on the Mississippi: The Photographs of Henry Peter Bosse* (Minneapolis: University of Minnesota Press, 2001); Charles Wehrenberg, *Mississippi Blue: Henry Bosse and His Views on the Mississippi River between Minneapolis and St. Louis, 1883–1891* (Santa Fe, N.Mex.: Twin Palms Publishers, 2002).

5. "In Memoriam, Alexander Mackenzie," *Annual Report of the Association of the Graduates of the United States Military Academy* (June 11, 1921): 1–6, quotes on 2, 4; Tweet, *Rock Island District*, 366.

6. U.S. Congress, House, "Mississippi River between Missouri River and St. Paul, Minn.," 59th Cong., 2d sess., Doc. 341, 8.

7. The height of the dams often depended on the reach. By 1908 they were generally raised to 4 feet above the low-water mark above the Des Moines Rapids, and 6 feet above low water below the rapids. C. McDonald Townsend, "Improvement of the Upper Mississippi River," *Journal of the Western Society of Engineers*" 14: 1 (February 1909): 35. House Doc. No. 341, 14; *Annual Report*, 1879, 111, see Figures 1, 2, and 3, and Plate 3.

8. Alberta Kirchner Hill, "Out with the Fleet on the Upper Mississippi, 1898–1917," *Minnesota History* (September 1961): 286, 291.

9. House Doc. No. 341, 8.

10. Ibid., 5, 14–15. Under the project as defined in 1897, the Engineers were to constrict the river to 400 feet between St. Paul and the St. Croix River, 600 feet between the St. Croix and Lake Pepin, 800 feet between Lake Pepin and the Wisconsin River, 1,000 feet between the Wisconsin River and Le Claire, 200 feet for the Rock Island Rapids, 1,200 feet between the Rapids and Quincy, 200 feet also for the Des Moines Rapids, 1,300 feet between the Des Moines Rapids and the Salt River, 1,400 feet between the Salt River and the Illinois River, and 1,600 feet between the Illinois River and the Missouri River.

11. House Doc. No. 341, 13; Townsend, "Improvement," 37.

12. *Annual Report*, 1895, 2103–4; *Annual Report, 1869*, 237; *Annual Report*, 1901, 2309; Raymond H. Merritt, *The Corps, the Environment, and the Upper Mississippi River Basin* (Washington, D.C.: U.S. Government Printing Office, 1984), 1; Raymond H. Merritt, *Creativity, Conflict, and Controversy: A History of the St. Paul District, U.S. Army Corps of Engineers* (Washington, D.C.: U.S. Government Printing Office, 1984), 68–74; Jane Carroll, "Dams and Damages: The Ojibway, the United States, and the Mississippi Headwaters Reservoirs," *Minnesota History* (spring 1990): 4–5.

13. *Annual Report*, 1882, 1755.

14. *Annual Report*, 1895, 2111; *Annual Report*, 1882, 1755.

15. *Annual Report*, 1880, 1495; *Annual Report*, 1882, 1756; *Annual Report*, 1887, 1627; *Annual Report*, 1890, 2037. Mackenzie, *Annual Report*, 1884, 1553, protested that "at some points where work is most desirable it cannot be commenced, for the reason that a sufficient allotment cannot be made for securing and protecting results." Between 1878 and 1907, Congress authorized $12,099,152 for the 4-foot channel project, of which about $725,000 went to maintenance. See *Annual Report*, 1908, 524. In his 1885 annual report, Mackenzie calculated the cost of the project at $20,000 per mile, and in the annual report of 1896, Mackenzie's successor, Lieutenant Colonel William R. King, repeated this figure. See *Annual Report*, 1885, 1671; *Annual Report*, 1896, 1778.

16. *Annual Report*, 1895, 2108; *Annual Report*, 1896, 1775.

17. *Annual Report*, 1885, 1667.

18. *Annual Report*, 1884, 1551; *Annual Report*, 1885, 1667.

19. *Annual Report*, 1896, 1777–78.

20. *Annual Report*, 1890, 2036, 1785; *Annual Report*, 1895, 2111.

21. Mark Twain, *Life on the Mississippi* (1896; New York: Bantam Books, 1990), 138–39.

22. *Annual Report*, 1885, 1719.

23. *Annual Report*, 1900, 2709.

24. Robert F. Fries, *Empire in Pine: The Story of Lumbering in Wisconsin, 1830–1900* (Madison: State Historical Society of Wisconsin, 1951), 160; Merritt, *The Corps*, 21.

25. *Annual Report*, 1879, 1115; *Annual Report*, 1880, 1500.

26. *Annual Report*, 1881, 1692–93.

27. *Annual Report*, 1885, 1677; *Annual Report*, 1888, 1505; *Annual Report*, 1898, 1762.

28. *Annual Report*, 1898, 1763; *Annual Report*, 1899, 2124–25.

29. *Annual Report*, 1889, 1729.

30. *Annual Report*, 1889, 1735. See also Fries, *Empire*, 156.

31. Fries, *Empire*, 160; Fries, chap. 9, argues that the Mississippi River Logging Company's success enabled it to buy out or dictate to nearly all the lumber manufacturers on the Chippewa, St. Croix, and upper Mississippi Rivers. In 1909 with the Chippewa pine reserves nearly exhausted, the West Newton works closed.

32. U.S. Congress, House, "Mississippi River from Cape Girardeau, Mo., to Rock Island, Illinois," Mississippi River Commission, House Doc. No. 628, 63d Cong., 2d sess., 6–7; Charles W. Durham, "Reclamation and Conservation of the Alluvial Lands in the Upper Mississippi Valley, Now and Formerly Subject to Overflow," *Engineering and Contracting* 37 (January 3, 1912): 21–24.

33. The Mississippi River Commission had had some flood control responsibilities on the lower Mississippi River since Congress established it in 1879. House Doc. No. 628, 6–7; Nani G. Bhowmik et al., *The 1993 Flood on the Mississippi River in Illinois* (Champaign: Illinois State Water Survey, Miscellaneous Publication, 1994), 151; Tweet, *Rock Island District*, 291; *Laws of the United States*, vol. 1, 419, 460, 511, 577, 637, 783; *Annual Report*, 1898, 1747; *Water Resources Development in Illinois 1991* (Chicago: U.S. Army Corps of Engineers, Chicago District, 1991), 48.

34. Rivers and Harbors Act of 1894, *Laws of the United States*, vol. 1, 704; *Annual Report*, 1896, 1776; *Annual Report*, 1898, 174; Rivers and Harbors Act of 1895, *Laws of the United States*, vol. 1, 732; Tweet, *Rock Island District*, 291–92; *Annual Report*, 1902, 1637–46; *Annual Report*, 1915, 1881. The Warsaw to Quincy reach included the Hunt, Lima Lake, and Indian Grave drainage districts, which were among the upper river's oldest and largest levee districts.

35. *Annual Report*, 1896, 1777–78. In an 1898 report for the Rock Island District, Captain C. McDonald Townsend complained that "the two methods of improvement are incompatible." To Townsend, the uncoordinated building of levees threatened the Corps' channel improvement works, and, he predicted, would "only lead to disaster." He recommended preparing a comprehensive plan to integrate levee construction and channel constriction, if Congress planned to authorize more levee work. *Annual Report*, 1898, 1748–49.

36. For a detailed history of the Meeker Island and Lock and Dam No. 1 projects, see John O. Anfinson, "The Secret History of the Mississippi's Earliest Locks and Dams," *Minnesota History* 54: 6 (summer 1995): 254–67.

37. House Doc. No. 341, 8; Roald Tweet, *A History of Navigation*

Improvements on the Rock Island Rapids: The Background of Locks and Dam 15 (Rock Island District: U.S. Army, Corps of Engineers, April 1980), 2-8; Tweet, *Rock Island District*, 35–38, 40–44, 75–105.

5. Highway of Empire

1. Upper Mississippi River Improvement Association (hereafter UMRIA), *Proceedings of the Upper Mississippi River Improvement Association, Convention Held at Moline, Illinois, October 22 and 23, 1907*, 14.

2. Carl N. Degler, *Age of Economic Revolution, 1876–1900*, 2d ed. (Glenview, Ill.: Scott, Foresman and Company, 1977), 17, 64–66.

3. Donald B. Dodd and Wynelle S. Dodd, *Historical Statistics of the United States, 1790–1970*, vol. 2, *The Midwest* (University: University of Alabama Press, 1973), 4–5, 10–11, 23–24, 46–47, 50–51; UMRIA, *Proceedings of the Upper Mississippi River Improvement Association, held in La Crosse, Wis., October 10 and 11, 1905* (Quincy, Ill.: McMein Printing Company, n.d.), 158.

4. *Annual Report*, 1887, 1621.

5. *Annual Report*, 1895, 2106; Raymond H. Merritt, *Creativity, Conflict, and Controversy: A History of the St. Paul District, U.S. Army Corps of Engineers* (Washington, D.C.: U.S. Government Printing Office, 1984), 164; Walter A. Blair, *A Raft Pilot's Log: A History of the Great Rafting Industry on the Upper Mississippi River, 1840–1915* (Cleveland: Arthur H. Clarke Co., 1930), 255–64, provides a list of sawmills on the river. Beginning with the *Annual Report*, 1893, 2198, the Corps presents a table of lumber manufactured on the upper Mississippi River. The table gives the amount of lumber and shingles produced on the main stem from Minneapolis to St. Louis, and on the St. Croix, Black, and Chippewa Rivers. This table and a similar or identical statement is given for the years 1893 to 1909. See *Annual Reports*, 1893–1910.

6. Robert F. Fries, *Empire in Pine: The Story of Lumbering in Wisconsin, 1830–1900* (Madison: State Historical Society of Wisconsin, 1951), 67–70; Roald D. Tweet, *History of Transportation on the Upper Mississippi and Illinois Rivers* (U.S. Army Water Resources Support Center, Institute for Water Resources, 1983), 30–31; Blair, *A Raft Pilot's Log*, 28–29.

7. Mark Twain, *Life on the Mississippi* (1896; New York: Bantam Books, 1990).

8. Sidney Glazer, *The Middle West: A Study of Progress* (New Haven, Conn.: United Printing Services, 1962), 55; John F. Stover, *American Railroads* (Chicago: University of Chicago Press, 1961), 174; Frank Haigh Dixon, *A Traffic*

History of the Mississippi River System, National Waterways Commission, Document No. 11 (Washington, D.C.: U.S. Government Printing Office: 1909), 49; Richard S. Prosser, *Rails to the North Star* (Minneapolis,: Dillon Press, 1966), 17, 30, 35, 38, 42, 56.

9. Mildred Hartsough, *From Canoe to Steel Barge* (Minneapolis: University of Minnesota Press, 1934), 203–6; Tweet, *Transportation*, 39; Sidney L. Miller, *Inland Transportation Principles and Policies* (New York: McGraw-Hill Book Company, 1933), 638, 668.

10. *Annual Report*, 1880, 1484, 1502; a table of the worst bars and depths over them from 1866 to 1879 appears on 1484; *Annual Report*, 1881, 1681.

11. *Annual Report*, 1884, 1548; *Annual Report*, 1888, 1476.

12. *Annual Report*, 1892, 1750, 1759–60.

13. *Annual Report*, 1895, 2103; *Annual Report*, 1899, 2101.

14. *Annual Report*, 1900, 2690–91.

15. Dixon, *Traffic History*, 51; Hartsough, *Canoe*, 186–87; Tweet, *Transportation*, 30. Steamboats increased in numbers until about 1892 and then leveled off. They grew in size, however, increasing the tonnage they could haul. Yet as the agricultural and industrial production in the upper Mississippi River valley soared, river traffic fell in real terms and, most dramatically, in relation to what railroads gained. By 1918 less than three hundred boats and even fewer barges worked the upper river.

16. Twain, *Life*, 274.

17. Raymond H. Merritt, "The Development of the Lock and Dam System on the Upper Mississippi River," *National Waterways Roundtable Papers, Proceedings: History, Regional Development, Technology, A Look Ahead* (Washington, D.C.: U.S. Government Printing Office [1980]), 94–95; *Annual Reports*, 1880–1920.

18. Roald Tweet, *A History of the Rock Island District, U.S. Army Corps of Engineers, 1866–1983* (Washington, D.C.: U.S. Government Printing Office, 1984), 237–44, reviews the arguments people have used to talk about the decline of commerce and the idea that river commerce had outlived its usefulness. He then rebuts these arguments by saying the critics have overlooked the fact that between 1890 and 1920 commerce shifted to more local and passenger traffic (ferried and excursion) and, other than lumber, did not decline much overall. The critics, however, have focused on the traffic used to justify federal spending on the river for navigation improvements.

19. Fries, *Empire*, 20; Merritt, "Lock and Dam System," 91; Tweet, *Transportation*, 31; *Annual Report*, 1907, 1560–61.

20. *Annual Report*, 1889, 1729; *Annual Report*, 1890, 2031; *Annual Reports*, 1886–1897.

21. *Annual Reports*, 1892–1912; quote from *Annual Report*, 1907, 1557.

22. *Annual Reports*, 1891–1903, the Corps used partial reports during the first eight years of the period and "tolerably complete" reports during the last five years.

23. *Annual Report*, 1904, 416; *Annual Report*, 1916, 2632.

24. UMRIA, *Proceedings of the Upper Mississippi River Improvement Convention, 1902* (Quincy, Ill.: Volk, Jones, and McMein Co., Printers, n.d.), 4–5.

25. Ibid., 8–9.

26. Ibid., 5.

27. Ibid., 6.

28. Ibid., 3.

29. UMRIA, *Proceedings of the Upper Mississippi River Improvement Association, Dubuque, Iowa, November 15 and 16, 1904* (Quincy, Ill.: McMein Printing, n.d.), 99–100.

30. Ibid., 100.

31. Philip V. Scarpino, *Great River: An Environmental History of the Upper Mississippi, 1890–1950* (Columbia: University of Missouri Press, 1985), 37. Scarpino and other critics of the 6-foot channel project argue that the UMRIA had been created largely to revive the river's urban economies and was, therefore, narrowly focused and not broadly supported.

32. UMRIA, *Proceedings*, 1902, 73.

33. Ibid., 36.

34. Ibid., 36–37, quote on 36.

35. Ibid., 45–47.

36. Richard Hoops, *A River of Grain: The Evolution of Commercial Navigation on the Upper Mississippi River* (Madison: Research Division of the College of Agriculture and Life Sciences, University of Wisconsin-Madison, 1993), contends that as rail rates climbed, "some commercial groups dug up old arguments for regulation of railroad rates by way of government support for commercial navigation" (29).

37. John Milton Cooper Jr., *Pivotal Decades: The United States, 1900–1920* (New York: W. W. Norton and Co., 1990), 51–53.

38. Ibid., 139; see also 69.

39. UMRIA, *Proceedings*, 1905, 24.

40. UMRIA, *Proceedings*, 1904, 36–37.

41. Ibid., 54.

42. Ibid., 100.

43. UMRIA, *Proceedings*, 1905, 13.

44. UMRIA, *Proceedings of the Upper Mississippi River Improvement Association, held in Minneapolis, Minn., October 10 and 11, 1906* (Quincy, Ill.: McMein Printing Company, n.d.), 90; quote on 89.

45. Samuel Hays, *Conservation and the Gospel of Efficiency: The Progressive Conservation Movement, 1890–1920* (Cambridge: Harvard University Press, 1959), 91–92; Degler, *Age of Economic Revolution*, 26–28.

46. UMRIA, *Proceedings*, 1906, 115; *Annual Report, 1905*, 167.

47. UMRIA, *Proceedings*, 1906, 14, 13–14, 151.

48. UMRIA, *Proceedings*, 1907, 7–8.

49. UMRIA, *Proceedings*, 1904, 9; UMRIA, *Proceedings*, 1906, 45.

50. UMRIA, *Proceedings*, 1905, 127; UMRIA, *Proceedings*, 1906, 153.

51. UMRIA, *Proceedings*, 1907, 14.

52. UMRIA, *Proceedings*, 1904, 30; quote on 31.

53. Ibid., 6–7, 24; quote on 25.

54. UMRIA, *Proceedings*, 1905, 51–52.

55. Ibid., 52.

56. Ibid., 53.

57. Ibid., 9, 53–54. The Secretary of War transmitted Major Riche's report to the Speaker of the House on December 21, 1906. See UMRIA, *Proceedings*, 1907, 26.

6. So Nearly Perfected by Nature

1. UMRIA, *Proceedings of the Upper Mississippi River Improvement Association, held in La Crosse, Wis., October 10 and 11, 1905* (Quincy, Ill.: McMein Printing Company, n.d.), 89–90.

2. U.S. Congress, House, "Mississippi River between Missouri River and St. Paul, Minn.," 59th Cong., 2d sess., Doc. 341, 1–18; Riche's comments are on 3 and 4. Durham based this figure on the exact quantities and costs that the Corps had kept for building wing dams, closing dams, and shore protection since 1878.

3. UMRIA, *Proceedings*, 1905, 69, 143, 149–50.

4. Ibid., 152–53.

5. UMRIA, *Proceedings of the Upper Mississippi River Improvement Association, held in Minneapolis, Minn., October 10 and 11, 1906* (Quincy, Ill.: McMein Printing Company, n.d.), 28–29, 30, 32, 34.

6. UMRIA, *Proceedings of the Upper Mississippi River Improvement Association, Convention Held at Moline, Illinois, October 22 and 23, 1907*, 26; UMRIA, *Proceedings*, 1906, 18.

7. UMRIA, *Proceedings*, 1906, 32–33.

8. Ibid., 69.

9. Ibid., 66–68.

10. Samuel Hays, *Conservation and the Gospel of Efficiency: The Progressive Conservation Movement, 1890–1920* (Cambridge: Harvard University Press, 1959); Rebecca Conard, "The Conservation Movement in Iowa, 1857–1942," National Register of Historic Places Multiple Property Documentation Form, Iowa State Historic Preservation Office (1991), E-2-6; W. J. McGee, "The Conservation of Natural Resources," *Proceedings of the Mississippi Valley Historical Association for the Year 1909–1910*, 3 (Cedar Rapids, Iowa, 1911): 361–79; Gifford Pinchot, *The Fight for Conservation* (1910; Seattle: University of Washington Press, 1967); Carolyn Merchant, ed., *Major Problems in Environmental History* (Lexington, Mass.: D. C. Heath and Company, 1993), chaps. 9–11; Kendrick A. Clements, "Herbert Hoover and Conservation," *American Historical Review* 89 (February 1984): 85–86.

11. Edward L. Pross, "A History of Rivers and Harbors Bills, 1866–1933" (Ph.D. diss., Ohio State University, 1938), 111–18.

12. Ibid., 101–2, 116–17, 120–21, 122.

13. Ibid., 92–94, 98.

14. Ibid., 98–100.

15. Hays, *Conservation*, 93–94; Pross, "Bills," 104–10.

16. Pross, "Bills," 106; Hays, *Conservation*, 93–94; Hays, 94, argues that the waterway boosters revived the National Rivers and Harbors Congress to counteract Burton and the Corps. Yet, many members of the Rivers and Harbors Committee and the Corps adamantly supported waterway projects; they wanted those projects to be more justified than they had been. The objective of the Rivers and Harbors Congress, and the primary reason for its rebirth, was to get Congress to spend more money on waterway projects so that more could be authorized and built. Leland Johnson, *The Falls City Engineers: A History of the Louisville District Corps of Engineers, United States Army* (Louisville, Ky.: Corps of Engineers, 1974), 171, says that the Rivers and Harbors Committee did not adopt the policy of taking projects only if the Corps had approved them until 1907. UMRIA, *Proceedings*, 1906, 66–69.

17. Hays, *Conservation*, 91–92; Pross, "Bills," 139.

18. W. J. McGee, "Our Great River," *World's Work*, February 13, 1907, 8576.

19. Ibid., 8578, 8584.

20. Pross, "Bills," suggests, "This great renaissance of the waterways movement was probably initiated by an International Waterways Convention, held in Cleveland on September 24–26, 1895" (140). However, with the Ohio River trip and the revitalization of the Rivers and Harbors Congress, the national waterway movement clearly entered a new phase. UMRIA, *Proceedings*, 1905, 11, 21–23; UMRIA, *Proceedings*, 1907, 77–78; Leland Johnson, *The Headwaters District* (Pittsburgh, Pa.: Corps of Engineers, 1978), 158–59; UMRIA, *Proceedings*, 1905, 11, 22–23, 77–78; Hays, *Conservation*, 234, says that Ransdell led support for a national waterway movement primarily to get funding for levee work on the lower Mississippi River.

21. UMRIA, *Proceedings*, 1905, 11, 79; for background on the 1901 organization, see 65–66.

22. UMRIA, *Proceedings*, 1907, 16, 79, 80.

23. UMRIA, *Proceedings*, 1906, 77; letter read to the convention from Captain J. F. Ellison, secretary of the National Rivers and Harbors Congress.

24. McGee, "Our Great River," 8577; Pross, "Bills," 131–32.

25. UMRIA, *Proceedings*, 1907, 80–81.

26. Robert H. Wiebe, *The Search for Order, 1877–1920* (New York: Hill and Wang, 1967); John Milton Cooper Jr., *Pivotal Decades: The United States, 1900–1920* (New York: W. W. Norton and Co., 1990); Louis L. Gould, ed., *The Progressive Era* (Syracuse, N.Y.: Syracuse University Press, 1974).

27. Hays, *Conservation*, 1–4; Donald Worster, *Rivers of Empire: Water, Aridity, and the Growth of the American West* (New York: Oxford University Press, 1985), 162; Conard, "Conservation Movement in Iowa," E-2-6; McGee, "Conservation of Natural Resources," 361–79; Pinchot, *The Fight for Conservation*; Merchant, *Major Problems*, chaps. 9–11; J. Leonard Bates, "Fulfilling American Democracy: The Conservation Movement, 1907 to 1921," *Mississippi Valley Historic Review* 44 (1957): 29–57; Wiebe, *The Search for Order*; James Penick Jr., "The Progressives and the Environment: Three Themes from the First Conservation Movement," in *The Progressive Era*, ed. Louis L. Gould (Syracuse, N.Y.: Syracuse University Press, 1974), 115–31.

28. Philip V. Scarpino, *Great River: An Environmental History of the Upper Mississippi, 1890–1950* (Columbia: University of Missouri Press, 1985), 62; Hays, *Conservation*, 90–91, 100.

29. Hays, *Conservation*, 90, 102–3.

30. McGee, "Our Great River," 8579–83.

31. UMRIA, *Proceedings of the Upper Mississippi River Improvement Association Dubuque, Iowa, November 15 and 16, 1904* (Quincy, Ill.: McMein Printing Company, n.d.), 28–29.

32. Ibid., 65.

33. Ibid., 88–89.

34. Ibid., 84–95.

35. UMRIA, *Proceedings*, 1905, 90; see 47–48 for which cities had contributed.

36. Ibid., 88.

37. Ibid., 88–95, 120–23.

38. UMRIA, *Proceedings*, 1906, 93.

39. Ibid., 84, 90–98; quote on 90.

40. *Congressional Record*, Representative James Lloyd speaking for the Rivers and Harbors bill, H.R. 24991, 59th Cong., 2d sess., February 5, 1907, pt. 41: 2307.

41. *Congressional Record*, Representative Joseph Ransdell speaking for the Rivers and Harbors bill, H.R. 24991, 59th Cong., 2d sess., February 5, 1907, pt. 41: 2308; *Congressional Record*, Representative Robinson speaking for the Rivers and Harbors bill, H.R. 24991, 59th Cong., 2d sess., February 5, 1907, pt. 41: 2308–9.

42. McGee, "Our Great River," 7577; Herbert Quick, *American Inland Waterways, Their Relation to Railway Transportation and to the National Welfare; Their Creation, Restoration, and Maintenance* (New York: C. Putnam's Sons, 1909), 77.

43. *Congressional Record*, Representative Robinson speaking for the Rivers and Harbors bill, H.R. 24991, 59th Cong., 2d sess., February 5, 1907, pt. 41: 2038; McGee, "Our Great River," 8577; U.S. Congress, House, Representative Joseph Ransdell speaking for the Rivers and Harbors bill, H.R. 24991, 59th Cong., 2d sess., January 31, 1907, *Congressional Record*, pt. 41: 2038.

44. *Congressional Record*, Representative Joseph Ransdell speaking for the Rivers and Harbors bill, H.R. 24991, 59th Cong., 2d sess., January 31, 1907, pt. 41: 2038.

45. Patrick James Brunet, "The Corps of Engineers and Navigation Improvement on the Channel of the Upper Mississippi River to 1939" (master's thesis, University of Texas, Austin, 1977), 77–79; UMRIA, *Proceedings*, 1907, 27–28. The 1907 Rivers and Harbors bill was large; and Pross, "Bills," 108, calls it Burton's best. Many projects were "pushed to completion, not one new project

was allowed unless the entire cost of appropriation was authorized, less than $500,000 was appropriated for local streams, and not one appropriation was made unless the project had the approval of the engineers." This represented a great change over previous Rivers and Harbors bills. Pross says that "as almost at one stroke the major weaknesses of rivers and harbors legislation were eliminated."

46. UMRIA, *Proceedings*, 1907, 6.

47. Gilbert C. Fite, "The Farmer's Dilemma, 1919–1929," in *Change and Continuity in Twentieth Century America: The 1920's*, ed. John Braemen, Robert H. Bremner, and David Brody (Columbus: Ohio State University Press, 1968), 67; James H. Shideler, *Farm Crisis, 1919–1923* (Los Angeles: University of California Press, 1957), 4.

48. UMRIA, *Proceedings*, 1906, 6.

49. UMRIA, *Proceedings*, 1907, 55.

50. Pross, "Bills," 290–94.

51. Roald Tweet, *A History of the Rock Island District, U.S. Army Corps of Engineers, 1866–1983* (Washington, D.C.: U.S. Government Printing Office, 1984), 237. He says this in a critique of those who have criticized the decline of river traffic as being inevitable. He emphasizes the importance of local and passenger traffic to argue that it remained important (238, 240–43). Richard Hoops, *A River of Grain: The Evolution of Commercial Navigation on the Upper Mississippi River* (Madison: Research Division of the College of Agriculture and Life Sciences, University of Wisconsin-Madison, 1993?), 31.

52. UMRIA, *Proceedings of the Upper Mississippi River Improvement Convention, 1902* (Quincy, Ill.: Volk, Jones and McMein Co., Printers, n.d.), 29–31; "Address by Mr. James J. Hill, President, Great Northern R.R.," *Proceedings of the National Rivers and Harbors Conference, Third Annual Convention*, Washington, D.C., Dec. 4, 5, and 6, 1907 (Cincinnati: Ebbert and Richardson Co., 1908), 191.

53. Hoops, *River of Grain*, says of navigation improvement organizations: "Instead of raising new questions that may have had no easy answers, these groups raised old and simple answers for questions that were irrelevant. These groups presented water transportation as a constraint on the power of railroads, a constraint that either was inefficient or unnecessary, given existing state and federal railroads regulations" (31). Pross, "Bills," 94–95, 117, 151–52, is consistently critical of the argument that waterways kept rail rates down.

54. *Annual Report*, 1906, 466–67.

55. McGee, "Our Great River," 8584.

7. Cradle, Home, and Place of Sojourn

1. Minneapolis Chapter Izaak Walton League of America, Announcement, "Child of the League, Mississippi Wild Life Refuge," no date (ca. 1928), Minnesota Historical Society, Izaak Walton League of America–Minnesota Division, papers, 151.F.17.13B. The announcement's author, presumably Judson L. Wicks, president of the Minnesota chapter, calls the refuge "the most monumental wild life sanctuary ever established by man," adding that it is "the cradle, home and place of sojourn of innumerable forms of animal and plant life." Philip V. Scarpino, *Great River: An Environmental History of the Upper Mississippi, 1890–1950* (Columbia: University of Missouri Press, 1985), chap. 4.

2. H. Bosse and A. J. Stibolt, *Map of the Mississippi River from the Falls of St. Anthony to the Junction of the Missouri River, in twenty-seven sheets, 1903–1905,* St. Paul District records; Roald Tweet, *A History of the Rock Island District, U.S. Army Corps of Engineers, 1866–1983* (Washington, D.C.: U.S. Government Printing Office, 1984), 134; the mileage figures for wing dams, closing dams, and shore protection are for the years 1878–1905.

3. W. A. Thompson and H. M. Anderly, "Improvement of Mississippi River from Winona to La Crosse in accordance with the 6-foot channel project adopted by Congress, March 2, 1907," *Professional Memoirs*, 9, U.S. Engineer Department, 304, 304–5; *Annual Report*, 1900, 2705; U.S. Congress, House, "Mississippi River between Missouri River and St. Paul, Minn.," 59th Cong., 2d sess., Doc. 341, 8; Bosse and Stibolt, *Map.*

4. *Annual Report*, 1880, 1495.

5. *Annual Report*, 1882, 1759; *Annual Report, 1884*, 1555; U.S. Congress, House, "Survey of Mississippi River between Missouri River and Minneapolis," House Doc. No. 137, 72d Cong., 1st sess., 57–58.

6. *Annual Report*, 1880, 1499–1500.

7. *Annual Report*, 1900, 2705.

8. *Annual Report*, 1875, Appendix CC, 459.

9. Raymond H. Merritt, *The Corps, the Environment, and the Upper Mississippi River Basin* (Washington, D.C.: U.S. Government Printing Office, 1984), 13; Raymond H. Merritt, *Creativity, Conflict, and Controversy: A History of the St. Paul District, U.S. Army Corps of Engineers* (Washington, D.C.: U.S. Government Printing Office, 1984), 138.

10. *Annual Report*, 1884, 1554, 1557–58.

11. *Annual Report*, 1881, 1679. See also *Annual Report, 1882*, 1750; and Mackenzie to Minnesota State River Commission, St. Paul, Minn., June 25,

1887, National Archives and Records Administration (NARA), Chicago, Record Group (RG) 77, Entry No. 1651, St. Paul District Records, Letter Book, Sept. 4, 1886, to Aug. 6, 1888, 142–43.

12. *Annual Report*, 1884, 1558; Merritt, *The Corps*, 18–19, 29, 31–39, and chap. 2; Mark R. Neuzil and Robert L. Craig, "Views on the Mississippi River: The Photographs of Henry Peter Bosse," paper delivered at the Association for Education in Journalism and Mass Communication, Anaheim, Calif., 1996, 10.

13. Merritt, *The Corps*, 19.

14. Ibid., 20.

15. U.S. Congress, House, "Mississippi River From Cape Girardeau, Mo., to Rock Island, Illinois," Mississippi River Commission, 63d Cong., 2d sess., House Doc. No. 628, 6–7.

16. Frederick J. Dobney, *River Engineers of the Middle Mississippi: A History of the St. Louis District, U.S. Army Corps of Engineers* (Washington, D.C.: U.S. Government Printing Office, 1978), 78–79. Rivers and Harbors Act of 1913, *Laws of the United States*, vol. 1, 1597.

17. Charles W. Durham, "Reclamation and Conservation of Alluvial Lands in the Upper Mississippi Valley, Now and Formerly Subject to Overflow," *Engineering and Contracting* 37 (January 3, 1912): 21.

18. Flood Control Act of 1917, *Laws of the United States*, vol. 2, 1703–5. In both the 1917 and 1928 Flood Control Acts, Congress limited levee work to the Mississippi River below Rock Island. Flood Control Act of 1928, *Laws of the United States*, vol. 2, 2004–7. This act "placed flood control on an equal footing with navigation improvement among the civil functions of the Corps," say Jamie W. Moore and Dorothy Moore, in *The Army Corps of Engineers and the Evolution of Federal Flood Plain Management Policy* (Boulder: University of Colorado, Institute of Behavioral Science, 1989), 4.

19. Frank T. Bell, "Proposals for a Solution of the Fishery Conservation Problem," *Progressive Fish Culturist* 15 (February 1936): 1.

20. Harriet Bell Carlander, *A History of Fish and Fishing in the Upper Mississippi River*, a publication sponsored by the Upper Mississippi River Conservation Committee, 1954, 26–28.

21. Carlander, *Fish and Fishing*, 26–27, says Missouri, Wisconsin, and Minnesota also established fish commissions in 1874. C. F. Culler, "Fish Rescue Operations," *Transactions of the American Fisheries Society* 50 (September 20–22, 1920): 247–48.

22. Patrick James Brunet, "The Corps of Engineers and Navigation

Improvement on the Channel of the Upper Mississippi River to 1939" (master's thesis, University of Texas, Austin, 1977), 143–44; Carlander, *Fish and Fishing*, 28.

23. Carlander, *Fish and Fishing*, 3, 30–31, 34, 37; Brunet, "The Corps," 144; U.S. Congress, Senate, Commerce Committee, *Hearing on S. 1558, a Bill to Establish the Upper Mississippi Wild Life and Fish Refuge*, 68th Cong., 1st sess., Feb. 15, 1924, 9; Rebecca Conard, "The Conservation Movement in Iowa," National Register of Historic Places Multiple Property Documentation Form, Iowa State Historic Preservation Office, 1991, 3.

24. Carlander, *Fish and Fishing*, 53.

25. Conard, "Conservation Movement," 4; Carlander, *Fish and Fishing*, 31–32; Culler, "Fish Rescue Operations," 247–48; Frank T. Bell, "Conservation Progress by the Bureau of Fisheries," *Progressive Fish Culturist* 28 (March and April 1937): 2. In 1920, Culler, "Fish Rescue Operations," 250, complained that the bureau could expand fish rescue if Congress would only allocate some funds.

26. Culler, "Fish Rescue Operations," 250; *Hearing on S. 1558*, 9–11; Brunet, "The Corps," 144.

27. Carlander, *Fish and Fishing*, 31, 35–37; Brunet, "The Corps," 144; U.S. Congress, House, Committee on Agriculture, *Hearing on H.R. 4088, A Bill to Establish the Upper Mississippi Wild Life and Fish Refuge*, Feb. 11, 12, and 13, 1924, 68th Cong., 1st sess., 41, 49.

28. Earl Simpson, "Conservation and Propagation of Fish in the Upper Mississippi River," *Transactions of the American Fisheries Society* 47 (1917): 36.

29. Clarence F. Culler, "Depletion of the Aquatic Resources of the Upper Mississippi River and Suggested Remedial Measures," *Transactions of the American Fisheries Society* (1930): 282.

30. Carlander, *Fish and Fishing*, 40; Scarpino, *Great River*, 84–86, 94–97, 99. Scarpino, *Great River*, 84, says the 1890 McKinley Tariff, which raised the tax on imported buttons, contributed to the boom in the button industry. The high price of marine shells and the poor quality of other materials made freshwater mussel shells especially desirable.

31. Scarpino, *Great River*, 86, 88–91.

32. Carlander, *Fish and Fishing*, 45; Robert E. Coker, "The Fairport Fisheries Biological Station: Its Equipment, Organization, and Functions," *Bulletin of the United States Bureau of Fisheries* 34 (1914): 387; Conard, "Conservation Movement," 19–20; Scarpino, *Great River*, chap. 3; on 104, Scarpino says only about 2 percent of the mussel larvae survived. Carlander, *Fish and Fishing*, 48,

notes that certain species of mussels lived on the gills of certain species of fish, and infecting millions of fish did little good if they were not the right fish. The ebony mussel, for example, relies on the skipjack herring as a host. House, *Hearing on H.R. 4088*, 57.

33. "Conservation Conference for Resources of Interior Waters, Held at United States Fisheries Biological Station, Fairport, Ia., June 8–10, 1921," National Archives and Records Administration (NARA), Record Group (RG) 22, Entry 121, Washington, D.C.; Carlander, *Fish and Fishing*, 46; Frank A. Stromsten, "Conservation Conference at the Fisheries Biological Station, Fairport, Iowa," *Iowa Conservation* 5 (1921): 26; Conard, "Conservation Movement," E-20-21.

34. Scarpino, *Great River*, 101–2.

35. Jill York O'Bright, *The Perpetual March: An Administrative History of Effigy Mounds National Monument* (Omaha: National Park Service, Midwest Regional Office, 1989), 47–48; Rebecca Conard, "Hot Kitchens in Places of Quiet Beauty: Iowa State Parks and the Transformation of Conservation Goals," *Annals of Iowa* 51, 5 (summer 1992): 441–79, discusses the origins and development of the park movement in Iowa. Many of the key figures in the Iowa state park movement were those pushing for the national park.

36. Brunet, "The Corps," 145; according to Brunet, this effort marked the beginning of a formal conservation movement in Iowa; Conard, "Conservation Movement," 96; George Bennett, "The National Park of the Middle West," *Iowa Conservation* 2, 3 (July–September 1918): 43–47; O'Bright, *Perpetual March*, 48.

37. Bennett, "National Park," 43.

38. O'Bright, *Perpetual March*, 48.

39. Bennett, "National Park," 46.

40. Bennett, "National Park," 46; C. H. McNider, "What the Mississippi Valley National Park Would Mean to Iowa," *Iowa Conservation* 1, 2 (April–June 1917): 30; Brunet, "The Corps," 146.

41. Harriet Bell Carlander, "The American School of Wildlife, McGregor, Iowa, 1919–1941," *Proceedings of the Iowa Academy of Sciences* 68 (1961): 294–96, quote on 295; Brunet, "The Corps," 146–47.

42. Conard, "Conservation Movement," 31.

43. Carlander, "The American School," 294–300; Conard, "Conservation Movement," 31; Brunet, "The Corps," 147–48.

44. Brunet, "The Corps," 146; Merritt, *The Corps*, 43.

45. Merton S. Heiss, "Will Dilg and the Early Days," *Outdoor America* 2 (January 1937): 4; Scarpino, *Great River*, 117–18, 131; see Will Dilg, "The Drainage Crime of a Century," *Outdoor America* 1 (July 1923): cover, 570, 600–601, 623.

46. *Hearing on H.R. 4088*, 35, 4, and passim.

47. Harry C. Oberholser, "Report on the Winneshiek Bottoms Drainage Project," Sept. 29, 1922, NARA, RG 22, Entry 162, 1–4.

48. Oberholser, "Winneshiek"; H. C. Oberholser, "The Winneshiek Drainage Project," *Iowa Conservation* 7 (1923): 9–10; Scarpino, *Great River*, 131.

49. *Hearing on H.R. 4088*, 79.

50. [Will Dilg, President, Izaak Walton League of America] to Hon. Henry C. Wallace, Secretary of Agriculture, October 25, 1923, NARA, RG 22, Entry 162.

51. *Saturday Evening Post* 196, 44 (May 3, 1924): 132. L. H. Pammel, professor of botany, Ames, Iowa, *Hearing on H.R. 4088*, 77, submitted a statement that said that "the project was promoted by Captain Thompson of La Crosse, Wis., in cooperation with a Mr. Clark." See also 77–80.

52. Scarpino, *Great River*, 144, 149; *Hearing on H.R. 4088*, 4, 5, 46.

53. *Hearing on H.R. 4088*, 93.

54. *Hearing on H.R. 4088*, 15; E. W. Nelson, Chief, Biological Survey, to Hon. Robert B. Howell, United States Senate, NARA, RG 22, Entry 162, Aug. 1, 1923.

55. *Hearing on H.R. 4088*, 24, 48, quote on 63.

56. Ibid., 85.

57. Ibid., 6–7, 40.

58. Ibid., 26.

59. Ibid., 26–27.

60. Culler, "Depletion," 279.

61. *Hearing on H.R. 4088*, 4, 17, 41–42, 49, 90.

62. [Dilg] to Wallace, Oct. 25, 1923, NARA, RG 22, Entry 162.

63. William T. Hornaday, "The Upper Mississippi Wild Life Refuge, Will H. Dilg's Monument," *Minnesota Waltonian*, April 1932, 15; Hornaday was quoting from Hawes's book, *My Friend the Black Bass*.

64. Scarpino, *Great River*, 9, 116–17, 135; Conard, "Conservation Movement," 35.

65. Scarpino, *Great River*, 130.

66. Ibid., 116.

67. Ibid., 124, 149–50.

68. Ibid., 147. Scarpino, *Great River*, 141–50, argues that the refuge movement anticipated environmental efforts of the post–World War II era in its level of sophistication.

69. Ibid., 143–50.

70. *Hearing on H.R. 4088*, 23–24, quote on 24.

71. Ibid., 6–7.

72. Carl Moneyhon, "Conservation as Politics," 360–66, in *Major Problems in American Environmental History*, ed. Carolyn Merchant (Lexington, Mass.: D. C. Heath and Company, 1993), argues that conservationists failed in many of their efforts because they divided into too many groups with separate agendas.

73. *Congressional Record*, "Upper Mississippi River Wildlife and Fish Refuge," 68th Cong., 1st sess., 1415–16; Merritt, *The Corps*, 45; Conard, "Conservation Movement," E-34.

8. A Marooned Interior

1. "An Inland Empire's Need," *St. Paul Pioneer Press*, May 12, 1928. The chapter title comes from the following quote: "In common with the impulses of all ambitious peoples, the Northwest's aspirations for growth, for prosperity, for power, find expression in demand for ready access to the sea. With its millions of population, its rich resources, and its unlimited possibilities for commercial growth, this region is like a giant, tied just beyond reach of a nobler destiny, straining at his chains. We are landlocked, a marooned interior, shut in by the barriers of costly overland carriage, to and from the common highway to the world's markets, the sea."

2. UMRIA, *Proceedings of the Upper Mississippi River Improvement Association, Convention Held at Clinton, Iowa, September 22, 23, 24, 1908*, 27; UMRIA, *Proceedings of the Upper Mississippi River Improvement Association, Convention Held at Winona, Minnesota, October 6 and 7, 1909*, 19–21; Carl H. Chrislock, *The Progressive Era in Minnesota, 1899–1918* (St. Paul: Minnesota Historical Society Press, 1971), 40–42.

3. UMRIA, *Proceedings of the Convention of the Upper Mississippi River Improvement Association, St. Paul, Minnesota, July 12–13, 1910*, 22.

4. Ibid., 22–23. On June 25, 1910, President Taft signed the Rivers and Harbors Act.

5. Ibid., 90.

6. Ibid., 87.

7. Ibid., 77, 90, 92.

8. Ibid., 24.

9. UMRIA, *Proceedings of the Upper Mississippi River Improvement Association Convention Held at Alton, Illinois, October 25 and 26, 1911* (Quincy, Ill.: McMein, n.d.), 51.

10. Ibid., 67–68, 88–89.

11. Ibid., 97, 65, 96, 52, 76, 79.

12. UMRIA, *Proceedings*, 1910, 136.

13. UMRIA, *Proceedings*, 1911, 124.

14. UMRIA, *Proceedings*, 1911, 98; Upper Mississippi River Improvement Association, *Extracts of Proceedings, Annual Convention, October 11–12, 1917*, 7.

15. *Annual Reports*, 1892-1909; Walter A. Blair, *A Raft Pilot's Log: A History of the Great Rafting Industry on the Upper Mississippi River, 1840–1915* (Cleveland: Arthur H. Clarke Co., 1930), 204; Roald D. Tweet, *History of Transportation on the Upper Mississippi and Illinois Rivers* (U.S. Army Water Resources Support Center, Institute for Water Resources, 1983), 32.

16. *Annual Report*, 1916, 2632; 28,444 tons of logs and lumber moved by barge in 1915 versus the 7,612 tons moved by raft.

17. *Annual Report*, 1919, 1239, states that in the Comparative Statements from 1914 to 1918 building material—sand, gravel, and crushed rocks—are included, but no ferry or government improvement traffic. *Annual Report, 1920,* 1215, provides gross tonnage figures based on this method from 1915 to 1919.

18. *Annual Report*, 1919, 2847; *Annual Report*, 1920, 3779; Frank Haigh Dixon, *A Traffic History of the Mississippi River System, National Waterways Commission, Document No. 11* (Washington, D.C.: U.S. Government Printing Office, 1909), 50, notes that the Census Report on Transportation by Water in 1906 gave the total receipts and shipments of the upper river, without logs and lumber, as 1,193,010 tons, of which 728,000 were stone and sand.

19. *Annual Report*, 1919, 2848; see note to Classified Freight traffic, 1918.

20. *Annual Report*, 1914, 2391.

21. *Annual Report*, 1918, 1169–70.

22. Ibid., 2767, 2727.

23. Mildred Hartsough, *From Canoe to Steel Barge* (Minneapolis: University of Minnesota Press, 1934), 213.

24. William H. Clark, *Railroads and Rivers, the Story of Inland Transportation* (Boston: L. C. Page and Company, 1939), 273–75; Hartsough, *Canoe*, 213–25;

Franklin Snow, "Waterways as Highways," *North American Review* 227 (May 1929), 592; Tweet, *Transportation*, 78.

25. H. Markham, "Railways," *Proceedings of the Eighteenth Convention of the National Rivers and Harbors Congress, December 6 and 7, 1922* (Washington, D.C.: Press of Ransdell, 1923), 108; James J. Hill, "Address by Mr. James J. Hill, President, Great Northern R.R.," *Proceedings of the National Rivers and Harbors Congress, December 4, 5 and 6, 1907* (Cincinnati: Ebbert and Richardson Co., 1908), 191–93, admitted that railroads could not keep up with demand, causing businessmen and farmers uncertainty and delays.

26. S. L. Wonson, "The High Cost of Inland Water Transportation," *Proceedings of the American Society of Civil Engineers* 63 (September 1937): 1248–50, says that the rapid growth of transportation needs occasionally overloaded railroad capacity, leading to public concern and a reevaluation of river transportation. But, he insisted, this "periodic inadequacy of the railroad plant" did not demonstrate a significant problem.

27. Tweet, *Transportation*, 77.

28. Herbert Hoover, "The Improvement of Our Mid-West Waterways," *Annals of the American Academy* 135 (January 1928): 15–24; he delivered this address before the Mississippi Valley Association on November 14, 1927. "Address at Louisville, Kentucky, October 23, 1929, in Celebration of the Completion of the Nine-foot Channel of the Ohio River...," William Starr Myers, ed., *The State Papers and Other Public Writings of Herbert Hoover*, vol. 1 (New York: Doubleday, 1934), 116–22; Tweet, *Transportation*, 77, says that the Midwest lost sales, manufacturers, and factories. See also Snow, "Waterways as Highways," 592.

29. Hartsough, *Canoe*, 223–24; see also xiii; Snow, "Waterways as Highways," 592. Proponents of navigation improvements cited the role of the Panama Canal in hurting the Midwest at every opportunity. The records of the Upper Mississippi Barge Line Company are filled with calls for compensating the Midwest for what the Panama Canal had done to it. See Upper Mississippi Barge Line Company (UMBLC), Wilmington, Delaware, Papers, 1919–1937, Minnesota Historical Society, Manuscript Notebooks, P331.

30. "Public Service Commission of Indiana et al. v. Atchison, Topeka and Santa Fe Railway Company," *Interstate Commerce Commission Reports, Decisions of the Interstate Commerce Commission of the United States*, vol. 66, January to March, 1922, No. 11388, 510, 512–22; vol. 88, No. 11388, February to April, 1924, 709–24; vol. 88, No. 13671, 728–42.

31. "Public Service Commission," 522.

32. Gilbert C. Fite, "The Farmer's Dilemma, 1919–1929," in *Change and Continuity in Twentieth Century America: The 1920's*, ed. John Braemen, Robert H. Bremner, and David Brody (Columbus: Ohio State University Press, 1968), 67; James H. Shideler, *Farm Crisis, 1919–1923* (Los Angeles: University of California Press, 1957), 4.

33. Shideler, *Farm Crisis*, 5.

34. Fite, "Farmer's Dilemma," 68, 69; Theodore Saloutos, *The American Farmer and the New Deal* (Ames: Iowa State University Press, 1982), 3–4, says that after an initial interruption in America's European markets, demand for American farm produce increased greatly.

35. Fite, "Farmer's Dilemma," 67–69.

36. Ibid., 71–72.

37. Fite, "Farmer's Dilemma," 67–72; Saloutos, *American Farmer*, 5, 12, 13, 71. Fite, "Farmer's Dilemma," 72, says that while "other segments of the economy were in trouble by 1921," farm "prices fell *first*, fell *fastest*, and fell *farthest*." Saloutos, *American Farmer*, 12–13, states that "their buying power, using 100 for the base period 1910 to 1914, fell from 102 in 1919 to 89 in 1928." The farm economy, he says, improved slightly between 1921 and 1925, suffered a minor slump from 1926 to 1927, and recovered somewhat in 1928.

38. Fite, "Farmer's Dilemma," 73–74.

39. Fite, "Farmer's Dilemma," 76; Saloutos, *American Farmer*, 6–7.

40. Saloutos, *American Farmer*, 7–12. Saloutos, notes that prior to the war the United States had been a debtor nation and had paid off part of that debt with farm products, providing a vent for some of America's surplus production (4). Fite, "Farmer's Dilemma," 76. Fite, 78, adds that the consumption of rye flour decreased by about 60 percent, and of barley products by nearly 90 percent.

41. Fite, "Farmer's Dilemma," 73–77; Saloutos, *American Farmer*, 7–12. Hartsough, *Canoe*, 222, wrote that "the prosperity of the Mississippi Valley was based upon a large export trade in farm produce, chiefly with Europe. But in the years since the war, our European trade has declined rapidly, to the distress particularly of the midwestern farmer. Tariff barriers have gone up in Europe, buy-at-home propaganda has become more and more emphatic, and currency and monetary difficulties have helped to cut off the European market for American goods."

42. Fite, "Farmer's Dilemma," 74-76.

43. "Thorpe Tells Commercial West Readers of New River Transportation Savings," *Commercial West* (August 27, 1927): 12.

9. Straining at the Chains

1. "Possibilities of Industrial Minneapolis," *The Realtor* 7, 29 (January 13, 1925): 1.

2. Ibid., 1. This article indicates that the board had begun considering how to attract new businesses by January 1923.

3. "Bartholomew on Industries," *The Realtor* 8, 30 (January 22, 1924): 1; "Report of the Industrial Committee," *The Realtor* 10, 25 (December 29, 1925): 2; Mildred Hartsough, *From Canoe to Steel Barge* (Minneapolis: University of Minnesota Press, 1934), xiii; W. W. Morse, "The Story of the Development of the Upper Mississippi for Navigation," *The Realtor* 13, 23 (December 11, 1928): 23.

4. "Report of the Industrial Committee," *The Realtor* 10, 25 (December 29, 1925): 2; "Minneapolis an Inland Port," *The Realtor* 10, 43 (May 4, 1926): 2–3.

5. "Making History," *The Realtor* 9, 44 (May 5, 1925): 2; "Minneapolis an Inland Port," *The Realtor* 10, 43 (May 4, 1926): 2; Hartsough, *Canoe*, 238–39.

6. "Report of the Industrial Committee," *The Realtor* 10, 25 (December 29, 1925): 2; "Minneapolis an Inland Port," *The Realtor* 10, 43 (May 4, 1926): 2.

7. Kenneth H. McCartney, "Government Enterprise: A Study of the Inland Waterways Corporation" (Ph.D. diss., University of Minnesota, 1958), 3–5. Michael C. Robinson, "The Federal Barge Fleet: An Analysis of the Inland Waterways Corporation, 1924–1939," *National Waterways Roundtable Papers, Proceedings: History, Regional Development, Technology, A Look Ahead* (Washington, D.C.: U.S. Government Printing Office, 1980), 107–12; Marshall E. Dimock, *Developing America's Waterways: Administration of the Inland Waterways Corporation* (Chicago: University of Chicago Press, 1935).

8. Dimock, *Developing America's Waterways*, 1–2, 5, 6–7.

9. Halleck Seaman, "What's the Matter with Iowa?" *Waterways Journal* 39, 18 (July 31, 1926): 5–6.

10. "Echoes from Last Thursday's Luncheon," *The Realtor* 9, 48 (June 2, 1925): 2. Seaman had come also to inspect the river terminals and transportation facilities along the Mississippi River in Minneapolis.

11. "An Outsider's View of Us," *The Realtor* 10, 7 (August 25, 1925): 3.

12. Ibid.; "Minneapolis an Inland Port," *The Realtor* 10, 43 (May 4, 1926): 2; "The Value of River Navigation as Viewed by a Member of the Inland Waterways Corporation," *The Realtor* 9, 45 (May 12, 1925): 2; Benton to Thorpe, July 29, 1925, UMBLC records, says that the National Rivers and Harbors Congress had sent Bailey to the Twin Cities "because of the interest of Minneapolis men

in reviving the river." "Stillwater to the Fore," *Waterways Journal* 38, 32 (November 7, 1925): 6.

13. "The Value of River Navigation as Viewed by a Member of the Inland Waterways Corporation," *The Realtor* 9, 45 (May 12, 1925): 2; Robinson, "The Federal Barge Fleet," 107–12; Dimock, *Developing America's Waterways*, 42–62.

14. Dimock *Developing America's Waterways*, 46–47, quote on 49. Dimock says that "in only one case has the board gone counter to the President on a matter of major policy. This was in the matter of extending the service to the upper Mississippi" (49). McCartney, "Government Enterprise," 58–63. McCartney, 7 n. 3, adds that in 1927, in recognition of Ashburn's work with the nation's inland waterways, the army promoted him to major general. When he retired in 1938, President Franklin Roosevelt convinced him to remain as the IWC's head. "Minneapolis an Inland Port," *The Realtor* 10, 43 (May 4, 1926): 2; Morse, "Story," 23.

15. "Minneapolis an Inland Port," *The Realtor* 10, 43 (May 4, 1926): 2; "A Signal Achievement," *The Realtor* 10, 7 (August 25, 1925): 2; Morse, "Story," 23.

16. Morse, "Story," 23.

17. Samuel S. Thorpe, Chairman, Upper Mississippi River Cities, Barge Line Committee, to H. W. Chittenden, September 15, 1925, Upper Mississippi Barge Line Company (UMBLC), Wilmington, Delaware, Papers, 1919–1937, Minnesota Historical Society, Manuscript Notebooks, P331 (hereafter, UMBLC records); *Annual Report of the Inland Waterways Corporation, Calendar Year 1927*, 2.

18. Public notice from the Upper Mississippi River Cities, Barge Line Committee, Minneapolis, Minn., October 10, 1925, UMBLC records; Samuel S. Thorpe to H. W. Chittenden, October 1, 1925, UMBLC records; Samuel S. Thorpe to H. W. Chittenden, October 5, 1925, UMBLC records.

19. "General Ashburn Explains Inland Waterways Corporation and Assures Operation of Upper Mississippi River Barge Line," *The Realtor* 10, 15 (October 20, 1925): 1.

20. Morse, "Story," 23. For a discussion of this legal problem, see *Annual Report of the IWC, Calendar Year 1927*, 2–3; Goltra entered into this lease on May 28, 1919. Goltra sought damages when the IWC broke the lease and repossessed the fleet, but failed to win; *Goltra v. Inland Waterways Corporation*, 1931, 49 F.2d 497, 60 AD.C. 115. U.S. 1941, *United States v. Goltra* 61 S. Ct. 487, 312 U.S. 203, 85 L. Ed. 779–80.

21. Carl A. Chrislock, *The Progressive Era, 1899–1918* (St. Paul:

Minnesota Historical Society, 1971), 189; "Report of River Navigation Meeting Held at the Minneapolis Club, Wednesday, Oct. 14, 1925," *The Realtor* 10, 15 (October 20, 1925): 4.

22. Chrislock, *The Progressive Era*, 183, 190–91; John E. Haynes, "Reformers, Radicals, and Conservatives," in *Minnesota in a Century of Change: The State and Its People since 1900*, ed. Clifford E. Clark Jr. (St. Paul: Minnesota Historical Society Press, 1989), 373–74; "Report of River Navigation Meeting Held at the Minneapolis Club, Wednesday, Oct. 14, 1925," *The Realtor* 10, 15 (October 20, 1925): 4.

23. "Report of River Navigation Meeting Held at the Minneapolis Club, Wednesday, Oct. 14, 1925," *The Realtor* 10, 15 (October 20, 1925): 4; William Starr Myers and Walter H. Newton, *The Hoover Administration: A Documented Narrative* (New York: Charles Scribner's Sons, 1936).

24. Richard Hoops, *A River of Grain: The Evolution of Commercial Navigation on the Upper Mississippi River* (Madison: Research Division of the College of Agriculture and Life Sciences, University of Wisconsin-Madison, 1993?), 51.

25. H. G. Benton, "Minneapolis Continues River Activity," *Waterways Journal* 38, 37 (Dec. 12, 1925): 10; "Strong for the River," *The Realtor* 10, 21 (December 1, 1925): 2; U.S. Congress, House, Committee on Rivers and Harbors, *Mississippi River between Missouri River and Minneapolis: Hearings on the Improvement of the Mississippi River between the Missouri River and Minneapolis*, House Doc. No. 137, 72 Cong., 1st sess., January 25, 26, 27, 1932 (Washington, D.C.: U.S. Government Printing Office, 1932), 1.

26. "Strong for the River," *The Realtor* 10, 21 (December 1, 1925): 2; H. G. Benton, "Minneapolis Continues River Activity," *Waterways Journal* 38, 37 (December 12, 1925): 10.

27. "Realtor Flashbacks, Greater Minneapolis Area Board of Realtors, 1887–1987," No. 11 of a series commemorating the board's one-hundredth anniversary, reprints from the *Minneapolis Realtor*; "Strong for the River," *The Realtor* 10, 21 (December 1, 1925): 2; Benton, "Minneapolis Continues River Activity," 10; "Minneapolis an Inland Port," *The Realtor* 10, 43 (May 4, 1926): 2; Morse, "Story," 23–24; *IWC Annual Report 1927*, 3.

28. "Strong for the River," *The Realtor* 10, 21 (December 1, 1925): 2; Benton, "Minneapolis Continues River Activity," 10; "Minneapolis an Inland Port," *The Realtor* 10, 43 (May 4, 1926): 2; Morse, "Story," 23–24; *IWC Annual Report*, 1927, 3; Willard W. Morse, George C. Lambert, and A. C. Wiprud, "Memorandum of the Upper Mississippi River Cities Committee Respecting the Need and

Method of Establishing Water Transportation on the Upper Mississippi between St. Louis and the Twin Cities, Submitted to the President of the United States," December 10, 1925, UMBLC records.

29. *IWC Annual Report*, 1927, 3.

30. Theodore Saloutos, "The Rise of the Equity Cooperative Exchange," *Mississippi Valley Historical Review* 32, 1 (June 1945): 31.

31. Saloutos, "Equity Cooperative Exchange," 31–62; C. L. Franks, "Inland Waterways Advocate, Col. George C. Lambert, Dies: Among Pioneers to Back Channel in Upper Mississippi," *Upper Mississippi River Bulletin* 3, 3 (March 1934): 1; David L. Nass, "The Rural Experience," in *Minnesota in a Century of Change: The State and Its People since 1900*, ed. Clifford E. Clark Jr. (St. Paul: Minnesota Historical Society Press, 1989), 143.

32. William E. Leuchtenburg, *The Perils of Prosperity, 1914–32* (1958; Chicago: University of Chicago Press, 1970), 96–98.

33. "Minneapolis an Inland Port," *The Realtor* 10, 43 (May 4, 1926): 2; "Report of the Secretary on the National Rivers and Harbors Congress Convention," *The Realtor* 10, 24 (December 22, 1925): 3; A. C. Wiprud to S. S. Thorpe, December 10, 1925, UMBLC records; Arne C. Wiprud, *The Search for Wider Horizons* (Richmond, Va.: William Byrd Press, 1970), 27–28; Morse, "Memorandum," December 10, 1925, UMBLC records, says, "As a practical result of this decision the former rate on first-class merchandise from Chicago to Fargo via [the] Twin Cities, which was $1.78 1/2 has been raised to $2.01, while the former rate on first-class merchandise from Chicago to Fargo direct of $1.78 has been changed to $1.65, making a difference of 36¢ in favor of shipping merchandise from Chicago to Fargo via the Twin Cities."

34. Morse, "Memorandum," December 10, 1925, UMBLC records.

35. Wiprud to Thorpe, December 11, 1925, UMBLC records.

36. Ibid.

37. Thorpe to Wiprud, December 12, 1925, UMBLC records.

38. "Sam Thorpe's Big Job," *The Realtor* 10, 25 (December 29, 1925): 1.

39. Morse, "Story," 23, 25; Ashburn, in his 1927 annual report, simply says that the brief filed by Wiprud and Congressman Newton, after the general counsel declared that the IWC did not have authority to lease equipment, had convinced the counsel to reverse his position; see *IWC Annual Report*, 1927, 3.

40. Hartsough, *Canoe*, xiii–xiv; "St. Louis–St. Paul Barge Line," *Waterways Journal* 38, 43 (Janurary 23, 1926): 5; Morse, "Story," 25; "The Upper Mississippi Barge Line Company," circa 1926, UMBLC records.

41. Hoops, *River of Grain*, 52, says that the War Department had yielded to lobbying from the Twin Cities group, implying that the leadership represented all there was to the movement.

10. An Inland Empire's Need

1. Theodore Saloutos, *The American Farmer and the New Deal* (Ames: Iowa State University Press, 1982), 21.

2. Joan Hoff-Wilson, *Herbert Hoover, Forgotten Progressive* (Boston: Little, Brown and Company, 1975), 104.

3. Gilbert C. Fite, "The Farmer's Dilemma, 1919–1929," in *Change and Continuity in Twentieth Century America: The 1920's*, ed. John Braemen, Robert H. Bremner, and David Brody (Columbus: Ohio State University Press, 1968), 79–80; Saloutos, *American Farmer*, 20.

4. Fite, "Farmer's Dilemma," 82–87; Saloutos, *American Farmer*, 20–23.

5. Fite, "Farmer's Dilemma," 90, 91–95.

6. Hoff-Wilson, *Forgotten Progressive*, 107; see also 102–8.

7. Fite, "Farmer's Dilemma," 96; Saloutos, *American Farmer*, 27–28.

8. "Steady Price Gains on Farm Products Forecast for N.W.," *Minneapolis Journal*, July 20, 1926; "Hoover Sees Midwest's Future in Waterways," *Minneapolis Morning Tribune*, July 21, 1926; "The Need for Comprehensive Inland Waterway Development," *Minneapolis Morning Tribune*, July 21, 1926; Herbert Hoover, "The Improvement of Our Mid-West Waterways," *Annals of the American Academy* 135 (January 1928): 15–24; "Hoover to Invite Lowden to Farm Aid Conference, He Says in Iowa Speech," *New York Times*, August 22, 1928; "Hoover Speech at Iowa Home-Coming," *New York Times*, August 22, 1928; "Address at Louisville, Kentucky, October 23, 1929, in Celebration of the Completion of the Nine-foot Channel of the Ohio River...," William Starr Myers, ed., *The State Papers and Other Public Writings of Herbert Hoover*, vol. 1 (New York: Doubleday, 1934), 116–22.

9. Hoover, "The Improvement of Our Mid-West Waterways," 17.

10. "Hoover Visions 9,000 Mile Waterways System Traversing 20 States," *Minneapolis Journal*, evening edition, July 20, 1926; "It is of supreme national concern," Hoover said, "that we conceive and develop our water resources as a whole if you are to receive your share of its benefits...." See also "Hoover Sees Midwest's Future," *Minneapolis Morning Tribune*, July 21, 1926; Hoover, "Our Mid-West Waterways," 15–24; Myers, "Address at Louisville," *State Papers*, 1: 116–22.

11. "Hoover Sees Midwest's Future," *Minneapolis Morning Tribune*, July 21, 1926.

12. *Official Report of the Proceedings of the Nineteenth Republican National Convention* (New York: Tenny Press, [1928]), 288; Hoover, "Our Mid-West Waterways," 15–24.

13. Hoff-Wilson, *Forgotten Progressive*, 108–9.

14. Ibid., 149–50.

15. *Republican National Convention*, 283, 286.

16. Ibid., 123.

17. Ibid., 285.

18. *The Campaign Book of the Democratic Party, Candidates and Issues in 1928* (New York: Democratic National Committee, Democratic Senatorial Committee, Democratic Congressional Committee, [1928]), 95, 336–37.

19. Ibid., 339.

20. Franklin Snow, "Waterways as Highways," *North American Review* 227 (May 1929): 592, observed that "when the people of the United States elected Herbert Hoover to the Presidency, they automatically cast their ballots in favor of intensive utilization of the vast network of inland waterways as arteries of transportation."

21. "The Northern Division of the Mississippi Valley Association presents its program of development" [1927], Upper Mississippi Barge Line Company (UMBLC), Wilmington, Delaware, Papers, 1919–1937, Minnesota Historical Society, Manuscript Notebooks, P331 (hereafter, UMBLC records); J. L. Record to A. C. Wiprud, February 19, 1928, UMBLC records, said that "it is absolutely necessary for our future prosperity. We must have adequate equipment, skillful management and in the shortest possible time the Nine Foot Channel that is necessary and will give us only what we are justly entitled to and we should be satisfied with nothing less."

22. *Congressional Record*, Appendix, 75th Cong., 1st sess., 2155; *Annual Report, 1927*, 1084.

23. Major General Edwin Jadwin, the Chief of Engineers, had informed Minneapolis businessmen in October 1926 that a plan for a 9-foot channel project would go before Congress during the winter session, with Corps backing. [Press release?] October 15, 1926, Minneapolis, Minn., UMBLC records.

24. U.S. Congress, House, "Mississippi River from Minneapolis to Lake Pepin. Report from the Chief of Engineers on Preliminary Examination and Survey of Mississippi River from Minneapolis to Lake Pepin, with a View to

Improvement by the Construction of Locks and Dams," Doc. No. 583, 69th Cong., 2d sess.

25. Ibid., 17.

26. Ibid., 19.

27. Ibid., 14–15.

28. Ibid., 14–15, quote on 14.

29. Ibid., 23, 48.

30. Raymond H. Merritt, *Creativity, Conflict, and Controversy: A History of the St. Paul District, U.S. Army Corps of Engineers* (Washington, D.C.: U.S. Government Printing Office, 1984), 195; Richard Hoops, *A River of Grain: The Evolution of Commercial Navigation on the Upper Mississippi River* (Madison: Research Division of the College of Agriculture and Life Sciences, University of Wisconsin-Madison, 1993?), 56–57.

31. "Unified and Standard Equipment for the River and the River Nine-Foot Channel Endangered by Attitude and Tactics of the Army and Particularly Through the Insistence of Major Hall That a Nine-Foot Channel Is Unnecessary" [Early January, 1929], UMBLC records.

32. Major C. L. Hall to Upper Mississippi Division, Inland Waterways Corporation, August 25, 1928, UMBLC records; Major Hall sent this letter to individuals, cities, and organizations interested in commerce on the upper river.

33. Major Robert C. Williams, St. Paul District Engineer, to C. C. Webber, August 16, 1928, UMBLC records. In replying to a letter from Webber dated August 14, Major Williams said that the St. Paul District portion of the survey had been completed in September 1927 and forwarded to Rock Island. Rock Island had put the whole report together and sent it to the Chief of Engineers in October, and it had been referred to the Board of Engineers for Rivers and Harbors. The Board sent the report back to Major Hall, requesting more information. As of August 16, 1928, Hall was still collecting data, and Williams said he could not disclose any of the report's conclusions. In 1926, Major Robert C. Williams had succeeded Major Charles F. Williams as St. Paul's District Engineer.

34. A. C. Wiprud to Cornelius Lynde, August 31, 1928, UMBLC records. This information comes from the following correspondence and records in the UMBLC records: Upper Mississippi Barge Line Company to Major General Edgar Jadwin, Chief of Engineers, August 27, 1928; A. C. Wiprud, Secretary and Counsel, Upper Mississippi Barge Line Company, to C. C. Webber, Deere & Company, August 27, 1928; General Edgar Jadwin to Upper

Mississippi Barge Line Company, August 28, 1928; press release, August 30, 1928, signed by the Upper Mississippi Barge Line Company, the Upper Mississippi and St. Croix River Improvement Commission of Minnesota, and the Mississippi Valley Association. Box 2, Folder for August 1928, UMBLC records, contains extensive correspondence on this subject.

35. Registration, Meeting with reference to the 9 Foot Channel held at the Nicollet Hotel–Friday, September 14, 1928, UMBLC records; "Final Battle Mapped for Deeper River," *Minneapolis Tribune*, September 15, 1928.

36. Theodore Brent to C. C. Webber, September 10, 1928, UMBLC records; Barge Line Company, the Upper Mississippi and St. Croix River Improvement Commission of Minnesota, and the Mississippi Valley Association to General Jadwin, August 31, 1928, UMBLC records; A. R. Rodgers to Major General Edgar Jadwin, October 6, 1928, UMBLC records; Major C. L. Hall to Minneapolis Civic and Commerce Association, October 10, 1928, UMBLC records; Hall sent similar letters to other interested parties. Raymond H. Merritt, "The Development of the Lock and Dam System on the Upper Mississippi River," *National Waterways Roundtable, Proceedings: History, Regional Development, Technology, A Look Ahead* (Washington, D.C.: U.S. Government Printing Office, [1980]), 97–98, says that because it was an election year, the Chief of Engineers asked Hall to reassess his survey, but the day after the election the chief called the project economically unjustified.

37. "Unified and Standard Equipment" [early January, 1929], UMBLC records.

38. A. C. Wiprud to Senator Henrik Shipstead, December 4, 1928, UMBLC records; S. S. Thorpe to Honorable Henrik Shipstead, December 28, 1928, UMBLC records, says that the meeting had been held at the "urgent request" of General Jadwin and Congressman Newton, and, consequently, valley interests had withdrawn their request for a public meeting; A. C. Wiprud "To the Stockholders," January 17, 1929, UMBLC records.

39. S. S. Thorpe to Honorable Henrik Shipstead, December 28, 1928, UMBLC records; Senator Henrik Shipstead to S. S. Thorpe, December 31, 1928, UMBLC records; A. C. Wiprud, "To the Stockholders," January 17, 1929, UMBLC records; "Unified and Standard Equipment" [early January, 1929], UMBLC records.

40. George C. Lambert, Chairman, Executive Committee, Mississippi Valley Shippers Conference, to Mr. A. C. Wiprud, Minneapolis Traffic Bureau, January 8, 1929, UMBLC records.

41. "Unified and Standard Equipment" [early January, 1929], UMBLC records.

42. Walter H. Newton to Mr. C. C. Webber, December 24, 1928, UMBLC records; George C. Lambert, Chairman, Executive Committee, Mississippi Valley Shippers Conference, to Mr. A. C. Wiprud, Minneapolis Traffic Bureau, January 8, 1929, UMBLC records.

43. "Resolution—Adopted by the Legislature of the State of Minnesota," February 27, 1929, Resolution No. 10, UMBLC records.

44. A. C. Wiprud to Theodore Brent, February 27, 1929, UMBLC records; City of St. Paul, Council Resolution, Council File No. 79690, February 28, 1929, UMBLC records.

45. A. C. Wiprud to Theodore Brent, February 27, 1929, UMBLC records; editorial, "Renewing the Channel Debate," *Minneapolis Morning Tribune*, February 27, 1929.

46. A. G. Godward, Executive Engineer, to Honorable Walter H. Newton, March 12, 1929, UMBLC records.

47. Ibid.

48. Unsigned letter to Mr. W. R. Dawes, April 13, 1929, UMBLC records.

49. George C. Lambert, Chairman, Mississippi & St. Croix River Improvement Association, to Hon. Frank Clague, M.C., May 29, 1929, UMBLC records; F. Trubee Davison, Acting Secretary of War, to George C. Lambert, Chairman, Mississippi and St. Croix River Improvement Commission of Minnesota, August 2, 1929, UMBLC records; Office of the Chief of Engineers, Administrative Files 1902–1942, "Minutes of Board Meetings June 20, 1922, to December 31, 1935," NARA, RG 77, Washington, D.C., 238, 241, 243.

50. George C. Lambert, Chairman, Mississippi & St. Croix River Improvement Association, to Hon. Frank Clague, M.C., May 29, 1929, UMBLC records; George C. Lambert, Mississippi and St. Croix River Improvement Commission, to Honorable James W. Good, August 31, 1929, UMBLC records.

51. F. Trubee Davison, Acting Secretary of War, to George C. Lambert, August 2, 1929, UMBLC records; John H. Carruth, Major, Corps of Engineers, Chief, Personnel Section, Special Orders No. 31, May 29, 1930, UMBLC records.

52. T. H. Jackson, Brigadier General, Corps of Engineers, to Lachlan Macleay, Secretary, Mississippi Valley Association, August 23, 1929.

53. George C. Lambert to Honorable James W. Good, Secretary of War, August 31, 1929.

54. Editorial, "Pre-judging the Nine-Foot Channel," *Minneapolis Journal*, August 23, 1929; Burton F. Peek to A. F. Dawson, Esq., September 7, 1929, UMBLC records; "Hall Removed as a Member of Channel Board," *St. Paul Pioneer Press*, October 26, 1929; Patrick James Brunet, "The Corps of Engineers and Navigation Improvement on the Channel of the Upper Mississippi River to 1939" (master's thesis, University of Texas, Austin, 1977)," 97.

55. The Board of Engineers entry for January 15, 1930, revealed its thoughts about the study. The board stated: "Interim F 1927 Report to be redrafted to state that the information available in advance of a complete survey is not sufficient for consideration of either a 9-foot project or definite changes in the 6-foot project, and recommending that the existing project be not modified at the present time." Chief of Engineers, "Minutes," RG 77, 269; see also 272.

56. C. C. Webber to Mr. Walter H. Newton, Secretary to the President, January 27, 1930, UMBLC records.

57. U.S. Congress, House, "Mississippi River, between Mouth of Missouri River and Minneapolis, Minn., Interior Report," 1st Cong., 2d sess., House Doc. No. 290, 9–11. On February 13 the chief sent the report to the secretary of war, who, two days later, sent it to Congress.

58. H. Doc. No. 290, 1–7; Hoops, *River of Grain*, 215.

59. Clarence Wiprud to C. C. Webber, February 14, 1930, UMBLC records.

60. R. Warner, Vice President, Mississippi Valley Association, to Herbert Hoover, President, March 6, 1930, UMBLC records.

61. Warner to Hoover, March 6, 1930, UMBLC records; Arne C. Wiprud, *The Search for Wider Horizons* (Richmond, Va.: William Byrd Press, 1970), 43.

62. C. C. Webber, President, Upper Mississippi Barge Line Company [Mid-February 1930], UMBLC records.

63. Ibid.

64. Ibid.

65. "Hearings before the Committee on Rivers and Harbors, House of Representatives, Seventy-First Congress, Second Session, on the Subject of the Improvement of the Mississippi River between Mouth of the Missouri and Minneapolis," March 13 and 27, 1930 (Washington, D.C.: U.S. Government Printing Office, 1930).

66. Ibid., 4.

67. Ibid., 26–27.

68. "Hearings," March 13 and 27, 1930, 7–8; Hoops, *River of Grain*, 222, notes that Dempsey had his statement removed from the official record.

69. "Hearings," March 13 and 27, 1930, 28–29.

70. A. F. Nelson, Secretary, Farmers Elevator Association of Minnesota, to Honorable Herbert Hoover, President, United States, April 4, 1930, UMBLC records; Cooperative Farmers Northwest Grain Corporation to Honorable Herbert Hoover, President, United States, April 5, 1930, UMBLC records; Cooperative Farmers Northwest Grain Corporation to A. C. Wiprud, April 10, 1930, UMBLC records; William Starr Myers and Walter H. Newton, *The Hoover Administration: A Documented Narrative* (New York: Charles Scribner's Sons, 1936), 530.

71. Theodore Christianson, Governor of Minnesota, et al., to Honorable Herbert Hoover, President of the United States, April 14, 1930, UMBLC records.

72. Walter H. Newton, Secretary to the President, to Charles C. Webber, Deere & Webber Company, April 17, 1930, UMBLC records; Myers, "Address at Louisville," *State Papers*, 1: 121.

73. C. C. Webber, President, Upper Mississippi Barge Line Company, to Walter H. Newton, Secretary to the President, April 19, 1930, UMBLC records. Evidencing his lack of patience, A. C. Wiprud, Secretary and Counsel, Upper Mississippi Barge Line Company, wrote to H. M. Hill, Janney, Semple, Hill & Co., March 10, 1930, UMBLC records, that "this is election year and if the Administration is to frown upon this proposed development, in the light of the President's Louisville address last October, there will be very little for the Republican congressmen to campaign on during the forthcoming primaries and election."

74. John Kerper, Chairman, Maritime Committee, Dubuque Chamber of Commerce, to the Secretary, Chamber of Commerce, April 24, 1930, UMBLC records.

75. "An Inland Empire's Need," *St. Paul Pioneer Press*, May 12, 1928.

11. This Noble River

1. William J. Aberg, "Winning Back the Winneshiek," *Outdoor America* 11: 3 (December–January 1933): 4.

2. Judson Wicks, "Clean the Mississippi," *Minnesota Waltonian* (November 1932): 10.

3. R. Dunlap, Acting Secretary [of Agriculture], to the Secretary of War, November 22, 1929, NARA, RG 22, Entry 162, Washington, D.C.; Patrick J. Hurley, Acting Secretary of War, to the Secretary of Agriculture, date stamped December 4, 1929, NARA, RG 22, Entry 162, Washington, D.C.

4. Henry Baldwin Ward, Izaak Walton League of America, to President Herbert Hoover, December 6, 1929, NARA, RG 22, Entry 162, Washington, D.C.

5. Arthur W. Hyde, Secretary of Agriculture, to the Secretary of War, March 19, 1930, NARA, RG 22, Entry 162, Washington, D.C.

6. Resolution, Harry V. Teegarden, Winona, Minnesota, n.d. [1930], NARA, RG 22, Entry 162, Washington, D.C.

7. Hyde to the Secretary of War, March 19, 1930, NARA, RG 22, Entry 162. Box 160 contains a number of draft letters from the president to the war secretary that the secretary of agriculture's letter finally embody.

8. F. Trubee Davison, Acting Secretary of War, to the Secretary of Agriculture, April 19, 1930, NARA, RG 22, Entry 162, Washington, D.C.

9. F. M. Uhler, "Report on a conference with U.S. War Department Engineers, relative to the proposed plan to improve navigation on the Upper Mississippi River by the construction of a series of dams to maintain a nine-foot stage of water, and the effects of such a project on the Upper Mississippi River Wild Life and Fish Refuge, Hearing held May 6, 1930, at St. Louis, Missouri," NARA, RG 22, Entry 162, Box 160, Washington, D.C.

10. Arne C. Wiprud, *The Search for Wider Horizons* (Richmond, Va.: William Byrd Press, 1970), 44; A. C. Wiprud to A. R. Rodgers, May 13, 1930, UMBLC records; A. C. Wiprud to Colonel George C. Lambert, May 21, 1930, UMBLC records; A. C. Wiprud to C. C. Webber, June 16, 1930, UMBLC records; Godfrey Goodwin, M.C., to A. C. Wiprud, June 24, 1930, UMBLC records.

11. Raymond H. Merritt, "The Development of the Lock and Dam System on the Upper Mississippi River," in *National Waterways Roundtable Papers, Proceedings: History, Regional Development, Technology, A Look Ahead* (Washington, D.C.: U.S. Government Printing Office, [1980]), 98; Philip V. Scarpino, *Great River: An Environmental History of the Upper Mississippi, 1890–1950* (Columbia: University of Missouri Press, 1985), 77, 171.

12. Scarpino, *Great River*, 76–77, 171.

13. U.S. Congress, House, Committee on Rivers and Harbors, *Mississippi River between Missouri River and Minneapolis: Hearings on the Improvement of the*

Mississippi River between the Missouri River and Minneapolis, House Doc. No. 137, 72 Cong., 1st sess., January 25, 26, 27, 1932 (Washington, D.C.: U.S. Government Printing Office, 1932), 55–63; Elmer Higgins, "Progress in Biological Inquiries, 1930," *Annual Report of the Commissioner of Fisheries to the Secretary of Commerce for the Fiscal Year Ended June 30, 1931* (Washington, D.C.: U.S. Government Printing Office, 1931), Appendix III, 623–25.

14. H. Doc. No. 137, Appendix C, 53–54; Higgins, "Progress," 623; Ray C. Steele, Superintendent, to Mr. Paul G. Redington, Chief, Bureau of Biological Survey, Washington, D.C., stamped received July 3, 1930, NARA, RG 22, Entry 162, Washington, D.C. Steele provided Redington with a list of issues to raise with the Senate committee. He stressed that the 9-foot project could benefit the refuge if the Corps held water levels steady and provided fish passage structures in the dams.

15. H. Doc. No. 137, Appendix C, 64–65, quote on 64.

16. Ibid., 65.

17. H. Doc. No. 137, Appendix C, 67–68; U.S. Department of Commerce, Bureau of Fisheries, *Annual Report,* 1932, 136.

18. F. M. Uhler, "Report on an Investigation of the Vegetation of the Lake Keokuk Section of the Mississippi River, with Reference to the Effects of the Keokuk Dam on the Waterfowl and Cover Plants, July 7 to 19, 1930," NARA, RG 22, Entry 162, Washington, D.C., 1–17.

19. Ibid., 16–17.

20. Ibid., 17.

21. Uhler, "Report," RG 22, Entry 162.

22. February 20, 1931, "TWO-BIG-MEETINGS," Minnesota Historical Society, Izaak Walton League of America–Minnesota Division, papers, 151.F.17.13B.

23. "Before the District Engineer, United States Army, In Re: The River and Harbor Act of Congress, approved July 3, 1930 providing for a Nine-foot Channel project for the Upper Mississippi River. Hearing at Wabasha, Minnesota, February 26, 1931 re: construction of dam at Alma, Wisconsin," (hereafter, "Hearing at Wabasha"), 28; materials gathered by Patrick O'Brien for Historic American Engineering Record Documentation project, 9-Foot Channel Locks and Dams 3–10, for St. Paul District, Corps of Engineers, from National Archives Record Group 77, (hereafter O'Brien files); C. F. Loweth, Chief Engineer, Chicago, Milwaukee, St. Paul and Pacific Railroad Company to Lieut. Col. Wildurr Willing, District Engineer, February 25, 1931, O'Brien

files; Wildurr Willing, Lieut. Col., Corps of Engineers, "Notice of Public Hearing," February 5, 1931, NARA, RG 22, Entry 162, Washington, D.C.

24. "Hearing at Wabasha," O'Brien files, 10–11, 23.

25. W. H. Pugh, President, Wisconsin Division, Izaak Walton League, to U.S. District Engineer, St. Paul, Minn., February 23, 1931, O'Brien files; Letter to Lieutenant Colonel Wildurr Willing, District Engineer, from O. L. Kaupanger, Executive Vice President, Minnesota Division, Izaak Walton League of America, February 26, 1931, O'Brien files; "Hearing at Wabasha," O'Brien files, 27.

26. La Crosse Chapter, Izaak Walton League of America, Letter to Colonel Wildurr Willing, District Engineer, February 25, 1931, Resolutions adopted at the executive meeting of the Board of Directors, O'Brien files; "Resolutions Drawn and Adopted by La Crosse Chapter of Izaac [sic] Walton League, February 4, 1931," O'Brien files.

27. Julius W. Haun, "A Statement for Actual Beauty versus Improbable Hope," February 25, 1931, "Hearing at Wabasha," Exhibit 16, O'Brien files.

28. Mr. Paul D. Klettner to Col. Wildurr Willing, February 25, 1931, "Hearing at Wabasha," Exhibit 15, O'Brien files.

29. W. C. Henderson, Associate Chief, U.S. Department of Agriculture, Bureau of Biological Survey, "Memorandum for Mr. Redington," March 18, 1931, NARA, RG 22, Entry 162, Washington, D.C., 1–5, with two-page statement from C. F. Culler attached.

30. Henderson, "Memorandum for Mr. Redington," RG 22, Entry 162, 2.

31. Ibid., 2.

32. W. C. Henderson, Acting Chief, Biological Survey, U.S. Department of Agriculture, U.S. Bureau of Biological Survey, "Memorandum for Hearing to be Held with the Army Engineers at Wabasha, Minn. On February 26, 1931," from "Hearing at Wabasha," Exhibit 1, 2, O'Brien files.

33. Ibid., 4.

34. Henderson, "Memorandum for Mr. Redington," RG 22, Entry 162, 2.

35. Henderson, "Memorandum for Mr. Redington," two-page statement from C. F. Culler, RG 22, Entry 162, 2.

36. *Winona Republican Herald*, March 7, 1931.

37. *Minneapolis Journal*, March 8, 1931.

38. *Winona Republican Herald*, March 9, 1931; the *Herald* printed his name as Blodgett whereas the *Minneapolis Journal* used Belitz.

39. *Winona Republican Herald*, March 9, 1931.

40. Memo: Public Hearing, Alma Dam, to Division Engineer, U.M.V.D., St. Louis, Mo., April 21, 1931, O'Brien files, 3.

41. Henderson, "Memorandum for Mr. Redington," 4.

42. Memo: Public Hearing, O'Brien files, 3, 5; *Winona Republican Herald*, March 7, 1931; *Winona Republican Herald*, March 9, 1931; *Minneapolis Journal*, March 8, 1931.

43. Letter from C. F. Culler, District Supervisor, Department of Commerce, Bureau of Fisheries, to Colonel Wildurr Willing, District Engineer, February 25, 1931, "Hearing at Wabasha," Exhibit No. 2, O'Brien files; *St. Paul Pioneer Press*, March 8, 1931.

44. "Hearing at Wabasha," O'Brien files, 8.

45. "Hearing at Wabasha," O'Brien files, 9; *Winona Republican Herald*, March 7, 1931.

46. *Winona Republican Herald*, March 9, 1931; *St. Paul Pioneer Press*, March 8, 1931.

47. *Winona Republican Herald*, March 9, 1931; Memo: Public Hearing, O'Brien files, 2; "Hearing at Wabasha," O'Brien files, 7–8.

48. "Hearing at Wabasha," O'Brien files, 6.

49. Ibid., 6–7.

50. H. Doc. No. 137, 20–22. The Engineers insisted, however, that maintaining the higher level would not be good below Muscatine, Iowa, where levees were more extensive.

51. Ibid., 20.

52. Ibid., 22–23, 26.

53. George W. Wood, "Editorial," *Outdoor America* 11: 1 (August–September 1932): 13; emphasis in the original.

54. Aberg, "Winning," 4.

55. Ibid., 4–5, quote from caption on 5.

56. *Outdoor America*, "National Convention Proceedings," 10: 11 (June 1932): 6; Scarpino, *Great River*, 171–73; on 171, Scarpino quotes a member of the league's executive board as saying local chapters were "'over-sensitive'" and "'too close to the subject to have the best judgement.'"

57. S. B. Locke, Conservation Director, Izaak Walton League of America, Inc., to Mr. Paul G. Redington, Chief, Bureau of Biological Survey, Washington, D.C., May 18, 1932; and resolutions of the April 1932 Izaak Walton League Annual Convention, NARA, RG 22, Entry 162, Washington, D.C.

58. Rudolph Dieffenbach, in Charge, Division of Land Acquisition,

"Memorandum for Mr. Redington," June 1, 1932, NARA, RG 22, Entry 162, Washington, D.C. Out of character with the bureau's official position, he wondered whether the new reservoirs would ruin the fish, wildlife, and scenic value of Winneshiek Bottoms and other areas in the refuge.

59. *Outdoor America*, "National Convention Proceedings," 10: 11 (June 1932): 6.

60. U.S. Congress, House, "Hearings before the Committee on Rivers and Harbors, Improvement of the Upper Mississippi River," 73rd Cong., 1st sess., May 2, 3, 4, and 5, 1933 (Washington, D.C.: U.S. Government Printing Office, 1933), 4–5, 46–48.

61. Ibid., 48.

62. Ibid., 4. Environmental interests had voiced some opposition at Rivers and Harbors Committee hearings held on January 25, 26, and 27, 1932, mustering telegrams from Burlington, La Crosse, and Winona. The telegrams expressed fears that barge traffic would hurt declining rail revenues, high water would damage sewage and water systems, the Upper Mississippi River Wildlife and Fish Refuge would be inundated, and the 9-foot project was too costly for a depression. But most of the testimony came from 9-foot channel supporters. See U.S. Congress, House Committee on Rivers and Harbors, "Mississippi River between Missouri River and Minneapolis: Hearings on the Improvement of the Mississippi River between the Missouri River and Minneapolis," 72 Cong., 1st sess., January 25, 26, and 27, 1932 (Washington, D.C.: U.S. Government Printing Office, 1932); Patrick James Brunet, "The Corps of Engineers and Navigation Improvements on the Channel of the Upper Mississippi River to 1939" (master's thesis, University of Texas, Austin, 1977), 108.

63. House, "Hearings, Upper Mississippi," 1933, 47.

64. Ibid., 47–48.

65. House, "Hearings, Upper Mississippi," 1933, 18; Seth E. Gordon, Conservation Director, Izaak Walton League of America, Inc., to Mr. Paul Redington, Chief, Bureau of Biological Survey, Washington, D.C., May 5, 1930, NARA, RG 22, Entry 162, Washington, D.C.; "Resolution Pertaining to the Proposed Canalization of the Mississippi River and the Probable Effect on the Upper Mississippi Wild Life and Fish Refuge. Passed at a Meeting of the National Executive Board of the Izaak Walton League of America on April 23, and at the League's National Convention on April 25th, 1931," NARA, RG 22, Entry 162, Washington, D.C., 1–3; S. B. Locke, Conservation Director, Izaak Walton League of America, Inc., to Mr. Paul G. Redington, Chief, Bureau of

Biological Survey, Washington, D.C., May 18, 1932, and resolutions of the April 1932 Izaak Walton League Annual Convention, NARA, RG 22, Entry 162, Washington, D.C.

66. House, "Hearings, Upper Mississippi," 1933, 7.

67. Ibid., 10.

68. Ibid., 7–8.

69. Ibid., 73–75, 77.

70. Judson Wicks, "Clean the Mississippi," *The Minnesota Waltonian* 4, 4 (January 1933): 11.

71. H. Doc. No. 137, 100; H. Doc. No. 290, 40–42, offered two alternatives for the reach from Hastings to the mouth of the Wisconsin River. One alternative called for seven low dams and the other for three high dams. The board, "for estimating purposes only," chose the low dams for the interim study. Under this alternative, the elevation of the Alma dam was to be 665.7; see 39. William Patrick O'Brien, Mary Yeater Rathbun, Patrick O'Bannon, edited by Christine Whitacre, *Gateways to Commerce, The U.S. Army Corps of Engineers' 9-Foot Channel Project on the Upper Mississippi River* (Denver: National Park Service, Rocky Mountain Region, 1992), 50–51.

72. Brunet, "Corps," 105–7.

73. House, "Hearings, Upper Mississippi," 1933, 11, 13.

74. Ibid., 88.

75. Ibid., 88–90.

76. Ibid., 90.

77. Ibid., 91.

78. Ibid., 104.

79. Ibid., 105, 107–8.

80. House, "Hearings, Upper Mississippi," 1933, 114–19; Brunet, "Corps," 118–21.

81. House, "Hearings, Upper Mississippi," 1933, 18, 50.

82. Ibid., 9.

83. Clarence F. Culler, "Depletion of the Aquatic Resources of the Upper Mississippi River and Suggested Remedial Measures," *Transactions of the American Fisheries Society* (1926): 281.

84. Judson Wicks, "Pollution of the Upper Mississippi River," *Transactions of the American Fisheries Society* 60 (1930): 287–92.

85. Culler, "Depletion," 280.

86. Capt. C. F. Culler, "Upper Mississippi River Problems," *Minnesota*

Waltonian (October, 1931): 4, 5; Raymond H. Merritt, *The Corps, the Environment, and the Upper Mississippi River Basin* (Washington, D.C.: U.S. Government Printing Office, 1984), 49–51; Scarpino, *Great River*, 105–10.

87. C. F. Culler, "Reclamation of Food Fishes and Mussel Propagation," *Transactions of the American Fisheries Society* (1926): 175.

88. Culler, "Depletion," 279–83.

89. Scarpino, *Great River*, 108.

90. Culler, "Depletion," 280–81.

91. Ibid., 281.

92. Ibid., 281–82. In "The Future of the Upper Mississippi River Fisheries," *Transactions of the American Fisheries Society* (1934): 328, Culler calls erosion "the ONE most serious factor" for the future of fisheries. *Annual Report, Bureau of Fisheries, Report to the Secretary of Commerce*, 1930, 208; Brunet, "Corps," 165.

93. Brunet, "Corps," 105, 111.

94. Martin Ross, *Shipstead of Minnesota* (Chicago: Packard and Co., 1940), 118; Richard Hoops, *A River of Grain: The Evolution of Commercial Navigation on the Upper Mississippi River* (Madison: Research Division of the College of Agriculture and Life Sciences, University of Wisconsin-Madison, 1993?), 76.

95. Ross, *Shipstead*, 118.

96. Ross, *Shipstead*, 119; Hoops, *River of Grain*, 76–77; Brunet, "Corps," 121–22; Roald Tweet, *A History of the Rock Island District, U.S. Army Corps of Engineers, 1866–1983* (Washington, D.C.: U.S. Government Printing Office, 1984), 274. The Corps built twenty-three locks and dams during the 1930s (3–26). Due to changes between the interim and final reports, the Corps added Lock and Dam 5A and deleted Lock and Dam 23. Locks and Dams 1, 2, and 19 had already been built, although the Corps had to build a new lock for No. 19 to make it match the 9-foot channel dimensions. Lower and Upper St. Anthony Falls Locks and Dams would be completed in 1956 and 1963, respectively. Lock and Dam No. 27 would be finished in 1964, bringing the total to twenty-nine.

Epilogue

1. U.S. Army Corps of Engineers, Waterborne Commerce Statistics Center, Preliminary CY-2000 Freight Table for the Upper Mississippi River.

2. Richard Hoops, *A River of Grain: The Evolution of Commercial Navigation on the Upper Mississippi River* (Madison: Research Division of the College of Agriculture and Life Sciences, University of Wisconsin-Madison, 1993?), 112.

3. *The 1997 Inland Waterway Review*, Draft, 3-16 to 3-17.

4. "Navigation Study Runs Aground," *Mississippi Monitor* 2, 6 (July 1998): 6; Bill Hord, "Farmers' Transportation Advantage Eroding, South America Giving U.S. Run for Its Money," *Mississippi Monitor* 2, 10 (November 1998): 3.

5. Hord, "Farmers' Transportation Advantage Eroding," 3; "Fixing Up Old Man River," *Mississippi Monitor* 2, 5 (June 1998): 3; originally published in *Prairie Farmer Magazine*.

6. Hord, "Farmers' Transportation Advantage Eroding," 3.

7. "Longer Locks Not Needed for Decades," *Mississippi Monitor* 2, 11 (Dec. 1998): 4.

8. Patrick Brunet, "The Corps of Engineers and Navigation Improvements on the Channel of Upper Mississippi River to 1939" (master's thesis, University of Texas, Austin, 1977), 167, 170–71; Upper Mississippi River Conservation Committee, "50 Years of Conservation through Cooperation," (UMRCC, ca. 1993), 4–9; Upper Mississippi River Conservation Committee, "Facing the Threat: An Ecosystem Management Strategy for the Upper Mississippi River, A Call for Action from the Upper Mississippi River Conservation Committee," December 1993; Dan McGuiness, "A River That Works and a Working River: A Strategy for the Natural Resources of the Upper Mississippi River System" (Upper Mississippi River Conservation Committee, January 2000).

9. Philip V. Scarpino, *Great River: An Environmental History of the Upper Mississippi, 1890–1950* (Columbia: University of Missouri Press, 1985), 177–86.

10. "Despite Gains, Pollutants Still Threaten Fishing and Swimming," *Mississippi Monitor* 2, 4 (May 1998): 5–6.

11. "Towards a Self-Sustaining River," *Mississippi Monitor* 2, 10 (November 1998): 14; McGuiness, "A River," 7–8, 17–18.

12. *Upper Mississippi River and Illinois Waterway Cumulative Effects Study, Preliminary Draft Report*, prepared by West Consultants, Inc., Bellevue, Wash., submitted to Rock Island District (July 1998), 73–74, 96, 151, 154.

13. Ibid., 14, 16, 82, 96.

14. Ibid., 82–83, 164.

15. *Cumulative Effects Study, Draft*, 92, 109–10, 120; McGuiness, "A River," 19.

16. *Cumulative Effects Study, Draft*, chap. 8, 38–40, 71.

17. Ibid., 40, 72.

18. McGuiness, "A River," 12–13.

19. *Cumulative Effects Study, Draft*, 51, 66; McGuiness, "A River," 28.

20. *Cumulative Effects Study, Draft*, 50–52.

21. Ibid., 51, 73. One positive effect is that the dam also blocks the invasion of exotic fish species.

22. Ibid., 51–52.

23. Ibid., 53.

24. "Towards a Self-Sustaining River," *Mississippi Monitor* 2, 10 (November 1998): 12–13; McGuiness, "A River," 13.

25. Donald Worster, *Rivers of Empire: Water, Aridity, and the Growth of the American West* (New York: Oxford University Press, 1991), 256, presents the Bureau of Reclamation in a similar way: "It had transcended its dreary, failed past and now could boast that it was, with minor exceptions, the technical master of water in the richest agricultural region in the world. In the early 1930s, it had been an agency tottering on the edge of extinction. With the Central Valley Project it had gained a new lease on life, a new role to play."

26. Floodplain management received little attention before 1960. After 1960, it would get greater notice, but old patterns would dominate floodplain and flood-control policy up to the present.

27. Richard White, *The Organic Machine: The Remaking of the Columbia River* (New York: Hill and Wang, 1995), 112.

28. Worster, *Rivers of Empire*, 329.

29. Ibid., 329.

30. Upper Mississippi River Basin Association, "Meeting the Challenge: The Upper Mississippi River System Environmental Management Program," n.d. The quote comes from the cover of the booklet, which references Section 103, Public Law 99-662, Upper Mississippi River Management Act of 1986.

31. Upper Mississippi River Basin Association, "Meeting the Challenge."

32. McGuiness, "A River That Works and a Working River," 27–28. The nine objectives include: (1) improve water quality; (2) reduce erosion and sediment; (3) restore the natural floodplain; (4) restore the river's seasonal pulse at the low flow end; (5) return connectivity between the main channel and backwaters; (6) open side channels, create islands, and sandbar habitat; (7) conduct channel maintenance and disposal in a way that supports the ecosystem; (8) stop exotics from coming into the river and limit their spread; and (9) provide fish passage past the dams. See page 14 for a summary.

Index

Abbot, Henry L., 38
Aberg, William, 257
Accault, Michael, 13
Adams, John Quincy, 23
Akerson, George E., 209–10, 235
Aird, James, 16
agricultural levees. *See* reclamation
agriculture: and demand for
    navigation improvements, 55;
    depression after Civil War, 56;
    and depression of 1920s, 192–94,
    328nn 37, 40–41; golden era, 192;
    growth of, 6, 53–55; and pollution,
    280–81; production, 101–2; too
    much for steamboats, 5, 6
Agriculture, Department of, 239–40,
    241
Agriculture Committee, 164, 166, 167
Alice, 43
Alma, Wisconsin, 249
Alton, Illinois, 5–6
American School of Wildlife
    Protection, 160, 229

Anderly, H. M., 147–48
Anti-Monopolists. *See* Anti-Monopoly
    parties
Anti-Monopoly parties, 61–63, 69
Argo Island, 14, 148
Arthur, Chester A., 129
Ashburn, T. Q., 202–3, 208, 330n 14,
    332n 39. *See also* Inland
    Waterways Corporation
Association of Railway Executives,
    262–64
Audubon Society, 160, 172
Auguelle, Antoine, 13, 21
Austin, Horace, 62

Bailey, Cornish, 201–2, 329–30n 12
Barbour, James, 24
Barge Line Committee. *See* River
    Cities Committee
Barge Line Company. *See* Upper
    Mississippi Barge Line Company
barges, 6
Baumgardner, A. L., 253

Beef Slough, 95, 97

Beirmann, Frederick, 259–60

Belitz, Pliny, 253

Beltrami, Giacomo, 1, 13, 22, 294n 2

Bennett, George, 159

Bernard, Simon, 42

Biddle, John, 3

biological survey: for 9-foot channel project, 244–48

Board of Engineers for Rivers and Harbors, 130, 223, 224, 227

Boepple, John F., 156

Bosse, Henry P., 82–83, 309n 4

Boswell, Lewis B.: and fund-raising, 136; initiates 6-foot channel movement, 115–17; lobbies for 6-foot channel, 119–20, 123–24, 140

Bowers, George M., 157

bridges, 33

Brown, Lytle, 231, 232

Buchanan, James, 26–27

Buck, Solon J., 60, 305n 7

buffalo, 21

Buford, Napoleon B., 25

Bureau of Biological Survey: and biological survey, 244, 247–48; and effects of 9-foot channel, 239–40, 242–43; does not oppose 9-foot channel, 252, 254. See also Henderson, W. C.; Steele, Raymond

Bureau of Fisheries: biological report on 9-foot channel, 244, 246–47; does not oppose 9-foot channel, 247, 254; dominates fish rescue, 155; and environmental effects of 9-foot channel, 239–40, 242–43, 247; succeeds Office of U.S. Commissioner of Fish and Fisheries, 154. See also Canfield, H. L.; Culler, Clarence F.; Ellis, M. M.

Burton, Theodore E., 123, 124, 130

Bryson, Alonzo, 119, 177

Caffrey, 42, 43, 44, 303–4n 42

Cairo, Illinois, 6

Canfield, H. L., 255

Carpenter, Cyrus, 63

Carver, Jonathan, 12

Cass expedition, 11. See also Schoolcraft, Henry Rowe; Trowbridge, Charles C.

Cass, Lewis, 11

Catlin, George, 21

Cavelier, Robert, sieur de la Salle, 13

channel constriction: environmental and physical effects of, 145–49; favored by Montgomery Meigs, 47–48; German influence, 47–48; rejected by Gouverneur K. Warren, 41. See also 4½ and 6-foot channels

cheap transportation movement, 66–68

Chicago, Illinois, 31, 32, 296n 16

Chicago and Illinois Canal, 31–32

Chicago and Rock Island Railroad, 5, 6, 33

Chicago River and Harbor Convention, 26

Chippewa River, 95, 97, 281

Christianson, Theodore, 205

Civil War, 6, 29–30, 31

Clark, William H., 189

Clay, Henry, 23, 25–26

clearing and snagging, 24

Cleveland, Grover, 129

closing dams, 266. *See also* channel
constriction; 4½ and 6-foot
channels

Coker, Robert, 158

Colhoun, James E., 21

Commerce, Department of, 239–40

Commerce Committee, Senate, 164,
243

connectivity, 283–85

conservationists: divide due to
condition of river, 248–49, 266,
268; and fish passage, 283; as
Progressives, 134–36; warn about
ecosystem collapse, 275. *See also*
Izaak Walton League; national
park movement; Upper
Mississippi River Wildlife and
Fish Refuge

conventions. *See* navigation
improvement conventions

Cooley, Lyman, 143

Coolidge, Calvin, 209–10, 213

Corps of Engineers. *See* U.S. Army
Corps of Engineers

Council on National Parks, Forests,
and Wild Life, 167

Crocker, A. L., 121

Cronon, William, 32

Culler, Clarence F., 155; considers

9-foot channel project a reprieve,
268; economic importance of
fishery, 168; and habitat destruction, 267–68; and 9-foot channel
project, 252, 254

Dakota Indians, 13–14

Daly, Nathan, 20

Davenport, Iowa: steamboat
arrivals, 4

Davidson, J. H., 126–27

Davison, F. Trubee, 242

Dawson, Albert F., 157

Democratic Party, 25, 129, 218–19

Dempsey, S. Wallace, 233–34

Des Moines Rapids, 15; calls for navigation improvements of, 33, 35,
36; delays shipping, 33; and
4-foot channel, 49; and 4½ foot
channel, 100; and funding for
work at, 26, 36; lightering cargo
around, *Virginia*, 15, 16; and
6-foot channel, 126; and surveys
by Napoleon Buford, 25; and
surveys by Robert E. Lee, 24;
and surveys by Gouverneur K.
Warren, 38; and surveys by
James H. Wilson, 39

Dieffenbach, Rudolph, 258, 343–44n
58

Dilg, Will, 161, 162, 163–65, 168–69,
170–72

Donnelly, Ignatius, 69

Doty, James Duane, 14

dredging, 41, 43

Dubuque, Iowa, 25, 26, 33

Dubuque Producers Exchange, 33, 34
Dunlap, R., 240
Durham, Charles W., 46, 125–26, 152, 315n 2
Dwinnel, Bruce, 263–64

Ecological Society of America, 167
ecosystem collapse, 291, 292
Effie Afton, 33
Eicher, Edward C., 260–61
Ellis, M. M.: and biological survey for 9-foot channel, 244, 246–47; criticized by A. C. Willford, 265; dams would not be responsible for condition of Mississippi River, 254; at St. Louis meeting with Corps, 242, 243
Environmental Management Program, 288–89
Equity Cooperative Exchange, 209
Esch, John J, 126
Ewing, William, 15–16
exotic species, 285

Fairport Biological Station, 157–58
farm crisis: after Civil War, 56; and Congress, 213–14, 215; of 1920s, 192–94, 328nn 37, 40–41; and president, 213
Farquhar, Frances U., 82
Featherstonaugh, George, 14–15
Federal Barge Line Service, 200, 202, 204
Fever River, 3
Fillmore, Millard, 26
fish management, 153, 158

fish migration, 283–85. *See also* fish passage
fish passage: Corps position on, 255, 256; issue at Winona meeting, 250, 251, 254, 255. *See also* fish migration
fish rescue, 153–56; and habitat destruction, 267; and mussel propagation, 157–58; in Winneshiek Bottoms, 164
Fitzgerald, John, 159
Flint Creek, Iowa: levee, 99
Flood Control Act of 1917, 152
Flood Control Act of 1928, 155, 321n 18
Fort Armstrong, 18
Fort Crawford, 11, 18
Fort Edwards, 16, 18
Fort Madison, Iowa, 183
Fort Snelling, 1
4-foot channel project, xvi, 29–32; authorized, 36–37; and Dubuque convention, 36; effect on Mississippi River, 50; experimental closing dams, 44; methods to achieve, 42; suggested by Alexander Ramsey, 302n 22; work on, 42–45; work at Des Moines and Rock Island Rapids under, 48–49
4½-foot channel project: in cheap transportation movement, 66–67; in Chicago grain elevator practices, 57; between Chippewa River and Winona 95–98; closing dams, 85–86; construction,

86–89; environmental and physical effects of, 145–49; funding of, 90–92, 310n 15; in Granger movement, 58–66; in high railroad rates, 53; limited success of, 105–6, 108; in midwestern population and agricultural expansion, 53–54; in natural character of upper Mississippi River, 53, 55, 57; and natural river, 93–94; planning of, 90–93, 94; and reclamation, 93; recommended by Windom Committee, 73; shore protection, 86; strategy/method, 87–89; survey and mapping for, 46–48, 82–83, 88; task of, 81; and timber industry, 93, 95–97; in urban demand, 66, 75–79; wing dams, 85, 309nn 7, 10; on work completed by 1905, 88. *See also* Granger movement; Windom Committee

fourth river, 275, 292

Fox Indians. *See* Sauk and Fox Indians

Galena, Illinois, 3, 6

Geiger, Ferdinand A., issues injunction, 261–62

General Barnard, 105

General Federation of Women's Clubs, 166, 168, 171–72

General Survey Act of 1824, 23–24, 25–26

Gillespie, J. L., 96

Goltra, Edward R., 204

Goltra fleet, 204

Goodwin, Godfrey G., 23

Gotwals, John C., 228

Grain elevators, Chicago: and farmer unrest, 57–58

Grange, the. *See* Granger movement

Granger Laws, 61, 62, 306n 22; thrown out by Supreme Court, 121

Granger movement: and Anti-Monopoly parties, 62–63, 69; Solon J. Buck on, 60, 305n 7; and cheap transportation, 66, 67; disagreement between leaders of, 60; founding of, 58; and Mississippi River as a navigation route, 64–66; and national railroad regulation, 63–64, 66; and navigation improvements, 306n 27; rapid growth of, 58–60. *See also* Kelley, Oliver

Grant, Ulysses, 69

Great Lakes, 32

Guttenberg, Iowa, 40, 93

habitat preservation, 157–58, 171

Hall, Charles L. 222–25, 227, 228, 229. *See also* Mississippi Valley Association, and 9-foot channel project; U.S. Army Corps of Engineers; Upper Mississippi Barge Line Company

Hanks, Stephan, 8

Harding, Warren G., 213, 214

Harding, Warren L., 160

Harrison, Benjamin, 129

Harrison, William Henry, 25

Haugen, Gilbert, 159, 214

Haun, Julius, 251

Hawes, Harry B., 165–66, 169

Hays, Samuel, 130–31, 135–36

headwaters reservoirs, 81–82, 89

Heiss, Merton S., 161

Heliopolis, 24

Henderson, W. C., 251–52, 254

Hennepin, Father Louis, 13, 20–21

Hill, Alberta Kirchner, 87

Hill, James J.: critical of 6-foot
channel, 142; criticizes status of
river terminals, 179; on railroad
car shortage, 139; spurs 6-foot
channel movement, 114–15

Hoops, Richard, 319n 53

Hoover, Herbert, 216; calls for
Fairport Station conference, 157;
and distribution problem,
215–17; helps Upper Mississippi
Barge Line Company, 210; and
national wildlife and fish refuge,
157, 169; and navigation
improvements, 333n 10, 334n 20;
and navigation improvements as
solution to farm and transportation
crises, 215, 217; and navigation
improvements as opposed to
McNary-Haugenism, 215,
217–18; opposes McNary-
Haugen bill, 214–15; opposes
9-foot channel project, 232; on
Panama Canal, 190; wins 1928
election, 219

Hornaday, William T., 160

Horse Shoe Bend, 94, 95–97

House Document 137, 255–56, 262

House Document 290, 244, 262,
345n 71

House Document 583, 220–22

Humphreys, Andrew A., 37, 38, 39

Hurley, Patrick J., 240

Hyde, Arthur, 241–42

hydraulic trap, 288

Indiana Rate Case, 191–92, 197, 210,
332n 33

Illinois River, 13

Inland Waterways Corporation
(IWC), 198, 200–201; and
extending Federal Barge Line
Service, 204; reverses position,
332n 39; and Upper Mississippi
Barge Line Company, 208, 212

Interstate Commerce Commission,
121–22, 191, 197, 204

Iowa Conservation Association, 160

islands: and natural river, 14–15

Izaak Walton League: Corps rebuts
arguments of, 253–55; distrust of
War Department, 240; and
Herbert Hoover, 240–41; Iowa
and Illinois divisions, 253; La
Crosse chapter, 251; Minnesota
and Wisconsin divisions, 250;
and national wildlife and fish
refuge, 161, 165, 168–69, 170,
239; notice of "Two Big Meetings,"
xi, 248; objects to 9-foot channel
survey, 241; opposes 9-foot
channel, xi, 250, 251, 253,

256–57; and *Outdoor America*, 256, 257–58; position of national organization on 9-foot channel, 257–58, 260, 343n 56; and Winona meeting on 9-foot channel, xi, 253–55

Jackson, Andrew, 23
Jackson, Thomas H; 228
Jadwin, Edgar, 334n 23
Jefferson, Thomas, 22
John Deere Company, 188, 199
Johnson, Hugh S., 214
Joint Committee of the Quincy Freight Bureau and Chamber of Commerce, 115

Keating, William, 15, 21
keelboats, 3
Keller, Charles, 179
Kelley, Oliver H., 58, 59, 60, 64, 65–66, 305n 12
Kenyon, William S., 159
Keokuk, Iowa, 15, 37, 39
Kerper, John, 236–37
King, William R., 92, 99
Kirchner, Albert, 87

La Crosse, Wisconsin, 6
Lake Cooper, 243, 244, 246
Lake Pepin, 8, 22, 254, 267
Lakes-to-the-Gulf Deep Waterway Association, 132
Lambert, George C., 209, 227
lead, 3, 11
leaning trees, 9, 14, 42–43

Le Dufphey, William, 22
Lee, Robert E., 24
levees, agricultural. *See* reclamation
Lewis, Henry, 20
lightering, 16
Lloyd, ames T., 127, 138
Lock and Dam No. 1, 100, 284
Lock and Dam No. 2, 220. *See also* House Document 583
Lock and Dam No. 4, 249–50
Lock and Dam No. 19, 284. *See also* Lake Cooper
Loire River, 42
Long, Stephen, 16, 18, 22, 38
Louisiana Purchase, 9
Lovell, Arthur J., 262
low water: of 1864, xvi, 30; and natural river, 16–17; and work on 4-foot channel, 43–44
lumber industry. *See* timber

Maas, Melvin J., 234
Mackenzie, Alexander, 83–84, 84; oversees 4½-foot channel project, 85, 90–93; on pollution from sawdust and garbage, 150; and timber industry, 97; and Upper Mississippi River Improvement Association, 123
Macleay, Lachlan, 201
Macomb, J. N., 44, 46, 303n 41
Madison, James, 22
Mansfield, Joseph J., 265
Markham, C. H., 189
Marshall, William R., 35
Maximum Freight Rate Case, 121

McKinley, William, 129

McNary, Charles L., 214

McNary-Haugen bill, 214, 215

McCabe, Robert, 22

McGee, W. J., 131–32, 133–34, 135–36

McGregor, Iowa, 159

Meeker Island Lock and Dam, 100

Meese, William A., 140

Meigs, Montgomery, 46–48

Merrick, George Byron, 19–20, 295n 5

Migratory Bird Act, 240

Mille Lacs Lake, 14

Minneapolis, Minnesota, 7, 40

Minneapolis Real Estate Board, 198–202, 206, 208

Minnesota Monthly, 64–65

Minnesota River, 1

Mississippi River Commission, 151–52, 311n 33

Mississippi River Logging Company, 97, 311n 31

Mississippi Valley Association, 201, 207; and appeal to the Board of Engineers, 226–27; lobbies President Hoover, 232; and 9-foot channel project, 220; response to Major Hall's first negative report, 223–24

Monroe, James, 22, 23

Montana, 42, 43, 44

Moore, Barrington, 167

Muscatine, Iowa: and pearl button industry, 156

mussels: depletion of by pearl button industry, 156, 157; propagation of, 157, 322n 32; and state regulations, 158; threatened by habitat destruction, 268; treated like crops, 158; zebra mussels, 285

National Agricultural Congress, 67

national heritage river, 287

national park movement, 158, 159–61

National Rivers and Harbors Congress, 133, 134, 176, 316n 16, 329–30n 12

natural river: beginning to change, 49–50; described in report by Montgomery Meigs, 46–47; fauna of, 2, 20–22; flora of, 12; forests of, 2, 9, 11, 12, 14; and high water, 17; islands of, 14–15; and leaning trees, 9; and low water, 16–17; navigating, 1, 9, 14–20; prairies along, 11, 12–13

navigation improvement conventions, 75; Cincinnati, Ohio, 133; Dubuque, Iowa, 33–36, 301n 13; Northwestern Farmers' Convention, 67; Quincy, Illinois, 117–18; St. Louis, 33; St. Paul, 75–79

navigation improvements: political attitudes toward, 22–23, 25–27, 129, 299nn 59, 61, 308n 65. *See also* 4-, 4½-, 6-, and 9-foot channel projects

New Orleans, Louisiana: inadequate harbor facilities, 31

Newton, Walter, 206, 209, 226, 235–36

9-foot channel project, 198; arguments for, 327n 29; authorized, 244; base of support, 206; biological survey for (*see* Ellis, M. M.; Uhler, Frances M.); and booster frustration over, 339n 73; call for, 334n 21; Chief of Engineers position on, 231, 232, 336n 36; completed, 274; construction of, 271, 272, 273, 274, 346n 95; cost as of 1940, 274; current debate over, xi–xv, 275, 288; current demand for navigation improvements, 277–79; environmental effects of, xii–xiii, 242–43, 279–84; and evolution of Corps role on upper Mississippi, 348n 25; and exotic species, 285; and farm organizations, 235; and fish passage, 283–84; funding for, 269, 272; future of, 290–92; and geomorphic changes, 282–83; and navigation boosters, 207, 231; opposition to, by Izaak Walton League, 248, 249, 250; opposition to, by others, 249, 250, 251; opposition to, by railroads, 240, 249, 261–64, 344n 62; and pollution, 280–81; and President Hoover, 234, 235–36; and Rivers and Harbors Committee, 233–34; Senate Commerce Committee includes in Rivers and Harbors bill, 242–43; and siltation, 281–82; survey for (*see* 9-foot channel survey); underlies power structure today, 287. *See also* House Document 137; House Dcument 290

9-foot channel survey, 334n 23; and Board of Engineers for Rivers and Harbors, 227, 231, 338n 55; and Chief of Engineers, 231, 232, 336n 36; Congress receives survey report (House Document 290), 230; and Hall, Major Charles L., 222–23, 225, 229; House Document 290 considered an interim report, 230; interim report inadequate, 233; and navigation boosters, 223–27; navigation boosters fear eastern opposition, 229; recommendations of, 230–31; and special board, 228, 229–30; submission of (House Document 290), 335n 33; third survey, 228; time running out, 227–28

Nininger Bluff Bar, 42

Nininger Slough, 42

Northern Light, 20

Northwestern Farmers' Convention, 67

Oberholser, Harry, 160, 163–64

Ohio River, 41, 42; inspection trip, 317n 20; Rivers and Harbors Committee inspection trip, 132

Ohio River Improvement Association, 132

Ottumwa Belle: takes last timber raft downriver, 183

Outdoor America, 165, 171

Panama Canal, 118–19, 190–91, 327n 29

Panic of 1837, 24, 25

Panic of 1857, 6

Panic of 1873, 56, 60, 67, 79

parity plan, 214. *See also* Haugen, Gilbert; Johnson, Hugh S.; McNary, Charles L.; McNary-Haugen bill; Peek, George N.

passenger pigeons. *See* pigeons

passenger traffic, 5, 109

Patrons of Husbandry. *See* Granger movement

pearl button industry, 156–58, 322n 30

Pearson, T. Gilbert, 160, 166–67

Peek, Burton F., 122, 140–41

Peek, George N., 214, 229

Permanent Wild Life Protection Fund, 160

Pierce, Franklin, 26–27

pigeons, 15

Pig's Eye Island, 44, 45

Pike, Zebulon, 10; describes islands, 14; Des Moines Rapids, 15–16; keelboat, 9; objectives for upper Mississippi River expedition, 9–10; on pigeon rookeries, 15; and sandbars, 17–18; and snags, 9, 11

Pillsbury, George B., 261

Polk, James K., 25, 26

pollution, 149–51, 266–67, 280–81

population: growth of, 5, 54

power structure, 286–87

Prairie du Chien, Wisconsin, 6

prairie fires, 13, 14, 297n 24

Prescott, Wisconsin, 19

Progressive Movement, 134–36

Public Service Commission of Indiana. *See* Indiana Rate Case

Pugh, W. H., 250

Quincy, Illinois, 6, 115; Freight Bureau, 115

railroad car shortages, 138–40, 189–90

railroads: arrangements with grain elevator operators and steamboat lines, 57, 62; belated protest against 9-foot channel project, 240; Chicago and Rock Island Railroad first to reach the Mississippi River, 5; expansion of, 5–6, 55, 103–4; and Lock and Dam No. 4, 249, 261–62; oppose 9-foot channel project, 261–64; overburdened, 327nn 25–26; promote river traffic, 5; as spur to navigation improvements, 29–30, 34, 53, 55, 56–57, 118, 121–22, 197–98, 201; take away steamboat traffic, 30–31, 32, 50, 55, 56–57, 103–4, 296n 16. *See also* Indiana Rate Case; railroad car shortages

Ramsey, Alexander, 302n 22
Ransdell, Joseph E., 128, 132
rapids. *See* Des Moines Rapids; Rock
    Island Rapids
rattlesnakes, 21–22
Realtor, The, 198, 199
reclamation, 82; Corps objects to, 98,
    99, 311n 35; during early
    twentieth century, 151–55, 266;
    economic and environmental
    effects, 166–68, 284–85; key issue
    in campaign for refuge, 163–68;
    levee districts, and 9-foot
    channel, 261; origins of on upper
    Mississippi River, 98. *See also* Flint
    Creek, Iowa, levee; Sny Island
    Levee and Drainage District;
    Winneshiek Bottoms
Record, M. K., 253
Red Wing, Minnesota: Dakota
    village, 22
Reform parties. *See* Anti-Monopoly
    parties
Report on Transportation Routes to
    the Seaboard, 46–48
Republican party, 25, 129, 218
Rhine River, 48
Richie, Charles, 123, 125–26
Richtman, Jacob, 87
river and harbor conventions. *See*
    navigation improvement
    conventions
River Cities Committee, 203, 204, 206
river commerce, 326nn 17–18;
    decline of, 112, 113, 114,
    180–88, 313nn 15, 18, 319n 51;

decline of, at Des Moines Rapids
    canal, 106, 108; decline of, at St.
    Louis, 107, 108; freight traffic
    declines, 103, 183–87; grain
    moved in sacks, 32, 301n 10; and
    inadequate terminal facilities, 31,
    32, 301n 10; low-water interrupts
    navigation, 105–6, 108; and
    9-foot channel, 276–77;
    passenger traffic, 103; railroads
    as cause of decline, 103–4; river
    as cause of decline, 104; through
    traffic ends in 1918, 188; value of
    commodities shipped, 187–88.
    See also timber
Rivers and Harbors Acts/bills:
    Congress revamps review process,
    129–30; 1824, 24; 1866, 36; 1890,
    150; 1894, 150; 1899, 150–51; 1905,
    124; 1907, 143, 318–19n 45; 1913,
    152; 1930, 233–34, 236, 243–44
Rivers and Harbors Committee, 130;
    calls for creation of National
    Rivers and Harbors Congress,
    133; and funding problem, 128;
    and 9-foot channel, 233–34, 236,
    262–65, 316n 16; and Ohio River
    inspection trip, 132; and 6-foot
    channel, 119–20, 122, 123–24.
    See also Burton, Theodore;
    Davidson, J. H.; Lloyd, James T.;
    railroad car shortage; Ransdell,
    Joseph
Rivers and Harbors Congress. *See*
    National Rivers and Harbors
    Congress

river terminals: status of, 177–79
River Transit Company, 199
Robb, P., 34–35, 301n 13
Rock Island, Illinois, 37
Rock Island District, 37
Rock Island Rapids, 15, 16, 26; calls for navigation improvements at, 33, 35, 36; and 4-foot channel, 48–49; funding for work at, 26, 36; and Robert E. Lee, 24; navigation improvements at during 4½-foot channel era, 100; and 6-foot channel, 126; and Gouverneur K. Warren, 38
Rollingstone Bar, 44–45
Rollingstone Slough, 94, 95, 96
Roosevelt, Franklin, 269
Roosevelt, Theodore, 121–22, 123, 129

Sac Indians. See Sauk and Fox Indians
St. Paul, Minnesota, 3–4, 6. See also navigation improvement conventions, St. Paul
St. Paul District, 37
St. Louis, Missouri, 4, 7, 31, 66, 280. See also navigation improvement conventions, St. Paul
St. Louis Merchants Association, 33
Salisbury, Robert: on William Windom, 74
sandbars, 17–18, 20, 43, 46–47
Saturday Evening Post: supports national fish and wildlife refuge, 165
Sauk (Sac) and Fox Indians, 3, 16

Scarpino, Philip V., 170–71, 325 n 68
Schoolcraft, Henry Rowe, 11–12, 18
Schulte, George F., 159
scraping. See dredging
Seaman, Halleck W., 200, 201
sedimentation, 266, 281–82
Senate Select Committee on Transportation to the Seaboard. See Windom Committee
Shaw, B. F., 154
Shipstead, Henrik, 205–6, 245; and funding for 9-foot channel project, 272; and injunction against construction, 262; and 9-foot channel construction, 269–70; and Senate Commerce Committee, 242
Shreve, Henry M., 24
sieur de la Salle, Robert Cavelier, 13
siltation, 266, 281–82
6-foot channel project, 115–18; arguments for, 118–19, 121–22, 314n 36, 319n 53; criticism of, 143–44, 319n 53; environmental and physical effects, 145–49; farmers do not join movement for, 141–42; focus of debate over, 142–43; funding for depends on river commerce, 176–77; goal to complete in ten years, 176; mostly Mississippi River cities and commercial interests, 141–42; national context of, 128, 134–36, 142; plans for, 126; and railroad car shortage, 138–40, 142; survey for, 125–26, 315n 2

Smedley, Colonel W. B., 66
Smith, Alfred E., 218
snagging and clearing, 24, 27
snags: and floodplain forests, 15;
    obstacles to navigation, 9; and
    Zebulon Pike, 9, 11; removal of,
    24, 27, 42, 43; types, 9
Sny Island Levee and Drainage
    District, 98–99
Spalding, George R., 228, 242, 243
steamboats: arrivals, 3–4, 295n 5;
    demand too great, 4–5, 6;
    heyday, 3–9; lead shipping, 3;
    lose traffic to railroads and east-
    ern route, 30–31, 300–301n 7,
    301nn 8, 10, 313nn 15, 18;
    passenger traffic, 5; reduce
    shipping costs, 3; reduce travel
    time, 3; timber traffic, 6. *See also*
    river commerce; individual boat
    names
steamboat traffic. *See* river commerce
Steele, Raymond, 254, 265, 341n 14
Stibolt, A. J., 83
Stillwater, Minnesota, 8
Stone, William M., 34
Surber, E. W., 242, 243
Surber, Thaddeous, 254–55

Tawney, James A., 176
Taylor, Harry, 203
Taylor, Zachary, 26
Thompson, William A., 97, 147–48
Thorpe, Samuel S., 206, 207–8, 211
Throckmorton, J., 44
timber: booming and rafting, 95, 96,

97; decline of, and shipping on
    upper Mississippi, 110, 111,
    112; growth of industry, 6–7, 8,
    102–3, 312n 5; influence on
    4½-foot channel project, 93, 95,
    97; note on statistics, 312n 5;
    production process, 7–8;
    raftboats, 80; raftboats and
    sawmill numbers decline, 110;
    shipping declines, 109–10, 114,
    179, 180, 183; and steam, 8
Totten, Joseph G., 42
Townsend, Charles McDonald,
    93–94, 115–17, 117–18
Trowbridge, Charles C., 18
turtles: nesting on islands, 15
Twain, Mark, 103, 108–9
Tweet, Roald, 5, 319n 51
Tyler, John, 25

Uhler, Frances M.: and biological
    survey for 9-foot channel, 244,
    247–48; opposes fluctuating
    river levels, 243; at St. Louis
    meeting with Corps, 242, 243
U.S. Army Corps of Engineers:
    agrees to fish passage if dams
    block migration, 255, 256;
    agrees with Bureaus of
    Biological Survey and Fisheries
    on low dams, 243; appeals
    process for negative survey
    reports, 224; dissatisfied Midwest
    not using upper Mississippi
    River, 203; and flood control
    mission, 98, 99, 154–55;

hosts St. Louis meeting, 242–43; hosts Wabasha meeting, 248, 249; modifies lock and dam design to satisfy environmental concerns, 252; opposes authorization of 9-foot channel, 236; rebuts criticisms of 9-foot channel, 253–55; role in navigation improvements, 30; supplies barges to help revive river traffic, 188

U.S. Commissioner of Fish and Fisheries, Office of, 153–54. *See also* Bureau of Fisheries

upper Mississippi River: Congress declares nationally significant ecosystem and navigation system, 288; defined, 293n 2; power structure on, 286–87

Upper Mississippi Barge Line Company, 203, 207; and extending Federal Barge Line Service, 208, 209–11, 212; and Lock and Dam No. 2, 222; and Charles L. Hall, 223–24; and 9-foot channel, 232

Upper Mississippi River Cities: Barge Line Committee. *See* River Cities Committee

Upper Mississippi River Conservation Committee: and ecosystem restoration, 279–80, 290; formed, 279; and 9-foot channel project, 279–80; restoration plan, 348n 32; warn of ecosystem collapse, 279

Upper Mississippi River Improvement Association: established, 117, 314n 31; final push to get 6-foot channel authorized, 140–41; fund-raising problems, 136–8; hosts Rivers and Harbors Committee inspection trip, 123; lobbies Rivers and Harbors Committee, 119–20, 122, 123–24; meets with Alexander Mackenzie, 123; meets with President Theodore Roosevelt, 123; and 1905 Rivers and Harbors bill, 124; and status of river commerce and terminals, 177–79; supports preservation of forests, 120–21; vision for the Mississippi River, 122; wants 6-foot channel completed in ten years, 176; wants $2 million annually, 127–28, 140; weak support base, 125, 138. *See also* Davidson, J. H.; Lloyd, James T.

Upper Mississippi River Wildlife and Fish Refuge: campaign for, 161, 163–73, 325n 68; defines landscape and ecology today, 172–73; demonstrates a new vision, 158; and Izaak Walton League, 320n 1; protected floodplains above Rock Island, 282

Upper Mississippi Waterway Association, 264

Van Buren, Martin, 25

Vance, John L., 119, 126

Van Sant, Samuel, 102, 119, 122, 177
Virginia, 1, 3; and Des Moines and
    Rock Island Rapids, 15, 16;
    dimensions, 294n 2; and passenger
    traffic, 5; and prairie fire, 13

Wabasha, Minnesota: Dakota village
    site, 22; meeting concerning
    elevation of Lock and Dam No.
    4, 248–51; opposes higher
    elevation for Lock and Dam No.
    4, 249
*Wabash, St. Louis, and Pacific Railroad
    v. Illinois*, 121
Wallace, Henry C., 165, 168
Ward, Henry Baldwin, 240–41
War Eagle, 43
Warner, R. P., 232
Warren, Gouverneur K., 37–38, 82,
    89; considers channel constriction,
    41; and dredge and snagboats,
    41; on dredging and scraping, 42;
    maps by, 40; and natural river,
    49–50; proposed navigation
    improvements, 39–40; on
    sandbars, 39–40; survey of upper
    Mississippi River, 39; on wing
    dams and closing dams, 40, 41
Warsaw to Quincy, Levee (Illinois), 99
Washburn, William D., 122
Washburne, E. B., 34
Waterhouse, Sylvester, 76–79, 80
water-level management: to mimic
    natural fluctuation, 289–90;
    natural fluctuation needed, 285;
    natural fluctuation prevented, 285

Webber, Charles, 231, 236
Western Rivers Improvement Act, 26
West Newton Chute, 95, 97
Weyerhaeuser, Frederick, 97. *See also*
    Mississippi River Logging
    Company
Wheat Ring, 62, 65, 67. *See also*
    railroads, arrangements with
    grain elevator operators and
    steamboat lines
Whig party, 25, 26
White, Richard, 288, 293–94n 4
white pine: characteristics, 6
Whitley, Frances E., 166, 171–72
Wicks, Judson: on pollution and
    vision for Mississippi River, 239;
    on Twin Cities pollution of
    Mississippi River, 266–67; on
    value of the Upper Mississippi
    River Wildlife and Fish Refuge,
    261
wild rice ("zizania"), 15
Wilkinson, James, 9
Wilkinson, Thomas: joins board of
    National Rivers and Harbors
    Congress, 133; president of
    UMRIA, 119; on status of river
    terminals, 179; supports
    preservation of forests to help
    navigation, 120–21; on UMRIA
    funding problems, 136; vision for
    the Mississippi River, 122;
Wilson, James H., 39
Willford, A. C.: opposes 9-foot
    channel project, 260, 265
Williams, Charles F., 205

Willing, Wildurr, 228, 252

Windom, William, 67, 68, 69, for railroad regulation and navigation improvements, 70; Robert Salisbury biographer, 74; on Senate Select Committee on Transportation to the Seaboard, 69. *See also* Windom Committee

Windom Committee, 69; assessment of, 74–75; biographer's comments on, 74; reaction to, 73–74; recommendations, 72–73; report, 307–8n 58; reviews alternatives to reduce transportation costs, 70–72. *See also* Windom, William

wing dams, 266, 309nn 7, 10. *See also* channel constriction; 4½- and 6 foot channels

Winneshiek Bottoms, 163–64, 253, 257, 258, 260. *See also* reclamation

Winona, Minnesota, 4, 50; Izaak Walton meeting in, xi, 250, 253–55

Wiprud, Arne C., 208–9, 232, 264, 265 339n 7

Wisconsin River, 7

Wisconsin state legislature: memorial to Congress, 36

Wood, George W., 256–57

Worster, Donald, 288

zebra mussel, 285

John O. Anfinson is a historian with the Mississippi National River and Recreation Area, a 72-mile national park corridor through the Minneapolis and St. Paul metropolitan area. For nearly twenty years before joining the National Park Service, he was the historian for the St. Paul District of the U.S. Army Corps of Engineers. He has frequently written and spoken about the Mississippi River to local, regional, and national audiences. He is a founding board member of the Friends of the Mississippi River, an organization that focuses on the health of the river in the Twin Cities.